Aspects of

India's Economic Growth and Reforms

The Author

R. Nagaraj is Professor at the Indira Gandhi Institute of Development Research (IGIDR), Mumbai. He obtained doctoral degree in Economics from the Jawaharlal Nehru University, New Delhi (at the Centre for Development Studies, Trivandrum, Kerala), and Masters degree from the Birla Institute of Technology and Science, Pilani, Rajasthan.

Aspects of

India's Economic Growth and Reforms

R. Nagaraj

Academic Foundation
NEW DELHI

Published in 2006 by

ACADEMIC FOUNDATION

4772-73 / 23 Bharat Ram Road, (23 Ansari Road),
Darya Ganj, New Delhi - 110 002 (India).
Phones : 23245001 / 02 / 03 / 04.
Fax : +91-11-23245005.
E-mail : academic@vsnl.com
www.academicfoundation.com

Aspects of India's Economic Growth and Reforms
by R. Nagaraj

ISBN 81-7188-430-X

Printed and bound in India

To My Parents

Contents

Part III

Some Aspects of Economic Policy

List of Figures and Tables

FIGURES

TABLES

Acknowledgements

In a collection of papers written over a decade, it is but natural to have accumulated considerable intellectual debt to a wide cross section of the academic community, though not all of them can be adequately acknowledged. As these studies are contributions to current policy issues, they generated intense debates among my colleagues and scholars, at the workplace and in academic meetings where I had the opportunity to present my findings. I have benefited a great deal by their comments and interactions that helped in sharpening my arguments and search for evidence. I am most grateful to Keshab Das, Bernard D'Mello, Errol D'Souza, Subir Gokarn, Ashima Goyal, Shikha Jha, Pradyumna Kaul, N. Krishnaji, A.C. Kulashreshtha, Sunil Mani, Veena Mishra, Sebastian Morris, Manoj Panda, Kirit Parikh, V.K. Ramachandran, K.V. Ramaswamy, G. Pakki Reddy, C. Rammanohar Reddy, Y. Venugopal Reddy, Cherian Samuel, J.C. Sandesara, S.L. Shetty, M.H. Suryanarayana, Madura Swaminathan, Suresh Tendulkar, Bagaram Tulpule, Shuji Uchikawa, Rajendra Vaidya and A. Vaidyanathan for sparing their valuable time to read and comment on many of the papers. I am also indebted to Jyoti Parikh, Kirit Parikh, R. Radhakrishna and T.L. Sankar, as the heads of the institutions where I have worked during these years, for granting the academic freedom to pursue my research interests unhindered by immediate institutional requirements.

Sound library resources are essential for research. Library staff at the Indira Gandhi Institute of Development Research, and other libraries that I have consulted extensively, has actively helped me in my academic work. I thank them all for putting up with many of my reasonable and unreasonable demands on their services.

Introduction

Studies included in this volume, carried out over a decade, represent an effort to grapple with a few contemporary issues of economic growth, industrial change and policy initiatives in India. These studies are motivated by the desire to carefully examine some of the widely held propositions on the aggregate and sectoral economic performance, premises of a few reform measures and the outcome of some aspects of the economic reforms initiated in the 1990s.

The Introduction provides a brief background to these studies, situates them in the relevant literature and indicates how they contributed to the ongoing discourse on economic analysis and policy. The two abiding concerns in these studies are (i) to examine the quality of statistics employed as they could have a bearing on research findings and their interpretation, and (ii) to provide analyses of a relatively long period to eschew hasty inferences from limited observations.

The 12 chapters included in this volume are thematically grouped into three parts. However, the Introduction follows a somewhat chronological order as it describes the evolution of the policy debate as well as the chain of reasoning of these studies. Part I consists of three chapters seeking to document economic growth and distribution during the last two decades and the effect of the policy reforms on the aggregate and sectoral performance. The following part, consisting of four chapters, focuses on the growth of the manufacturing sector and factors influencing it. Five chapters in Part III deal with a few specific aspects of the economic policy: two of them are concerned with the public sector and one each with the industrial labour market, capital market and inward foreign direct investment.

Improvements in Economic Performance in the 1980s

In the early 1980s, India's economic outlook appeared gloomy. Though the economic shocks of the 1970s, originating mainly from crop failures and energy crises, were successfully overcome the economy continued to grow only at around 3½ per cent per year, with continued mass poverty and inequality. The persistence of the "Stagnant Parameters"—to borrow the title of late Raj Krishna's popular piece in the *Seminar* in January 1984—in spite of a perceptible rise in domestic saving rate, growing food stocks and (briefly) trade surplus in the late 1970s was indeed a puzzle that challenged many economists and policymakers alike.

However, as the evidence began to trickle in, there emerged a cautious optimism around the mid-1980s. While the policymakers were quick to take the credit for the incipient signs of acceleration, professional economists, accustomed as they were to many such false dawns, were cautious in changing their outlook. The circumspection was perhaps also justifiable on account of their suspicion of the quality of the macroeconomic data that were used to buttress the optimistic view.

Chapters 1 and 4 of this volume are perhaps the earliest attempts to subject the optimistic view to systematic statistical enquiries. They demonstrate that there has indeed been an improvement in the trend growth rate of domestic output and manufacturing sector performance since 1980-81. Chapter 1 also suggests that the improved output growth was shared by primary, secondary and tertiary sectors. Though, by 1980 the share of the tertiary sector in domestic output was the largest, contrary to the widely held view, it was not the fastest growing one.

Findings reported in Chapter 4 show that (i) the output growth in organised manufacturing in the first 7 years of the 1980s was distinctly higher than that in the previous 15-year period (1965-80) of 'relative stagnation,' and (ii) the growth rate in the 1980s was comparable to that recorded during 1959-66. Admittedly, the *National Accounts Statistics* (NAS) data on domestic output (GDP) in registered manufacturing analysed in this study had some limitations, as information for the two most recent years was based on the revised *Index of Industrial Production* (IIP) that had been widely contested for possible overestimation.

Chapter 5 seeks to remedy the shortcomings by utilising the *Annual Survey of Industries* (ASI) data for 1980-81 to 1987-88. Using a variety of price deflators, it is conclusively shown that the upturn in the industrial output growth in the 1980s was indeed real. The chapter, then, looks for an explanation for the upturn in terms of the various hypotheses identified in the literature for the persistence of the 'relative stagnation.' We found that (i) a step-up in fixed investment/GDP ratio since the mid-1970s, (ii) a shift in the composition of investment in favour of industry and infrastructure, and an improvement in their output growth, and (iii) a steady rise in public sector's share in investment could have contributed to the industrial upturn. The study also suggests that domestic deregulation too could have played a part in releasing supply constraints, and does not rule out the positive role of the shift in trade policy from quotas to tariffs (albeit fixed at very high levels).

Chapter 8 further explores public sector's improved performance in the 1980s. Usually the balance sheet data of central public sector enterprise (PSEs), or public finance data, are analysed to show its meagre contribution to the government revenues. Both these data sources, and the widely used statistical ratios, seem to have their limitations as they fail to adequately capture the performance of PSEs. We believe public sector transactions, as recorded in the NAS, provide a comprehensive picture. Our analysis of this less used data source shows that the non-financial public sector enterprises' performance gradually improved since the late 1970s (albeit from a low base). This was true—measured as the ratio of gross profits to capital employed—even excluding the petroleum firms whose profits contained an element of tax on account of the administered prices of their output. The study further contends that the improved profitability of PSEs was also on account of a faster rise in public sector prices relative to the GDP deflator in the 1980s. This, in itself, need not be undesirable since public sector output was generally subsidised in the earlier years and the government's inability to raise public sector prices seen as part of the problem.

If there is one area where the economic reforms of the 1990s departed most from the past policy, it is public sector. From being the 'commanding heights' of the economy, public sector was quickly and summarily castigated as a 'millstone' around the government's neck.

In other words, after the reforms, it is a widely shared belief that the financial losses of the PSEs were largely responsible for the unsustainable growth in fiscal deficit that spilled into the external sector. Do the financial losses of the PSEs really account for a large and growing share of the fiscal deficit?

Continuing our earlier effort, we examined the preceding question by applying a widely accepted methodology to the NAS data (Chapter 9). When the fiscal deficit of the centre and states was decomposed to distinguish between the PSEs and government administration, it was discovered that the PSE deficits were a steadily declining share of the total. The finding remained unchanged, even after excluding the surpluses of public sector petroleum companies. Moreover, the budget constraint for the PSEs had been steadily hardening during the 1980s, that was probably responsible for the improved financial performance. Further, these improvements were the results of raising the administered prices of public sector output (as reported in the previous study) as well as of a sustained improvement in capacity utilisation (as a measure of efficiency).

These results imply that the government administration's expenditure policies were mainly responsible for the growing fiscal deficit, not the financial losses of PSEs. When the above measures were extended to the 1990s, they showed that PSEs sustained the improvement in their performance despite the changes in the policy environment (Chapter 2). These results perhaps question the widely held views on the public sector performance and, by implication, the policies of disinvestment that follow from them.

Indian economic performance in the 1980s was significant in many ways. It was an improvement over its record of the past three decades; it withstood the slow down of the world economy and was unaffected by debt and inflation that ravaged much of the developing world. The 1980s' performance provided a basis for hope that judicious policies could make a difference within the constraints of institutions and politics. As there is a renewed interest in understanding the genesis of the reforms, the above-mentioned studies could be of value in understanding the continuity and change in economic policy and performance over the last two decades. As Dani Rodrik and Arvind Subramanian (*Economic and Political Weekly*, Vol.39, No.16, 2004) have recently discovered, the reforms of the 1990s were built on the improved performance of the previous decade.

Aspects of Economic Reforms: Some Critical Analyses

One of the principal tenets of the economic reforms is that the excessive protection of the organised industrial working class in India has created a rigid labour market. Reportedly, the growing bargaining power of the organised labour has increased labour cost, resulting in a substitution of capital for labour, hurting the prospects of labour-intensive industries and their exports. The 'jobless growth' in registered manufacturing in the 1980s is a widely accepted evidence of such a proposition. Further, the job security legislations brought in 1976 (their further tightening in 1982) that ruled out employers' ability to retrench even a single worker (without the state's permission) is widely acknowledged as emblematic of all the ills of the industrial labour market.

A careful re-examination of a variety of data sources in Chapter 10 does not corroborate such a proposition. For instance, the much publicised acceleration of wage growth was unfounded, when adjusted for the increase in days (hours) worked. Similarly, the rise in mandays lost due to strikes and lockouts dropped sharply since the mid-1970s, when measured as a proportion of total mandays—challenging the rigidity hypothesis.

A variety of measures widely used in labour economics suggest a decline in the strength of the organised labour since around the mid-1970s. The study also documents the diffusion of employment into smaller-sized factories within the organised sector, and a decline in the factory sector's share in total manufacturing employment—all of which have contributed to the weakening of the bargaining power of the trade unions. Therefore, the hypothesis of growing rigidity of the labour market seems unsustainable.

A well-functioning stock market is widely regarded as the centrepiece of a market economy that mobilises risk capital and efficiently allocates financial resources among competing borrowers. Since around the mid-1980s a series of changes were initiated to promote the primary stock market as a source to mobilise funds. The pace quickened after 1991 to move away from a bank-centric financial system, to one based on the stock market. What did it imply for the economy's domestic saving, capital formation and efficiency of resource use? Evidence reported in Chapter 11 suggests that it mainly meant disintermediation in the financial markets, with little effect on financial saving, private fixed investment and corporate profitability. We then raised the question whether the development of the market for corporate control could remain far behind the growth of the primary stock. It is a moot point if the subsequent developments in the secondary stock market have turned out to be an adequate and efficient mechanism to contest corporate control and enforce efficiency.

Since 1991 the inflow of foreign direct investment (FDI) has been perceived as a source of additional capital, technology and scarce managerial skills—overturning the earlier consensus on the need to regulate foreign investment and technology imports. What has been India's experience with the change in the policy? How does it compare with China's? In seeking answers to these questions, Chapter 12 highlights the growing limitations of the existing official data sources—since the FDI is now taking different legal forms that circumvent the disclosure norms. Based on illustrative information from a variety of sources, the chapter raises issues that need to be carefully examined to fully understand the effects of FDI on domestic economy. Enlisting the shortcomings of the Chinese official statistics, the study explains why foreign investment in China seems overstated. A careful comparison would suggest that FDI inflows, as a proportion of the domestic output in the two countries, are perhaps roughly of the same order. Therefore, what one should be concerned about is perhaps not so much the quantum of the inflow, but where it flows, and what it does to augment potential output, domestic capability and net exports.

Assessment of the Aggregate Economic Performance

Economic reforms are believed to have raised the growth rate of domestic output, and reduced the incidence of poverty at a faster rate. A careful statistical analysis seems to provide little evidence to support such a proposition (Chapters 2 and 3). It suggests that the decades of 1980s and 1990s should be seen as roughly continuous periods of improved growth (of about 5.6 per cent per year) compared with the earlier three decades (1950-80).

However, Chapter 3 contends that the improved growth during the last two decades is accompanied by increased inequalities: across states, between rural and urban areas, between organised and unorganised sectors and between profits and wages. As reported in Chapter 6, inequality in the organised manufacturing output across major states has also increased in the 1990s, reversing the declining trend in the previous decade. Thus, the improved growth performance is accompanied by a polarisation of the economy.

The much deliberated poverty reduction after 1980 also seems suspect since there is little statistically valid association across major Indian states between (i) the growth rates of per capita output and (ii) the decline in poverty levels. Further, the lack of poverty reduction seems to be associated with the slowdown of employment growth across all sectors of the economy during this period.

The remaining two chapters (6 and 7) in this Part deal with the effects of the reforms on the industrial sector. Contrary to some apprehensions, India did not witness a 'deindustrialisation,' either in terms of output or employment. However, the tariff reforms adversely affected the capital goods industries' output growth. But the prices of capital goods, relative to the GDP deflator, have come down, improving the productivity of investment. There is no statistically valid evidence to suggest a rise in industrial output growth rate after 1991 (as with domestic output). However, in terms of regions, the backward states of Uttar Pradesh and Bihar and agricultural states of Punjab and Haryana witnessed a deceleration of output growth after the reforms. But, significantly, the 1990s witnessed a boom in output and investment in the first half of the decade, which went bust after 1995-96, that has persisted since then.

Why didn't the policy reforms lead to a sustained improvement in the growth of labour-intensive manufacturing and its exports? Why was the boom of 1992-96 so short lived? Would the hastening of the reforms have sustained the boom? We have argued in Chapter 7 that the reason for the deceleration after the mid-1990s is the lack of industrial demand caused by the collapse of public investment since the late 1980s, and a slowdown of agricultural productivity in the 1990s; both of which perhaps are the victims of the economic reforms. We contend, unless these issues are addressed seriously, deepening of the reforms is unlikely to turnaround the industrial sector on a sustainable basis.

Conclusions

Since the early 1980s, India witnessed an acceleration of economic growth compared to the first three decades of planned economic development. It also represents a period of sustained diversification of the economic structure with a greater openness to external trade and investment and with a greater ability to withstand external and internal shocks.

Yet, it has also been a period of growing inequality, with increased nutritional poverty, despite the economy's capacity to augment foodgrains output and the government's ability to garner a growing share of it for public distribution. Stagnant domestic saving and a decline in tax collection, as proportions of domestic output, also accompany improved growth performance—which is well reflected in our inability to achieve budgetary balance.

Surely, the gradualism in the policy changes has helped avoid a debt crisis of the Latin American kind as well as the economic implosion of the East Asian variety. However, the acceleration that we have witnessed seems modest in comparison with what China has reportedly achieved. Can India hope to catch up with East Asia in general and China in particular, with more thoroughgoing (or deepening of) economic reforms, as many have advocated? Or do we need to alter the course of the economic policy? One hopes that the studies in this volume would contribute towards finding suitable answers to such questions.

Part I

Macroeconomic Performance

1

Growth Rate of India's GDP, 1950-51 to 1987-88

Examination of Alternative Hypotheses

The long-term trend growth rate of India's (measured) gross domestic product at factor cost in real terms (hereafter simply GDP) has been a widely debated issue in recent years. While the dominant opinion appears to hold the view of a more or less constant growth rate of about 3.5 per cent per annum [Bardhan, 1984, for instance] with considerable yearly fluctuation around the trend,[1] there have been some who seem to perceive an improvement in the growth rate since the middle or the late seventies. It was perhaps Raj [1984] who for the first time explicitly stated this proposition. To quote him: "I would venture to place it [the growth rate] now at not less than 4 to 4¼ per cent per annum, certainly much above the so-called 'Hindu' rate of growth" [Raj, 1984: p 1802].[2] Commenting on the supposedly rapid increase in the capital-output ratios resulting in sluggish macroeconomic performance in relation to savings and investment in Indian Economy, Chakravarty [1987] suggested that the incremental capital-output ratio "appears to have come down somewhat in the course of the last two Five-Year Plans ... *since the annual average rate of growth of GDP has been around 5 per cent over the period 1975-85*" (p 54, emphasis added). More recently, commenting on the effects of the policy reform initiated in the eighties, Ahluwalia [1988] has argued that "the growth rate over the past ten years or so averages about 4.5 per cent and this is an average over a period in which growth rate was accelerating. The underlying growth rate of the economy in the mid-eighties is nearer 5 per cent per year" (p 347).

Besides the differences in the perception on the overall performance of the economy considerable concern has been expressed over the perceptible change in the composition of the domestic output in favour of the tertiary sector in general and (within it) of 'public administration and defence' (PAD) in particular. Mitra [1988] said: "There is therefore a seeming disproportionality in the recent shift in the composition of India's national income. The explosion in service activities cannot be readily attributed to any impulse transmitted by the sectors engaged in material production ... . In this context, the fact that within the service sector the highest rate of growth is being registered in public administration and defence, that is, in the arena of government activities, is of considerable significance" (p 6).[3]

A systematic statistical examination of these propositions using a consistent and up-to-date time series data since 1950-51 could be of considerable value not only to secure a more realistic and accurate summary measure of the underlying long-term trends in the economy, but also to provide a firmer empirical basis for the debate on the (recent) changes in the economic policies. The above-mentioned propositions could be translated into the following testable hypotheses:

(i) The trend growth rate of India's GDP since 1950-51 shows no perceptible variation and it has been growing at a constant rate of about 3.5 per cent per annum.

(ii) There has been a trend acceleration in the GDP growth rate over the entire period since 1950-51.

(iii) A distinct break is descernible in GDP at 1975-76/1979-80 with a higher trend growth rate in the following period.

(iv) Growth rate of the tertiary sector has been higher than that of the primary and secondary sectors since 1980-81.

(v) Growth rate of GDP originating in PAD has been the highest among all the sub-sectors of GDP since 1980-81.

This paper attempts to subject these hypotheses to a rigorous test using mainly the revised (with 1980-81 as the base year) series of *National Accounts Statistics* [CSO, 1989a and b] for the period 1950-51 to 1987-88. In order to do so we have applied the known (but not uncontentious) methods of statistical trend fitting to the time series data.[4]

I

DATA SOURCE

In 1988, Central Statistical Organisation (CSO) published a revised series of *National Accounts Statistics* (NAS) with 1980-81 as the base year, which, more or less, follows the methodology of the earlier series with 1970-71 as the base year. Most of the commentators [Dutta Roy Choudhury, 1988 and Gothoskar, 1988] have, by and large, reacted favourably to the changes that have been introduced as they are said to overcome some of the widely acknowledged shortcomings in the previous series. Reservations expressed over the non-comparability of the old and the revised series to draw meaningful long-term trends in the economy [Mukherjee, 1988] have been unfounded as CSO has now published long-term estimates of national accounts since 1950-51 with the new base year [CSO, 1989b]. However, as the official publication does not provide any explanatory notes as to the methodology used for carrying backward the revised estimates, we have little basis to assess their quality.

As our interest lies not so much in absolute magnitudes but in the trends in GDP we prepared index numbers (with 1950-51 as 100) of the old and the revised series of GDP (and its principal sectors) to discern any perceptible divergence in the movements of the pairs of series (Figures 1.1 to 1.4). While the index numbers for the old and revised series of GDP (Figure 1.1) show a perfectly correlated movement over the entire period from 1950-51 to 1984-85 (the latest year for which data according to the old series are available), it is not so for its major sectors. As a result of the changes in the estimation procedures, while the secondary sector shows a slightly faster growth rate in the eighties (Figure 1.3), the tertiary sector has recorded a relatively slower growth rate (Figure 1.4). Within the tertiary sector most perceptible and significant difference between the old and the revised series (from the point of view of our exercise) is in PAD.[5] While the two series of PAD move in almost perfect unison between 1950-51 and 1972-73, they begin to diverge thereafter, with the new series moving up at a relatively slower rate compared to the old series (Figure 1.5). The gap between the two series seems to get pronounced after 1977-78. This anomaly is brought out more sharply when PAD is measured as a percentage of GDP (Figure 1.6). In the new series

Figure 1.1

Index No. of Gross Domestic Product

1970-71 and 1980-81 Prices

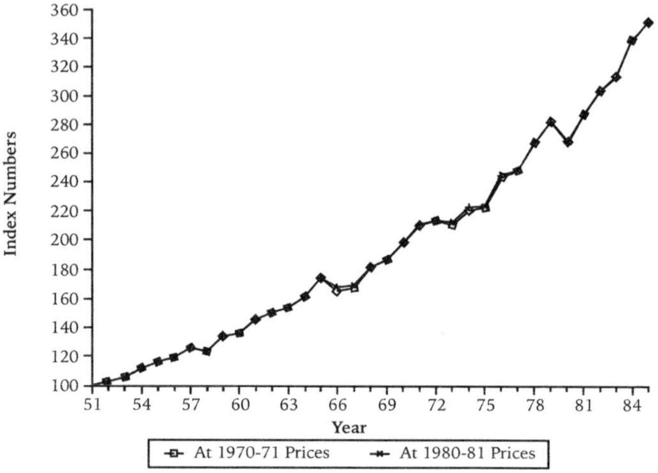

Figure 1.2

Index No. of Primary Sector

1970-71 and 1980-81 Prices

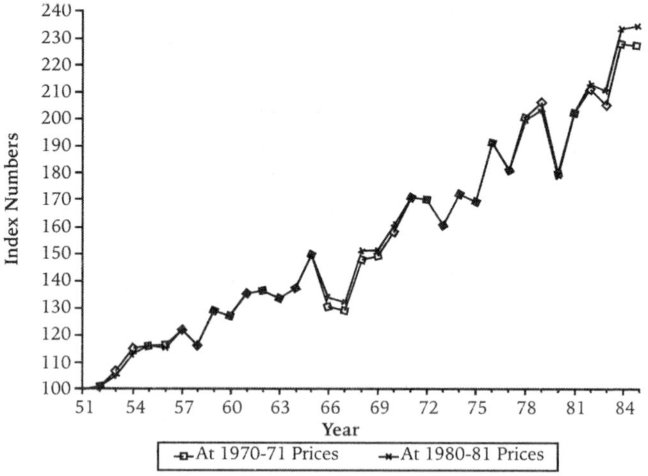

Figure 1.3

Index No. of Secondary Sector

1970-71 and 1980-81 Prices

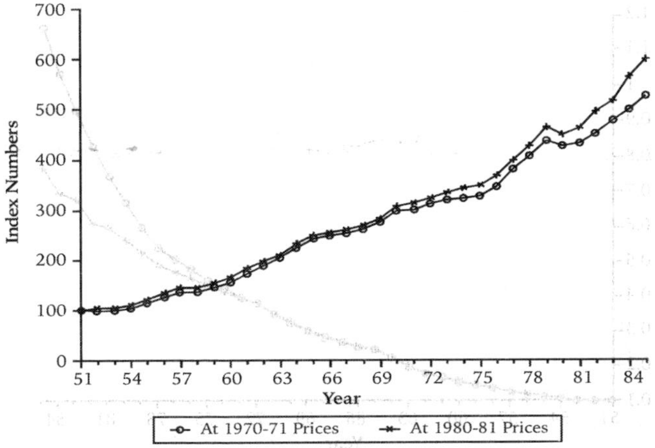

Figure 1.4

Index No. of Tertiary Sector

1970-71 and 1980-81 Prices

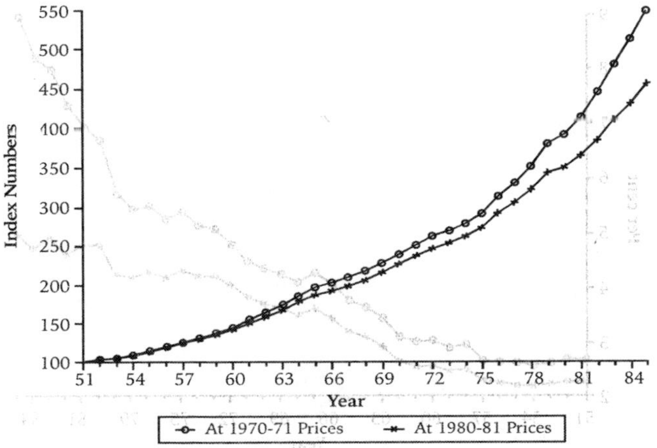

Figure 1.5

Index No. of Public Administration and Defence

1970-71 and 1980-81 Prices

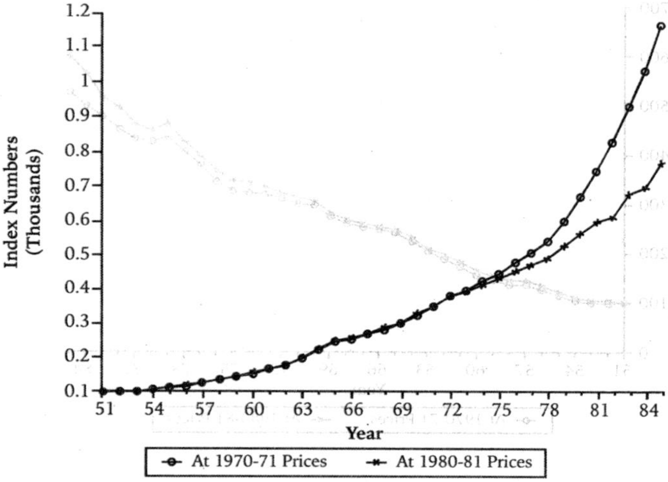

Figure 1.6

Share of Public Administration and Defence in GDP

1970-71 and 1980-81 Prices

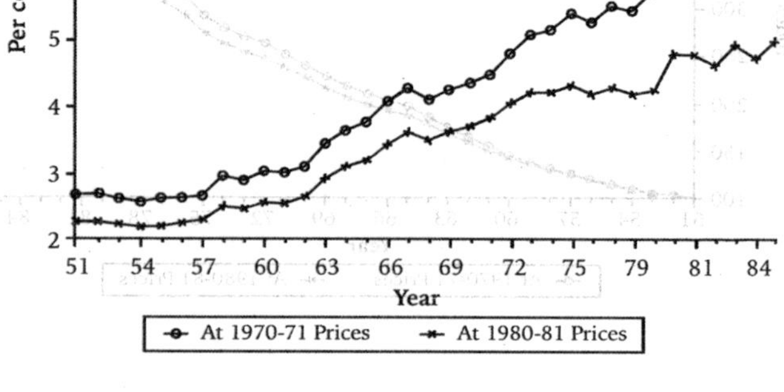

the share of PAD in GDP does not only grow at a slower rate compared to that in the old series, but its initial value for 1950-51 has also got reduced by half a percentage point. As a result of a lower base and a slower growth rate the share of PAD in GDP in the new series for 1984-85 gets reduced to roughly one half (less than 5 per cent of GDP) of that according to the old series.

The extent of the difference in the movements of the two series noted above can perhaps be better captured by a comparison of their growth rates (Table 1.1). It shows that during 1977-78 and 1984-85 (the period when the gap is growing sharply) while the growth rate of GDP originating in PAD according to the old series is 11.7 per cent per annum it is only 6.4 per cent per annum as per the new series.[6]

Table 1.1

Growth Rate of PAD according to Old and Revised Series 1972-73 to 1984-85

Period	*Trend Growth Rate (Per cent per annum) According to*	
	1970-71 Series	*1980-81 Series*
1972-73 to 1984-85	9.6	5.7
1977-78 to 1984-85	11.7	6.4

Note: All growth rates are statistically significant at 95 per cent level.
Source: *National Accounts Statistics*, various issues.

A discrepancy of this magnitude has apparently been on account of some changes in the methodology of estimation. CSO [1988] has provided the following explanation for the observed divergence between the old and the revised series of PAD at constant prices.

> ... a comparison between the new series and the 1970-71 series, at constant prices, is possible broadly through growth rates only. In the new series, the methodology for conversion of the value added of various industry groups, at current prices, to those at constant prices, is the same as that adopted hitherto, except in the industry group, public administration and defence. In this industry group, hitherto, the practice had been to deduct amounts of dearness allowance, etc., from the total disbursement of salary and related allowances, to arrive at the incidence of outgo at constant prices. This practice was causing considerable

> difficulties on account of the absence of separate figures relating to dearness allowance, especially in respect of the employees of some of the state governments and local bodies. An overestimation of income in real terms, seems to have resulted as a consequence. In view of the fact that most of the state governments are now following the dearness allowance pattern of the central government, which is based on the recommendation of the Central Pay Commissions, the practice has now been adopted of deflating the current price estimates in the public administration and defence, by the consumer price index of industrial workers, which is the index being utilised for determining the dearness allowance pattern of government employees. *The effect of this adjustment has been that the rate of growth of this sector over the years is now around half of that under the 1970-71 series* (p 15, para 2.33 emphasis added).

We are not in a position to assess the validity of the changes in the estimation procedure as there has been little discussion on this aspect.[7] However, it may not be inappropriate to suggest that the argument of the relatively faster growth of PAD in the eighties[8] (hypotheses No. 5 in the previous section) rests on contestable data and therefore, we are not in a position to test the hypothesis. However, we will use these findings later in the study to compute growth rate of GDP, excluding PAD.

II

PRELIMINARY ANALYSIS OF GROWTH OF GDP

As a first step in our attempt at understanding the long-term trends, following Rao [1983], we have estimated growth rates[9] over successive decades for GDP and its main sectors (namely, primary, secondary and tertiary sectors), though, however, such a periodisation may not be particularly meaningful for analytical work. Table 1.2 shows that GDP has grown at a distinctly high rate at 4.9 per cent per annum during the eight-year period of the eighties compared to the earlier three decades. Moreover, the higher rate of growth has been shared by all the three sectors of the economy.

While the growth rate of the primary sector in the eighties is slightly higher than that of the sixties and the seventies, the tertiary sector has witnessed a steady increase in its growth rate over the successive decades. However, it is interesting to note, contrary to the

Table 1.2

Growth Rate of Real GDP and its Main Sectors, 1951-52 to 1987-88

	Primary	*Secondary*	*Tertiary*	*GDP*
1951-52/1959-60	2.7	6.0	4.0	3.6
1960-61/1969-70	1.6	5.3	4.3	3.2
1970-71/1979-80	1.8	4.6	4.5	3.4
1980-81/1987-88	2.1	6.9	6.3	4.9

Source: Central Statistical Organisation [1989a and 1989b].

widely held view, that in the eighties the secondary sector has grown at a faster rate[10] (at 6.9 per cent per annum) than the tertiary sector (at 6.3 per cent). The relatively faster growth of the secondary sector in the eighties over the other sectors is brought out more sharply in Figure 1.7. The observed faster growth of the secondary sector in the eighties at 6.9 per cent per annum has not only halted the declining trend of the previous two decades, but has also improved over its performance of the fifties at 6 per cent per annum.

Figure 1.7

Sectoral GDP at Constant Prices

1980-81 to 1988-89 Prices

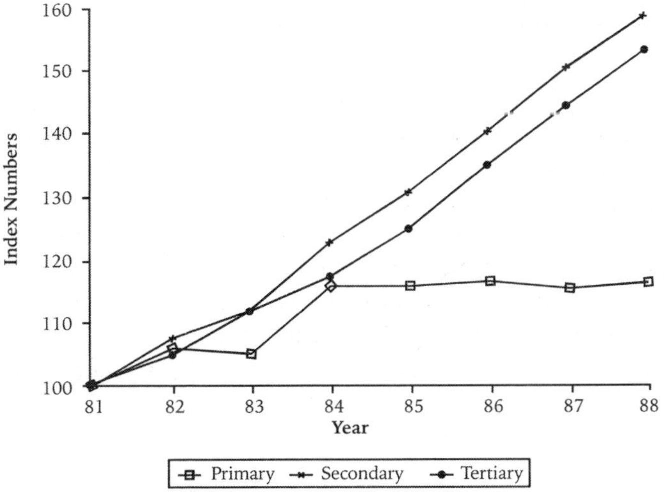

A similar exercise at a disaggregated level shows (Table 1.3) that the majority of components of GDP registered higher growth rates in the seven-year period of the eighties[11] than in the earlier three decades, with the sub-sector 'banking and insurance' recording the highest growth rate of 10.3 per cent per annum, followed by 'mining and quarrying' (10.2 per cent per annum) and 'electricity, gas and water' (9.9 per cent per annum).

Table 1.3

Growth Rate of GDP and its Sub-Sector over Successive Decades

Industry	*1950-51/ 1959-60*	*1960-61/ 1969-70*	*1970-71/ 1979-80*	*1980-81/ 1986-87*
1. Agriculture, forestry and fishing	2.7	1.5	1.7	2.3
1.1 Agriculture	2.9	1.3	1.9	2.6
2. Mining and quarrying	4.1	5.0	4.6	10.2
3. Manufacturing	6.1	4.7	4.9	8.2
4. Electricity, gas and water supply	10.2	11.5	7.4	9.9
5. Construction	5.9	6.9	3.1	3.0
6. Trade, hotel and restaurant	5.1	4.5	4.9	5.4
7. Transport, storage and communication	5.7	5.5	6.4	7.8
8. Finance and real estate	3.1	3.1	4.4	6.1
8.1 Banking and real estate	7.7	5.0	7.8	10.3
9. Community, social and personal services	3.5	5.2	3.7	6.2
9.1 Public administration and defence	5.2	7.6	4.9	7.5
Gross domestic product	3.7	3.3	3.4	5.1

Note: All growth rates are statistically significant at 95 per cent.
Source: *Central Statistical Organisation* [1989a and 1989b].

To ascertain if the observed trend growth rate of GDP during 1980-81 and 1987-88 at 4.9 per cent per annum is higher than that recorded during the earlier periods of equal length of time, we have computed growth rates for all the successive eight-year periods from 1950-51 to 1987-88. (Table 1.4). It shows that during the entire period of 38 years a growth rate of over 5 per cent per annum was achieved only once between 1979-80 and 1986-87. Further, up to the end of the seventies growth rates were less than 4 per cent per annum in all the periods of eight-year duration except in two cases. On the contrary, growth rates have been over 4 per cent per annum in the recent periods. These results seem to indicate that the relatively better performance record during the eight-year period since the late seventies and the eighties were perhaps not so common in the earlier three decades.

Table 1.4

Growth Rate of Real GDP for Successive Eight-Year Periods, 1951-52 to 1987-88

Year	*Growth Rate (per cent per annum)*	*Year*	*Growth Rate (per cent per annum)*
1951-58	3.6	1967-74	3.6
1952-59	3.7	1968-75	2.9
1953-60	3.6	1969-76	3.0
1954-61	3.7	1970-77	2.9
1955-62	3.8	1971-78	3.4
1956-63	3.8	1972-79	4.2
1957-64	3.9	1973-80	3.9
1958-65	4.4	1974-81	3.7
1959-66	3.7	1975-82	3.7
1960-67	3.2	1976-83	3.4
1961-68	3.0	1977-84	3.9
1962-69	3.0	1978-85	4.0
1963-70	3.3	1979-86	4.6
1964-71	3.5	1980-87	5.2
1965-72	3.6	1981-88	4.9
1966-73	3.9		

Note: All growth rates are statistically significant at 95 per cent level.
Source: *Central Statistical Organisation* [1980a and 1989b].

III

STATISTICAL TESTING OF ALTERNATIVE HYPOTHESES

Having made a preliminary exercise on the trends in the growth rate of GDP (and its various sectors and sub-sectors) we are now in a position to test the alternative hypotheses outlined earlier using the following functional forms:[12]

1. $log\ Y = a + bt$
2. $log\ y = a + bt + ct^2$
3. $log\ y = a + a_1(D) + bt + b_1(Dt)$

where *Y* is GDP (or its components), '*t*' is 'time' and '*D*' is the dummy variable which takes values '*0*' or '1' to distinguish different sub-periods.

While the equation (1) provides constant growth rate,[13] equation (2) tests the hypothesis of acceleration/deceleration in the trend growth rate on the basis of the estimated coefficient of '*c*' and its sign. To test whether there has been a 'break' in the series resulting in a change in the slope of the curve and to estimate the trend growth rate in different sub-periods a dummy variable is included [Rao and Miller, 1972][14] in a log-linear equation. In equation (3) coefficient of '*t*' gives the compounded growth rate for the first period and the sum of the coefficient of '*t*' and '*Dt*' gives the compound growth rate for the second period. Whether the growth rate during the two sub-periods is same or not is tested by the statistical significance of coefficient of 'Dt'. However, before applying the regression method to test the hypotheses we considered it appropriate to 'explore' the data to get a 'feel' of the pattern in the time series.[15] A box-and-whisker plot[16] (Figure 1.8) of the yearly growth rate of GDP shows that the observation for 1979-80 (when there was a sharp fall in GDP of 5.2 per cent over the previous year) is a clear outlier[17] indicating a possible break in the series at that point. However, on *a priori* considerations we have also tested for possible breaks in the series at 1965-66 (fall in GDP of 3.7 per cent over the previous year due to crop failure; and changes in economic policies and agricultural technology since then) and 1975-76 (indicated by Chakravarty and Ahluwalia as a possible turning point in the growth rate of GDP) and attempted to statistically verify them by the trend analysis.

Table 1.5 presents estimated trend equations for GDP under alternative functional specifications. According to the log-linear curve, GDP has grown at 3.6 per cent per annum[18] for the entire period of 38 years since 1950-51.[19] Log-quadratic equation does not show a statistically significant acceleration in the trend, though the estimated coefficient has a positive sign.[20] Therefore, the hypothesis of trend acceleration in the growth rate of GDP is not supported by the data.

Figure 1.8

Box-and-Whisker Plot

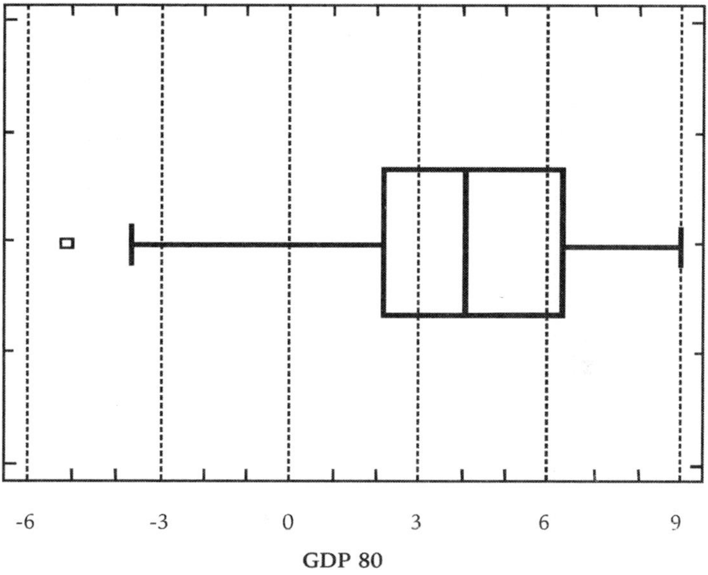

Equations 3, 6, 7 and 8 (Table 1.5) clearly reject the hypothesis of any break in the series at 1965-66 implying that despite the changes in the economic policies and the introduction of the newer agricultural technology around that time the economy has continued to grow at an unchanging growth rate. Various estimated equations in the same table, however, do not reject the hypothesis of a possible break in the series at 1975-76/1979-80 and an increase in growth rate thereafter. According to equation 5 while the growth rate of GDP up to 1974-75 is 3.5 per cent per annum, it increased to 4.2 per cent per annum thereafter. Similarly, while the growth rate of GDP up to 1979-80 (equation 6) is 3.8 per cent per annum, in the eight-year period after it witnessed a trend growth rate of 5.0 per cent per annum with a statistically significant break in the series. However, when the dummy variable to indicate breaks in the series at 1975-76 (D_3) and 1979-80 (D_2) are taken together (equation 8) the former turns statistically not significant with a negative sign suggesting perhaps the relatively 'strength' break in the series at 1979-80.

Table 1.5

Growth Rate of GDP, 1950-51 to 1987-88

Functional Form	b	c	b_1	b_2	b_3	R^2	Growth Rate (per cent per annum)
1. Log-linear	0.036390					0.9950	3.6
2. Log-quadratic	0.025085	0.000083				0.9953	
3. Log-linear with D_1	0.037685		0.000832			0.9955	
4. Log-linear with D_2	0.035286			0.012909		0.9965	3.5 up to 1979-80 and 4.8 thereafter
5. Log-linear with D_3	0.035233				0.006652	0.9960	3.5 up to 1974-75 and 4.2 thereafter
6. Log-linear with D_1 and D_2	0.037685		(-) 0.002401	0.01291		0.9967	3.8 up to 1979-80 and 5.0 thereafter
7. Log-linear with D_1 and D_3	0.037685		(-) 0.004683		0.008884	0.9963	
8. Log-linear with D_1, D_2 and D_3	0.037685		(-) 0.004683	0.018711	(-) 0.003519	0.9967	

Source: *Central Statistical Organisaiton* [1989a and 1989b].

The above trend analysis, to recapitulate, rejects the hypotheses of a trend acceleration over the entire period and a break in the series at 1965-66. The hypothesis of a constant growth rate is also rejected as the breaks in the series at 1975-76/1979-80 and an increase in growth rate thereafter are statistically significant. Moreover, the break in the series at 1979-80 and a higher growth rate in the eighties appears to be a statistically stronger proposition than the break in the series at 1975-76.

Admittedly the above inference could be influenced by the presence of the statistical outlier (as revealed by Figure 1.8) in the data for the year 1979-80. To verify if the significantly higher growth rate of GDP in the eighties is on account of it, we dropped the value for the year 1979-80 and re-estimated the trend equations (Table 1.6). Though the growth rate according to the log-linear equation does not show any perceptible change, the estimated coefficient of quadratic term turns out to be statistically significant with a positive sign indicating a trend acceleration in GDP.[21] Further, the dummy variable test (equation 3) clearly shows a statistically significant break in the series at 1978-79 and the estimated equation has a higher slope thereafter indicating a clear increase in trend growth rate in the eighties, uninfluenced by the presence of the outlier.

Table 1.6

Growth Rate of GDP, 1950-51 to 1987-88
(Excluding the year 1979-80)

Functional Form	*b*	*c*	b_2	R^2	*Growth Rate (per cent per annum)*
1. Log-linear	0.036554			0.9957	3.7
2. Log-quadratic	0.025466	0.000081		0.9961	3.8 in 1977-78
3. Log-linear with D_2	0.035642		0.012552	0.9969	3.6 up to 1978-79 and 4.8 thereafter

Source: Central Statistical Organisation [1989a and 1989b].

Thus the hypothesis of an unchanging growth rate over the entire period 1950-51 to 1987-88 is not a valid proposition as there has been a statistically significant break in the series at 1975-76/1979-80 and a higher growth rate thereafter. However, the argument of such a break at 1979-80 appears to be statistically stronger proposition. This inference is valid even when the value for 1979-80, an outlier, is dropped. The hypothesis of a trend acceleration based on log-quadratic equation does not find adequate support as the statistical significance of the estimated value of the quadratic term seems to be influenced by the presence (or absence) of the outlier.

IV

GROWTH RATE OF GDP EXCLUDING 'PUBLIC ADMINISTRATION AND DEFENCE'

As noted earlier, the relatively rapid growth of PAD since the late seventies or the early eighties has attracted considerable attention. Since GDP originating in this sector is simply public expenditure it may perhaps be meaningful to look into trends in GDP excluding PAD.[22]

However, the hypothesis of relatively rapid growth of PAD is not sustainable, as noted in Section I, with the revised series due to changes in the estimation procedure. As one is not sure about the validity of the changes incorporated, we have arrived at a re-estimate of PAD series from 1977-78 to 1986-87 using its observed growth rate (at 11.6 per cent per annum for the period 1977-78 to 1984-85) according to the old series. Implicit in such a procedure is the assumption that PAD has continued to grow at the same rate even after 1984-85, as has been suggested by Minhas [1990]. We have subtracted the estimated value of PAD from the revised GDP to arrive at an adjusted 'GDP-PAD' series, at 1980-81 prices.

Table 1.7 shows that according to the log-linear curve, the adjusted 'GDP-PAD' has grown at 3.5 per cent per annum over the 38-year period since 1950-51. Log-quadratic equation does not show a statistically significant trend acceleration though the coefficient, as in the earlier cases, has a positive sign. Break in the series at 1979-80 is statistically significant. While the growth rate of the adjusted GDP-PAD up to 1979-80 is 3.4 per cent per annum, it is 4.6 per cent per annum thereafter. Table 1.8 provides broadly similar results for 'GDP-PAD' excluding the outlier value for the year 1979-80.

Table 1.7

Growth Rate of (GDP-PAD), 1950-51 to 1986-87

Functional Form	*b*	*c*	b_2	R^2	*Growth Rate (per cent per annum)*
1. Log-linear	0.034661			0.9949	3.5
2. Log-quadratic	0.032884	0.000013		0.9948	
3. Log-linear with D_2	0.034240		0.011359	0.9961	3.4 up to 1979-80 and 4.6 thereafter

Source: *Central Statistical Organisation* [1989a and 1989b].

Table 1.8

Growth Rate of (GDP-PAD), 1950-51 to 1986-87
(Excluding the year 1979-80)

Functional Form	*b*	*c*	b_2	R^2	*Growth Rate (per cent per annum)*
1. Log-linear	0.03431			0.9943	3.5
2. Log-quadratic	0.03365	(0.00)		0.9942	
3. Log-linear with D_2	0.03386		0.012764	0.9951	3.4 up to 1978-79 and 4.8 thereafter

Source: *Central Statistical Organisation* [1989a and 1989b].

V

CONCLUSIONS

This paper has attemtped to rigorously examine the alternative hypotheses on the long-term trend growth rate of India's GDP, using mainly the revised (with 1980-81 as the base year) series of *National Accounts Statistics*. A comparison of the old (with 1970-71 as the base year) and the revised series shows that while the movements of GDP over the period 1950-51 to 1984-85 are identical, a sharp decline in the growth rate of 'public administration and defence' is discernible in the revised series, since 1972-73 and especially so since 1977-78. This apparently is on account of changes in the estimation procedure whose validity we are not in a position to ascertain. On account of this, the hypothesis of relatively rapid growth of PAD in the eighties cannot be tested adequately.

GDP as well as its major sectors have grown at a faster rate between 1980-81 and 1987-88 compared to the earlier three decades, with the secondary sector leading the other two. The observed growth rate of GDP during 1980-81 and 1987-88 at over 4.9 per cent per annum were not found in any period of the same length of time during the previous three decades.

Long-term trend analysis rejects the hypothesis of a constant growth rate over the entire period between 1950-51 and 1987-88 since there have been statistically significant breaks in the series. The proposition of trend acceleration as reflected in log-quadratic trend equation, does not get adequate statistical support. The hypothesis of a break in the trend at 1979-80 with an increase in growth rate thereafter cannot be rejected statistically. These findings do not get vitiated when the data for the year 1979-80, a statistical outlier, is excluded. On the contrary, when the outlier is dropped the hypothesis of trend acceleration in growth rate gets a statistically significant coefficient with a positive sign.

Since the growth of 'public administration and defence' has been a matter of dispute—and moreover it simply constitutes public expenditure—we attempted to look into trends in GDP excluding PAD. To overcome the observed lowering of its growth rate in the revised series, we re-estimated it for the period 1972-73 to 1986-87 with the growth rate observed with the old series between 1977-78 and 1984-85 and deducted it from GDP at 1980-81 prices to arrive at a more accurate measure of 'GDP-PAD.' Trend analysis of this series yields more or less identical results (even after dropping the outlier) to those observed with GDP, thus providing a more reasonable basis to suggest a clear increase in the trend growth rate of real GDP in the eighties. This statistical exercise, we believe, could provide a firmer basis for more meaningful debate on India's macroeconomic performance.

Notes

1. Graph A taken from Kumar [1989] seems to capture the widely held perception of an unchanging growth rate of the economy since 1950-51. The author calls the constant growth rate of about slightly less than 4 per cent per annum as "the low growth trap which the economy finds itself in..." (p. 1780).

Graph A

Annual Growth Rates of Indian Economy

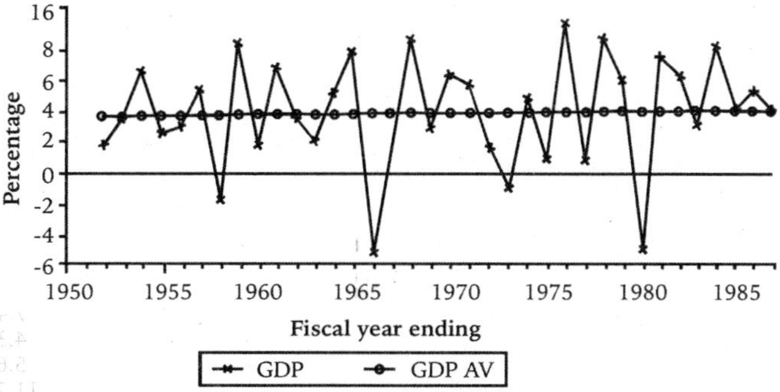

2. Though Rudra [1985] was critical of Raj's method for lack of statistical rigour, little effort appears to have been made as yet to subject his hypothesis to a careful scrutiny.
3. Although similar concern has been expressed by a number of scholars [Kurien, 1989], some, like Minhas [1987], make a distinction between the impact of services sector in general (which need not be particularly adverse) and that of PAD.
4. Unless mentioned otherwise, we have used the actual series and not smoothened them by taking moving average.
5. A similar, though perhaps not of the same magnitude, divergence is discernible in sub-total 'Finance and Real Estate' as noted in Graph B. For the period 1964-65 to 1984-85 when the two series begin to diverge while the old series recorded a growth rate of 5 per cent per annum it is only 4 per cent per annum according to the revised series.

Graph B

Indices of Finance and Real Estate

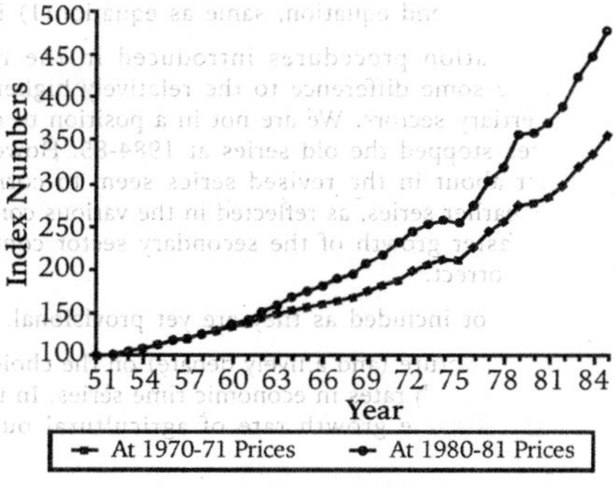

6. Table A shows, as has also been pointed out by Minhas [1987 and 1990], that during the period 1977-78 to 1984-85 the growth rate of PAD was highest among all sectors of GDP.

Table A

		Trend Growth Rate (Per Cent Per Annum)
1.	Agriculture	2.2
2.	Forestry	-6.4
3.	Fishing	2.8
4.	Mining and quarrying	7.4
	Sub-total: Primary	2.2
5.	Manufacturing	3.9
6.	Construction	1.1
7.	Electricity, gas and water supply	6.7
	Sub-total: Secondary	3.5
8.	Transport, storage and communication	7.1
	i. Railways	2.8
	ii. Transport other than railways	8.6
	iii. Communication	8.0
9.	Trade, hotel and restaurant	4.6
	Sub-total: Transport, communication and trade	5.5
10.	Banking and insurance	7.4
11.	Real estate	4.3
	Sub-total: Finance and real estate	5.6
12.	Public administration and defence	11.7
13.	Other services	4.8
	Sub-total: Community, social and personal services	9.0
	Gross domestic product, at factor cost	4.1

Note: All the trend growth rates are statistically significant at 95 per cent level.
Source: National Accounts Statistics, (1987)

7. On this specific issue Uma Dutta Roy Choudhury [1988] merely stated the changes without commenting on it. According to CSO [1988] the changes incorporated in the revised series were discussed at two annual seminars of the Indian Association for Research in National Income and Wealth. However, their publication, *The Journal of Income and Wealth,* does not seem to contain any paper concerning this particular aspects.

8. Minhas [1990] has reiterated his earlier stand [Minhas, 1987] that PAD has continued to grow in the more recent years at the same rate as between 1977-78 and 1985-86. To quote him: "The only sector in which real NDP has grown steadily, between 1977-78 and 1985-86 [*I can now extend this proposition right up to 1987-88]*, is Public Administration and Defence" (p. 464), emphasis added.

9. We have used log-linear trend equation, same as equation(1) in the next section.

10. Changes in the estimation procedures introduced in the revised series could, admittedly, have made some difference to the relatively higher growth rates of the secondary and the tertiary sectors. We are not in a position to capture the difference as the official sources stopped the old series at 1984-85. However, considering that the changes brought about in the revised series seem to correct for the observed shortcomings, of the earlier series, as reflected in the various comments, our inference about the relatively faster growth of the secondary sector compared to the tertiary sector may not be incorrect.

11. Data for 1987-88 are not included as they are yet provisional.

12. There is considerable literature (and a lively debate) on the choice of functional forms to be used to describe growth rates in economic time series. In the Indian context the debate, a decade ago, on the growth rate of agricultural output, has yielded up

considerable literature on analytical and empirical complexities involved in 'trend fitting' exercises. For a very clear exposition of the issues, see, Dandekar [1980]. While we could have chosen some non-linear functional forms (in fact we tried some) the interpretation of the results could perhaps be not without dispute; therefore, we have reported here the results based on the simpler (and also perhaps more widely accepted) functional forms. We are quite aware, as Rudra [1978] has cautioned, that the dispute on growth rate cannot be settled merely on the basis on statistical test of 'goodness of fit'.

13. Anti-log of 'b' minus 1 multiplied by 100 is the estimated value of the underlying compound growth rate of Y.
14. Equation (3) can have more than one dummy variable to test 'breaks' in the series.
15. Author is grateful to Chandan Mukherjee for introducing him to the exploratory data analysis for a more meaningful time series analysis.
16. Box-and-Whisker plot is an effective way to display summary statistics graphically. It allows one to detect outliers and note asymmetric behaviour since the plot divides the data into four areas of equal frequency.
17. Outliers are defined as those observations which are beyond 1.5 times the inter quartile range.
18. All trend equations reported in this note have been tested for statistical significance at 95 per cent confidence level, unless otherwise stated.
19. We have not included the observation for the year 1988-89 when GDP increased over the previous year by over 10 per cent since such a sharp 'rise in the terminal year of the series could severaly distort the value of the estimated coefficient.
20. The coefficient (with estimated 't' value of 1.974) is, however, statistically significant at 90 per cent confidence level.
21. Log-quadratic trend equation for the 3-year moving average of GDP without excluding the observation for the outlier, i.e., 1979-80, also shows a statistically significant acceleration.

$$\log Y = 9.199 + \underset{(6.198)}{0.026\, t} + \underset{(2.632)}{0.000079\, t^2}$$

$$R^2 = 0.9976 \qquad N = 38$$

Where Y is smoothened GDP and figures in brackets refer to estimated 't' values. Both the independent variables are statistically significant at 95 per cent confidence level.

22. Minhas has, in fact, used this category in his recent analysis [Minhas 1987].

References

Ahluwalia, Montek S. (1988). "India's Economic Performance, Policies and Prospects" in Robert E.B. Lucas and Gustav F. Papanek (eds.), *The Indian Economy: Recent Development and Future Prospects*, Oxford University Press, Delhi.

Bardhan, Pranab (1984). *The Political Economy of Development in India*, Oxford University Press, Delhi.

Central Statistical Organisation (1988). *New Series on National Accounts with 1980-81 as Base Year, 1980-81 to 1985-86*, Government of India, New Delhi.

———. (1989a). *National Accounts Statistics, 1980-81 to 1986-87*, Government of India, New Delhi.

———. (1989b). *National Accounts Statistics, (New Series) 1950-51, 1979-80*, Government of India, New Delhi.

Chakravarty, Sukhamoy (1987). *Development Planning: The Indian Experience*, Clarendon Press, Oxford.

Dandekar, V.M. (1980). "Introduction," *Indian Journal of Agricultural Economics*, Vol. 35, No. 2, April-June.

Gothoskar, S.P. (1988). "New Approach in National Account Statistics," *Economic and Political Weekly*, September 24.

Kumar, Arun (1989). "Unemployment, Technological Dynamism and Need for Government Intervention: A Closer Look at 1989-90 Budget," *Economic and Political Weekly*, August 5.

Kurien, C.T. (1989). "Indian Economy in the 1980s and on to the 1990s," *Economic and Political Weekly*, April 15.

Minhas, B.S. (1987). "The Planning Process and the Annual Budgets: Some Reflections on Recent Indian Experience," *Indian Economic Review*, Vol. 22, No. 2.

————. (1990). "NSS Consumer Expenditure Data: Further Comment," *Economic and Political Weekly*, March 3.

Mitra, Ashok (1988). "Disproportionality and the Service Sector: A Note," *Social Scientist*, No. 179, April.

Mukherjee, M. (1988). "New National Income Estimates: Some Observations," *Economic and Political Weekly*, Vol. 23, No. 48, November 26.

Raj, K.N. (1984). "Some Observations on Economic Growth in India over the period 1952-53 to 1982-83," *Economic and Political Weekly*, Vol. 19, No. 41, October 13.

Rao, Patluri and Roger Le Roy Miller (1972). *Applied Econometrics*, Wiley Eastern, Delhi.

Rao, V.K.R.V. (1983). *India's National Income, 1950-1980*, Sage Publication, New Delhi.

Roy Choudhury, Uma Dutta (1988). "New Series on National Accounts Statistics: Some Comments," *Economic and Political Weekly*, Vol. 23, No. 30, July 23.

Rudra, Ashok (1978). "Organisation of Agriculture for Rural Development: The Indian Case," *Cambridge Journal of Economics*, December.

————. (1985). "Economic Growth in India," *Economic and Political Weekly*, Vol. 20 No. 15, April 13.

Economic and Political Weekly, Vol. 25, No.26, June 30, 1990.

2

What has Happened since 1991?

Assessment of India's Economic Reforms

Faced with rising inflation and a balance of payment crisis in mid-1991, India's new (minority) government introduced a fairly comprehensive, orthodox, policy reform package—with currency devaluation as its centrepiece.[1] A sudden drying up of inward remittances and the West Asian markets because of the Gulf War and the collapse of the Soviet economy—then India's largest trading partner—were the proximate economic causes of the crisis. Moreover, domestic political instability accentuated the economic troubles, as critical decisions got postponed and fiscal discipline loosened.[2] Collapsed Soviet Union and rapidly advancing Chinese economy with a greater use of market coordination formed the international background for initiating these policy changes.

Attributing the crisis to unsustainability of the previous policy regime, the reforms tried to consciously fashion the new policy as close to the 'Washington consensus' as permitted by domestic conditions [Williamson 1990]. Long-time critics of India's development strategy widely welcomed this change. For example, for Behrman and Srinivasan, the reforms meant getting rid of an internationally discredited statist development paradigm. To quote them, "The dethronement of the dominant paradigm and elevation to a higher status, if not enthronement, of openness, competition and the market in development is best illustrated by India, the earliest articulator of, and the last among major developing countries to abandon, the dominant paradigm" [Behrman and Srinivasan, 1995: 2468].

Over the last six years, these initiatives have generated an intense debate and considerable popular resistance. The desirability of the reforms and their effects remain contentious issues, and opinions continue to be divided. To illustrate, Kirit Parikh thinks "... the reforms have put the Indian economy on a higher growth path ... . With more sensible policies, we have an opportunity to accelerate our growth further and take off into a high growth trajectory" [Parikh, 1997: 1151]. However, Arun Ghosh believes "... in no sector or manner has the NEP [new economic policy] succeeded" [Ghosh, 1997: 1139].

This study tries to assess some aspects of the reforms, focusing mainly on a few macroeconomic indicators, and the industrial, corporate and public sectors.[3] This attempt is preliminary for many reasons. The reforms were reasonably comprehensive, but we do not yet have adequate information to take a definitive position on many features. Moreover, since many structural aspects of the policy changes are microeconomic in nature, their effects will take some more time to yield measurable results.

For such an assessment to be meaningful, it is perhaps necessary to appreciate the 'initial conditions' of the reforms. India's 1991 balance of payment crisis came after an 11-year period of (relatively) improved and stable growth performance, lower inflation and a steady decline in the proportion of population in poverty. The reforms were preceded by policy changes in 1980-81, associated with a $5 billion IMF credit that India took after the second oil shock. Continuing these, in mid-1980s, there was a deregulation of industry and trade, diversification of financial sector and promotion of stock market [Narasimham Committee on Controls, 1984; Raj, 1986; Patel, 1987].[4] While this period witnessed giving up of prudence that characterised India's long-term macroeconomic policy [Bardhan, 1991], Burgess and Stern (1993) have called the 1980s as an ambitious decade that witnessed a rapid rise in revenue expenditure. Thus, in some respects, the 1991 initiatives represent continuation of the move toward greater market co-ordination of economic decision-making. Therefore, there is a need for caution in attributing changes to these initiatives as evidence reported might be capturing results of earlier efforts.

For the assessment, we follow the 'before and after' approach, as we now have some reasonably sound aggregate data for comparable lengths of time. This method could have some limitations. Analytically, such a comparison may be inappropriate, if the economic performance before the reforms was considered unsustainable.[5] Empirically, in this method we would be artificially truncating a longer trend. Since we (mostly) use average of annual growth rates, they might exaggerate short period fluctuations. Such averaging could at times understate the recovery of economic magnitudes after stabilisation. Therefore, we describe the magnitudes (and changes in them) with considerable care.

I

ANALYTICAL DEBATE: A SYNOPTIC VIEW

Structural adjustment is defined as "a process of market-oriented reforms in policies and institutions, with the goals of restoring a sustainable balance of payments, reducing inflation, and creating conditions for sustainable growth in per capita income. Structural adjustment programmes generally start with a conventional stabilisation programme, intended to restore the viability of the current account and the budget, but they are distinguished from pure stabilisation programmes by the inclusion of a set of microeconomic-institutional policy reforms" [Corbo and Fisher, 1995: 2847].

As there is a widespread appreciation of strengths and shortcomings of the orthodox reform programme, we will not repeat them here.[6] However, what is perhaps missed in much of the recent India debate on reforms is the consensus that has emerged in the literature, based on experience over last two decades, and on some recent advances in economic theory. Lance Taylor said, "... There has been a convergence of views over the past 10 to 15 years about initiatives that are likely to self-destruct, as bold programmes of both orthodox and heterodox intellectual persuasions have failed spectacularly" [Taylor, 1993:40]. Dornbusch considers, "There are plenty of examples now of heterodoxy gone wrong. And there are examples of failed orthodoxy" [Dornbusch, 1993:2]. For instance, there is considerable consensus on the need for fiscal balance, though there are no definitive views on how to achieve it. To quote Lance Taylor once again, "Fiscal equilibrium is desirable, but can be devilishly difficult to attain...Reducing a fiscal deficit is always tricky in political terms; in some corners of the world, distributional conflicts make it well-nigh inconceivable" [Taylor, 1993: 87].

Responding to some of the criticisms against the orthodoxy, John Williamson has recently updated the consensus (Washington

Consensus II) to incorporate the importance of social spending, social insurance and safety nets [Williamson 1996]. Commenting on the modified consensus, Dani Rodrik said, "The equity and social dimensions of policy are now returning to centrestage in the wake of the less than thrilling consequences that market-oriented reforms in Latin America and Eastern Europe have produced along these dimensions" [Rodrik 1997: 413].

More fundamentally, the question still remains, whether the orthodoxy offers an adequate analytical frame to understand the development process of an agrarian, labour surplus economy like ours. Bhaduri (1993) argues that it does not. He shows that development of such an economy involves a rise in the output per worker. This can be decomposed into an (i) increase in participation rates, (ii) changes in sectoral composition of the workforce, and (iii) sectoral labour productivities. Since about two-thirds of India's workforce is still in agriculture, with an unchanging workforce participation rate, and substantial inter-sectoral labour productivity differentials; a development strategy that tries to raise the participation rates and shift workforce away from agriculture can secure large economywide productivity gains.

To quote Bhaduri, "... in the presence of substantially under-utilised labour, an extensive growth strategy may still form an essential element in the early phase of development process ... indeed *there is something strange about so much attention being paid to 'efficient allocation of resources' and the price mechanism while ignoring the blatant inefficiency of massive under-employment*" [Bhaduri, 1993: 11] (emphasis added).

II

ASSESSMENT

Macroeconomic Performance

On average, the Indian economy grew at 5.3 per cent per year during the first five years since the reforms (1992-96), compared to 5.9 per cent during 1986-91 (Table 2.1(a)).[7] Primary and secondary sectors' annual growth rates since 1991-92 were lower at 2.5 per cent and 6.3 per cent, compared to 3.7 and 7.4 per cent, respectively during 1986-91. The tertiary sector, with about two-fifths share in the

GDP, grew fastest in the 1990s (6.8 per cent per year). Within this sector, 'trade, hotel and restaurant' witnessed a sizeable rise (1.7 per cent) in its annual growth rate, from 6.4 per cent (Table 2.2).

Table 2.1(a)

GDP and its Sectoral Growth Rates, 1981-96

(Per cent per year)

Avg. of Years	*Primary*	*Secondary*	*Tertiary*	*GDP*
1981-85	5.8	6.1	5.4	5.6
1986-91	3.7	7.4	7.1	5.9
1992-96	2.5	6.3	6.8	5.3
1981-96	4.0	6.6	6.5	5.7

Source: *National Accounts Statistics*, various issues.

Table 2.1(b)

Trends in Prices, 1982-96

(Per cent per year)

Avg. of Years	*GDP Deflator*	*WPI*	*CPIiw*
1982-85	8.5	6.6	8.7
1986-91	8.4	7.3	9.3
1992-96	9.8	10.1	9.7
1982-96	9.1	8.1	9.4

Note: CPIiw refers to consumer price index for industrial workers.
Sources: *National Accounts Statistics* and *Economic Survey*, various issues.

Admittedly, these estimates are sensitive to yearly variations—an unavoidable problem in comparing growth rates over relatively short time spans. We estimate trend equations—for 1981-91 and 1981-96—to find out if the growth rate in the second period is very different from that during 1981-91 (Table 2.3). Since the trend growth rates for 1981-96 are broadly similar to those for 1981-91, we can reasonably infer that the economy continued to grow at roughly the same rate in 1990s as it did in the previous decade. To ascertain if there is a discontinuity in the trend since 1991, we re-estimated the trend equations with a dummy variable. This was not statistically significant for all the cases, except for the secondary sector.[8] Thus, the GDP and the primary and tertiary sectors maintained their growth rate in the 1990s. Though modest, the secondary sector witnessed a statistically significant slowing (0.4 per cent) since 1991, from 6.8 per cent per year during 1981-91.

Table 2.2

GDP Growth Rates—Disaggregated Trends

(Per cent per year)

Industry (1-digit NIC)	1981-85	1986-91	1992-96	1981-96
1. Agriculture and allied	5.5	3.3	2.3	3.7
2. Mining	8.1	9.2	4.4	7.3
3. Manufacturing	6.2	7.5	6.4	6.7
4. Electricity, gas, water	7.9	8.9	8.5	8.5
5. Construction	4.8	6.3	3.8	5.0
6. Trade, hotel, restaurant	5.4	6.5	8.2	6.7
7. Transport, comm, etc.	6.4	7.3	6.9	6.9
7.1 Railway	3.0	4.8	2.6	3.5
7.2 Other transport	7.3	8.4	6.7	7.5
8. Financial institutions, real estate, etc.	5.3	8.0	7.3	6.9
8.1 Banking, insurance	8.6	13.8	10.4	11.1
8.2 Real estate	3.6	3.5	3.5	3.5
9. Services	5.2	6.7	4.6	5.6
9.1 Pub. admn. and defence	6.5	7.2	3.6	5.9
9.2 Other services	4.1	6.3	5.5	5.3
GDP	5.7	5.9	5.3	5.6

Source: *National Accounts Statistics*, various issues.

Table 2.3

Trend Growth Rate of GDP and its Principal Sectors

(Per cent per year)

Years	Primary	Secondary	Tertiary	GDP
1980-81 to 1990-91	3.5	7.0	6.7	5.6
1980-81 to 1995-96	3.3	6.5	6.6	5.4

Note: Trend growth rates are estimated using log-linear trend equation. All the growth equations are statistically significant at least at 5 per cent significance level.

Source: *National Accounts Statistics*, various issues.

The economy has become more open—share of merchandise imports plus exports in current GDP at market prices has gone up to

17.6 per cent in the 1990s, up from 12.4 per cent during 1986-91 (*Economic Survey*, 1996-97). This did not mean a faster growth of the traded goods sector, specially manufacturing (more later). Inflation up to 1996, however measured, is higher in the 1990s, although all signs suggest it has distinctly slowed down since then (Table 2.1(b)). Balance of trade is less unfavourable than in 1980s, and foreign exchange reserves are adequate for 5-6 months of import requirement [World Bank, 1997]. In relatively open financial markets, whether the present level of reserves is adequate to withstand an external shock is debatable—with a variety of non-resident repatriable deposits continuing to account for the majority of the reserves.

India's fiscal deficit, however measured, has also narrowed; but the revenue deficit, the main cause of concern as it means borrowing for current consumption has, if anything, deteriorated (Figure 2.1). The tax-GDP ratio has stagnated around 12-13 per cent in 1990s, despite an improvement in direct and corporate taxes. They barely compensate for the fall in indirect tax revenue that resulted from tariff cuts and accompanying rationalisation of excise duties (Figure 2.2). Interestingly, during the nine years since 1987-88, while the GDP rose 5.5 per cent a year, the tax-GDP ratio declined a half percentage point. Thus, faced with a growing need to borrow for consumption and a stagnant tax revenue, government tried to rein in public finances by cutting mainly public investment, and to a lesser extent, public spending (as proportions of GDP). The anticipated reduction in government employment to save current spending did not occur (Figure 2.3).[9]

Certainly, India has been able to quickly recover from the 1991 crisis, and the stabilisation effort that followed. Economic growth during the 1990s is close to that during the previous decade, though with a somewhat changed composition.[10] A deep cut in public investment and a modest reduction in public expenditure are broadly consistent with *a priori* expectation and comparative experience [Corbo and Fisher, 1995]. Then, the question arises, who and which sectors bore the burden of these adjustments? Has private (including foreign) investment come into the industries 'vacated' by the public sector? Do these aggregate trends suggest that the economy is on a sustainable growth path? In other words, what is the quality of adjustment?

Figure 2.1

Fiscal and Revenue Deficits of Non-Financial Consolidated General Government, as per cent of Current GDP at Market Prices

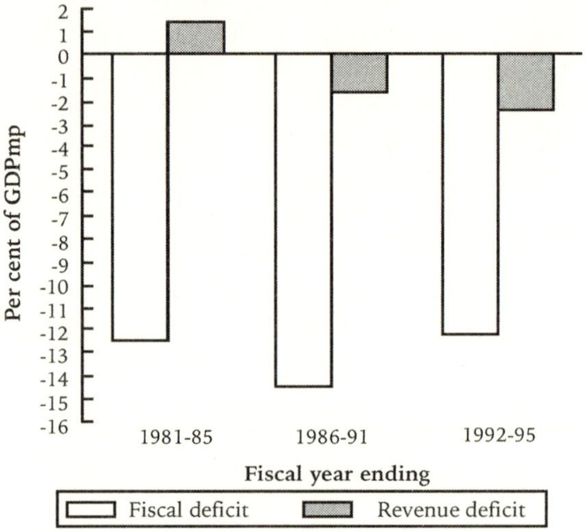

Source: *National Accounts Statistics*, various issues.

Figure 2.2

Tax Revenue, as per cent of Current GDP at Market Prices

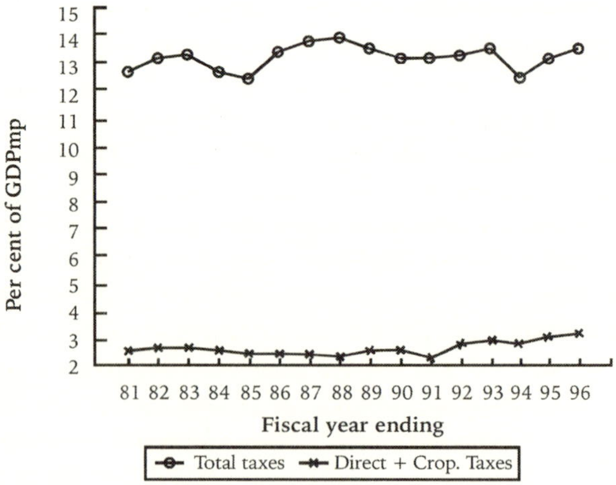

Source: *National Accounts Statistics*, various issues.

Figure 2.3

Public Sector Employment

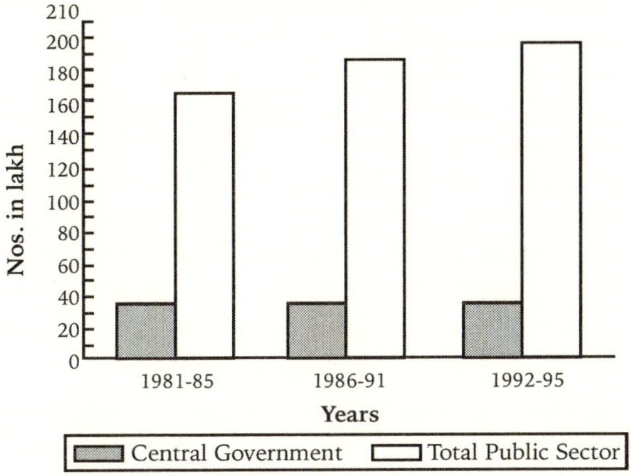

Source: *Economic Survey*, various issues.

This study will address some of these questions. We take a closer look at public spending and investment performance in the aggregate; and then at three interrelated sectors that have been the focus of structural reforms, namely, industry, public and corporate sectors.

Social Sector Spending

Has there been a significant cut in social service spending since 1991? This is a vital question, as it affects the largest segment of the population—the poor. Since the orthodox reforms adversely affected poor in many countries, there has been a concern of a similar effect in India also. Moreover, many studies based on meagre and preliminary budgetary data have found adverse effects of the reforms on these spending [Baru 1993; Guhan 1995; Seeta Prabhu 1996].[11] We now take another look at this question using *National Accounts Statistics* data for four years since 1991-92 that is complete and consistent.

Tables 2.4 and 2.5, respectively show disaggregated trends in (a) economic and purpose classification of expenditure of administrative departments, and (b) government final consumption expenditure, as proportions of (i) total expenditure, and (ii) GDP (all at current prices). As noted earlier, government expenditure as proportion of

GDP has declined, from 11 per cent during 1986-91 to 10.1 per cent during 1992-95 (Table 2.5). However, the sum of spending on health, education, housing and social services has remained constant at 2.9 per cent of GDP during 1992-95. The same measure as a proportion of total government final expenditure rose from 26.2 to 28.1 (Table 2.5). Sectors that witnessed bulk of spending cuts are defence and economic services. Government final consumption expenditure on defence fell from 4.1 per cent of GDP during 1986-91 to 3.3 per cent during 1992-95 (Table 2.5). In the same period, current expenditure of administrative departments on economic services fell from 6 per cent to 5.2 per cent of GDP (Table 2.4).

Table 2.4

Economic and Purpose Classification of Expenditure of Administrative Departments as proportions of (i) Total Expenditure and (ii) Current GDPfc

(Per cent of total in current prices)

Average of Years	*Gen. Public Service*		*Defence*		*Edu. and Health*		*Edu.+Health+ Soc.+Husg. Service*		*Econ. Service*		*Total Exp. as per cent of GDPfc*
	1	*2*	*1*	*2*	*1*	*2*	*1*	*2*	*1*	*2*	
					Current expenditure						
1981-85	16.0	2.5	19.6	3.0	25.7	4.0	32.2	5.0	30.2	4.7	15.5
1986-91	15.1	2.9	21.2	4.1	24.2	4.7	31.3	6.1	30.7	6.0	19.4
1992-95	17.9	3.2	18.8	3.4	25.4	4.6	33.4	6.0	28.8	5.2	17.9
1981-95	16.1	2.8	20.0	3.6	25.0	4.4	32.2	5.7	30.0	5.3	17.7
					Capital expenditure						
1981-85	7.8	0.7	0.2	—	2.2	0.2	12.2	1.0	30.2	6.6	8.5
1986-91	7.7	0.6	0.2	—	2.8	0.2	16.5	1.2	30.7	5.6	7.5
1992-95	5.6	0.3	0.4	—	3.1	0.2	21.5	1.2	28.8	4.1	5.7
1981-95	7.2	0.5	0.3	—	2.6	0.2	16.4	1.2	30.1	5.2	7.3

Notes: (1) As per cent of expenditure of the administrative departments; (2) As per cent of current GDPfc. Row totals do not add up to 100 as some expenditure items are excluded.

Source: *National Accounts Statistics*, various issues.

Thus, contrary to earlier apprehensions, social spending, averaged over four years since the reforms, did not suffer, as defence and economic services bore bulk of the adjustment burden. Why are our results different from the earlier studies and popular perception? It is largely because our information includes centre's as well as states' spending, and we have data for more years. It is perhaps true that during stabilisation, there was, in fact, a significant cut in social service spending. As Guhan (1995) showed, actual expenditure on rural development and social services declined by 0.4 per cent of GDP between 1990-91 and 1992-93. As the economy recovered, this expenditure appears to have been restored.[12]

Table 2.5

Government Final Consumption Expenditure by Purpose as proportions of (i) Total Expenditure, (ii) Current GDPfc

(Per cent of total at current prices)

Average of Years	*Gen. Public Service*		*Defence*		*Edu. and Health*		*Edu.+Health+ Soc.+ Husg. Service*		*Econ. Service*		*Total Exp. as per cent of GDP*
	1	*2*	*1*	*2*	*1*	*2*	*1*	*2*	*1*	*2*	
1981-85	22.9	2.1	33.1	3.0	21.1	1.9	26.5	2.4	15.3	1.4	9.1
1986-91	22.0	2.4	36.9	4.1	21.1	2.3	26.2	2.9	13.5	1.5	11.0
1992-95	24.4	2.5	32.9	3.3	22.2	2.3	28.1	2.9	13.5	1.4	10.1
1981-95	22.9	2.3	34.6	3.5	21.4	2.2	26.8	2.7	14.1	1.4	10.2

Notes: (1) As per cent of government final consumption expenditure; (2) As per cent of current GDPfc. Row totals do not add up to 100 as some expenditure items are excluded.

Source: *National Accounts Statistics*, various issues.

Investment Performance

Contrary to *a priori* expectation, and comparative experience, India's physical investment ratio improved after the reforms [World Bank, 1988]. Gross fixed capital formation (GFCF), as a proportion of GDP, rose from about 20 per cent in 1989-90 to about 23 per cent in 1995-96 (Figure 2.4). However, the GFCF growth rate after the reform is lower at 8 per cent, 1 per cent less than before (Table 2.6). Agriculture, mining, registered manufacturing, (non-rail) transport and communication, and banking and finance improved their GFCF growth rates, while unregistered manufacturing, electricity, gas and water witnessed a decline.

Figure 2.4

Investment Performance: GCF and GFCF as per cent of GDP

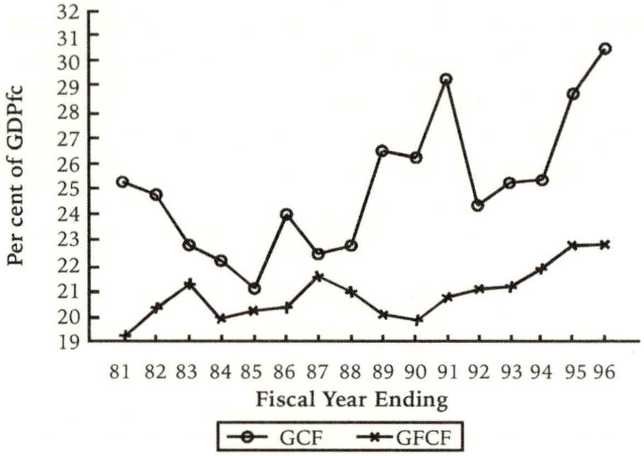

Source: *National Accounts Statistics*, various issues.

Table 2.6

GFCF Growth Rates by Industry, 1982-96

(Per cent per year)

Industry (NIC-1 digit)	*1982-85*	*1986-91*	*1992-96*	*1982-96*
1. Agriculture	(-)1.3	1.6	6.7	2.5
2. Mining	25.8	6.2	11.9	13.4
3. Manufacturing	10.7	8.0	9.1	9.4
3.1 Regd. mfg.	13.0	8.2	11.2	10.4
3.2 Unregd. mfg.	5.9	7.8	5.9	6.6
4. Electricity	7.5	8.9	4.8	7.1
5. Trade, hotel, etc.	9.3	8.2	2.8	6.7
6. Transport and comm.	11.4	6.4	8.8	8.8
6.1 Railway	5.2	4.5	4.9	4.9
6.2 Others	12.9	5.8	7.4	8.2
7. Financing, insurance, real estates and business services	2.6	9.8	8.7	7.5
7.1 Banking and finance	19.8	30.1	23.6	25.2
7.2 Real estate	1.4	7.2	3.6	4.5
8. Public admin.	4.4	1.8	3.9	3.2
9. Other services	5.7	6.9	2.0	5.0
10. Total	4.0	9.0	8.0	7.3

Source: *National Accounts Statistics*, various issues.

As noted earlier, public sector, as percentage of GDP, came down sharply after the reforms (to around 9 per cent), although the decline started a little earlier, in 1987-88—from around 12 per cent (Figure 2.5). Public sector's share in GCF during 1992-95 (40.4 per cent) is lower than any five-year period since 1960-61 (Figure 2.6). Infrastructure's share in GFCF reduced sharply—from 37 per cent in 1986-87 to 26 per cent a decade later (Figure 2.7). However, public investment's composition continues to grow in favour of infrastructure (irrigation, mining, utilities and transport), while the manufacturing sector's share steadily declined, to around 10 per cent (Figure 2.8).[13]

Along with the public sector, the share of household sector has also declined by 4 per cent since 1991, to about 30 per cent of the total GFCF (Table 2.7). Decline in physical investment shares of public and household sectors is compensated by a rise in that of the private corporate sector (corporate sector, hereafter). Thus, by kind of organisation, the corporate sector has emerged as the economy's 'leading sector' since the reforms, accounting for nearly 45 per cent of machinery and equipment investment. The corporate GFCF growth rate nearly doubled, to 18 per cent per year during 1992-96. However, much of it has gone into the tertiary sector (probably in finance) as the growth rate of GFCF in registered manufacturing rose only 3 per cent. Thus, contrary to *a priori* expectation, structural adjustment seems to have propelled investment in non-traded goods sector.

Table 2.7

Proportion of GFCF by Institutions and by Type of Assets

(Per cent of total)

Average of Years	*Total GFCF*			*GFCF in Machinery and Equipment*		
	Public Sector	*Corp. Sector*	*Household Sector*	*Public Sector*	*Corp. Sector*	*Household Sector*
1981-85	49.9	18.6	31.5	43.1	30.1	26.8
1986-91	46.7	18.7	34.6	40.9	27.4	31.7
1992-96	37.8	32.0	30.2	33.4	44.7	21.9
1981-96	44.9	22.8	32.3	39.4	33.6	27.1

Source: *National Accounts Statistics*, various issues.

Figure 2.5

Public Investment, as per cent of GDP

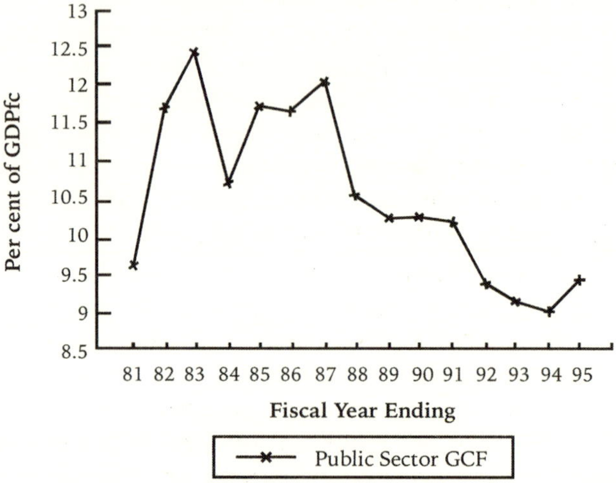

Source: *National Accounts Statistics*, various issues.

Figure 2.6

Public Sector's Share in Total Investment, 1961-95

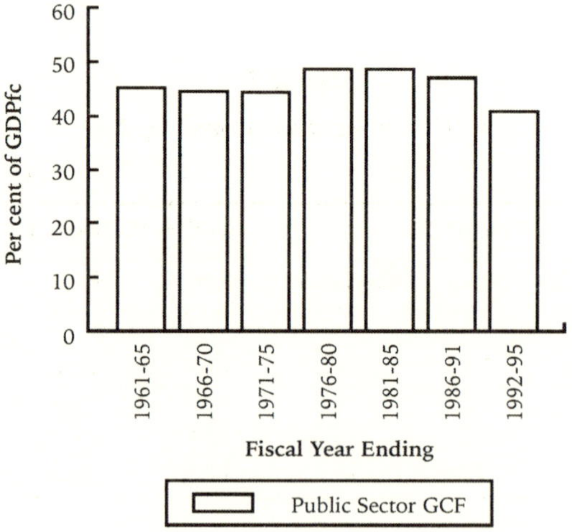

Source: *National Accounts Statistics*, various issues.

Figure 2.7

Share of Infrastructure in GFCF

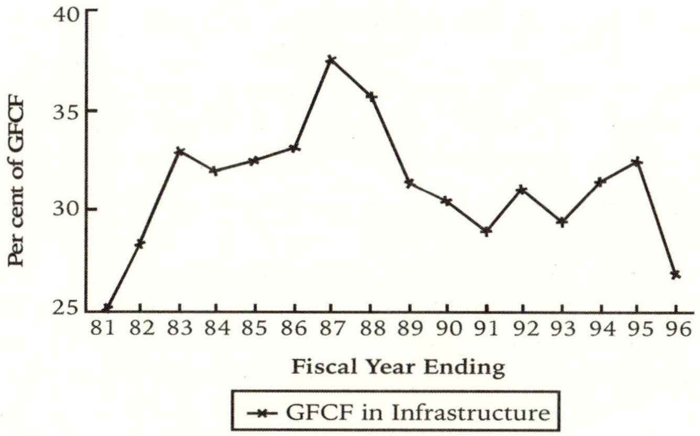

Source: *National Accounts Statistics*, various issues.

Figure 2.8

Composition of Public Investment

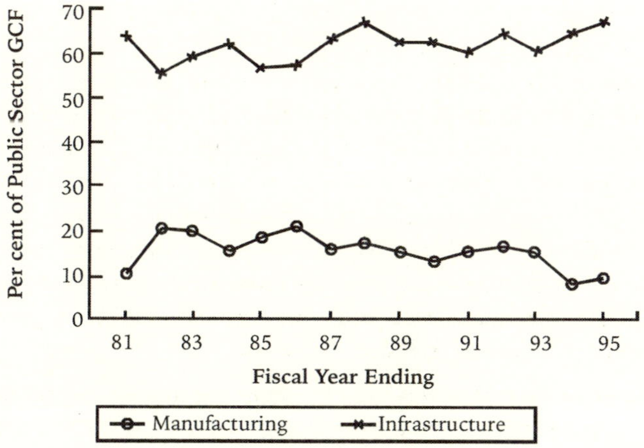

Source: *National Accounts Statistics*, various issues.

While a strong physical investment growth during an orthodox reform process is a (pleasantly) surprising development, its changed composition—away from infrastructure and (unregistered) manufacturing—could adversely affect potential output and export growth, as the corporate sector is a net importer. Decline in household physical investment in general, and unregistered manufacturing in particular, perhaps, reflects the high interest rates and a decline in the banking sector's priority sector lending.[14]

There is, perhaps, more to the investment performance than recorded in these aggregate trends. Since 1991, the office of the Controller of Capital Issues (CCI) was abolished investments by non-resident Indians (NRIs) and foreign institutional investors (FIIs) were allowed in the corporate sector and (larger) Indian firms could now secure long-term low cost resources from international capital markets. As we know, the Indian primary stock market boomed and the supply of long-term loanable funds to Indian (large) firms rose sharply. They perhaps, partly explain the recent corporate investment boom. But, is it commensurate with this sector's access to investible resources? Probably not. Reportedly, a sizeable proportion of these funds was diverted elsewhere, as the ratio of GFCF in manufacturing to supply of long-term funds came down significantly during 1992-96.[15] Then, question arises, where did the rest of the resources go?

Preliminary information suggests they went into (i) intercorporate investment and (ii) real estate.[16] The availability of low cost, untied funds perhaps fuelled the property boom of 1992-94 (Figure 2.9). These are evident from the rise in the corporate sector's non-operating profits in the last few years that boosted corporate results.[17] Another investment avenue was probably financing of mergers and takeover, precise dimensions of which are yet to be analysed. Though speculative, these propositions could form working hypotheses for understanding the effect of the reforms on domestic investment activity. While definitive evidence on these tendencies might be hard to get, the experience with such reforms elsewhere suggests the plausibility of a similar trend in India too.

A sizeable part of investible resources has been used for trading existing capital stock leading to speculative activities. Such asset price bubbles certainly do not augur well for the economy's real sector in the long run. If this tentative proposition is valid, then our assessment of the effects of the reforms on investment activity leads to a more cautious conclusion.

Figure 2.9

Real Estate Prices in Mumbai, per sq. ft. of Built Area

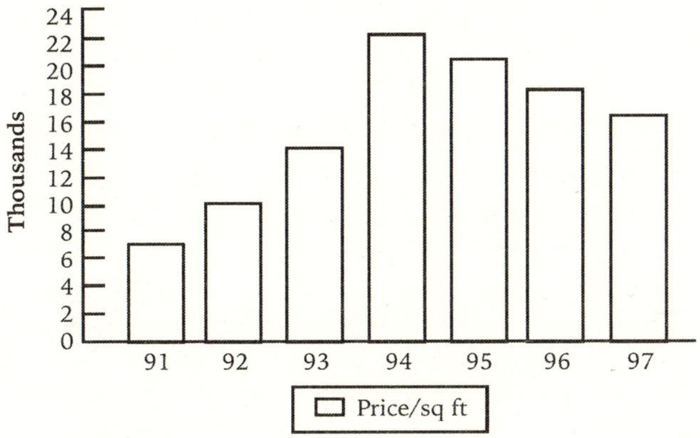

Source: HDFC, Mumbai.

Foreign Direct Investment

Though realised inward foreign direct investment (FDI) in India is only about a fifth of the approved amount (at Rs. 95,690 crore) during 1992-96, it nonetheless represents a significant jump over the previous decade.[18,19] Even ignoring the much debated FDI composition —potato chips *versus* computer chips, for the moment—popular (and official) concern seems to have ignored some vital issues. To what extent FDI represents capital formation? Despite access to large long-term resources, foreign firms' share in fixed asset formation in corporate sector remained a meagre 10 per cent in the 1990s [CMIE, 1997]. Moreover, compared to Indian firms, foreign firms use a smaller share of their investible resources in physical investment: during five years since 1991-92, the ratio of gross fixed assets to total uses of funds for foreign private sector was less than that for Indian private sector by about 13 per cent [CMIE 1997]. Therefore, we suspect that a sizeable proportion of FDI represents a rise in, and acquiring of, managerial control in existing firms, effects of which on efficiency are debatable.[20] Such transactions of existing assets by foreign controlled firms do not represent rise in the economy's potential output and investment demand. So, the effects of such investment on the real sector are likely to be limited.

Industrial Growth Performance

What has happened to industrial output since the reforms? In principle, trade and industrial policy reforms, by removing (reported) anti-export bias, are expected to move resources into the tradable goods sector (specially manufacturing) and raise its growth rate.

After the (expected) sharp negative growth in the first two years of the reforms, industrial growth recovered after 1993-94 or so. Table 2.8(a) suggests that the annual growth rate of manufacturing sector, measured by index of industrial production (IIP), during six years since the reform is lower (6.4 per cent) than that during 1986-91 (8.9 per cent).[21] This is broadly consistent with *National Accounts Statistics* estimates: total manufacturing growth rate is lower at 6.6 per cent during 1992-96, compared to 7.5 per cent in 1986-91 (Table 2.8(b)). Growth rate of unregistered manufacturing—which, if at all, is marginally included in the IIP—suffered more, as it declined by a quarter, to 5.7 per cent per year.

Table 2.8(a)

Industrial Growth, 1982-97—IIP Series

(Per cent per year)

Average of Years	*Index of Industrial Production (IIP)*				*Use-Based Classification of IIP*					
	Mining	*Mfg.*	*Elec.*	*Total*	*Basic Goods*	*Capital Goods*	*Inter-mediate*	*Cons Goods*	*CD Goods*	*CND Goods*
Weights	11.46	77.11	11.43	100.00	39.42	16.43	20.51	23.65	2.55	21.10
1981-85	12.7	5.7	8.9	7.0	8.7	6.3	6.0	5.3	14.4	4.0
1986-91	5.5	8.9	9.1	8.5	7.3	14.9	5.8	7.6	13.4	6.4
1992-97	3.5	6.4	6.9	6.1	6.6	6.4	6.1	5.4	9.2	4.5
1981-97	6.5	7.2	8.2	7.2	7.4	9.6	6.0	6.2	12.1	5.1

Note: Cons-Consumer Goods; CD-Consumer Durable Goods; CND-Consumer Non-Durable Goods.

Sources: *Economic Survey*, various issues, *Economic and Political Weekly*, Vol.32, No. 29, July 19-25, 1997.

Table 2.8(b)

Manufacturing Sector Growth, 1981-96—
National Accounts Series

(Per cent per year)

Average of Years	*Total Manufacturing*	*Registered Manufacturing*	*Unregistered Manufacturing*
1981-85	6.2	7.7	4.1
1986-91	7.5	7.5	7.6
1992-96	6.6	7.1	5.7
1981-96	6.8	7.5	5.9

Source: National Accounts Statistics, various issues.

The decline in the growth rate is evident across IIP's all use-based categories, except intermediate goods industries. Consumer durable goods (weightage: 2.6 per cent) continued to grow the fastest, although slower than before.

The capital goods sector suffered most, as its growth rate fell nearly 60 per cent, to 6.4 per cent per year. By two-digit industry groups, annual growth rate of electrical machinery fell from 20 per cent during 1986-91 to 6.4 per cent during 1992-97 (Table 2.8(c)). This happened, as noted above, not because of a fall in (physical) investment rate, but perhaps because of import competition – as the tariffs on capital goods were substantially reduced. The flip side of it is that capital goods have become cheaper: investment goods prices, relative to the GDP deflator, specially of machinery and equipment, have fallen since late 1980s (Figure 2.10).[22]

Thus, contrary to the widely held view, the manufacturing growth rate since the reforms is lower and its composition uneven.[23] Though these trends suggest a fairly quick recovery from the stabilisation efforts, the recovery is nevertheless partial. In principle, unregistered manufacturing—representing labour-intensive traded goods sector—is expected to improve its growth performance. This did not happen.

While manufacturing output growth recovered, though partially, the mining sector decelerated, largely representing a decline in petroleum production. This sector's annual growth rate came down from 5.5 per cent in 1986-91, to 3.5 per cent in the post-reform

Figure 2.10

Capital Goods Prices, Relative to GDP Deflator

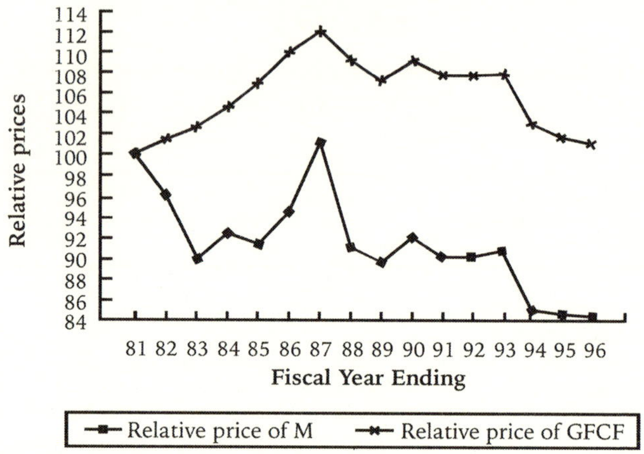

Source: *National Accounts Statistics*, various issues.

Figure 2.11

Import Dependence: Share of Import in Total POL Consumption

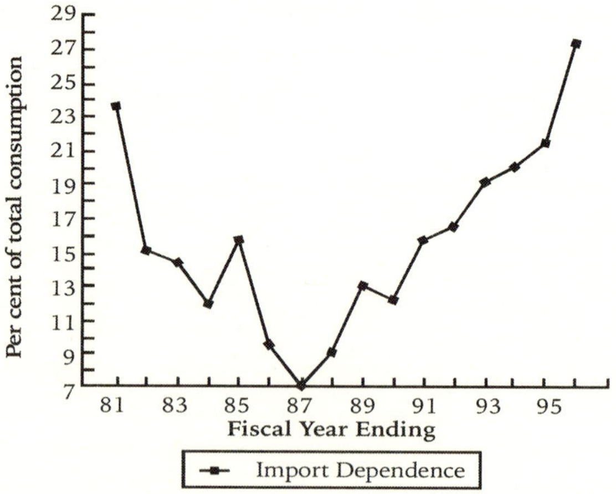

Source: *Economic Survey*, various issues.

period; thus, the dependence on imported oil nearly doubled since 1991, to about 28 per cent of domestic consumption (Figure 2.11).[24]

Table 2.8(c)

Manufacturing Growth Rates by 2-Digit Industry Groups, 1982-97—IIP Series

(Per cent per year)

NIC Code	*Industry Group*	*1982-85*	*1986-91*	*1992-97*	*1982-97*
20-21	Food	5.1	5.8	4.2	5.1
22	Beverages, tobacco	2.9	(-)0.2	10.4	4.4
23	Cotton textiles	0.9	4.6	5.6	3.7
25	Jute	1.0	(-)1.0	(-)1.9	(-)0.2
26	Other textiles	(-)1.0	3.1	(-)0.7	1.2
27	Wood	23.0	(-)0.9	2.8	6.8
28	Paper	7.5	6.4	7.7	7.4
29	Leather	10.6	4.1	3.3	6.1
30	Rubber	10.4	2.3	2.9	4.8
31	Chemicals	9.4	9.1	6.2	8.5
32	Non-metallic minerals	8.7	6.0	6.7	6.9
33	Basic metals	2.1	6.7	10.8	7.1
34	Metal products	1.7	3.6	4.3	4.0
35	Machinery	6.3	5.5	5.3	6.1
36	Elec. machinery	10.7	20.0	6.4	14.6
37	Transport equipment	7.1	5.5	11.0	8.4
38	Others	9.5	13.7	(-)1.6	8.8

Source: Same as Table 2.8(b).

Public Sector Performance

As part of the stabilisation effort, public investment and expenditure ratios are expected to fall; they did so in India, as noted earlier. However, interestingly, public sector output growth and surplus generation improved in 1990s. The public sector's share in GDP rose 1.3 per cent, to 24.8 per cent during 1992-95. Share of public sector in manufacturing rose—a sector that witnessed rapid fall in tariffs, abolition of non-price protection measures and raise in domestic competition (Table 2.9). In institutional terms, much of this growth occurred in non-department enterprises as their share in GDP steadily rose while administrative departments and departmental enterprises (mainly railways and communication) recorded growth rates less than that of GDP (Figure 2.12).

Table 2.9

Public Sector's Share in GDP by Industry, 1981-95

(Per cent)

Avg. of Years	*Ag.*	*Mining*	*Mfg.*	*Regd. Mfg.*	*Elec. Gas, Water*	*Const.*	*Trade, Hotel*	*Trans-port, Comm.*	*Bank-ing, Finance*	*Other Service*	*GDP*
1981-85	2.1	98.8	12.4	21.1	93.3	16.8	5.3	52.9	83.7	42.2	20.3
1986-91	2.1	115.2	14.1	23.1	92.5	19.2	4.5	46.9	85.8	44.3	23.5
1992-95	1.9	109.4	14.8	23.6	94	18.6	3.0	41.7	80.5	41.3	24.8

Note: Since mid-1980s, there is an anomaly in the GDP estimates for mining sector: public sector GDP is greater than GDP of the sector as a whole. This is apparently because of different methods used for estimating the GDP in public and private sectors.

Source: *National Accounts Statistics*, various issues.

Figure 2.12

Public Sector Output Growth, by Type of Institution

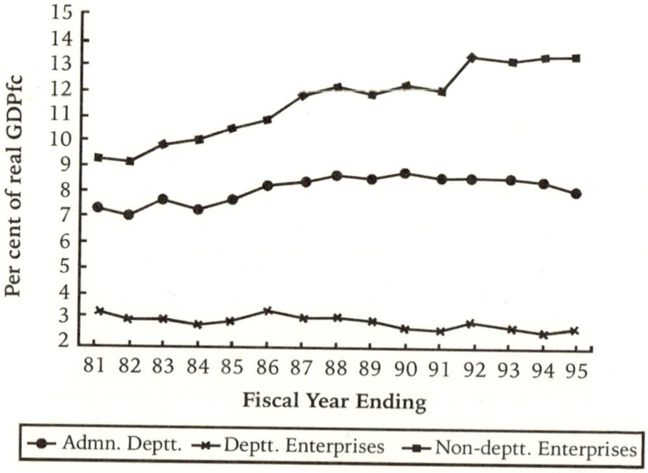

Source: *National Accounts Statistics*, various issues.

Along with output growth, public sector's internal resource generation ratio also improved (Figure 2.13) and, correspondingly, external finance's (domestic and foreign) share in capital formation declined.[25] A sharp rise in profitability (gross profit as percentage of capital employed) of central government public sector enterprises (PSEs)—even excluding petroleum enterprises—is also evident (Figure 2.14). Moreover, PSEs' share in fiscal deficit of non-financial consolidated general government declined (Figure 2.15).[26] These improvements are not because of a faster rise in public sector prices.[27] In fact, price of public sector output (relative to GDP deflator) did not rise in 1990s (Figure 2.16).

At least so far, in the aggregate, public sector has clearly withstood the 1991 policy shock, and continues to improve its performance.[28] This can be illustrated by a steady rise in physical efficiency of thermal power plants, most of which are in the public sector. The average plant load factor of thermal power plants rose nearly 10 per cent in six years in 1990s, continuing the trend of the previous decade (Figure 2.17). However, since public investment has been cut severely, it is a moot point if the improvement can be sustained.

Figure 2.13

Financing of Public Sector Enterprises' GCF

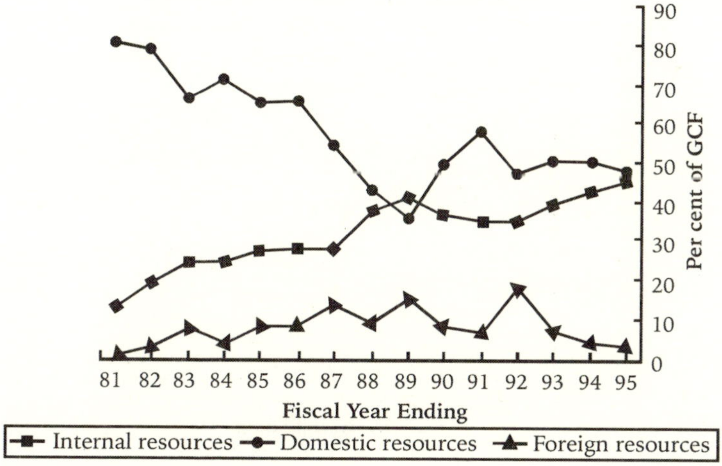

Source: *National Accounts Statistics*, various issues.

Figure 2.14

Profitability of Central Government Public Sector Enterprises

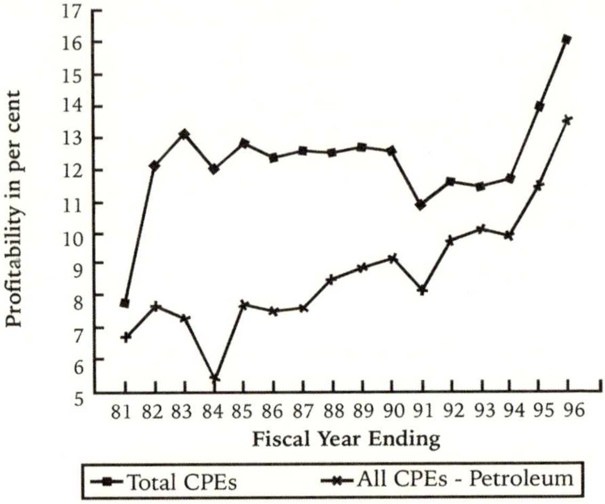

Source: *Public Enterprises Survey*, various issues.

Figure 2.15

PSEs' Share in Fiscal Deficit of Non-Financial General Government

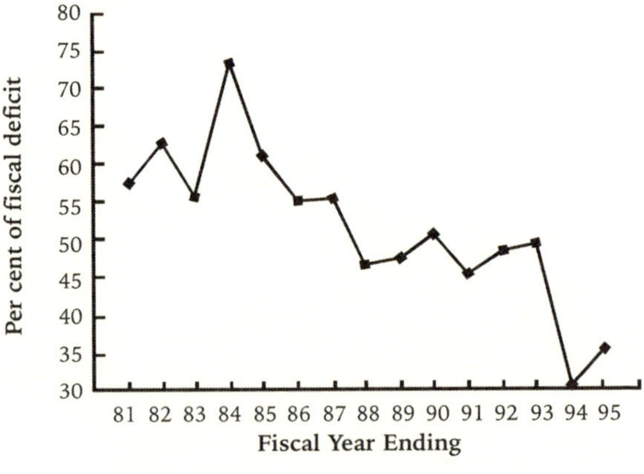

Source: *National Accounts Statistics*, various issues.

Figure 2.16

Public Sector Deflator, Relative to GDP Deflator

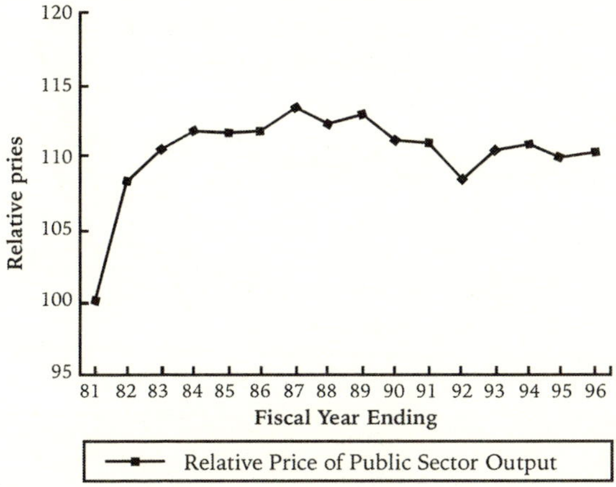

Source: *National Accounts Statistics*, various issues.

Figure 2.17

Average Plant Load Factor of Thermal Power Plants

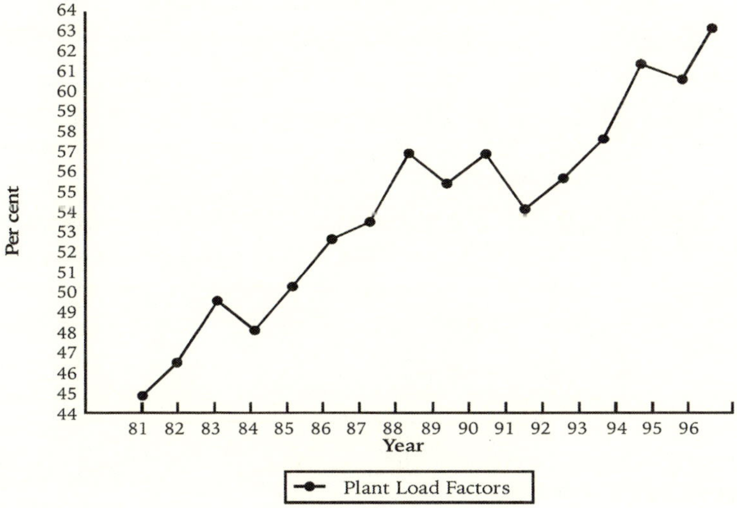

Source: *Economic Survey*, various issues.

III

SUMMARY AND CONCLUSION

This study has tried to understand what happened to the Indian economy since the orthodox economic reforms were initiated in mid-1991. It is preliminary, as we have looked at evidence for only 4 to 5 years since the reforms were made, and many tendencies might confound the effects of earlier initiatives. Therefore, attributing changes mainly (or solely) to the 1991 policy changes may, at times, be simplistic. This attempt is partial as well, since we have examined only a few, though important, aspects of the reform package, and only some sectors of the economy.

Nonetheless, our attempt offers a sober, yet significant picture of the changes that have occurred. After stabilisation, the economy got back on the growth path charted in the 1980s. The secondary sector shows a modest, yet statistically significant decline in its growth rate since 1991-92. The fiscal balance appears better, at the expense of a deep cut in public investment, and to a lesser extent, public spending. Borrowing for consumption (the revenue deficit) has gone up, as the much publicised reduction in public employment to reduce current spending did not occur; the tax-GDP ratio has stagnated in 1990s, though direct and corporate taxes collection improved.

Contrary to much apprehension, there was practically no fall in social service spending ratios, as the axe fell mainly on defence and economic services. Whether economising on defence spending is the best way to correct the fiscal imbalance is something that cannot, perhaps, be judged on economic considerations alone.

Again, contrary to *a priori* expectation, the economy's aggregate investment ratio improved since the reforms, though the physical investment growth rate is 1 per cent lower than in the pre-reform period. Moreover, its changed composition is certainly a cause for concern.

Manufacturing sector growth recovered from the adverse stabilisation effect. But the average growth rate for six years since the reforms is clearly lower than the pre-reform period. Moreover, the recovery is uneven, with a sharp decline in the growth rates of capital goods and unregistered manufacturing (accounting for about 40 per cent of gross manufacturing value added). Capital goods growth rate fell, with the fall in tariffs. But capital goods prices have also fallen, relative to the GDP deflator. Therefore, we need to weigh the price advantage against the learning effects foregone.

Public investment witnessed a deep cut. Yet public sector output growth and profitability improved, public sector enterprises' share in the fiscal deficit of (non-financial) consolidated general government has also come down. These trends evidently suggest a better resource utilisation, reducing much criticised high incremental capital-output ratio in public sector. However, we cannot be sure if this improvement can persist after the deep cut in public sector's potential output growth.

If India's post-independence economic experience is any guide, then the decline in public investment could have severe consequences for sustaining the 5.5 per cent annual growth rate that we have recorded since 1980-81.[29]

In sum, the good news (so far) is that there is no major, unqualified, bad news. In the aggregate, many of the potentially adverse effects of such orthodox reforms were avoided. The picture that emerges is, as is perhaps often the case—the proverbial half filled glass – permitting selective use of evidence to buttress one's preferred view. But overall, do the favourable changes call for a celebration of a higher and sustainable growth path, led by private initiative?

Probably not, as our closer look shows some dark clouds in the horizon. Some of the adverse effects were avoided at the expense of a better fiscal balance. Many of the favourable features are secured at the expense of the future, (potential) growth and export possibilities. Therefore, it is hard to believe that the economy has been put on a more sustainable path. Further, such an assessment is based on not only what is achieved in the 1990s, but what has been missed out—the lost growth potential by (implicitly) viewing the problem in the orthodox perspective.

Posing the problem as Bhaduri did, as discussed before, we find some unfavourable developments that might have something to do with the increasingly market-oriented policy perspective in the recent years. Recent employment statistics show that in 1993-94 still nearly two-thirds of Indian workforce was in agriculture [NSS, 1997].

Table 2.10

Workforce Distribution and Labour Productivity

Sector	*Workforce Distribution in 1977-78 (per cent)*	*Percentage Change in Workforce Distribution*			*Real GDP Per Worker (Index)*
		1983 over 1977-78	*1987-88 over 1983*	*1993-94 over 1987-88*	
Primary	71.22	(-)4.22	(-)2.20	(-)1.40	100
Secondary	12.10	1.60	1.70	(-)0.80	386
Tertiary	16.70	2.20	0.80	2.30	381

Source: *National Sample Survey*, various reports: *National Accounts Statistics*, various issues.

Interestingly, the intersectoral shift in the workforce from agriculture to non-agriculture has slowed down during 1988-94, and the secondary sector's share has also come down. Since labour productivity in the non-agriculture sectors, in 1993-94, is nearly four times that in agriculture, slowing down of the workforce transformation implies an immense loss of (potential) productivity gains. This potential loss perhaps far outweighs the efficiency gains (possibly) secured by eliminating 'little triangles' of price distortions.

If this assessment is correct, then we need to ponder over how to regain the lost momentum of workforce transformation and better utilisation of surplus labour that is at the heart of equitous growth in a large agrarian economy like ours.

Notes

1. In many countries, in recent years, new political regimes have initiated similar policies by discrediting previous governments on past economic failures. Haggard and Kaufman find, "Incoming governments ... have capitalised on honeymoon periods and the disorganised or discrediting of the opposition to launch ambitious new reform initiatives" [Haggard and Kaufman, 1992: 30].
2. Whether these proximate causes were significant is debatable. Bhagwati and Srinivasan (1993), and Joshi and Little (1994) dismiss these to argue that the crisis was mainly 'made in India', due to the unsustainable policy regime of the 1980s. However, characterising the 1991 episode as merely a liquidity crisis, Arjun Sengupta has questioned the necessity of initiating such a complete package of reforms. To quote him: "What is novel about the economic reforms of 1991 is the timing and the fact that it was introduced as a package of measures to meet a specific liquidity crisis for which such an elaborate package was really not necessary" [Sengupta, 1995: 40].
3. This effort is motivated by the concern that I.G. Patel expressed about the new initiatives. He said, "... indeed, so great is the area of agreement that the new economic policies themselves are in danger of becoming a new ideology or orthodoxy—and surely, that is the time to watch out, to look more closely at things and options ..." [Patel, 1992: 40].

4. Some commentators believe that industrial reforms in 1991 were quite superfluous, as much of it was already done in 1985 [Mani, 1992].

5. Unsustainability of a policy regime refers to size and growth public debt. Analytically and empirically, this is a very debatable issue, except when GDP growth rate is lower than interest rate (both in nominal or real terms). Despite much analytical refinement, Evsey Domar's following much quoted comment is still valid: "If all the people and organisations who work and study, write articles and make speeches, worry and spend sleepless nights—all for fear of the debt—could forget about it for a while and spend even half of their efforts trying to find way of achieving a growing national income, their contribution to the benefit and welfare of humanity—and to the solution of the debt problem—would be far greater" [Domar, 1957: 64].

6. The essence of the orthodox reforms is an abiding faith in the power of markets in (static) efficiency in allocation of resources, a deep distrust of state intervention, and 'sound money.' The following list broadly summarises the Washington consensus:

   (1) balanced budget, with deficit of a few per cent of GDP, spending controls and broad based taxation with low marginal rates;

   (2) sound macroeconomic policy with some limited social safety nets;

   (3) price reforms, positive real interest rates and weak and stable exchange rates;

   (4) trade and investment liberalisation;

   (5) privatisation of state-owned enterprises; and,

   (6) deregulation of markets, including the labour market.

7. Unless otherwise mentioned, variables in this study are at constant (1980-81) prices; growth rates are average of annual percentage change over the previous year; years refer to fiscal year ending, for example, 1992-96 refers to period 1991-92 to 1995-96; and GDP refers to GDP at factor cost.

   Our estimates of average growth rates suffer from the well known problems of yearly fluctuations and terminal years chosen. To reduce their misinterpretation and permit a balanced judgement of these numbers, we provide estimates for 1981-85, and for the entire period, 1981-96.

8. We estimated Log Y = a+bt+D(t), where D is 0 up to 1991, and 1 for 1992-96.

9. Contrary to the popular view, growth rate of public employment steadily came down, close to zero, during the 1980s. This trend was not sustained in 1990s, clearly suggesting the absence of a political consensus on this, and the minority government's inability to take hard decisions, despite much public rhetoric.

10. Based on 1995-96 growth rate of 7 per cent, there is much popular, including official, optimism about India entering into a higher trend growth rate after the reforms. In 1980s, when the trend growth rate was about 5.5 per cent, in three years annual growth rate was over 7 per cent. We have to be cautious against such 'opportunistic biases,' to borrow Gunnar Myrdal's phrase. He had warned, "The fact that conceptions about reality ... are influenced by the interests as commonly perceived by the dominant groups in the society ... and that they so come to deviate from truth in a direction opportune to these interests ..." [Myrdal, 1970: 21].

11. To quote Guhan, "In the final outcome, what is of concern is that the GDP ratio of outlays at both [centre and states] levels taken together has declined in the first four years of adjustment" [Guhan, 1995: 1096-97].

12. These aggregates, though very important, probably hide more than they reveal. Since the reforms, there was a greater emphasis on wage employment generation, rather than self-employment and asset creation programmes. Moreover, there has probably been a proliferation of 'schemes' to suit political ends. To quote Guhan again, "... one cannot escape the conclusion that the centre's anti-poverty portfolio is riddled with much needless confusion and complexity in its conceptualisation, design and administration. ... this is to be attributed to the use of a limited set of instruments for promoting diverse multiple objectives... and, at the same time, some pocket money for members of parliament" [Guhan, 1995: 1099].

13. Much of the widely held opinion against public investment is in manufacturing, as it is believed to represent investment in inefficient import substituting industries [Joshi and Little 1994]. Such criticism has little basis since the manufacturing sector's share in public investment has been small and declining, as evident in the same figure.

14. This result is consistent with findings based on a cross-country analysis. Greene and Villanueve (1991) find, for a sample of 23 less developed countries, over 1975-87, a negative and statistically significant effect of real interest rates on investment.

15. The ratio of corporate gross fixed capital formation to long-term sources of finance (primary capital mobilisation, 'euro issues' and development finance institutions' disbursements) came down from 121 per cent during 1986-91, to 64 per cent during 1992-96.

16. All intercorporate investment may not be undesirable. If firms take minority stake in suppliers' and distributors' firms, such investment could have long-term positive effects, as has been widely documented in Japanese industry. But if intercorporate investment, mediated by 'finance companies,' is used as a vehicle for hostile takeovers, and other measures that reduce competition, or divert resources for unproductive activities, then such investment may have undesirable consequence. More important, if intercorporate investment is ill regulated, finance companies could take advantage of the widely noted imperfections in the financial markets as is feared to have happened recently in India leading to socially undesirable results.

17. ICICI's annual study of financial performance of its 675 assisted companies supports our contention. Although this report emphasises year to year variations, the underlying point is that non-operating profits were a dominant influence. To quote the report, "Other income rose by 23.4 per cent in 1995-96 compared to 35.8 per cent in 1994-95... . Therefore, other income, which was a significant factor in influencing profits in 1993-94 and 1994-95 did not play a major role in 1995-96. The major sources of other income in the past were interest on inter-corporate deposits (ICDs), dividend receipts, profit on sale of investments, lease rentals, investment in units and sale of real assets. In 1995-96, a dormant secondary capital market militated against a substantial rise in other income through sale of investments. However, some cash-rich companies were able to earn large other income by lending in the ICD market at high interest rates" [ICICI 1997].

18. This estimate is based on the comprehensive data on FDI collated in *Economic and Political Weekly*, May 10, 1997 (p.987).

19. Realised FDI being a small fraction of approvals is not peculiar to India. For China, the ratio is about one-third [computed using data in Table 3 of Broadman and Sun 1997].

20. Effects of corporate takeovers on efficiency is a much contested issue in economics. Appreciating limitations of this mechanism of corporate control, a significant professional opinion holds that the developing countries should avoid replicating this anglo-saxon institution. To quote Ajit Singh, "The important question is whether the evolution of such a market [for corporate control] would be conducive to Indian industrialisation and for fast economic growth. The review of the analysis and evidence on the markets for corporate control in the US and the UK indicate several drawbacks, particularly from the perspective of Economic Development... . A developing country like India simply cannot afford the burden of an extremely expensive and hit-and-run system of management change which takeovers represent" [Singh 1997:35-36].

21. Index of industrial production (IIP) with 1980-81 as the base is widely used to assess the recent industrial production trends. Primary information for construction of the index is voluntary reporting of output by firms above a certain size. Quality of the index has been widely questioned for some time now. One suspects that problem has become acute after the recent policy changes since the firms now have little incentive for timely supply of this information. Therefore, we suspect that the index has increasingly become unrepresentative. However, for lack of anything better, we still use these estimates, with great caution.

22. K.N. Raj repeatedly emphasised that developing capital goods industries in Indian planning was precisely to cheapen these goods which will in turn, reduce prices of final consumption goods. In 1970s, when GDP growth rate did not pick up despite significant

rise in domestic saving and investment, he attributed it partly to growing relative price of capital goods, [Raj, 1986]. This has now happened after import liberalisation.

23. Arvind Virmani's recent study illustrates the popular perception: "The manufacturing sector has shown the greatest improvement in performance. The growth of manufacturing (GDP at factor cost) is likely to average about 8.9 per cent during the Eighth Plan period. This is 1.2 per cent higher than during the Seventh Plan period, 1.9 per cent points higher than during 1980s. It is not a coincidence that it has seen the most extensive reforms" [Virmani, 1997: 2064].

24. Decline in domestic petroleum production was partly due to 'overexploitation' of certain oilfields in late 1980s. But it was a short-term problem. More enduring reason was perhaps the cut in public investment.

25. These estimates are for non-departmental non-financial enterprieses. This is probably the most comprehensive category of public sector enterprises, as given in *National Accounts Statistics*. For a discussion on merits of using this data source, refer to Nagaraj (1991).

26. Computed using *National Accounts Statistics*, this comprehensive measure of the deficit, includes not only the central government, but also the states and public sector enterprises. For details see, Nagaraj (1993).

27. Bardhan (1993) sought to ignore our contention of improved public sector enterprise performance in 1980s, by suggesting that it was largely due to a faster rise of PSEs prices. The development in 1990s, vindicates our earlier position as PSEs profitability has improved, despite a fall in their relative prices.

28. World Bank believes the singular achievement of the 1991 reforms is its success in reducing public sector's role in the Indian economy. To quote its latest official assessment: "The declining role of the public sector since the start of the reform programme in 1991, both as producer of good and services and economic regulator, is one of India's most fundamental change since independence" [World Bank, 1997:i].

    True. If this were the real agenda, then the reforms were quite a success. But, perhaps, PSEs proved their critics wrong by improving their output growth and financial performance, suggesting that they have been—at least so far, in the aggregate—able to withstand the policy changes.

    We have not assessed if public sector's role as an economic regulator has declined; if yes, is it desirable. Probably it is not, as the 1997 *World Development Report* argues.

29. Studies on India's macroeconomic performance clearly brings out centrality of public investment, most of which has been mainly on infrastructure [Nayyar 1994; Pandit 1995]. Unless this stylised fact has been undone, India surely faces an infrastructure supply constraint.

References

Bardhan, Pranab (1991). "India's Macro-Economic Performance in a Comparative Political Economy Perspective" in Dipak Banerjee (ed.), *Essays in Economic Analysis and Policy*, Oxford University Press, Delhi.

———— (1993). "Market Socialism and Public Sector Reform" in Kaushik Basu *et al.*, (eds.) *Capital, Investment and Development*, Blackwell, Oxford.

Baru, Sanjay (1993). "New Economic Policy: Efficiency, Equity and Fiscal Stabilisation," *Economic and Political Weekly*, Vol. 28, April 10.

Behrman, Jere and T.N. Srinivasan (1995). "Introduction," T.N. Srinivasan and Jere Behrman (eds.), *Handbook of Development Economics*, Vol. 3B, Elsevier, Amsterdam.

Bhaduri, Amit (1993). "Orthodox Development Theories and their Application to Less Developed Countries" in Gianni Vaggi (ed.), *From Debt Crisis to Sustainable Development: Changing Perspectives on North-South Relationship*, St. Martin's Press, London.

Bhagwati, Jagdish and T.N. Srinivasan (1993). *India's Economic Reforms*, Ministry of Finance, Government of India.

Broadman, Harry G. and Xiaolun Sun (1977). "The Distribution of Foreign Direct Investment in China," *The World Economy*, Vol. 20, No. 3, May.

Burgess, Robin and Nicholas Stern (1993). "Tax Reform in India," *DEP* No. 45, Development Economics Research Programme, London School of Economics.

Centre for Monitoring Indian Economy (1997). *Corporate Sector*, Mumbai.

Corbo, Vittorio and Stanley Fisher (1995). "Structural Adjustment: Stabilisation and Policy Reform — Domestic and International Finance" in J Behrman and T.N. Srinivasan (eds), *Handbook of Development Economics*, Vol. 3, Elsevier Science BV, Amsterdam.

Domar, Evsey (1957). "The 'Burden of the Debt' and the National Income," Essays in the *Theory of Economic Growth*, Oxford University Press, New York.

Dornbusch, Rudiger (1993). *Stabilisation, Debt and Reform*, Harvester-Wheatsheaf, New York.

Ghosh, Arun (1997). "Budget 1997-98: Underlining NEP," *Economic and Political Weekly*, Vol. 32, Nos. 20-21 May.

Government of India (1985). *Report of the Committee to Examine Principles of a Possible Shift from Physical to Finance Control* (Chairman: M. Narasimham), New Delhi.

Greene, J. and D. Villanueva (1991). "Private Investment in Developing Countries: An Empirical Analysis," *IMF Staff Papers*, Vol. 38, No. 1.

Guhan, S. (1995). "Social Expenditures in the Union Budget: 1991-96," *Economic and Political Weekly*, Vol. 30, Nos. 18-19, May 6-13.

Haggard, S. and Robert K. Kaufman (eds.) (1992). *Politics of Economic Adjustment*, Princeton University Press, New Jersey.

ICICI (1997). *Financial Performance of Companies: ICICI Portfolio, 1991-92 to 1995-96*, Mumbai.

Joshi, Vijay and IMD Little (1994). *India: Macroeconomics and Political Economy, 1964-91*, World Bank, Washington, DC.

Mani, Sunil (1992). "New Industrial Policy, Barriers to Entry, Foreign Investment and Privatisation," *Economic and Political Weekly*, Vol. 27, No. 35.

Myrdal, Gunnar (1970). *The Challenge of World Poverty*, Penguin, Harmondsworth.

Nagaraj, R. (1991). "Public Sector Performance in the Eighties: Some Tentative Findings," *Economic and Political Weekly*, Vol. 26, No. 50, December 14.

————. (1993). "Macroeconomic Impact of Public Sector Enterprises: Some Further Evidence" paper presented at the Seminar in IIM Calcutta in August.

National Sample Survey (1997). "Employment and Unemployment in India, 1993-94," *Fifth Quinquennial Survey, NSS 50th Round* (July 1993-June 1994), Report No. 409, Government of India, New Delhi.

Nayyar, Deepak (ed.) (1994). *Industrial Growth and Stagnation*, Oxford University Press, Delhi.

Pandit, V.N. (1995). "Macroeconomic Character of the Indian Economy: Theories, Facts and Fancies" in Prabhat Patnaik (ed.), *Macroeconomics*, Oxford University Press, Delhi.

Patel, I.G. (1987). "On Taking India into the Twenty First Century: New Economic Policy in India," *Modern Asian Studies*, Vol. 21, No. 2.

————. (1992). "New Economic Policies: A Historical Perspective," *Economic and Political Weekly*, Vol. 27, January 11.

Parikh, Kirit (1997). "India's Economy: Poised for Take-Off," *Economic and Political Weekly*. Vol. 32, Nos. 20-21, May 23-30.

Raj, K.N. (1986). "New Economic Policy," *V.T. Krishnamachari Memorial Lecture*, Oxford University Press, Delhi.

Rodrik, Dani (1997). "The 'Paradoxes' of the Successful State," *European Economic Review*, Vol. 41, Nos. 3-5.

Seeta Prabhu, K. (1996). "The Impact of Structural Adjustment on Social Sector Expenditure: Evidence from Indian States" in C.H. Hanumantha Rao and Hans Linneman (eds.) *Economic Reforms and Poverty Alleviation in India*, Sage, Delhi.

Sengupta, Arjun (1995). "Financial Sector and Economic Reforms in India," *Economic and Political Weekly*, Vol. 30, No 1, January 7.

Singh, Ajit (1997). *Liberalisation, The Stock Market and the Market for Corporate Control: A Bridge Too Far for the Indian Economy?* University of Cambridge, mimeo.

Taylor, Lance (1993). "Stabilisation, Adjustment and Reform" in Lance Taylor (ed.), *The Rocky Road to Reform*, MIT Press, Cambridge, Massachusetts.

Virmani, Arvind (1997). "India: Crisis, Reform and Growth," *Economic and Political Weekly*, Vol. 32, No. 32, August 9-15.

Williamson, John (1990). "What Washington Means by Policy Reform" in John Williamson (ed.), *Latin American Adjustment: How Much Has Happened?*, Institute for International Economics, Washington, DC.

————. (1996). *Washington Consensus Revisited*, Institute for International Finance, (mimeo).

World Bank (1998). "Adjustment Lending: An Evaluation of Ten Years of Experience," *Policy and Planning Research Series Paper* 1, Washington, DC.

————. (1997). "India – 1997 Economic Update: Sustaining Rapid Growth," *Report No. 16506-IN*, Washington, DC.

Economic and Political Weekly, Vol.32, No.44-45, November 8-14, 1997.

3

Indian Economy since 1980

Virtuous Growth or Polarisation?

I

INTRODUCTION

Picture the economic discourse in the early 1980s. There was widespread gloom about India's macroeconomic performance—perhaps, best captured in the words of Raj Krishna:

> A review of the economic development of India in the last three decades reveals an astonishing fact: a large number of the indicators of development have remained stuck at very unsatisfactory levels ... The stability of numerous parameters would not be a matter of concern but for the fact that their stable values epitomise a large and a growing mass of unrelieved suffering ... For 32 years the rate of growth of national income has been stagnating around a miserable mean of about 3.5 per cent. This rate keeps India as low as 71st in the list of 104 countries ordered according to the rate of growth of income per capita [Raj Krishna, 1984: 62-63].

Now, consider the discourse, one and half decades later. Intervening in a popular debate on the development policy, T.N. Srinivasan illustrated his arguments with an assessment of India's recent economic performance:

> During 1980-90, the rate of growth increased to 5.8 per cent and was exceeded by only eight out of 113 countries. During 1990-98, the growth rate further increased to 6.1 per cent and was exceeded by only 9 out of 131 countries ... Only after the growth accelerated in the 1980s, was there a significant declining trend in poverty, a trend that appears to have continued after the recovery from the 1991 crisis and reform [*The Financial Times*, September 27, 1999].

That the (orthodox) economic reforms initiated in 1991 have improved economic growth with a continued positive effect in reducing poverty has made scholars optimistic that accelerating the growth further will banish poverty very quickly. Participating in the same debate, Deepak Lal argued:

> ... dispute about the poverty numbers in India merely reflects the fact that rapid growth has not occurred or has not been sustained to make a marked dent on poverty. The stalled reforms have failed to raise growth rate appreciably. Some estimates that ... I have made ... show that if the growth rate rises to 9-10 per cent that China has seen, by 2006 the poverty ratio can fall from its current rate of over 30 per cent to just over 5 per cent [*The Financial Times,* October 8, 1999].

These views reflect the dramatic change in the professional perception about the Indian economic performance and prospects—especially in the international circles—over the last two decades.[1] Vijay Kelkar also echoed a similar view recently: "There is, in fact, some evidence that during the nineties the growth rate in India has shown some acceleration." He further contended, "As we enter the new century, the economy stands at the crossroads. It can take either the 'business as usual' road which means continued poverty and the low-growth trap or the high road to prosperity through accelerated reforms" [Kelkar, 1999: 2326, 2329].

Thus, the emerging consensus is:

1. Improved economic growth since in 1980-81 has reduced poverty significantly.
2. The growth rate improved as a result of the economic reforms initiated since 1991, without affecting the trend decline in poverty.
3. Therefore, more reforms—popularly called the 'second generation reforms,' or 'completing the reform agenda'—will further improve the growth rate and reduce poverty.[2]

More recently, there is a growing view in popular writings that Indian economy is increasingly driven by services, as the tertiary sector now accounts for close to one-half of GDP. Therefore, India is perceived as a post-industrial society—a 'knowledge' based economy. Such optimism is perhaps largely based on the recent spurt in software exports and the perceived potential of trade in services such as information technology, communications and entertainment.

The foregoing views and perceptions have considerable significance, both for the current policy initiatives in India, as well as for the development discourse in general. Therefore, there is a need for a careful examination of these propositions, both for their analytical soundness and empirical validity.

Whether the reforms—as defined by stabilisation and structural adjustment programme, or as popularly called the 'Washington Consensus'—result in a superior economic performance has been seriously questioned in the literature. Dornbusch had warned a decade ago; "Stabilisation may be inevitable but is not a ticket to prosperity .... One should not presume that the market automatically solves the coordination problems ..." [Dornbusch, 1991: 42-43].

More recently, there has been considerable rethinking on the neo-liberal orthodoxy (Washington Consensus) within the mainstream economics.[3] This is perhaps best illustrated in the writings of Joseph Stiglitz. According to him,

> The goal of the Washington Consensus was to provide a formula for creating a vibrant private sector and stimulate economic growth. In retrospect, the policy recommendations were highly risk-averse—they were based on the desire to avoid worst disasters. Although the Washington Consensus provided some of the foundations for well functioning markets, it was incomplete and sometimes even misleading [Stiglitz, 1998: 30].

Empirically, there is little unambiguous positive association between the reforms and economic growth. The 1999 annual report of the World Bank Operation Evaluation Department has reported some startling facts. In its assessment of the World Bank lending for 28 countries between 1981 and 1997, the annual report came to the following conclusions. To quote the report,

The facts of growth and poverty in the 28 countries between 1981 and 1997 are sobering:

- In 40 per cent of the countries, per capita income either failed to grow or shrank.
- In 25 per cent, the share of population in absolute poverty increased.
- In 23 per cent, life expectancy declined.
- In 54 per cent, the people experienced stagnating per capita income, rising poverty and declining life expectancy, or a combination of these events.

- In 85 per cent, per capita income grew 1 per cent a year or less in the 1990s.
- In 59 per cent, gross savings as a percentage of GDP were low (less than 10 per cent) or declining.
- In 67 per cent, investment efficiency was less than 10 per cent or declining.

These findings confirm the view ... that the battle against poverty is being lost and that business as usual will not accomplish the objectives of the development community [World Bank, 2000: 17].

In a careful assessment of the structural adjustment in Latin America since 1980, Agarwal and Sengupta (1999), conclude that there is no evidence of a positive association between reforms and growth.

In addition to growth and poverty, there is a considerable evidence of growing inequality among countries that have systematically followed the reforms. Growing inter-regional disparities in China after market-oriented reforms were initiated in 1978 is, by now, a well-accepted proposition [Tsuui, 1996]. In the context of similar reforms in the 1980s in Thailand, John Lewis and Devesh Kapur (1990) had warned of a growing rural-urban divide.

Quite apart from the question of how the reforms affect income distribution, recent economic literature has witnessed a renewed interest on the effects of growth on inequality, from a variety of analytical perspectives.

Bringing Income Distribution Back In

In the Keynesian literature, income distribution is central to the pace and pattern of economic growth in terms of its implications for aggregate demand. Within the mainstream economic discourse, micro-economic arguments are increasingly brought in to understand how greater equality is conducive to faster economic growth.[4] Yet another strand in the recent years, following the public choice theoretic literature, has shown how income distribution influences economic growth as it affects voting behaviour in a democracy [Tanzi and Chu, 1998]. In this genre of literature, there are several chains of causation, in which initial level of inequality affects economic outcomes. These are perhaps best described in Alberto Alesina's words:

> Several channels imply an inverse relationship running from initial income inequality to growth. A fiscal channel suggests that income inequality creates a demand for redistributive fiscal policy. In a median voter model, the key measure of inequality is the level of income or wealth of the median voter relative to the average. The poorer the median voter, relative to the average, the larger the amount of redistribution that a majority of voters will favour. More generally, a large, impoverished fraction of the population creates political pressure for redistributive policies. The pressure may take different forms in different institutional contexts, but it is generally felt in both democracies and dictatorships. In fact, in order to survive, even dictators cannot totally ignore popular demands. Redistributive fiscal polices lead to high levels of taxation, which negatively affects growth. Thus, the chain of causation goes from high initial income inequality to high taxes and from large redistributions to low growth. An alternative argument is that the rich in very unequal societies have the political and economic resources to escape taxation by exiting the economy with capital flight or by tax evasion. Thus, demand for redistribution policies with a vanishing tax base may lead to large budget deficits.
>
> A second channel linking inequality and macroeconomic performance goes through political instability. Income inequality fosters social discontent and unrest. The associated threats to property rights, policy volatility and government fragility depress productive investment, promote capital flight and ultimately reduce growth [Alisena, 1998: 301].

Empirically, it has been found that in the OECD countries, in the post-war period, economies with less unequal income distribution have performed better.[5] Similarly, comparing the performance of the east Asian economies with those of Latin America, Jeffery Sachs contended, "... high income inequality ... [In Latin America] contributes to intense political pressure for macroeconomic policies to raise income of lower income groups, which in turn contributes to bad policy choices and weak economic performance" [Sachs, 1989: 9].

Seen in this background, a near total lack of interest in how the gains of the improved growth in India since the 1980s are distributed is surprising.[6] Perhaps, it is implicitly believed that the problem of absolute poverty is more acute in India, and that a decline in it implies an improvement in income distribution. Since there is a widespread consensus on the positive effects of growth on poverty reduction over the last quarter century or so, concerns of income distribution seem to have taken a back seat.

The brief discussion above on growth, reforms and inequality—both from analytical and comparative economic perspectives—provides a meaningful background to formulate working hypotheses to examine the recent Indian experience. In light of the foregoing, we will examine the following propositions:

- Has GDP, or any of its major components, shown a statistically valid change in its growth rate since 1991?
- How valid is the postulated association between economic growth, poverty and the policy reform? Does the inverse relationship between growth and poverty reduction hold at the disagregated level?
- How has the improved growth rate since the 1980s been distributed across rural and urban areas, between the organised and unorganised sectors, across the major Indian states, and between the factors of production in the private corporate sector?

II

DATA SOURCES AND THEIR LIMITATIONS

This study mostly uses the *National Accounts Statistics* (NAS). Recently a new series of NAS has been introduced with the base year 1993-94, replacing the earlier one with the base year 1980-81. As the new series are available only from 1993-94, and the old series stopped with 1996-97, we had to use a chain index to convert the data for the recent years to the old base year. To this extent, the findings reported here are tentative. As the data for 1998-99 and 1999-2000 are based on quick and revised estimates respectively, they are subject to revision. Hence, our growth estimates are tentative on this count also.

State Domestic Product (SDP) data, though available in time series, have many limitations for comparability across states [Nagaraj, 1998]. Planning Commission computes 'comparable estimates' of SDP that are used for the finance commission awards.[7] Apparently, these estimates, though comparable across states, are not comparable over time. Therefore, in principle, it is difficult to be sure, which series is superior. Thus, it would be useful to check if the two series give similar results. However, such a question will remain hypothetical, as the 'comparable estimates' are not made public.

Data on poverty and employment are based on the widely used five yearly surveys conducted by the NSS. We avoided using the results based on the yearly 'thin sample' surveys, which are found to have a large variance, and hence unreliable. We have followed the official definition of poverty and used the head count ratio.

Since the unorganised sector accounts for over 60 per cent of NDP and over 90 per cent of workforce, 'mixed income' forms a large share of India's national income. As mixed income is a composite of wage income and property income, it is difficult to study factor incomes systematically. Therefore, we examine the distribution of income across broad structural categories like rural and urban, organised and unorganised and across regions. However, we study factor incomes in the private corporate sector since the mid-1980s, as systematic accounts for this sector are available.

In analysing growth rates, we use semi-log trend analysis; and employ a dummy variable to test for statistically significant breaks in the trends. We use as long a time series as possible to minimise problems caused by the omitted years. Where data are available for discrete time points, we have computed implicit growth rates using compound growth rate principle.

III

FINDINGS

Trends in GDP

Table 3.1(a) provides estimated growth rates for GDP, and its main sectors, between 1980-81 and 1999-2000; and, tests of significance of the dummy variable. Evidently, there is no statistically valid break in the series at 1991, implying that, so far, on a trend basis, GDP has continued to grow since 1991-92 at the same rate as it did during the previous decade – at 5.7 per cent per year.[8] This result holds, even when the year 1991-92 is excluded. There is no change in the trend growth rate between the 1980s and the 1990s for the primary sector as well, at 3.2 per cent per year.

Table 3.1(a)

Trend Growth Rate of GDP and its Principal Sectors, 1980-81 to 1999-2000

(Per cent per year)

Sector	*1980-81 to 1990-91*	*1980-81 to 1999-2000*	*Dummy Variable*	
			Sign	*Significance*
Primary	3.4	3.2	-	Not significant
Secondary	7.0	6.8	-	Significant**
Tertiary	6.7	7.1	-	Not significant
GDP	5.6	5.7	-	Not significant
GDP#	5.6	6.2	+	Not significant

Notes: Data for 1999-2000 represents the revised estimates, released in June 2000.
Excluding 1991-92.
** Statistically significant at 99 per cent confidence interval.
Sources: *NAS*, various issues, and the official press releases.

Table 3.1(b)

GDP Growth Rates—Disaggregated Trends, 1980-81 to 1999-2000

(Per cent per year)

	Industry (1-digit NIC)	*1980-81 to 1990-91*	*1980-81 to 1999-2000*	*Dummy Variable*	
				Sign	*Significance*
1	Agriculture and allied	3.1	3.1	-	Not significant
2	Mining	7.7	5.8	-	Not significant
3	Manufacturing	7.4	7.0	-	Significant**
	3.1 Reg Mfg	8.3	7.7[t]	-	Significant
	3.2 Unregd Mfg	6.1	5.8[t]	-	Significant
4	Electricity, gas and water	8.9	8.3	+	Not significant
5	Construction	4.6	5.1	+	Not significant
6	Trade, hotel and restaurant	6.1	7.3	-	Not significant
7	Transport, communication	7.3	6.2	+	Not significant
	7.1 Railways	4.1	3.4[t]	-	Not significant
8	Finance and real estate	7.4	8.1	+	Not significant
	8.1 Banking and insurance	13.0	13.1[t]	+	Not significant
9	Services	6.5	6.2	-	Significant
	9.1 Public admin and defence	7.7	6.2[t]	-	Significant
	GDP	5.6	5.7	-	Not significant

t - These estimates are for the period, 1980-81 to 1997-98, based on the NAS.
Sources: NAS, Economic Surveys, various issues, and the official press releases.

Though modest, there is a statistically significant slow down in the growth rate of the secondary sector, after 1991-92. Thus, the widely held view that there has been acceleration in the GDP growth rate since the introduction of the reforms is not statistically correct. The same holds true for the tertiary sector as well. However, since the secondary sector growth rate has modestly slowed, the tertiary sector has become the fastest growing sector in the 1990s—but not because its growth rate has improved in that decade, statistically significantly.

A further disaggregation of GDP suggests that none of the industry group (at one digit level) show a statistically significant improvement in its growth rate after the reforms. However, (i) total manufacturing and (ii) public, social and personal services—constituting around 30 per cent of GDP in the 1990s—have witnessed a statistically significant slow down since 1991-92.

Growth and Poverty Reduction

Figure 3.1, describes the official estimates of poverty levels (right-hand scale) and the absolute number of persons below the poverty line (left-hand scale) since 1973-74, for all-India combined for rural and urban areas (*Economic Survey, 1998-99*). It shows that the proportion of population living in poverty has steadily come down

Figure 3.1

Poverty in India, 1973-74 to 1993-94

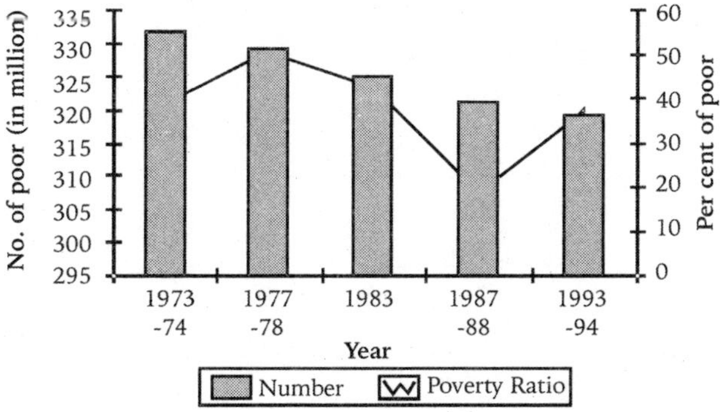

from 55 per cent in 1973-74, to 36 per cent in 1993-94. Evidently, the widely believed poverty reduction started in the 1970s, quite a few years before the economy got on to the higher growth path after 1980-81. Thus, Srinivasan's propositions that poverty began to decline only after the growth rate improved and, that the growth accelerated in response to the reforms in 1991—as we have seen above—are not sustainable.

Admittedly, the official estimates for all-India do suggest an inverse relationship between growth and poverty, at least since the 1980s. But does it hold across the states? To find it out, we estimated two kind of correlation: one, between the levels, and two, between the growth rates. This we did for the years since 1973-74 across 13 major states for which data are available—5 for the levels, and 4 for the growth rates. There is an unambiguous, statistically significant, inverse relationship between per capita SDP and levels of poverty across the states, for all the years (Table 3.2(a)). But, no such relationship was found between growth in per capita SDP and change in poverty for all the four periods (Table 3.2(b)). This is true, both with simple correlation coefficient as well as with the rank correlation coefficient. Thus, our finding provides a basis to question the widely believed virtuous association between output growth and poverty reduction at a disaggregated level.

Table 3.2(a)

Correlation between Levels of Poverty and Per Capita SDP across Major Indian States

(No. of Observations = 14)

Year	*Simple Correlation Coefficient*	*Rank Correlation Coefficient*
1973-74	– 0.683*	– 0.535*
1977-78	– 0.525*	– 0.341
1983	– 0.722*	– 0.605*
1987-88	– 0.702*	– 0.627*
1993-94	– 0.596*	– 0.682*

* Statistically significant at 95 per cent confidence level.

Table 3.2(b)

Correlation between Growth in Per Capita SDP and Change in Poverty Level across Major Indian States

(No. of Observations = 13)

Change Over the Years	*Simple Correlation Coefficient*	*Rank Correlation Coefficient*
1977-78 over 1973-74	– 0.043	– 0.007
1983 over 1977-78	– 0.254	– 0.118
1987-88 over 1983	– 0.493	– 0.350
1993-94 over 1987-88	– 0.493	– 0.484

Source: EPWRF (1998), Economic Survey (1998-99).

However, since the bulk of poverty is in rural areas, with agriculture as the main source of livelihood, we estimated the association between growth in SDP per capita in the primary sector and poverty reduction in rural India across the major Indian states (Table 3.2 (c)). The association is negative and statistically significant in only one out of two cases. Thus, it seems reasonable to infer that the suggested inverse relationship between primary sector growth and poverty reduction in rural India is at best a weak one.[9]

Table 3.2 (c)

Correlation between Growth in Per Capita SDP in Primary Sector and Change in Rural Poverty Level across Major Indian States

(No. of Observations = 14)

Change Over the Years	*Simple Correlation*	*Rank Correlation*
1987-88 over 1983	– 0.738*	– 0.654*
1993-94 over 1987-88	– 0.273	– 0.375

* Statistically significant at 95 per cent confidence level.

As officially reported, if poverty has indeed declined by about 20 per cent in the two decades after 1973-74, it would be reasonable to expect a steady improvement in average per capita consumption, especially of the bottom half of the population. Expectedly, as Suryanarayana (2000) has shown, the monthly per capita consumption expenditure in rural India has increased by 32 per cent during the two decades from the level of Rs. 18.40 in 1973-74.

However, on a closer examination, the whole process largely appears a statistical mirage. If one takes a longer period since 1960, as Suryanarayana has documented, there was a drop of about 20 per cent in the average consumption during 1960-65. And, it took over a decade (ending in 1977-78) to recover this consumption loss. Nevertheless, during the subsequent 16 year period, between 1977-78 and 1993-94, the average consumption grew annually at 0.9 per cent. More significant, the average for the bottom half of rural population increased annually at 1.5 per cent.[10] Though modest, these trends indeed suggest a process of growth with redistribution in rural India.

But the growth in per capita consumption did not result in any improvement in the nutritional status of the poor, mainly for the following reasons.

- Since the 1970s, to acquire the same level of nutrition, the poor had to substitute expensive cereal like rice and wheat for *jowar, bajra* and other millets whose production has fallen sharply in per capita terms.
- The decline in the institution of permanent farm servants and an increase in casualisation of rural workforce resulted in monetisation of the rural economy. This required (i) a 'diversification' of consumption of the poor to include fuel and other complementary items, and (ii) an increase in 'overhead' cost of acquiring the same level of nutrition. In other words, changes in the cropping pattern and the institutional setting in rural India seem to have wiped out the potential benefits of improved—albeit modest—average consumption growth in value terms.

Thus, when measured in terms of nutritional status there is, in fact, a definite evidence of an increase in poverty in India (Figure 3.2). The proportion of the rural population not getting adequate nutrition has gone up by 10 percentage points from 65 per cent in two decades after 1972-73.

Admittedly, a nutrition-based measure of poverty has limitations [Lipton and Ravallion, 1995]. But considering the problems of

Figure 3.2

Poverty Ratio

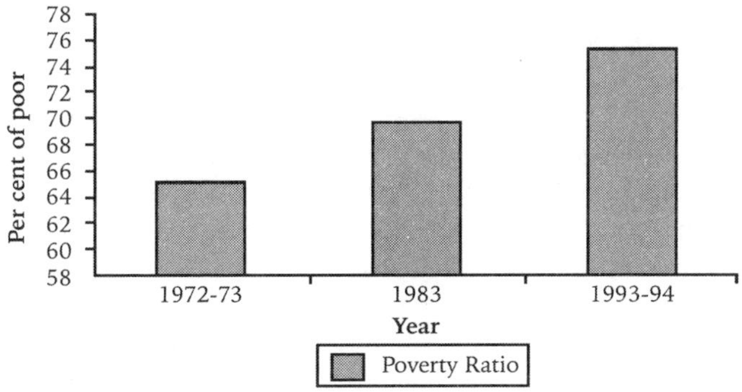

measurement when changes in the rural economy and the cereal output mix significantly affect consumption patterns, it may nevertheless be valuable to know how a nutrition-based poverty measure has performed. Therefore, a simple yet, robust nutrition-based measure perhaps has some merit. This is particularly so, since food still accounts for about 80 per cent of the consumption basket of the bottom half of the rural population.

If the above finding is valid, then the question arises, how is it that in spite of a sustained growth in per capita income for nearly two decades since 1980-81, there has been no real improvement in the nutritional status of the poor. Intuitively, one could argue that a large-scale subsidised food distribution could have, in principle, improved the nutritional status. In the absence of such a programme, perhaps one should look at how the labour market has performed, since it is only through gainful employment on a large scale that demand for food could go up, and thus improve the nutritional status of the poor. As Amit Bhaduri rightly reminded us,

> It is through the labour market that both the stimulus to economic growth and the process of social justice could largely operate. And, the extent of increase in gainful employment opportunities provides the crucial bridge between economic growth and efficiency on the one hand and social justice on the other ... Economic reforms, no matter labelled 'capitalist or socialist'—are bound to falter without enough popular support, unless they meet this latter test [Bhaduri, 1996:15].

Trends in Employment

Since the incidence of poverty and unemployment as highly correlated, one would expect that if poverty has really declined, then it would have reduced unemployment and underemployment. But we find that since 1973-74, there has been an economy-wide decline in employment elasticity of output (Table 3.3).[11] For instance, the elasticity for the economy as a whole has declined from 0.61 between 1972-73 and 1977-78, to 0.47 between 1987-88 and 1993-94. The fall is more pronounced in the secondary and tertiary sectors. Although there has been a modest decline in the proportion of population in agriculture since the 1970s, and there has been some diversification of rural workforce into non-farm activities especially in the 1980s, there is no evidence of a sustained reduction in unemployment levels, however measured [Ghose, 1999].[12]

Table 3.3

Employment Elasticity of Output, by Industry

	1-Digit Industry Group	*1977-78 Over 1972-73*	*1983 Over 1977-78*	*1987-88 Over 1983*	*1993-94 Over 1987-88*
1	Agriculture	0.54	0.49	0.26	0.54
2	Mining	0.95	0.67	0.81	0.36
3	Manufacturing	1.05	0.68	0.35	0.39
4	Electricity	1.67	0.74	0.74	0.53
5	Construction	0.35	1.00	3.43	0.01
6	Transport, storage and comm.	0.76	0.92	0.39	0.62
7	Trade, hotel and restaurants			0.76	0.59
8	Services	0.80	0.90	0.52	0.68
	8.1 Services including trade			0.39	0.76
9	Total	0.61	0.55	0.32	0.47

Source: Bhalla (1997: 217).

On the contrary, there is a distinct deterioration in the quality of employment. Between 1977-78 and 1993-94, the share of

- the organised sector in total workforce declined from 8.7 per cent to 8.1 per cent;

- wage employment in the unorganised sector went up from 6.6 per cent to 7 per cent;
- self-employed in total workforce declined from 56.5 per cent to 51.7 per cent; and,
- casual wage employment went up from 28.2 per cent to 33.2 per cent.

Some of these changes, in principle, could have improved labour market flexibility.[13] However, they could have been equally responsible for the changes in the level and composition of aggregate demand that could have adversely affected the consumption growth of the unemployed.[14] If the suggested implications for the labour market have any value, then the observed growth process is likely to have been inequalising. In other words, as the improved growth since the 1980s did not result in a proportionate increase in employment (and poverty reduction), it is very likely that the growth has helped only those persons, regions, or segments of the economy that are already employed or better off. To test this proposition, we now look at some dimensions of income distribution.

Trends in Income Distribution

As in most developing economies, there is no information on personal income distribution since over 9/10th of the workforce is in the unorganised sector where the majority of the population is self-employed. As a proxy, the consumption distribution is widely used. As noted earlier, there has been a modest improvement in the per capita consumption of the bottom half in rural India in value terms, since 1977-78. But it has not improved their nutritional status mainly as they have been compelled to consume costlier cereals like wheat and rice, since the output of inferior cereals has fallen sharply.

However, there is evidence to suggest that the distribution of income measured in other structural and institutional categories has deteriorated over the last two decades. Figure 3.3 shows the rural (nominal) per capita income as a proportion of urban per capita income. Evidently, the ratio, which improved in favour of rural India between 1970-71 and 1980-81, deteriorated during the subsequent 14-year period. The per capita rural income has declined relative to urban per capita income, from 42 per cent in 1980-81 to 38 per cent in 1993-94.[15]

Figure 3.3

Ratio of Rural-Urban Per Capita Income

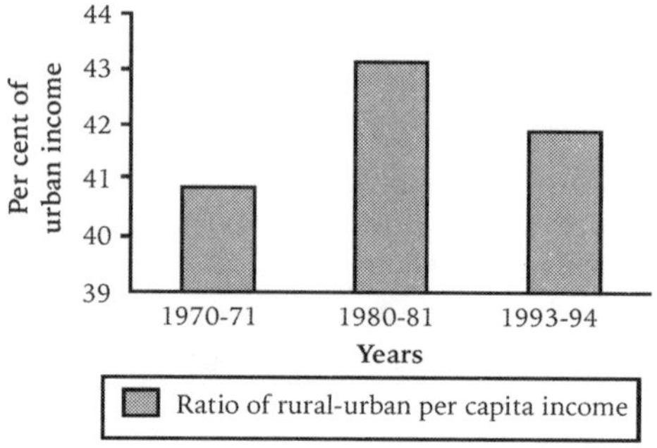

A similar comparison of (nominal) per capita income in the organised and unorganised sectors is even more revealing (Figure 3.4). Over the decade since 1983, the per capita NDP in the unorganised sector as a proportion of that in the organised sector has steadily gone down by 3 per cent. This decline is not just because of a faster growth in employment in that sector, but its output growth has also been slower.

Figure 3.4

Ratio of Unorganised to Organised Sector NDP Per Capita

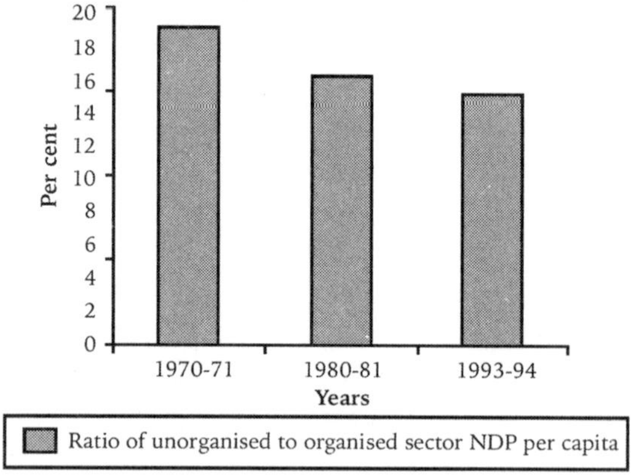

Another aspect of income distribution in a heterogeneous country like India is inter-regional inequality. This inequality, measured by the coefficient of variation in per capita SDP across the major states, has nearly doubled in 25 years since 1970-71, from about 0.2 to 0.4

(Figure 3.5). However, more significantly, the divergence in per capita income between the top three and the bottom three states has widened sharply since 1986-87 (Figure 3.6). In 1980-81, the average per capita SDP of the bottom three states (Bihar, Orissa and Assam) was 43 per cent of that of the top three states (Punjab, Haryana and Maharashtra). This ratio fell to 27 per cent in 1995-96. Moreover, in absolute terms, the per capita SDP of the bottom three states was lower in 1995-96, compared to 1988-89.[16]

Figure 3.5

Coefficient of Variation of SDP Per Capita

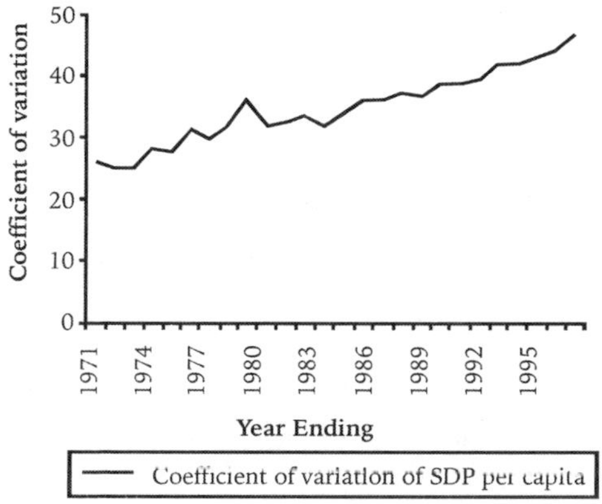

Figure 3.6

Per Capita SDP of Top and Bottom Three States

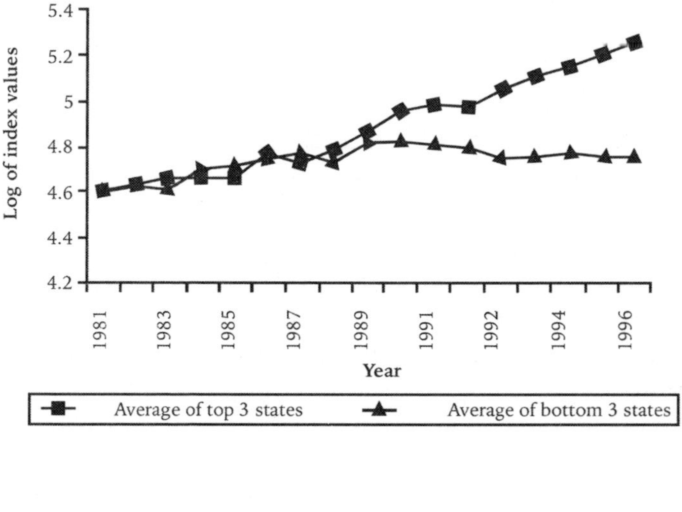

Finally, we look at the distribution of value added between wages and profits in the private corporate sector.[17] Although this sector accounts for roughly about a tenth of GDP in the 1990s, it uses a much greater share of domestic savings and attracts a disproportionately large attention of policy-makers. As Figure 3.7 shows, the share of wages in value added, in current prices, has fallen from about 35 per cent in 1985-86 to about 20 per cent in 1996-97. During the same period, the profit share (measured by profit before tax, after depreciation and interest) has gone up by about 15 percentage points—roughly equal to the fall in the wage share. Although such a simplistic comparison may have analytical limitations, perhaps the sharp changes in factor incomes, in just over a decade does indicate, however crudely, a distinct change in income distribution in favour of owners of capital, and against workers.[18]

Figure 3.7

Wages and Profits in Private Corporate Sector

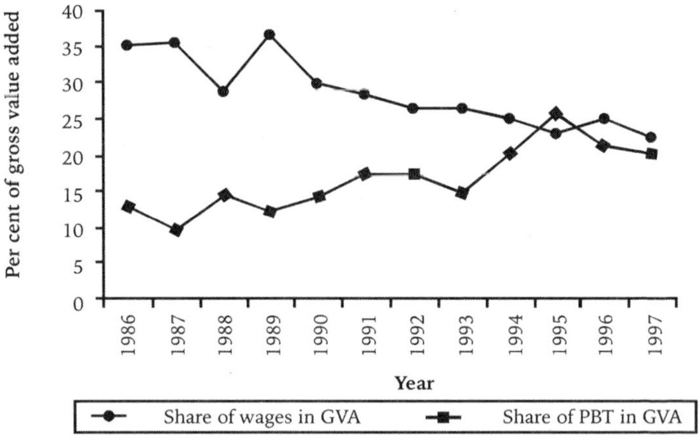

In a highly diverse and heterogeneous economy like ours, perhaps one can document many more dimensions of economic inequality. But perhaps our limited inquiry does suggest an unambiguous increase in inequality in Indian economy over the last two decades or so.

IV

CONCLUSIONS

What does all this add up to? Between 1980-81 and 1999-2000, on a trend basis, the domestic economy has grown annually, at about 5.7 per cent. The growth is likely to have been faster in per capita terms in the 1990s, when the population growth rate is said to have declined noticeably. The growth is laudable in a comparative perspective as well, as Srinivasan noted. While debt and inflation ravaged large parts of the developing world in the 1980s, India improved its growth rate, with a greater stability. Moreover, India withstood the 1991 external payment crisis as well as the recent East Asian contagion, without any slow down in the growth momentum.

It is widely believed—especially among the policymakers and in the development profession—that India's economic performance during the last quarter century or so has been a virtuous one: growth with poverty reduction. Moreover, the economic reforms initiated since 1991 are believed to have improved the growth rate further, without adversely affecting the trend reduction in poverty. The findings reported in this study question these stylised views of the recent economic performance. We found:

1. There is, at least as yet, no statistically significant acceleration in India's growth rate after 1991-92. This holds excluding 1991-92 as well, the year of external payment crisis. Thus, on a trend basis, GDP growth rate between 1991-92 and 1999-2000 is the same as it was between 1980-81 and 1990-91.
2. The secondary sector growth rate witnessed a modest, statistically significant, slow down after 1991-92.
3. Contrary to the popular view, there is no statistically significant acceleration in the growth rate of the tertiary sector in the 1990s. On a trend basis, the primary and the tertiary sectors, like GDP, have grown at the same rates as in the 1980s.
4. As the widely believed, decline in poverty started before the growth rate improved in the 1980s—and the reforms in 1991—there is no association between the widely believed

poverty reduction with the improved growth rate, or with the economic reforms.

5. There is no statistically significant association between the growth in per capita income (SDP) and poverty reduction across the major Indian states. Further, the correlation between the growth in primary sector SDP per capita and poverty reduction is found to be ambiguous. This evidence contests the widely held view of an inverse relationship between growth and poverty reduction in India, at a disaggregated level.
6. Moreover, the widely believed poverty reduction is probably a statistical mirage. The nutritional status—a contentious yet robust measure of poverty—of the average (as well as that of the bottom half) in rural India has not improved at all in the entire period since the early 1970s. Recent research cited, in fact, suggests that rural poverty, measured in terms of nutritional deficiency, has gone up by 10 percentage points since 1972-73, from 65 per cent.

The absence of an association between growth and poverty reduction across the major Indian states—contrary to much popular and scholarly writing—is perhaps not surprising (or intuitively understandable), if one looks at the labour market performance. After all, if the growth is poverty reducing, it should then, in principle, work through a large-scale rural employment creation, especially in poorer states, as the unemployed and underemployed form the bulk of the poor.

The study shows that while the growth rate improved since 1980-81, there is no sustained reduction in unemployment rates, however measured. Although employment growth roughly kept pace with the growth in workforce—as has been widely documented—there has been an economy-wide decline in employment elasticity of output since the mid-1970s, suggesting that the fruits of higher growth are largely restricted to those already employed. Further, the quality of employment has deteriorated during the 16 years since 1977-78. For instance, there has been (i) a decline in the share of regular wage employment in the organised sector, (ii) an increase in the share of wage employment in the unorganised sector, (iii) a decline in self-employment in rural India, and (iv) an increase in casualisation of the workforce. While these changes may have reduced some of the widely perceived rigidities in the industrial labour market, they have not resulted in greater labour absorption—as anticipated in the mainstream economic theory. Considering these, the widely held inverse association between growth and poverty reduction in India, during the last two decades or so, seems suspect.

In recent years, attention has been mainly focused on the widely believed virtuous effects of growth on poverty reduction, overlooking how the improved growth since the 1980s is distributed. Such a neglect of concerns of equity is surprising, since there has been a renewed interest in this question in the recent economic discourse, both from analytical and comparative economic perspectives. There is an increasing appreciation—both in theory and experience—that greater equality is conducive for growth. Further, recent evidence suggests that the economic reforms have, more often than not, accentuated inequalities since the 1980s across the developing world. It is with this concern that we looked at some aspects of inequality in India over the last two decades. The results, though limited to a few dimensions of the problem, appear quite startling:

- The ratio of rural to urban (nominal) per capita income, which improved during the 1970s, deteriorated during 14 years after 1980-81.
- There is a secular deterioration in the ratio of the unorganised to organised (nominal) per capita income since 1982-83.
- Since 1970, there has been a steady increase in inequality across the major states, as measured by the coefficient of variation in SDP per capita.
- The ratio of per capita income of the bottom three states, as a proportion of that of the top three states, has widened significantly since 1986-87. Further, the level of per capita SDP of the bottom three states is lower in 1995-96, compared to seven years earlier.
- In the decade since the mid-1980s, in the private corporate sector, the share of (nominal) gross value added accruing to labour has steadily declined by about 15 per cent, while that

of capital (profit before tax, after depreciation and interest) has gone up correspondingly.

These changes in income distribution do seem to indicate that the growing inequality—as in the case of poverty—represent long-term tendencies in India. However, it may be reasonable to infer that the increasing market orientation of the economy since the early 1980s probably hastened the process of widening of disparities.

If the above findings and inferences are valid, then the gains of faster economic growth since 1980-81 have been unequally shared by different sections of the Indian society. Growth has favoured urban India, organised sector, richer states and property owners—against rural India, unorganised sector, poorer states and wage earners. To answer the question posed in the title of this study: India's growth process during the last two decades does not seem to have been a virtuous one—it has polarised the economy. It has been a period of growth with inequality.[19]

Interestingly, such an inequalising process of economic growth has occurred at a time when there is a distinct diffusion of political power towards the erstwhile disenfranchised classes and castes, which broadly represent those left behind in economic development.[20] To quote Pranab Bardhan's recent assessment of the political changes in India:

Along with political power drifting from the centre to the regions, there is an associated drift towards the backward and lower castes. This is clearly a sign of democratic progression in an unequal society. The numerical strength and increased assertiveness of some of the historically subordinated groups have compelled the upper classes and castes to form downward alliances and brought to the fore political actors from backward communities and regions. These players may not be initiated in the etiquette of parliamentary democracy and social grace of modernity, but are quite astute in pursuing the interests of their constituencies (and, of course, their own self-interest) [Bardhan, 1988: 132].

If such an iniquitous growth process is not corrected—and corrected quickly—Indian society may have to pay a huge political price for it.

Notes

1 Reviewing books on India in the *Times Literary Supplement*, Jagdish Bhagwati wrote, "... India's liberal and outward oriented economic reforms, began in earnest after the external-payment crisis of 1991, have been accomplished by a sustained increase in a growth rate that had remained stuck at a dramatically low level of around 3.5 per cent over nearly three decades of illiberal and autarkic policies. The 1980s, treated to only a small dose of such reforms, were already registering higher growth rates... " (March 31, p 28).

2 The meaning of the term, 'second generation reforms' is far from clear, except to broadly mean a continuation of the market-oriented changes in policies initiated earlier. Reportedly, Sebastian Edwards coined the term in an unpublished note in 1996 to mean (i) central bank independence, (ii) budgetary constraint on all levels of government, (iii) creation of an efficient civil service, (iv) improvement in citizens' security, and (v) judicial reforms to strengthen the rule of law.

3 This is best illustrated by the deliberations of a group constituted by the United Nations "to review some of the key questions that arise in formulating strategies for development in the contemporary world," in the foreword by Edmond Malinvaud and Amartya Sen [Malinvaud *et al.*, 1997:v].

4 For a fine set of recent essays on this issue, see Solimano (1998). Also, see Osmani (1996) for a lucid review of various strands of thought on the relationship between economic growth and income distribution.

5 There is a large literature on this issue. See Persson and Tabellini (1994).

6 One could contend that our emphasis on inequality is misplaced since what matters in India is not so much inequality as much as the need to focus on human development. Since there has been a steady improvement in human development, one could argue for improving it further rather than focus on inequality. Such a view can be contested both on empirical and analytical considerations. Empirically, improvement in human development across the Indian states depends on public expenditure, and not on GDP growth [Dutta *et al.*, 1997]. Analytically, whether public spending is used for improving human development or for providing subsidised services for the better-off would in turn depend on income distribution. Therefore, inequality would be central to how public resources are raised and the pattern of their spending.

7 These estimates are not made public. Uma Dutta Roy Choudhary (1993) published these estimates for the years 1966-76 to 1985-86. As the data for more recent years are not available, we could not crosscheck our findings with the another data source.

8 Unless mentioned otherwise, all estimates reported in this study are at constant prices.

9 Ahluwalia's (1978) evidence on the relationship between rural poverty and agriculture growth was ambiguous. Recently, Ravallion and Dutt (1999) have sought to address somewhat similar questions. However, they seem to have overlooked simple yet robust associations that we have reported.

10 I gratefully acknowledge M.H. Suryanarayana for providing these estimates.

11 There is a sharp fall in the elasticities between 1983 and 1987-88, and an improvement during the subsequent 5-year period. This is due to the severe drought in 1987-88. However, this does not vitiate the long-term decline in the employment elasticities.

12 Undoubtedly, during this period, there has been a significant growth in real wages in agriculture, both for men and women. Between 1977-78 and 1993-94, real wage rate for men and women rose at 2.9 per cent and 3.1 per cent per year, respectively. However, since the absolute level of wages are so low that wage growth did not enable rural poor to acquire adequate consumption to come out of poverty.

13 Robert Solow has recently argued that the much discussed employment elasticity with respect to labour market flexibility may be modest. To quote him, "... the issue is whether lower wages, on average, will more or less automatically provide new jobs.... I think it is fare to say that the measured responsiveness has been disappointedly small" [Solow, 1998: 30-31].

14 Further, as Bhaduri explained, "... a more flexible market permitting lower real (more exactly product) wage rates would induce profit maximising firms to produce more through greater employment, until the diminishing marginal product equals that lower wage rate. This neo-classical view in which the economic transmission mechanism operates from the 'active' labour market to the 'passive' product market may be contrasted against the 'Keynesian' view, which claims the opposite." [Bhaduri, 1996: 15].

15 A decade ago, in a popular lecture, K.N. Raj (1990) hinted at the growing rural-urban divide—a caution that was largely ignored.

16 One of the reasons for it could be the sharp fall in public investment—much of which is in infrastructure—as we know it has a dampening effect on increase in equality (Nagaraj *et al.*, 2000). Significance of inadequate public infrastructure investment in absolute decline of states like Bihar is being increasingly appreciated among the policy-makers. Recently, Raja Chelliah (1999) advocated a special development programme for Bihar.

17 This is based on CMIE data.

18 Roughly during the same period, a similar pattern is evident in Europe as well. Oliver Blanchard (1997) found a steady rise in profit share in Europe in the 1980s. I am grateful to Kaushik Basu for this reference.

19 One may nevertheless draw comfort from the fact that the observed growth process is following the Kuznetsian inverted U. Alternatively, one may defend the process as being Pareto superior. These arguments are of questionable validity. Evidence during the last half a century of development experience does not support the Kuznets hypothesis unequivocally. Invoking Pareto could be misleading, as it ignores initial income distribution. As Frances Stewart had warned, "If a given income distribution is considered to be wrong, then maximising on that may lead to a worse outcome than taking a Pareto-inferior decision that leads to a better income distribution. Welfare conclusions ... cannot occur independently of an assessment of income distribution in two situations" [Stewart, 1988-286].

20 We are aware, our inference, in turn, raises many questions. For instance, if political power has really shifted in favour of the erstwhile disenfranchised classes and castes, why have they not been able to grab a larger share of the domestic output? We have no answer at the moment, as the question lies outside the scope of the present study.

References

Agarwal, Manmohan and Dipankar Sengupta (1999). "Structural Adjustment in Latin America: Policies and Performance," *Economic and Political Weekly*, Vol. 24, No. 44, October 30.

Ahluwalia, Montek S. (1978). "Rural Poverty in India: 1956-57 to 1973-74," *India: Occasional Papers*, World Bank Staff Working Paper No. 279, Washington, DC.

Alisena, Alberto (1998). "The Political Economy of Macroeconomic Stabilisations and Income Inequality: Myths and Reality" in Vito Tanzi and Ke-young Chu (eds), *Income Distribution and High Quality Growth*, MIT Press, Cam Massachusetts.

Bardhan, Pranab (1998). *Political Economy of India*, Second edition, Oxford University Press, Delhi.

Bhaduri, Amit (1996). "Employment, Labour Market Flexibility and Economic Liberalisation in India," *Indian Journal of Labour Economics*, Vol. 39, No. 1.

Bhalla, Sheila (1997). "Trends in Poverty, Wages and Employment in India," *The Indian Journal of Labour Economics*, Vol. 40, No. 2.

Blanchard, Oliver (1997). "The Medium Term," *Brooking Papers on Economic Activity*, No. 2, Washington, DC.

Chelliah, Raja J. (1999). "Economic Reforms Strategy for the Next Decade," *Economic and Political Weekly*, Vol. 24, No. 36, September 4-10.

Roy Choudhury, Uma Dutta (1993). "Inter-State and Intra-State Variation in Economic Development and Standard of Living," *Journal of Indian School of Political Economy*, Vol. 5, No. 1, January-March.

Dornbusch, Rudiger (1991). "Policies to Move from Stabilisation to Growth," *Proceedings of the World Bank Annual Conference on Development Economics*, 1990, World Bank, Washington, DC.

Dutta, Bhaskar, Manoj Panda and Wilima Wadhwa (1997). "Human Development in India," in S Subramanian (ed.), *Measurement of Inequality and Poverty*, Oxford University Press, Delhi.

Ghose, Ajit (1999). "Current Issues in Employment Policy in India," *Economic and Political Weekly*, Vol. 24, No. 36, September 4-10.

Kelkar, Vijay (1999). "India's Emerging Economic Challenges," *Economic and Political Weekly*, Vol. 24, No. 33, August 14-20.

Krishna, Raj (1984). "Stagnant Parameters," *Seminar*, January.

Lewis, John and Devesh Kapur (1990). "Updating a Country Study: Thailand's Needs and Prospects in 1990s," *World Development*, Vol. 18, No. 10, October.

Lipton, Michael and Martin Ravallion (1995). "Poverty and Policy" in Jere Behrman and T.N. Srinivasan (eds.), *Handbook of Development Economics*, Vol. 3B, North Holland, Amsterdam.

Malinvaud, Edmond, *et al.* (1997). *Development Strategy and Management of the Market Economy*, Vol. 1, Clarendon Press, Oxford.

Nagaraj, R. (1998). *India's National Accounts and Balance of Payments*, a Study done for the Data Archives Committee of the Indian Council of Social Science Research, New Delhi.

Nagaraj, R., A. Varoudakis and M.A. Veganzones (2000). "Long-Term Growth Trends and Convergence across Indian States," *Journal of International Development*, Vol. 12, No. 1, January.

Osmani, S.R. (1996). "Is Income Equality Good for Growth?" in Abu Abdullah and Azizur Rahman (eds.), *State, Market and Development*, Oxford University Press, Delhi.

Persson, Torstern and Guido Tabellini (1994). "Is Inequality Harmful for Growth? Theory and Evidence," *American Economic Review*, Vol. 28.

Raj, K.N. (1990). "Bridging Rural-Urban Gap," *Economic and Political Weekly*, January 6.

Ravallion, Martin and Gaurav Datt (1999). "When is Growth Pro-poor? Evidence from the Diverse Experiences of India's States," *Policy Research Working Paper* WPS 2263, World Bank, Washington, DC.

Sachs, Jeffrey (1989). "Social Conflicts and Populists Policies in Latin America: Labour Relations and Economic Performance," *NBER Working Paper* No. 2897, Cam. Mass.

Solimano, Andres (1998) (ed.) *Social Inequality: Values, Growth and the State*, Michigan University Press, Ann Arbor.

Solow, Robert (1998). *Work and Welfare*, Princeton University Press, Princeton.

Stewart, Frances (1988). "The Fragile Foundations of the Neoclassical Approach to Development," *Journal of Development Studies*, Vol. 25

Stiglitz, Joseph (1998). *More Instruments and Broader Goals: Moving Toward the Post-Washington Consensus*, World Institute for Development Economics Research, Lecture No. 2.

Suryanarayana, M.H. (2000). "How Real is the Secular Decline in Poverty?," *Economic and Political Weekly*, Vol. 35, No. 25, June 17-23.

Tsuui, Kai-yuen (1996). "Economic Reforms and Interprovincial Inequities in China," *Journal of Development Economics*, Vol. 50, No. 2, August.

Williamson, John (1996). "Washington Consensus Revisited" in Louis Emmerij (ed.), *Economic and Social Development into the XXI Century*, Inter-American Development Bank, Washington, DC.

World Bank (2000). *1999 Annual Review of Development Effectiveness*, World Bank Operations Evaluation Department, The World Bank, Washington, DC.

Economic and Political Weekly, Vol. 35, No. 32, August 5, 2000.

Part II

Industrial Growth

4

Growth in Manufacturing Output since 1980

Some Preliminary Findings

Trends in the growth of the manufacturing sector in India have been a much debated issue for quite sometime now. Ahluwalia's statistical exercise conclusively demonstrated the relatively slower growth of the registered manufacturing net value added at constant prices between 1966-67 and 1979-80 as compared to the earlier seven-year period of 1959-60 to 1965-66 [Ahluwalia, 1985]. She added that, "There was no difference in results whether the period analysed is up to 1979-80 or includes the first two years of the eighties to end in 1981-82, implying continuation of the 'relative stagnation'."

Before her decisive statistical account was published, Raj's graphical analysis of smoothened time series of *total* manufacturing gross value added for the period 1952-53 to 1982-83 questioned the persistence of the relative stagnation or deceleration [Raj, 1984]. He advanced the view that, "even though one cannot yet firmly support it with adequate statistical evidence (in fact not perhaps for another decade till sufficiently long time series is available), there has been possibly some increase in the rate of growth of industrial output since the middle of the 1970s raising it closer to the levels achieved in the 1950s and 1960s [Raj, 1984: 1802]."

Drawing a different periodisation on the basis of a certain understanding of policy regimes, Alagh [1985] arrived at a similar conclusion: "Even ignoring the unregistered manufacturing sector, industrial output in India grew at a rate of 7.6 per cent per annum for the period 1976-77 onwards compared to 4.6 per cent per annum in the period 1971-76..."

Arguing that the improved industrial performance (secured as a result of the policy initiatives since 1980) is not getting fully reflected in the *index of industrial production* (IIP)[1] *Economic Survey, 1985-86* provided data to support its view (Table 4.1). It showed that during 1974-75 to 1982-83, the output growth in real terms was 8.0 per cent per annum according to *Annual Survey of Industries* (ASI), whereas IIP recorded a growth rate of only 4.4 per cent.[2]

Table 4.1

Indices of Industrial Production

(Base: 1973-74 = 100)

Year	*Based on*	
	Index of Industrial Production	*Annual Survey of Industries*
1974-75	101.8	105.0
1975-76	106.6	115.8
1976-77	117.4	127.6
1977-78	122.8	140.6
1978-79	132.1	156.5
1979-80	128.8	156.9
1980-81	133.6	159.0
1981-82	143.6	176.1
1982-83	147.1	199.1
Growth Rate	4.4	8.0

Source: *Economic Survey, 1985-86*.

To overcome the shortcomings of the IIP (with 1970-71 as base year), a revised (or new) index with 1980-81 as the base year was introduced. The revised index, showing a distinctly higher growth rate in the eighties, is widely criticised for the alleged overestimation of output due to arbitrary replacement of supposedly slow growing industries with faster growing ones [Chandrasekhar, 1988, and Kurien, 1989]. However, despite the scepticism over the validity of the new IIP, there now appears to be a cautious admission of a moderate improvement, though it is not strong enough to change the long-term trend of relative stagnation in industrial output observed since the mid-sixties: "The most recent trend rate is still well short of the expansion seen in the first decade and a half after the launch of planned development" [Chandrasekhar, 1988: 2359].

In this context, especially as serious doubts have been expressed on the accuracy of the revised IIP, there appears to be a need to assess the trends in the eighties with possibly more reliable and recent data. A modest attempt at such an exercise is now possible with the availability of *National Accounts Statistics* (NAS), 1989. This note describes trends in the manufacturing sector in the eighties and compares them with the performance in the earlier periods. Though our exercise has a limited purpose of reporting the findings which seem to merit attention, the observed changes in the eighties could have implications for the long-term trends in industrial output.

I

NAS, 1989, the second issue with new series with 1980-81 as base year, provides data on gross value added at constant prices separately for both registered and unregistered manufacturing disaggregated at two-digit National Industrial Classification (NIC). Estimates on registered manufacturing, like in the earlier series, is based on ASI data though with a changed base year. Estimates for the unregistered manufacturing have been revised on the basis of production of cloth in the decentralised sector and changes in the benchmark estimates using NSSO data [CSO, 1988]. Considering that the estimation procedures have remained by and large the same, the revised series can perhaps be taken to be reasonably satisfactory for analysing broad trends in the manufacturing sector.[3]

Taking these remarks into consideration we find a significant difference in the estimates of gross value added in the new series. The share of unregistered segment in the total manufacturing which came down from 48 per cent in 1953 to 37 per cent in 1979-80 (according to the 1970-71 series) increased to 43 per cent in 1980-81 in the revised series. However, it has declined since then (Figure 4.1).

A comparison of the share of unregistered manufacturing to the total at 1970-71 prices and 1980-81 prices for the year 1980-81 shows (Table 4.2) that the upward revision in the new series is mainly on account of industry groups beverages and tobacco (22)[4] and textiles (23-26). Decline in the share of unregistered manufacturing is discernible in industry groups food (20-21), paper and printing (28), leather and fur (29), rubber and petroleum (30), non-metallic minerals (32), transport equipment (37) and others (38).

Table 4.2

Relative Shares of Unregistered Manufacturing at 1970-71 and 1980-81 Prices for Disaggregated Industry Groups

(Per cent)

NIC Code	*Industry Group*	*Share of Unregistered Manufacturing in 1980-81 at*	
		1970-71 Prices	*1980-81 Prices*
20-21	Food products	48.8	45.8
22	Beverages, tobacco, etc.	59.4	65.2
23-26	Textiles	42.0	67.7
27	Wood, furniture, etc.	89.7	89.3
28	Paper and printing, etc.	36.3	34.7
29	Leather and fur products	82.2	80.6
30	Rubber, petroleum, etc.	16.7	12.4
31	Chemicals, etc.	14.6	12.3
32	Non-metallic mineral products	54.0	51.0
33	Basic metal industries	1.4	1.2
34	Metal products	55.4	54.7
35	Non-elec. machinery	23.1	22.7
36	Electrical machinery	13.5	13.4
37	Transport equipment	19.0	17.4
38	Other manufacturing	53.6	50.6
39	Repairing services	68.7	68.7
	Total gross value added	37.6	42.9

Source: NAS (1987) and NAS (1989).

Table 4.3 provides trend compound growth rate[5] and annual average growth rate for total, registered and unregistered manufacturing.[6] The results show that during 1980-81 to 1986-87 total (registered plus unregistered) manufacturing gross value added at constant prices grew at 8.3 per cent per annum. While the registered segment of manufacturing recorded a growth rate of 10.4 per cent per annum the unregistered segment increased at 5.3 per cent per annum. A similar trend is noticeable according to the measure of annual average rate also.

Table 4.3

Growth Rate of Manufacturing Output 1980-81 to 1986-87

(Per cent)

NIC Code	Industry Group	Trend Compound Growth			Annual Average Growth Rate $\left(\frac{X_1-X_0}{X_0}\right)\times 100$
		Registered	*Unregistered*	*Total Manufacturing*	*Total Manufacturing*
20-21	Food products	13.1 (0.82)	3.2 (0.63)	9.2 (0.85)	9.6
22	Beverages, tobacco, etc.	9.9 (0.52)	-0.8 (0.11)*	3.3 (0.37)*	3.2
23-26	Textiles	3.3 (0.66)	5.8 (0.97)	4.9 (0.94)	4.6
27	Wood, furniture, etc.	6.1 (0.84)	-4.4 (0.90)	-3.0 (0.88)	-1.8
28	Paper and printing etc.	9.5 (0.90)	8.7 (0.89)	9.2 (0.90)	6.0
29	Leather and fur products	16.6 (0.99)	3.2 (0.96)	6.5 (0.98)	6.4
30	Rubber, petroleum, etc.	12.3 (0.82)	7.5 (0.51)	11.6 (0.85)	11.2
31	Chemicals, etc.	11.1 (0.97)	8.2 (0.96)	10.8 (0.98)	11.4
32	Non-metallic mineral products	16.2 (0.97)	2.1 (0.50)	9.9 (0.98)	9.3
33	Basic metal industries	4.1 (0.77)	4.9 (0.41)*	3.9 (0.79)	4.9
34	Metal products	6.8 (0.94)	4.9 (0.63)	5.7 (0.93)	6.1
35	Non-elec. machinery	10.3 (0.97)	5.5 (0.97)	9.3 (0.98)	8.9
36	Electrical machinery	20.6 (0.96)	16.9 (0.94)	20.1 (0.96)	20.2
37	Transport equipment	9.1 (0.97)	6.4 (0.99)	8.6 (0.97)	8.8
38	Other manufacturing	20.6 (0.99)	9.0 (0.40)*	15.0 (0.88)	19.6
39	Repair services	13.3 (0.98)	9.9 (0.97)	11.0 (0.98)	11.0
	Total gross value added	10.4 (0.99)	5.3 (0.96)	8.3 (0.99)	8.4

Notes: Figures in bracket refer to R^2.

* Statistically not different from zero even at 90 per cent significance.

Source: NAS (1989).

Total manufacturing gross value added grew at a faster rate than average growth rate in industry groups rubber and petroleum (30), chemicals (31), non-metallic minerals (32), non-electrical machinery (35), electrical machinery (36), others (38) and repair services (39).[7] Beverages and tobacco (22) recorded the lowest positive growth while wood and furniture (27) experienced a negative growth. Unregistered manufacturing grew at a lower rate than the registered in all industry groups excepting in textiles (23-26). Comparison between the growth

Figure 4.1

Share of Unregistered Manufacturing, 1950-51 to 1986-87

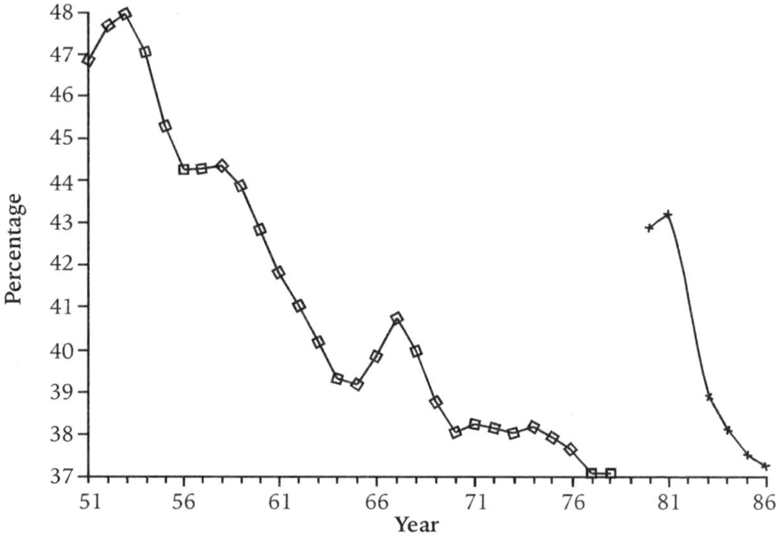

rates according to NAS 1989 and the revised IIP for manufacturing shows that the output increase by the latter measure is not only lower (6.7 per cent per annum) than that of the registered manufacturing (at 10.4 per cent per annum), but also of the total manufacturing (at 8.3 per cent per annum). This appears to be significant in the context of the serious doubts expressed over the accuracy of the revised IIP. As the observed higher growth rate according to NAS compared to IIP is similar to the pattern observed for the earlier periods by Ahluwalia, the arguments of overestimation of output by IIP do not appear to be tenable. If we accept that the trends depicted by the IIP are broadly correct, though on a conservative side (Figure 4.2), then it may not be inappropriate to utilise the IIP to discern some patterns in the observed growth in the eighties.

Use-based classification of the revised IIP for the period 1980-81 to 1986-87 shows that consumer durables accounting for 2.55 per cent of manufacturing grew the fastest at 14.7 per cent per annum[8] followed by capital goods (weightage 16.4) at 10 per cent per annum (Table 4.4).

Figure 4.2

Trends in Manufacturing Output, 1980-81 to 1986-87

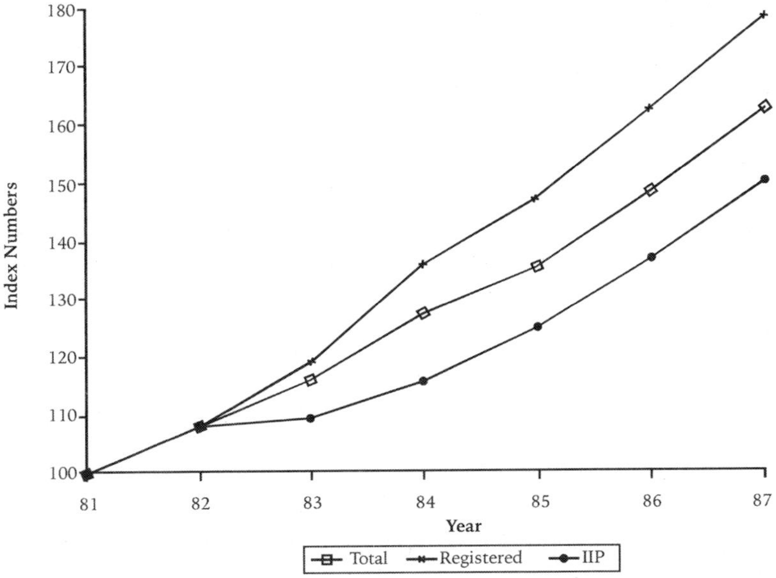

Table 4.4

Growth of Manufacturing Output according to Use-based Classification (Using Revised IIP), 1980-81 to 1986-87

	Industry Group	*Weight*	*Compared Annual Average Growth Rate (in per cent)*
1	Basic goods	39.42	8.1
2	Capital goods	16.43	10.0
3	Intermediate goods	20.51	5.8
4	Consumer goods	23.65	6.9
	(a) Consumer durables	2.55	14.7
	(b) Consumer non-durables	21.10	5.7

Source: Economic Survey, 1988-89.

II

Having described the growth of manufacturing sector in the eighties in a few limited dimensions, we compare them with the record of the earlier periods though such an attempt has a number of limitations. First, comparison of results based on a short time period of seven years with long-term trends could yield misleading results. Secondly, as the data for different time periods are based on different base years a strict comparison is not possible. Thirdly, as there have been changes in the industrial classification a rigorous comparison would require more disaggregated data. Considering these limitations our exercise could at best be taken as an indication of the broad changes. To accommodate for the statistical problems mentioned above, variation in growth rate in different periods up to 2 percentage points are not taken into account.[9]

Our preliminary attempt could perhaps be justified, despite being fully aware of the shortcomings since it appears to us to be important to have such a comparative empirical basis to assess the changes in the policy regime in the eighties.

Table 4.5 provides growth rates in value added[10] in registered manufacturing for three time periods, namely, 1959-60 to 1965-66 (period I), 1966-67 to 1979-80 (period II) and 1980-81 to 1986-87 (period III).[11] Growth rate in registered manufacturing in period III at 10.4 per cent per annum is not only higher than that attained in period II (at 5.5 per cent), but also that in period I (at 7.6 per cent). Growth rate at the disaggregated level in period II is lower than that in period III (after applying a discount of 2 percentage points) in all industry groups except textiles (23-26), wood and furniture (27) and basic metals (33). A similar comparison between period I and period III shows that the following industry groups constituting about two-fifths of the value added (in 1986-87) experienced a higher growth rate in the latter period as compared to the former: food products (20-21), leather products (29), rubber and petroleum (30), non-metallic mineral products (32), electrical machinery (36) and miscellaneous (38).

Table 4.5

Growth Rates in Gross/Net Value Added in Registered Manufacturing in Different Sub-period at Disaggregated Level

(Per cent)

	Industry Group	Period I (1959-60 to 1965-66)	Period II (1966-67 to 1979-80)	Period III (1980-81 to 1986-87)
1	Food products	0.7*	3.8	13.1
2	Beverages	9.3	7.3	9.9
3	Tobacco, etc.	1.5*	1.3	
4	Textiles	3.9	4.4	3.3
5	Footwear, etc.	15.3	14.5	16.6
6	Leather and fur products	0.5*	3.1	
7	Wood and cork	1.1	5.4	6.1
8	Furniture and fixtures	11.7	6.3	
9	Paper and paper products	11.4	7.3	9.5
10	Printing and publishing	6.8	1.7	
11	Rubber products	4.6	4.2	12.3
12	Petroleum products	-5.9	6.2	
13	Chemicals and chemical products	10.7	9.1	11.1
14	Non-metallic mineral products	7.0	3.0	16.2
15	Basic metal	15.0	5.1	4.1
16	Metal products	12.0	2.5	6.8
17	Non-elec. machinery	17.9	7.5	10.3
18	Electrical machinery	14.7	9.8	20.6
19	Transport equipment	10.3	4.6	9.1
20	Miscellaneous	14.2	4.5	20.6
21	Repair services			13.3
	Total gross/net value added	7.6	5.5	10.4

* Statistically not different from zero even at 90 per cent significance.

Sources: (1) Ahluwalia (1985), pp 30-31; (2) *National Accounts Statistics* (1989).

The above findings indicate that the observed expansion of registered manufacturing output in the first seven years in the eighties appear to be comparable, if not better, than the achievement in the seven year period preceding the mid-sixties, a period is widely accepted as a phase of high growth.

To sum up: In the context of the continued debate on the relative stagnation of the manufacturing sector since the mid-sixties we considered it meaningful to examine the trends in this sector in the eighties. As the official view of an upturn in the growth rate based on the revised index of industrial production has been questioned we considered it appropriate to examine the issue using the data provided in the NAS, 1989. Our findings show that while the total manufacturing gross value added grew at over 8 per cent per annum in real terms during 1981-87, the registered manufacturing segment recorded a growth of over 10 per cent per annum. According to the new series of NAS, the share of unregistered manufacturing has gone up, mainly on account of an upward revision of output in beverages and tobacco (22) and textile (23-26) industries. However, the rate of growth of unregistered sector has been considerably lower than that of the registered sector. In terms of use-based classification (of the revised IIP) consumer durable industries having a weightage less than 3 per cent witnessed fastest growth rate of over 14 per cent per annum followed by capital goods industries at 10 per cent per annum.

A careful comparison—since such an attempt has several limitations—of the experience of the eighties with those of the earlier periods for the registered manufacturing (even after discounting of growth rate of 2 percentage points to account for the statistical adjustments) suggests that the growth rate between 1980-81 and 1986-87 is higher than that during 1966-67 to 1978-79. It also seems to be comparable to, if not better than, the growth rate achieved during 1959-60 to 1965-66. The above pattern seems to be true for a wide range of industry groups accounting for about two-fifths of the registered manufacturing output. If our findings, based on limited data and rudimentary statistical method, are valid then the observed changes in the eighties would warrant a closer examination so as to understand their underlying causes.

Notes

1 This is said to be so on account of changes in the composition of output and the inadequate coverage of the supposedly fast growing industries in the small-scale sector.

2 Discussing the limitations of IIP, Ahluwalia (1985) has clearly demonstrated the underestimation of output by the index. Since the method of collecting information has not changed the shortcomings outlined by her would seem to continue in the new series as well.

3 We are quite aware that this inference may appear somewhat hasty. As the 'sources and methods' for the revised series is yet to be published, we are unable to check for the quality of the revised estimates. However, accepting the view of Dutta Roy Choudhury (1988) we are inclined to accept that the revised estimation of output is not significantly different from that of the earlier series.

4 Figures in brackets refer to industry group according to two-digit NIC.

5 We have fitted log linear trend function where anti log of 'b' minus one, multiplied by 100, gives annual average growth rate. Our method is identical to Ahluwalia's.

6 Annual average growth rate is simply average of annual percentage change over the period. This is same as the method used by Raj (1984). However, we have not smoothened the series due to lack of adequate number of observations.

7 Differences in growth rate up to 1 percentage point are not taken into account.

8 Relatively rapid growth of consumer durables has been widely commented upon as a reflection of a certain pattern of luxury goods oriented growth strategy implicit in the liberalised policy regime in the eighties [Kurien 1989, Chandrasekhar 1988]. Table A providing growth rates of industrial output according to use-based classification shows that since 1951 growth of consumer durables has been consistently higher than that of the non-durables. Without questioning the commodity composition of the consumer durables category, if the ratio of growth rate of durables to non-durables is taken as a measure of the 'luxury goods orientedness' of industrial output then this was highest 6.7 during 1955-60 as compared to 1980-87 when it was 2.6. Moreover, the weight of consumer durables in successive IIPs has steadily come down from 5.68 per cent in 1960-61 to 2.55 per cent in 1980-81 (see Table A).

Table A

	1951-55	*1955-60*	*1960-65*	*1965-70*	*1970-75*	*1975-79*	*1981-87*
Basic goods	3.8	12.0	10.5	6.3	5.2	6.6	8.1
Capital goods	15.1	13.7	19.7	-1.7	5.1	5.9	10.0
I goods	6.4	6.2	7.0	2.5	2.6	5.3	5.8
DC goods	12.3	25.5	10.8	8.5	2.4	8.5	14.7
NDC goods	3.7	3.8	3.8	2.6	1.5	5.4	5.7

Notes: I goods: Intermediate goods
DC goods: Durable consumer goods
NDC goods: Non-durable consumer goods.

Sources: Desai (1981), *Economic Survey, 1988-89.*

9 This, admittedly, is arbitrary. We have no *a priori* reason for using any specific discount factor.

10 Growth rate estimates for periods I and II from Ahluwalia [1985: 30-31] are for *net* value added while our estimates for the eighties and for *gross* value added. Since we are concerned about growth rates and not about absolute value the discrepancy is unlikely to make any difference.

11 Ahluwalia's study completely ignored the unregistered manufacturing which, though declining, was not insignificant at a little over two-fifths of the total manufacturing output in 1980-81, according to the new series.

References

Ahluwalia, I.J. (1985). *Industrial Growth in India: Stagnation Since the Mid-Sixties,* Oxford University Press.

Alagh, Y.K. (1985). "Some Aspects of Planning Policies in India," *Govind Vallabh Pant Memorial Lecture.*

Chandrasekhar, C.P. (1988). "Aspects of Growth and Structural Change in Indian Industry," *Economic and Political Weekly,* Special Number.

Central Statistical Organisation (1988). *New Series on National Accounts Statistics,* Government of India.

Dutta Roy Choudhury, Uma (1988). "New Series on National Accounts Statistics: Some Comments," *Economic and Political Weekly,* July 23.

Kurien, C.T. (1989). "Indian Economy in the 1980s and on to the 1990s," *Economic and Political Weekly,* April 15.

Raj, K.N. (1984). "Some Observation on Economic Growth in India over the Period 1952-53 to 1982-83," *Economic and Political Weekly,* October 13.

Economic and Political Weekly, Vol.24, No.26, July 1, 1989.

5

Industrial Growth

Further Evidence and Towards an Explanation and Issues

The rate and the pattern of growth in manufacturing sector in the eighties has attracted considerable attention. While the official sources as well as the proponents of the policy changes introduced in the eighties have viewed the improved growth rate as vindication of their stand, many others are not only sceptical of their claim on empirical grounds but have attributed any possible improvement in the growth rate mainly to a spurt in the production of consumer durables secured largely by import liberalisation—giving rise to the term, 'import led growth.'

Providing some evidence, using the *National Accounts Statistics* [CSO, 1989a], we [Nagaraj, 1989] suggested that the growth rate of real manufacturing gross value added during 1980-81 to 1986-87 is not only higher than that during 1965-66 and 1979-80, but could also perhaps be comparable to that attained during 1959-60 and 1965-66 —even after making an allowance of 2 percentage points in growth rate to account for any possible statistical discrepancy. Further, these results also questioned the alleged overestimation of the growth of output by the revised (with 1980-81 as the base year) *Index of Industrial Production* (IIP).

Endorsing the validity of the IIP on the basis of our findings, Kelkar and Kumar (1990) described the pattern of manufacturing output at a disaggregated level and have outlined a policy prescription to reinforce the favourable conditions of the eighties to foster an internationally competitive manufacturing sector to realise India's potential comparative advantage. The discussion so far on the recent industrial growth appears to have remained mainly either statistical or on the need (or desirability) of the policy reform[1] with the implicit assumption of its positive effect on increase in output, investment and efficiency of resource use without perhaps adequately analysing the influence of real economic factors on the observed growth. This appears striking as the debate on the causes for the rapid growth during 1950 and 1965 and period of (relative) stagnation that followed up to the late seventies or so centred around various structural reasons, especially those emanating from the demand side—Patnaik and Rao (1977), and Nayyar (1978), to name a few.

This paper—after adducing some further evidence on the recent experience—makes a modest attempt to seek an explanation for the observed industrial change in the eighties by empirically examining some of the prominent hypotheses outlined in the 'stagnation' debate. Such an attempt could also help indicate, though perhaps not in quantitative terms, the scope and limitations of the policy changes in securing a sustained higher growth rate of manufacturing output. Moreover, such an analysis could also possibly enable one to identify the potential constraints on—and the means for overcoming the limitations of—the observed improvement. We have then sought to raise a number of issues for a more reasoned discussion on the implications of the policy reform on the possibility of sustaining the higher growth. Our effort in this direction seems to acquire a greater significance in the present context of the renewed attempts at further reinforcing the policy changes initiated in the eighties.

This paper, consisting of six sections, sets out (in Section I) by offering some more results on the growth rate of manufacturing sector since 1980-81 and its composition, mainly using the *Annual Survey of Industries* (ASI). Since the allegedly rapid growth of consumer durables in the eighties has been widely noted with a deep concern—as it is said to reflect a growing undesirable pattern of consumption demand indicating a possible increase in inequality—we assess the problem in Section II, though such an attempt may, at the first instance, appear somewhat a digression. Some of the main hypotheses of growth and relative stagnation of the industrial sector in the light of the evidence of the eighties are re-examined in Section III. Drawing attention, on the basis of such an exercise, to some of the potential microeconomic (or sectoral) areas of concern for sustaining the improved growth rate (Section IV), we have sought to raise a few issues which, in our view, merit a closer scrutiny (Section V). The final section contains the conclusion.

I

SOME FURTHER EVIDENCE

The data on the real gross value added in registered manufacturing reported in the *National Accounts Statistics* [CSO, 1989a], using which the earlier findings were reported, has a limitation. The figures for 1985-86 and 1986-87—the most recent years—are based[2] on the IIP (with 1980-81 as the base year), as is evident from the following:

> Latest ASI data relate to 1984-85. The estimates for later years have been prepared using the indexes of industrial production at 2-digit level of NIC, and corresponding indices of wholesale price [CSO, 1989a: 204-205].

Since the revised IIP is said to overestimate industrial output, the NAS data for the most recent years have also been subjected to the same criticism. Perhaps a more acceptable measure (and which can also test for the alleged overestimation of output by the revised IIP) is to compare the growth rates computed by using the NAS figures and the ASI factory sector data, though such a comparison is not without some shortcomings.

While the ASI reports value added, the IIP refers to output. As there is considerable time lag in the publication of the results of the ASI, such a comparison presently gets limited to only six years of the eighties, namely, 1980-81 to 1985-86. Moreover, the ASI and the revised IIP do not have exactly the same coverage as the latter is said to have been expanded to include some industries in the small-scale sector which may partly comprise of small firms in the unregistered manufacturing sector.[3] However, considering that the weight of the small-scale sector is not very substantial, a comparison of the growth rates according to the ASI and the revised IIP may not be totally inappropriate for our limited purpose.

Table 5.1 provides annual average growth rates of manufacturing output/real gross value added as revealed by the different sources of data for the period 1980-81 to 1985-86. Growth rate according to the revised IIP (6.6 per cent) is higher than that according to the older series (with 1970-71 as the base year) by only about 1 percentage point. Growth rates recorded using the NAS data for the registered manufacturing are higher than those according to the ASI factory sector data.[4] Moreover, both for NAS and ASI, the growth rates when deflated by implicit deflator used in the NAS for registered manufacturing,[5] are lower than those deflated by the Wholesale Price Index (averages of months). As a result of these variations one gets a range of four growth rates from 7.2 per cent for the ASI (when deflated by implicit NAS deflator for registered manufacturing) to 10.7 for the NAS current price data (deflated by Wholesale Price Index).

Table 5.1

Annual Average Growth Rate of Manufacturing Output/Value Added according to Different Measures, 1980-81 to 1985-86

	Alternative Measures of Industrial Production	*Per cent Per annum*
I	Index Numbers of Industrial Production	
	(a) 1970-71 as base year	5.5
	(b) 1980-81 as base year	6.6
II	Annual Survey of Industries, factory sector gross values added	
	(a) Deflated by WPI, averages of months	8.3
	(b) Deflated by implicit price deflator used for registered manufacturing in NAS	7.2
III	National Accounts Statistics	
	(a) Gross Value Added at 1980-81 prices	9.6
	(b) Gross Value Added deflated by WPI, (average of months)	10.7

Note: In this table we have computed average annual growth rates as the number of observations are limited.

Sources: 1. *Annual Survey of Industries*, Summary results of the factory sector various issues.
2. Central Statistical Organisation (1989a).
3. WPI various issues.
4. *Reserve Bank of India Bulletin*, various issues.

However, significantly the growth rate even at 7.2 per cent per annum is higher than that recorded by the revised IIP at 6.6 per cent per annum. Therefore, the proposition that IIP overestimates industrial growth rate [Chandrasekhar, 1988; Kurien, 1989], does not appear to be consistent with the available data.

While considerable concern has been expressed over the alleged arbitrariness in the deletion of the so-called slow growing industries[6] and their replacement by allegedly fast growing ones—as also items like cloth production in the decentralised sector—no attempt appears to have been made to draw attention to the *method* of collection of data for computing the IIP, which apparently continues to be on a voluntary basis. We are inclined to believe, as has been indicated by Ahluwalia (1985) and reiterated by Alagh (1985), that the real problem with the IIP seems to be the inability of the official machinery to obtain accurate and up-to-date production figures from a reasonably satisfactory sample of manufacturing firms on a regular basis.

A comparison of IIP with ASI at 2-digit level of NIC, for the period 1980-81 to 1985-86, shows that the growth rate according to the former are not uniformly lower than those according to the latter as in the case of aggregated data (Table 5.2). In industry groups cotton textiles (NIC 23); wood, wood products, furniture and fixtures (NIC 27); paper, paper products and printing industries (NIC 28); leather and fur products (NIC 29); electrical machinery, apparatus and appliances (NIC 36); and transport equipment (NIC 37), the growth rates according to the IIP are higher than the corresponding figures from the ASI. Considering the divergence between the results obtained by using the IIP at the aggregated and the disaggregated levels one has to be cautious in using the disaggregated data.[7]

An analysis of net value added at constant prices at the level of 3-digit NIC for the same time period shows some interesting trends (Table 5.3). Barring a minority of industry groups, bulk of the manufacturing sector accounting for about three-fifths of the number of industries with an almost equal weight in terms of net value added recorded annual average growth rates ranges from 5 per cent to 30 per cent per annum. Seventy-one industries with a weight of two-fifths of total net value added in ASI factory sector registered growth rates ranging from over 10 per cent to 50 per cent per annum. It is, however, not possible for us to describe the growth according to use-based classification as it would require a more disaggregated data.

Table 5.2

Comparison of Annual Average Growth Rate as Recorded by Revised IIP and ASI, Factory Sector, 1980-81 to 1985-86, at 2-Digit NIC

Industry Group	*Industry*	*Annual Average Growth Rate*	
		ASI	*IIP*
20-21	Food products	18.7	5.0
22	Beverages, tobacco and tobacco products	11.8	2.4
23	Cotton textiles	0.0	2.3
25	Jute, hemp and mesta products	—	—
26	Textile products	5.9	2.8
27	Wood, wood products, furniture and fixtures	1.9	19.0
28	Paper, paper products and printing industries	3.0	8.5
29	Leather and fur products	10.0	12.7
30	Rubber, plastic, petroleum and coal products	—	9.1
31	Chemical and chemical products	9.0	9.2
32	Non-metallic mineral products	13.1	9.7
33	Basic metal and alloy products	2.9	3.5
34	Metal products and parts	2.6	3.2
35	Machinery and machine tools and parts	8.0	5.5
36	Electrical machinery, apparatus and appliances	8.1	15.5
37	Transport equipment and parts	5.0	6.4
38	Other manufacturing industries	—	12.5

Sources: 1. *Annual Survey of Industries*, Summary Results for the Factory Sector, various issues.
2. *Economic Survey*, 1988-89.

A significant aspect of the observed growth appears to be that despite a steady increase in the number of capital goods under the 'open general licence'—that is, shifting of these items from physical to tariff based controls—their domestic production does not seem to have been adversely affected. For instance, production of machine tools [NIC 357] increased at an annual average growth rate of 13.4 per cent per annum between 1980-81 to 1985-86. Though, admittedly, some industries which include consumer durable, like manufacturing of radios, TVs, etc., [NIC 364] have grown at 28.1 per cent per annum, the higher growth rates are also discernible in machinery manufacturing like prime movers, boilers, etc., [NIC 352] at 18.7 per cent per annum (more about it later).

Table 5.3

Frequency Distribution of Average of Annual Growth Rates of Net Value Added in Manufacturing Industries, at 3-Digit Level

Class Interval of Growth Rate (per cent per annum)	*3-Digit Industry Groups*	*Number of 3-Digit Industry Groups*	*Share in Manufacturing NVA Excluding Services*
(1)	*(2)*	*(3)*	*(4)*
(-)10 to (-)50	251, 292	2	1.2
(-)5.0 to (-)9.9	272, 325, 370	3	0.3
(-)0.1 to (-)4.9	214, 231, 246, 261, 263, 275, 281, 312, 331, 343, 353, 361	13	12.8
0.0 to 5.0	200, 217, 225, 228, 268, 271, 280, 284, 285, 307, 314, 320, 323, 330, 333, 334, 340, 345, 362, 377, 379, 385, 389	23	15.1
5.1 to 10.0	210, 213, 226, 229, 236, 243, 247, 269, 270, 273, 290, 291, 302, 313, 329, 332, 336, 341, 350, 351, 354, 356, 359, 360, 371, 372, 373, 374, 376	31	24.1
10.1 to 15.0	207, 208, 211, 212, 219, 220, 232, 264, 287, 299, 301, 310, 327, 339, 347, 357, 363, 380	18	9.8
15.1 to 20.0	201, 203, 209, 222, 241, 248, 259, 260, 267, 300, 303, 316, 319, 321, 328, 352, 355, 366, 367, 375, 382	22	13.3
20.1 to 30.0	204, 206, 223, 233, 234, 235, 239, 242, 245, 261, 274, 283, 288, 292, 311, 317, 318, 344, 358, 364, 369, 387	24	10.5
30.1 to 40.0	202, 315, 324, 342	4	3.7
40.1 to 50.0	205, 221, 250	3	1.7
Greater or less than 50 per cent	227, 240, 249, 265, 266, 279, 286, 293, 304, 305, 306, 322, 335, 365, 378, 381, 383, 384, 386	19	8.0

Notes: 1. Share in NVA is computed using the data for 1985-86 at current prices.

2. The exceptionally high/low growth rates of over (+)/(-) 50 per cent appear to be on account of some error in the data.

3. As the data are limited for six years only, we have computed average of annual growth rates and not trend growth rates.

4. We have used Chaudhuri (1989) Table 6 for getting equivalence between NIC industry groups and corresponding commodity groups in wholesale price index.

5. Values in column 4 may not add up to 100 due to rounding off error.

Sources: Annual Survey of Industries, Summary Results for the Factory Sector, various issues, WPI.

II

ON GROWTH OF CONSUMER DURABLES

A rapid growth of consumer durables (CDs), taken as a proxy for luxury goods, at a trend growth rate of 16 per cent per annum during 1980-81 to 1988-89 according to the revised IIP [*Economic Survey*, 1989-90]—as against 7.4 per cent per annum for the manufacturing sector as a whole during the same period—has attracted considerable criticism [for instance, Economic Advisory Council, 1989]. Since the observed higher growth rate of CDs is widely perceived to be a new phenomenon[8] as reflecting the emerging pattern of manufacturing output we have considered it appropriate to examine the empirical and analytical basis of such a proposition.

As noted earlier [Nagaraj, 1989], the weight of CDs in the successive indices of industrial production has come down from 5.68 in the 1960-61 series to 2.55 per cent in the 1980-81 series.[9] Moreover, the ratio of the growth rates of durables to non-durable consumer goods has declined from 6.7 during 1955-60 to 3.3 per cent during 1980-89, indicating that over time the rate of increase in the growth rate of non-durables has been higher than that in durables—thus contesting the widely held view.

Analytically, the growth rate of CDs have to bear a relationship with the growth rate of national output. Countering Ahluwalia's (1985) characterisation of growth of consumer goods industries at 5.6 per cent per annum during 1965-66 and 1979-80 as "slow and indifferent," Raj (1985) argued that the observed growth rate was in conformity with the implicit income elasticity of demand. He further added that "a much higher rate of growth of consumer goods industries is possible only if the overall rate of growth of the economy as a whole is considerably accelerated."

Extending Raj's argument for the eighties, the higher growth rate of consumer goods at 6.4 per cent per annum (and within them of CDs at 16 per cent per annum) during 1980-89 appears to be broadly compatible with the higher trend growth rate of real (measured) GDP, at 4.8 per cent per annum as compared to 3.5 per cent per annum recorded during 1950-51 and 1979-80.[10]

Therefore, *prima facie* the hypothesis of an unduly higher growth rate of CDs in the eighties does not seem to be sustainable on either analytical or empirical grounds. However, it may be instructive to re-examine the appropriateness of the IIP data for testing the proposition.[11] Furthermore, it may perhaps be meaningful to use one's intuitive understanding of the recent developments to arrive at a more reasonable assessment of the issue. What follows in this section, therefore, would necessarily be somewhat tentative.

Industries (or their products) categorised as CDs by various studies and indices of industrial production (with different base years) are shown in the Appendix A-5.1. It seems to suggest that items included under this category by different studies/indices vary considerably. Moreover, the various categories listed in the Appendix A-5.1 contain items like hurricane lanterns which, though a durable good, cannot perhaps be taken as a luxury item even at India's low level per capita income. On the other hand, none of the classifications seem to include items like video cassette recorders, cameras, washing machines and so forth, which probably are the widely visible indicators of luxury goods implicit in the popular argument.

Conceptually, equating CDs with luxuries and non-durable goods with the 'necessities' is also perhaps a little simplistic, especially with the widening of the domestic manufacturing base and with a steady increase, though from a very low level, in the per capita income. While there appears to have been some diffusion of CDs, like inexpensive single band transistor radio sets, a growing variety of non-durables catering to the upper income groups are perhaps not captured as luxuries in the empirical studies.

Even ignoring the conceptual difficulties, changing size structure of manufacturing sector, with the rapid growth of the 'modern' small scale sector appears to make the task of capturing of output increasingly difficult. If there is a basis to assume that a greater share of non-durable consumer goods are produced in 'small' and unorganised sectors then their growth is likely to be more underestimated relative to that of the CDs. Thus there appears to be a serious limitation of using CDs as a proxy for luxuries and hence empirical verification, the popular hypothesis, in any satisfactory manner.

III

TOWARDS AN EXPLANATION

The recovery of the lost momentum of growth of the pre mid-sixties, after a prolonged period of nearly one and half decade, calls for a serious examination as is its causes. Though, admittedly, the changes in the industrial and trade policies initiated in the eighties could have had a favourable effect on the output, to ascribe the improvement to them entirely would appear too simplistic an explanation, especially in the context of various hypotheses of structural constraints for sustaining the growth after the mid-sixties, as discussed in the stagnation debate. Therefore, any careful attempt to explain the observed improvement in the growth rate has to, perhaps, go beyond the policy induced changes to explore the underlying causal factors. Such an exercise could possibly also enable one to examine whether the increased growth rate is contingent upon transient, once over changes in the regulatory regime or whether it rest, among others, on a more secure foundation of improved demand and supply conditions, of capital formation and its efficient use. Our exercise, therefore, takes the stagnation debate of the seventies as the point of departure as it provides a sound basis to inquire into the factors to account for the changes in the eighties.

Agricultural Growth: Any attempt at explaining the growth in the manufacturing sector in India, for the well known reasons, has to begin with the agricultural performance.[12] Table 5.4 provides long-term trend growth[13] rates of agricultural output for the period 1949-50 to 1987-88[14] using the official index numbers. The results show a constant growth of crop output with little sign of neither a trend acceleration nor statistically significant break with a higher growth rate in the eighties (more about it later).

Although the real GDP originating in agriculture during 1980-81 to 1987-88 shows a higher growth rate than those witnessed during the previous two decades (Table 5.5), the proposition is not sustainable on a trend basis when the time series for the period 1950-51 to 1987-88 is considered (Table 5.6). Nor has there been a statistically significant 'break' in the series with a higher growth rate in the eighties.[15,16]

Table 5.4

Trend Analysis of Agricultural Output, 1949-50 to 1987-88

t	t^2	D_1	D_2	D_3	R^e	*Growth*	*Rate per cent per annum*
(1)	(2)	(3)	(4)	(5)	(6)	(7)	(8)
All Commodities							
I Log-linear	0.0255*					0.957	2.6
II Log-quadratic	0.0307*	(-)0.00004				0.956	
III Log-linear with D_1	0.0308*		(-)0.00296			0.961	
IV Log-linear with D_2	0.0250*			(-)0.00276		0.956	
V Log-linear with D_3	0.0254*				(-)0.0085	0.956	
Foodgrains							
I	0.0258*					0.935	2.6
II	0.0217	0.00003				0.934	
III	0.0291*		0.00032			0.939	
IV	0.0241*			(-)0.00131		0.934	
V	0.0251*				(-)0.00677	0.933	
Non-foodgrains							
I	0.0253*					0.970	2.5
II	0.0487*	(-)0.00017*				0.974	
III	0.0348*		(-)0.00981*			0.979	
IV	0.0270*			(-)0.00500		0.970	
V	0.0261*				(-)0.00974	0.970	

Contd ...

.... *Contd* ...

(1)	(2)	(3)	(4)	(5)	(6)	(7)	(8)
Cereals							
I	0.0288*					0.950	2.9
II	0.0295	0.0				0.948	
III	0.0318*		(-)0.000231			0.951	
IV	0.0278*			(-)0.00359		0.949	
V	0.0286*				(-)0.01049	0.948	
Rice							
I	0.0246*					0.909	2.5
II	0.0320	(-)0.000050				0.907	
III	0.0343*		(-)0.00664			0.921	
IV	0.0242*			(-)0.00031		0.904	
V	0.0242*				(-)0.00126	0.904	
Wheat							
I	0.0571*					0.960	5.7
II	0.0310	0.000189				0.960	
III	0.0391*		0.02115*			0.966	
IV	0.0546*			(-)0.01135		0.962	
V	0.0575*				(-)0.02655	0.950	
Coarse Cereals							
I	0.0119*					0.651	1.2
II	0.0723*	(-)0.000438*				0.736	
III	0.0220*		(-)0.015479*			0.697	
IV	0.0157*			(-)0.02342		0.725	
V	0.0152*				(-)0.03753	0.727	

Contd ...

... Contd ...

(1)	(2)	(3)	(4)	(5)	(6)	(7)	(8)
Pulses							
I	0.0030					0.063	0.03
II	0.0004	0.00002				0.037	
III	0.1384*		(-)0.005202			0.207	
IV	0.0003			0.00392		0.042	
V	0.0010				0.00610	0.051	
Oilseeds							
I	0.0197*					0.826	2.0
II	0.0574*	(-)0.00027				0.839	
III	0.0340*		(-)0.015151*			0.852	
IV	0.0229*			(-)0.00756		0.827	
V	0.0208*				(-)0.00998	0.820	

Notes: Dummy variables were used to distinguish the following time periods:

D_1 takes value 0 from 1949-50 to 1964-65 and 1 from 1965-66 to 1987-88.

D_2 takes value 0 from 1949-50 to 1974-75 and 1 from 1975-76 to 1987-88.

D_3 takes value 0 from 1949-50 to 1979-80 and 1 from 1980-81 to 1987-88.

* Refers to statistical significance at 95 per cent confidence level. The same level of significance is used in all the regression reported in this paper, unless otherwise stated.

Source: Economic Survey, various issues.

Table 5.5

Growth of Value Added in Agriculture, 1950-51 to 1987-88

	1950-51/ 1959-60	*1960-61/ 1969-70*	*1970-71/ 1979-80*	*1980-81/ 1987-88*
Agriculture and allied	2.7	1.5	1.7	1.9
Agriculture	2.9	1.3	1.9	2.2
Forestry	0.3	3.3	0.6	-3.4
Fishing	5.6	3.9	2.9	5.7

Source: CSO (1989b) and CSO (1990).

Table 5.6

Trend Growth Rate of GDP Originating in Agriculture at 1980-81 Prices, 1950-51 to 1987-88

Functional Form	*t*	*t^2*	*D_2*	*R^2*	*Growth Rate per cent per annum*
I Agriculture and allied activities					
1 Log linear	0.22*			0.966	2.2
2 Log quadratic	0.018	0.00003		0.965	
3 Log linear with D	0.022*		(-)0.003	0.965	
II Agriculture					
1 Log linear	0.22*			0.956	2.2
2 Log quadratic	0.156	0.00011		0.957	
3 Log linear with D	0.22*		(-)0.0002	0.958	

Note: Dummy variable D taken value '0' for the years 1950-51 to 1979-80 and '1' for 1980-81 to 1987-88.

Source: CSO (1989b) and CSO (1990).

Changes in Input Use in Agriculture: While a constant growth rate of agricultural output could not have provided any additional source of consumption demand from that sector, increase in the use of manufactured inputs per unit of cultivated area (or output) could have been, as suggested by Chakravarty (1987), an important source of further demand for a certain range of manufacturing industries. Thamarajakshi (1990) has shown that the percentage of purchased inputs to total inputs (taken as a proxy for demand for industrial inputs in agricultural production) has roughly doubled from 16.4 per cent in 1970-71 to 35.6 per cent in 1983-84.

Intersectoral Terms of Trade: A fairly stable intersectoral barter terms of trade since 1951-52 up to the early sixties, followed by a sharp movement in them against non-agricultural sector (or 'industry') for over a decade, as estimated by Thamarajakshi (1969 and 1977) formed an important basis for some influential hypothesis for the relative stagnation[17] of the manufacturing sector.

In his application of the Lewis model to elucidate the main features of the Indian economic development in the post-independence period, Chakravarty (1974) found the adverse movement in intersectoral terms of trade against industry to be a reflection of the behaviour of the agricultural output. Given the constant product wage in the organised sector, he argued that, such a tendency could reduce the saving rate in the economy, thus constraining the growth of the modern (or 'industrial') sector. Mitra (1977), on the other hand, posing the problem in a Kaleckian perspective attributed the slowing down of industrial growth after the mid-sixties to a relative fall in the demand for manufactures consequent upon the shift in the terms of trade in favour of agriculture leading to a decline in the profitability in the private corporate sector.

Thamarajakshi's (1990) updated estimates of barter terms of trade offers us an opportunity to reassess the postulated relationships outlined above for the entire period since the early fifties. Figure 5.1 provides indices of real total gross value added in manufacturing and barter terms of trade for the period 1951-52 to 1987-88. It shows that after steadily moving in favour of agriculture since 1961-62 the terms of trade reached a peak in 1973-74 and shows a decline[18] thereafter, though with considerable fluctuations. Interestingly the terms of trade for the non-agriculture in the eighties appears to be at more or less at the same level as in the pre mid-sixties period.

Table 5.7 shows that, consistent with Chakravarty's reasoning, the movement in the terms of trade favourable to non-agriculture after the early seventies appears to have slightly improved the savings rate in the private corporate sector from the relatively low level it had reached during the latter half of the sixties.[19] However, contrary to Mitra's reasoning, improved terms of trade in the eighties do not seem to have resulted in any increase in the profitability for the private corporate sector. As can be seen from Table 5.8, 'profit before

Figure 5.1

Total Manufacturing Output and Terms of Trade 1951-52 to 1987-88

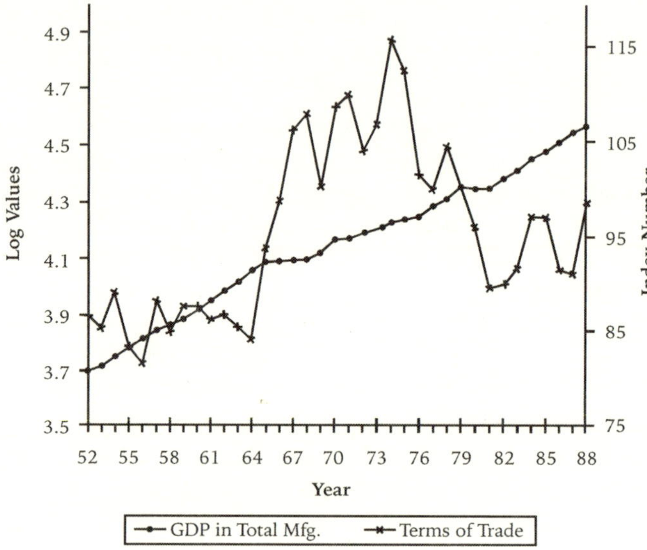

Sources: Thamarajakshi (1990), CSO (1989b) and CSO (1990).

Table 5.7

Savings in Private Corporate Sector as a Proportion of Gross Domestic Product, 1950-51 to 1988-89

Years	*Per Cent*
1950-51 to 1954-55	1.0
1955-56 to 1959-60	1.1
1960-61 to 1964-65	1.7
1965-66 to 1969-70	1.3
1970-71 to 1974-75	1.7
1975-76 to 1979-80	1.5
1980-81 to 1984-85	1.6
1985-86 to 1988-89	1.8

Source: Economic Survey, 1989-90.

tax' and 'profit after tax' as percentages of income (both indices used by Mitra for the period 1960 to 1970) have steadily declined, especially in the eighties despite an improvement in the terms of trade for the non-agricultural sector. 'Profit after tax as percentage of net worth' has also declined since 1960-61 though, however, with considerable fluctuation.

Table 5.8

Indices of Profitability in Private Corporate Sector, 1960-61 to 1986-87

Year	*Profit Before Tax as per cent of Total Income*		*Profit After Tax as per cent of Total Income*		*Profit After Tax as per cent of Net Worth*	
	Actual	*Index*	*Actual*	*Index*	*Actual*	*Index*
1960-61	9.1	100.0	5.6	100.0	11.1	100.0
1961-62	9.0	98.9	5.1	91.0	10.0	90.1
1962-63	9.1	100.0	4.3	76.8	8.7	78.4
1963-64	9.3	102.2	4.6	82.1	9.4	84.7
1964-65	8.6	94.5	4.2	75.0	9.3	83.8
1965-66	8.0	87.9	4.0	71.4	8.8	79.3
1966-67	7.6	83.5	4.0	71.4	9.1	82.0
1967-68	6.2	68.1	3.2	57.1	7.3	65.8
1968-69	5.8	63.7	2.9	51.8	6.9	62.2
1969-70	6.8	74.7	3.9	69.6	9.5	85.6
1970-71	7.2	79.1	4.1	73.2	10.0	98.2
1971-72	7.0	76.9	3.8	67.9	10.8	97.3
1972-73	6.8	74.7	3.6	64.3	10.4	93.7
1973-74	7.6	83.5	4.0	71.4	11.6	104.5
1974-75	8.1	89.0	4.2	75.0	13.7	123.4
1975-76	5.7	62.6	2.4	42.9	8.2	73.9
1976-77	5.4	59.3	2.1	37.5	7.9	71.2
1977-78	5.4	59.3	2.3	41.1	8.8	79.3
1978-79	6.0	65.9	2.9	51.8	11.5	103.6
1979-80	6.8	74.7	3.6	64.3	14.5	130.6
1980-81	6.3	65.2	3.5	62.5	14.6	131.5
1981-82	5.3	58.2	3.1	55.4	13.4	120.7
1982-83	4.5	49.5	2.8	50.0	11.6	104.5
1983-84	3.5	38.5	1.8	32.1	6.8	54.1
1984-85	3.9	43.9	1.9	33.9	7.5	67.6
1985-86	4.3	47.3	1.7	30.4	8.3	74.8
1986-87	3.0	33.0	1.3	23.2	5.4	48.6

Note: To arrive at continuous time series we have taken simple average for the overlapping years of the RBI's quinquennial surveys.

Source: Reserve Bank of India Bulletin, various issues.

Though broadly inverse relationship between the movement of terms of trade and the growth of manufacturing output over the 38-year period under consideration is clearly discernible, the causal links suggested, especially by Mitra, appear tenuous. The above evidence showing the long-term movements in the economic variables perhaps calls for a closer analytical specification taking into account perhaps specific features of India's agricultural and industrial economy. However, for the limited purpose of our exercise the data seem to indicate that a shift of terms of trade in favour of industry or, more appropriately, a decline in the adverse movement of terms of trade observed after 1972-73 appears to be positively associated with a higher rate of industrial growth in the eighties, though, neither the precise chain of causation nor the exact strength of the relationship seems to be evident.[20]

Public Investment: Centrality of public investment[21] in India's growth process, though viewed in differing theoretical perspectives, has been widely acknowledged [Patnaik and Rao, 1977 and Srinivasan and Narayanan, 1978]. More recently Ahluwalia (1985) has provided considerable evidence to suggest the deleterious effect the slowing down of public investment after the mid-sixties had on the industrial growth in general and on the infrastructure industries in particular.

Capital formation in the eighties in the light of the experience of the previous three decades, seems to indicate some interesting trends (Table 5.9). Although real gross capital formation as a percentage of GDP (at market prices) has remained more or less constant at around 21 per cent in the eighties,[22] its composition appears to have undergone some discernible changes. The rate of real gross fixed capital formation which stagnated for over a decade after reaching 16.7 per cent in 1965-66 increased since 1979-80 attaining a level of 19.5 per cent in 1982-83. Moreover, within gross fixed capital formation the share of 'machinery and equipment' has gone up from 48.1 per cent in 1980-81 to 61.6 per cent in 1987-88, with a corresponding decline in the share of 'construction'.[23,24] Further, the share of public sector in gross domestic capital formation has also shown a distinct increase to over 50 per cent in the eighties.[25] These changes in the pattern of capital formation in general and public investment in particular appear to have been overlooked by studies

Table 5.9

Trends in Capital Formation in India at 1980-81 Prices, 1950-51 to 1987-88

(Per cent)

Year	*GDCF as per cent GDP*	*GFCF as per cent GDP*	*Share of Machinery and Equipment in GFCF*	*Share of Public Sector in GDCF (Adjusted for Errors and Omissions)*
(1)	(2)	(3)	(4)	(5)
1950-51	14.7	10.7	40.5	
1951-52	16.6	11.3	40.9	
1952-53	10.7	10.1	40.4	
1953-54	11.5	8.7	36.5	
1954-55	12.1	11.1	32.7	
Average 1951-1955	**13.1**	**10.4**	**38.2**	
1955-56	16.4	12.8	40.6	
1956-57	20.0	13.7	43.8	
1957-58	19.5	14.6	52.9	
1958-59	15.0	12.7	38.4	
1959-60	15.7	12.8	39.7	
Average 1956-1960	**17.3**	**13.3**	**43.1**	
1960-61	18.1	14.4	41.1	38.9
1961-62	16.0	13.5	42.5	42.5
1962-63	18.1	15.1	45.8	43.5
1963-64	17.9	15.4	44.8	46.5
1964-65	18.2	15.2	45.9	44.9
Average 1961-1965	**17.7**	**14.7**	**44.0**	**43.2**
1965-66	20.8	16.7	45.0	43.9
1966-67	21.9	16.3	38.2	37.0
1967-68	18.6	15.2	35.5	41.1
1968-69	16.9	14.1	36.0	39.2
1969-70	18.2	14.1	36.5	34.1
Average 1966-1970	**19.3**	**15.3**	**38.2**	**39.1**
1970-71	18.7	13.6	36.3	36.9
1971-72	19.3	13.9	39.6	38.4
1972-73	18.2	15.9	40.3	48.6
1973-74	22.4	14.9	45.6	37.9
1974-75	20.0	14.5	45.6	41.0
Average 1971-1975	**19.7**	**14.6**	**41.5**	**40.2**

Contd ...

... *Contd* ...

(Per cent)

Year	*GDCF as per cent GDP*	*GFCF as per cent GDP*	*Share of Machinery and Equipment in GFCF*	*Share of Public Sector in GDCF (Adjusted for Errors and Omissions)*
(1)	*(2)*	*(3)*	*(4)*	*(5)*
1975-76	18.9	15.5	42.5	50.1
1976-77	20.4	15.9	42.9	51.0
1977-78	20.7	15.7	41.6	39.7
1978-79	23.6	16.5	44.8	39.4
1979-80	22.3	17.0	47.4	45.9
Average 1976-1980	**21.2**	**16.1**	**43.8**	**45.2**
1980-81	22.7	19.3	48.1	45.4
1981-82	22.3	19.4	50.6	49.3
1982-83	20.4	19.5	55.6	54.9
1983-84	19.9	18.4	57.6	51.1
1984-85	18.9	18.4	58.5	55.5
Average 1981-1985	**20.8**	**19.0**	**54.1**	**51.4**
1985-86	21.2	18.4	57.9	51.2
1986-87	19.7	18.7	61.1	56.2
1987-88	20.0	18.4	41.6	48.2
Average 1986-1988	**20.3**	**18.4**	**61.6**	**52.1**

Notes: GDCF–Gross domestic capital formation, GFCF – Gross fixed capital formation, GDP–Gross domestic product at market price.

Source: CSO (1989b), CSO (1990).

suggesting continuation of a relative stagnation in them since the mid-sixties [Chandrasekhar, 1988, for instance].

As can be seen from Tables 5.10 and 5.11, the sectoral composition of public investment also appears to have undergone a distinct shift in the eighties. While agricultural sector has witnessed a negative growth rate in real capital formation, industry, i.e, (a) manufacturing, (b) electricity, gas and water, and (c) mining and quarrying experienced an increase. Further, the share of industry and infrastructure [(a) mining and quarrying, (b) electricity, gas and water, and (c) transport] have gone up from 52.1 per cent and 43.3 per cent, respectively in 1980-81 to 61.9 per cent and 55.2 per cent in 1987-88, respectively.

Table 5.10

Growth of Public Investment by Sectors
(Net Domestic Capital Formation at Constant Prices)

		Per Cent Per Annum			
		1960-61 to 1965-66	1965-66 to 1975-76	1975-76 to 1980-81	1980-81 to 1986-87
1	Agriculture	7.9	3.0	12.0	–5.4
2	Manufacturing	6.6	1.7	8.2	3.2
3	Infrastructure	16.7	2.1	8.3	8.4
	(a) Railway	(12.5)	(–7.7)	(9.1)	8.2
	(b) Electricity, gas and water	(23.7)	(4.2)	(5.6)	7.4
	(c) Mining	(2.4)	(13.8)	(6.4)	10.3
4	Public administration and defence	0.6	–0.1	(11.6)	3.5
5	Trade, hotel and restaurants	69.5	21.3	–30.2	
6	Others	10.9	8.1	–5.7	
7	Total	9.2	3.9	3.6	4.9

Sources: Ahluwalia (1985) and CSO (1989a).

Table 5.11

Composition of Public Sector Gross Capital Formation at 1980-81 Prices, 1960-61 to 1987-88

Year	Share of Industry*	Share of Infrastructure**
1960-61	35.7	34.1
1965-66	42.1	42.4
1970-71	40.1	43.4
1975-76	44.0	40.8
1980-81	52.1	43.4
1987-88	61.9	55.2

Notes: * Industry includes (1) mining and quarrying, (2) manufacturing and (3) electricity, gas and water.

** Infrastructure includes (i) mining, (ii) electricity, gas and water and (iii) transport.

Source: CSO (1989b), CSO (1990).

Improvement in Performance of Public Sector: Table 5.12 suggests that the share of public sector in total gross value added in manufacturing

Table 5.12

Share of Public Sector in Total Manufacturing Gross Value Added at 1980-81 Prices, 1960-61 to 1987-88

(Per cent)

Year	*Share of Public Sector in Total Gross Value Added in Manufacturing*
1960-61	5.4
1961-62	7.5
1962-63	9.6
1963-64	9.9
1964-65	10.1
Average 1961-1965	**8.5**
1965-66	10.8
1966-67	10.7
1967-68	11.0
1968-69	11.3
1969-70	10.5
Average 1966-1970	**10.9**
1970-71	10.5
1971-72	9.6
1972-73	10.2
1973-74	10.9
1974-75	12.3
Average 1971-1975	**10.7**
1975-76	11.5
1976-77	12.0
1977-78	12.5
1978-79	14.6
1979-80	11.9
Average 1976-1980	**11.9**
1980-81	13.0
1981-82	11.8
1982-83	12.4
1983-84	12.5
1984-85	12.3
Average 1981-1985	**12.4**
1985-86	12.7
1986-87	14.0
1987-88	13.6
Average 1986-1988	**13.4**

Source: CSO (1989b), CSO (1990).

at 1980-81 prices, after remaining constant for nearly a decade since around the mid-sixties, has shown an increase, especially after 1980. As the bulk of the public sector output is likely to consist of capital and intermediate goods, it is quite conceivable that an improvement in this segment of manufacturing could have also contributed positively towards increasing the growth rate of the industrial sector as a whole through the well known linkages between the public and private sectors.

An important aspect of the behaviour of public sector in the eighties appears to have been the attempts at a relatively greater selectivity in newer projects and concentration of the available resources in completing the ongoing ones. Though we do not have evidence to substantiate the proposition this could perhaps be taken as a hypothesis for a closer examination.[26] However, an indication to validate our proposition is available in the following official assessment.

The seventh Five-Year Plan has emphasised the consolidation of the existing manufacturing capacity rather than a widespread creation of entirely new capacity. Thus, the plan has laid stress on modernisation and technological upgradation of existing facilities in order to obtain higher production through increased productivity, improved product quality and higher capacity utilisation. Additional capacity is sought to be created by expansion of existing plants wherever possible rather than investment in entirely new green field projects [Planning Commission, 1988: 103].

As a response to the changes in the magnitude and pattern of public investment, and a greater selectivity in the projects with an increasing emphasis on modernisation (and also possibly some improvement in decision-making), infrastructure industries seem to have improved their performance in the eighties. Since their poor growth during 1965-66 and 1979-80 is shown to have had adverse effect on the growth of manufacturing output [Ahluwalia, 1985], an improvement in the infrastructure could, by the same argument, have resulted in, other things remaining same, a higher growth rate of manufacturing sector. Figures 5.2 to 5.6 show a distinct increase in the rate of growth output of coal, electricity, nitrogenous fertiliser, phosphatic fertilisers and cement.[27]

Figure 5.2

Coal Production, 1950-51 to 1988-89

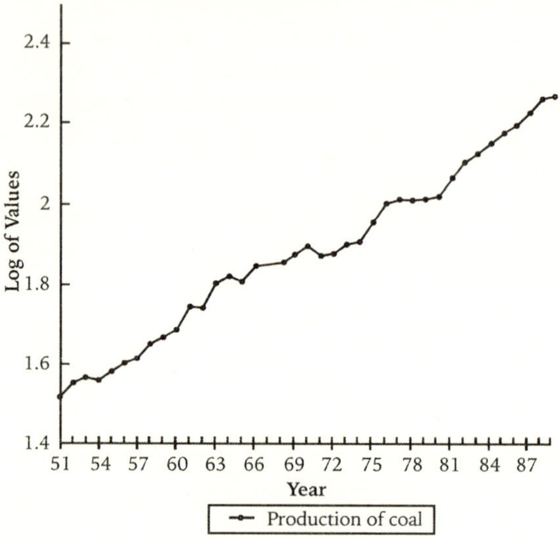

Source: *Economic Survey*, various issues.

Figure 5.3

Total Electricity Generated in Utilities, 1951-52 to 1988-89

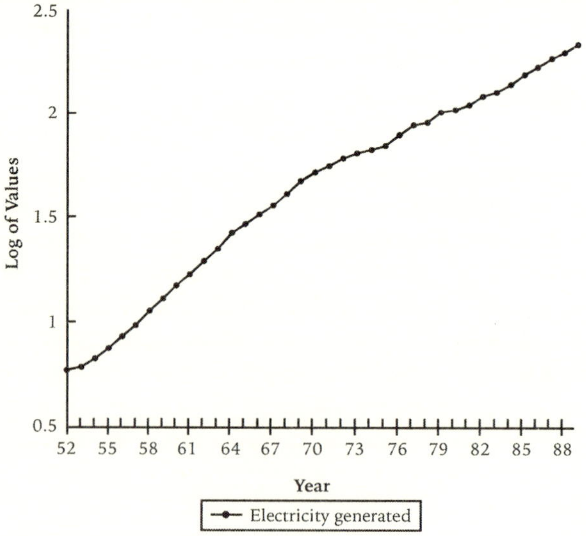

Source: *Economic Survey*, various issues.

Figure 5.4

Production of Nitrogenous Fertiliser 1951-52 to 1987-88

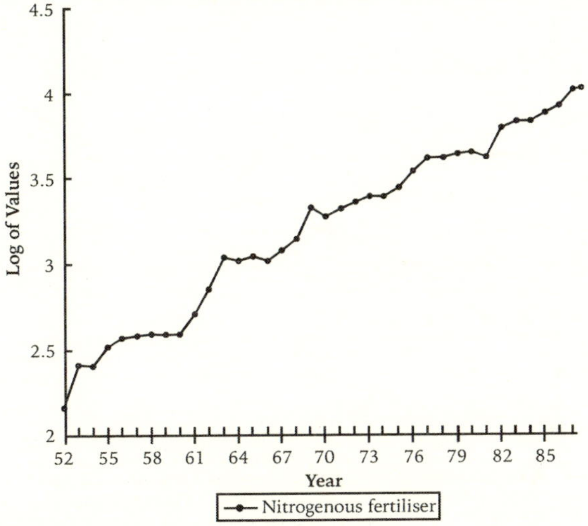

Source: *Economic Survey*, various issues.

Figure 5.5

Production of Phosphatic Fertiliser, 1951-52 to 1987-88

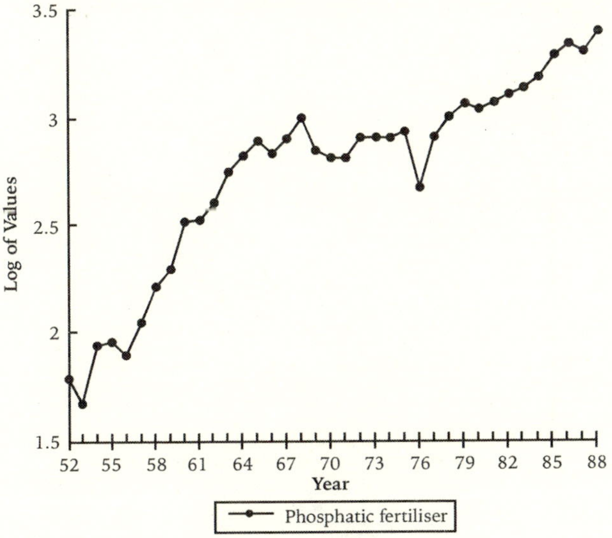

Source: *Economic Survey*, various issues.

Figure 5.6

Cement Production, 1950-51 to 1988-89

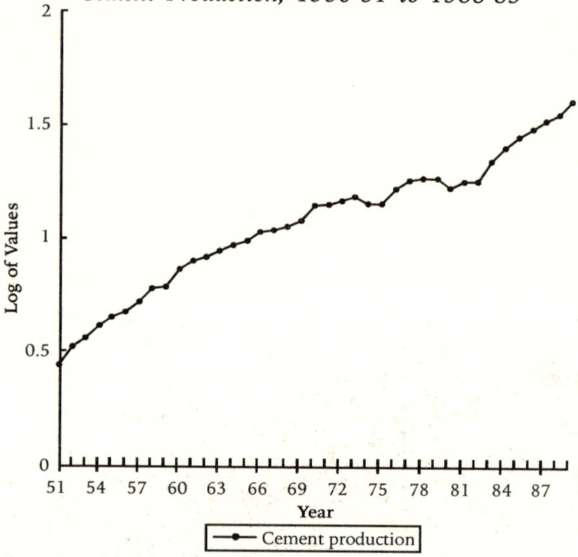

Source: *Economic Survey*, various issues.

Figure 5.7

Plant Load Factor of Thermal Power Plants in India, 1975-76 to 1987-88

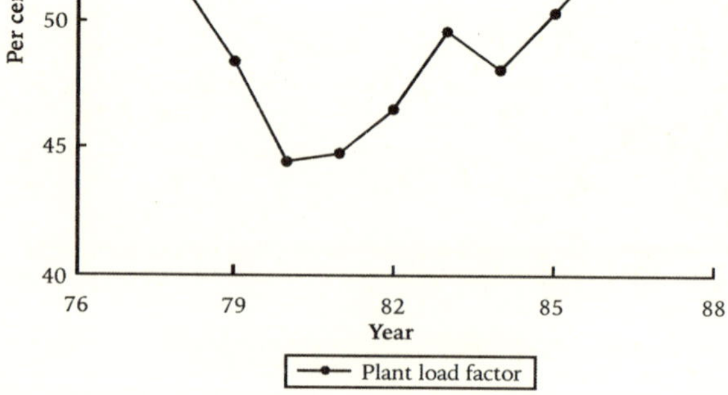

Source: *Economic Survey*, various issues.

Figure 5.8

New Direct Exchange Lines Added, 1961-62 to 1988-89

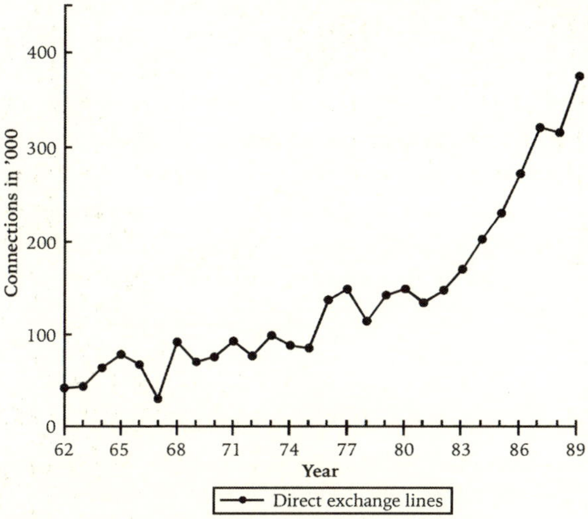

Source: *Economic Survey*, various issues.

Figure 5.9

Growth in Revenue Earning Traffic in Railways, 1975-76 to 1988-89

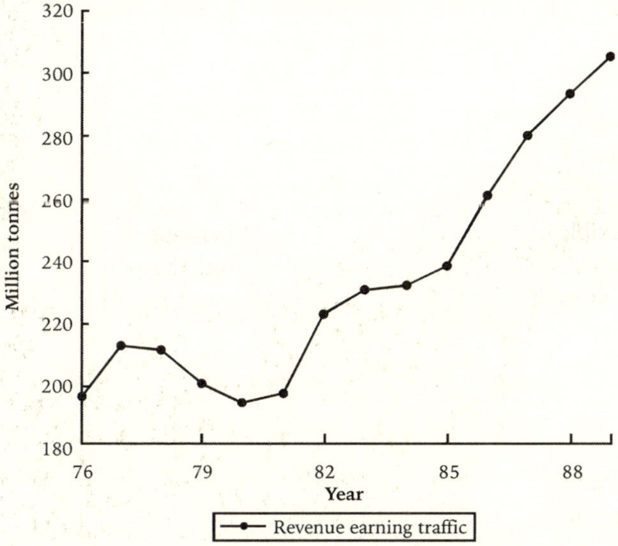

Source: *Economic Survey*, various issues.

Admittedly the sharp increase in growth of cement output is perhaps more in response to the partial (and later total) decontrol introduced since 1982. However, being an energy intensive industry rapid growth in its output could possibly not have been secured without a simultaneous improvement in the generation of electricity which is almost entirely in the public sector. Performance of this sector in the eighties can perhaps be better captured by the recorded increase in plant-load factor of thermal power plants (Figure 5.7), constituting two-thirds of total electricity generated in 1988-89. However, admittedly, as is evident from Figure 5.3, the growth rate of electricity output in the eighties is considerably lower than that obtained during the fifties and up to the late sixties. In the services sector, growth in telecommunication (as measured by new direct exchange lines added) and railways (as recorded by revenue earning traffic) since 1981 are notable (Figures 5.8 and 5.9).

However, it is important to highlight some of the shortcomings in the performance of infrastructure. Production of steel, (NIC 330), as can be seen from (Table 5.3),[28] has displayed no growth at all during the period 1980-81 to 1985-86[29] resulting in a sharp increase in imports of the basic metal from 6.8 lakh tonnes to 2.4 million tonnes during the same period [*Economic Survey,* 1989-1990].[30] Thus, it may not be incorrect to infer that better performance of infrastructure industries in general, barring some industries like basic steel, could have had a positive influence on the growth of manufacturing sector as a whole.

Admittedly, the process of liberalisation, besides the real factors discussed in this section, could have played a role in reducing the delays in decision-making, introduction of some additional (primarily domestic) competition[31] and enabling firms to use their resources in a more flexible manner. However, it would perhaps be premature, as would be discussed below, to be categorical on the role of the policy reform in stimulating the growth of output and investment.[32]

IV

EMERGING CONSTRAINTS

The forgoing analysis clearly suggests that the improved growth rate of manufacturing output since 1980 is empirically valid and that it appears to have been secured not merely by the changes in the industrial and trade policies but, perhaps more importantly, on account of some identifiable improvements in the composition of public investment, performance of most of the infrastructure industries, increasing use of manufactured inputs in crop production and also probably due to a decline in the unfavourable intersectoral terms of trade. In the absence of a significant improvement in the trend growth rate of either agriculture or of exports [at least up to 1985-86[33] as shown by Nayyar, 1988], greater willingness to use imports to dampen inflationary potential[34] and release-supply constraints on raw material and intermediate inputs—even at the risk of an increasingly adverse current account and revenue deficits—appear to have been the main elements in the macroeconomic policy stance to facilitate higher industrial growth under relatively liberal domestic policy regime.

While the strategy appears to have, at least in the medium-term, yielded some favourable results—given the reasonably favourable 'initial conditions'[35] for initiating such a policy change—its sustainability in the long run, other things remaining the same, could be constrained by serious macroeconomic imbalance as has been suggested by a number of studies [Economic Advisory Council, 1989, for instance]. In this section we would attempt to highlight some of the emerging microeconomic (or sectoral) problems which, unless corrective steps are initiated, could become binding constraints and/ or accentuate internal as well as external imbalance.

The changes in the trade and industrial policies initiated in the eighties are widely believed to have enabled firms and industries to operate in a more market sensitive manner to secure increased output and efficiency by a better utilisation of capacity with greater inducement to invest. Figures 5.10 and 5.11 showing indices of real gross value added and real gross domestic capital formation for total and registered manufacturing sectors respectively, for 1950-51 to 1987-88 suggest some interesting trends. While a sharp increase in the growth rate of gross value added since 1980-81 is clearly discernible, rate of growth in gross capital formation, especially in the registered manufacturing sector, has remained very low since the late seventies. This seems to indicate that though the process of liberalisation, in conjunction with other real factors discussed earlier,

Figure 5.10

GDP and GCF in Total Manufacturing at 1980-81 Prices, 1950-51 to 1987-88

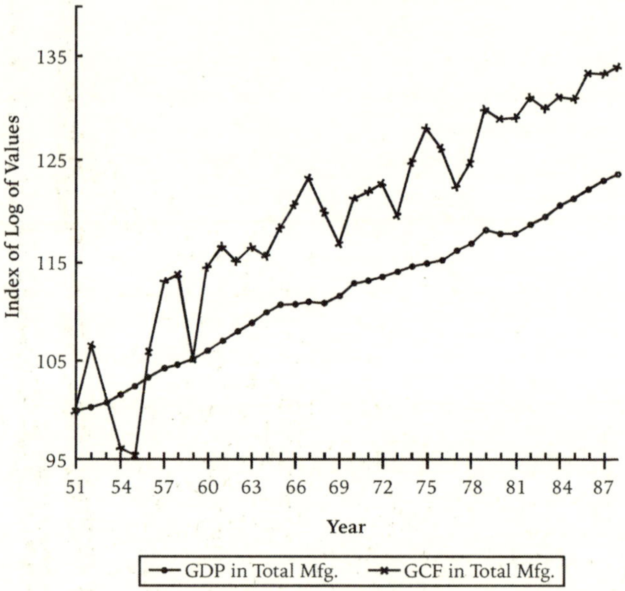

Source: CSO (1989b) and CSO (1990).

has contributed towards improving capacity utilisation leading to an increase in productivity,[36] the policy changes appear to have had little effect, at least so far, in stepping up the rate of investment in the manufacturing sector. This is particularly significant in the context of the widely publicised improvements in the investment climate—as reflected in, among other measures, the number of licences issued (despite considerable reduction in the entry barriers), foreign technical (and financial) collaborations approved and mobilisation of resources through the capital market.

Interpreting the long-term-trends in the economy the Working Group on Savings [Chairman: K.N. Raj] had pointed out that a possible reason for the continued slower growth of domestic output up to the late seventies, despite significant increases in the rates of savings and investment, could be—quite contrary to the historical

Figure 5.11

GDP and GCF in Registered Manufacturing at 1980-81 Prices, 1951-52 to 1987-88

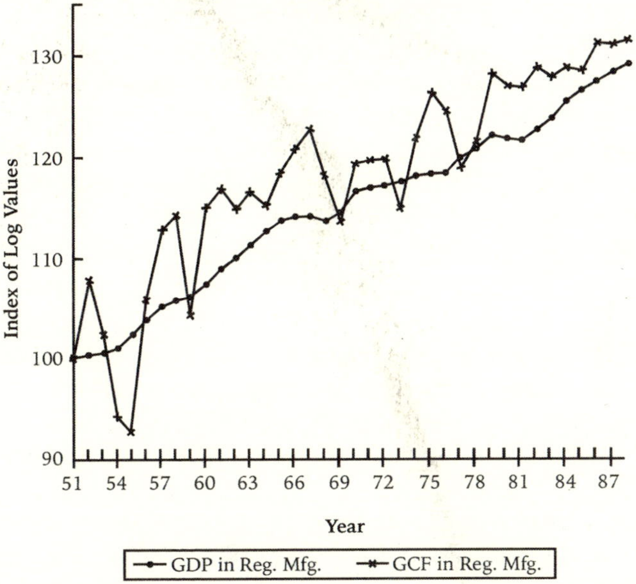

Source: CSO (1989b) and CSO (1990).

trends in the presently developed economies—the relatively faster rise in prices of commodities that go into fixed capital formation than the implicit GDP deflator since 1973-74 [Reserve Bank of India, 1982]. Highlighting the findings of the Working Group, Raj (1981) said:

> A closer examination of the estimates of investment in the economy brings out, of course, a number of important qualifications that must be made straight away about the extent of increase in the rate of investment itself and the nature of such investments. For instance, part of the apparently large increase in the rate of gross fixed capital formation is traceable simply to the prices of capital goods having risen much more sharply than the prices of other commodities. So, instead of capital goods getting cheaper, they have become dearer (p 10).

Indices of implicit price deflators of GDP and gross fixed capital formation at 1980-81 prices for the period 1950-51 to 1987-88

(Figure 5.12) shows that the adverse trend observed by Raj for the period 1973-74 to 1979-80 seems to have got further accentuated in the eighties with the continued rapid rise of the former relatively to that of the latter, suggesting that despite a perceptible increase in the rate of fixed capital formation in the eighties (with a sharp increase in the share of machinery and equipment in GFCF as noted in the previous section) its effect on the output growth appears to be getting eroded due to faster increase in prices of items constituting fixed capital formation. Interestingly the adverse trend seems to have got further strengthened despite the relatively liberal import of capital goods (intended to improve the productive capacity of the industrial sector) and rapid growth of domestic capital goods industries at 9.8 per cent per annum during 1980-81 to 1988-89 (according to the revised IIP).

Thus, it may not be inappropriate to infer that despite various attempts to strengthen the domestic capital goods sector by a freer import of technology and capital, and reduction in the extent of various physical controls, neither the rate of investment in manufacturing in general nor the efficiency of capital goods sector in particular seems to have witnessed any perceptible improvement. This, in our view, appears to be an increasingly serious shortcoming of the domestic manufacturing base which seems to warrant a much closer examination.

Admittedly greater investment in infrastructure seems to have had a positive effect on industrial growth in the eighties. However, considering the prolonged period of inadequate investment, the backlog of renovation and modernisation appears to be so large that it perhaps calls for sustaining the increased investment to regain the momentum lost around the mid-sixties. To illustrate as can be seen from Figure 5.13, the real gross capital formation in railways in the eighties, despite an increase in its growth rate since 1977, has not recovered the level attained in 1963-64.

Though agricultural output has maintained a constant growth rate some unfavourable features seem to be persisting. As noted in Table 5.4, coarse cereals and non-foodgrains have recorded a trend deceleration in growth rate during the entire period since 1950-51. Oilseeds[37] show a statistically significant slower growth rate since 1965-66 a trend which has not been reversed in the eighties. More

Figure 5.12

Implicit NAS Deflators at 1980-81 Prices, 1951-52 to 1987-88

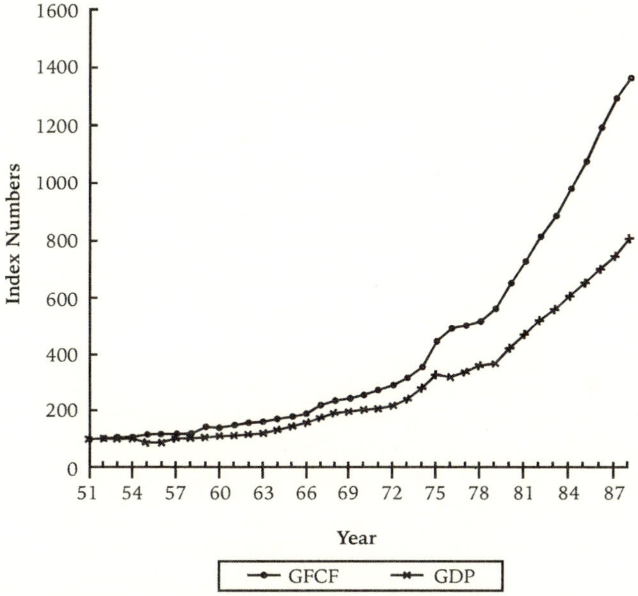

Source: CSO (1989b) and CSO (1990).

alarming is the fact that over the entire 39 year period there is no statistically significant trend growth rate in pulses. These tendencies could find their reflection in further adverse movement in inflation and balance of payments.

Figure 5.14 shows that while the real domestic capital formation in the secondary and tertiary sectors have maintained a reasonably steady growth, it has witnessed a negative growth in the agricultural sector since 1977-78.[38] A reflection of this adverse trend seems to be discernible in some of the main physical indicators of agricultural development (Table 5.13). For instance, the rate of creation of additional irrigation potential and spread of yielding varieties (HYV) of seeds appear to have come down in the latter half of the eighties. Such a negative growth rate of investment in agriculture, not witnessed earlier, could seriously impair the long-term growth potential of not only manufacturing sector, but also of a self-reliant growth.

Figure 5.13

GCF in Railways at 1980-81 Prices, 1951-52 to 1987-88

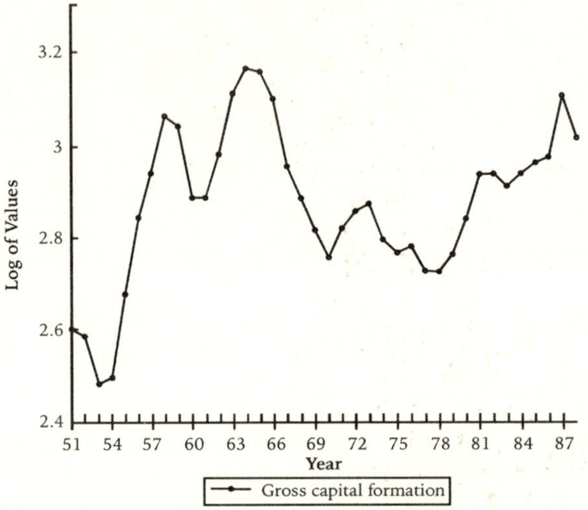

Source: CSO (1989b) and CSO (1990).

Figure 5.14

Real GCF in Agriculture, Industry and Tertiary Sectors, 1951-52 to 1987-88

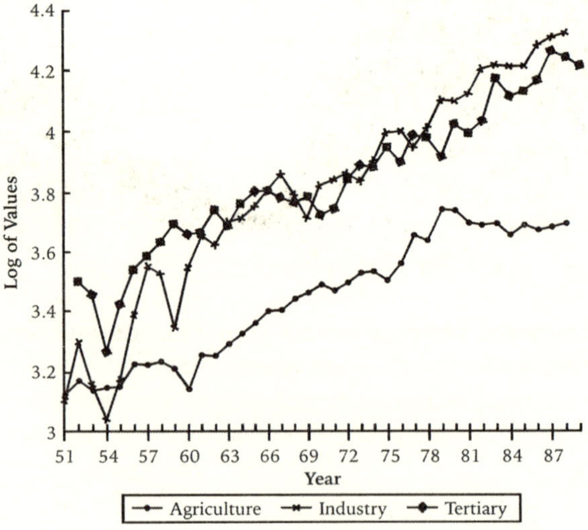

Source: CSO (1989b) and CSO (1990).

Table 5.13

Physical Indicators of Agricultural Development, 1967-68 to 1987-88

(Million hectares)

Year	*Area Under High Yielding Varieties HYV Seeds*	*Irrigation Potential*	*Soil Conservation*
1967-68			
1968-69			
1969-70	11.40		
1970-71	15.38	38.0	13.37
1971-72	18.17		
1972-73	22.09		
1973-74	26.02	42.3	17.10
1974-75	27.01	43.6	
1975-76	31.89	45.3	18.90
1976-77	34.48	47.4	19.60
1977-78	38.93	48.5	21.70
1978-79	40.13	50.6	22.57
1979-80	38.38	52.6	23.40
1980-81	43.07	54.1	24.37
1981-82	46.49	56.1	25.39
1982-83	47.48	58.2	26.52
1983-84	53.74	58.6	27.98
1984-85	54.14	60.5	29.38
1985-86	55.42	62.4	30.48
1986-87	56.12	64.4	31.22
1987-88	51.23	63.3	32.07

Source: Economic Survey, various issues.

V

ISSUES FOR FURTHER ENQUIRY

If the evidence reported in this study has any validity then they perhaps raise a number of issues warranting further investigation not only for securing a better understanding of the process of industrial change in India, but also for policy reform.

Though our exercise has provided a reasonably firm basis to reject the hypothesis of overestimation of industrial output by the revised

IIP, there appear to be many problems with the index which need to be carefully examined. Why has the list of items included in the revised index kept at 290 when there has been such a rapid diversification of production structure? It is puzzling to discover, as noted in Section II, that despite very rapid growth of consumer durables in the seventies and an unchanging number of items included in the index (though with some re-classification), the share of CDs has come down from 2.92 to 2.55. A close review of the revised IIP could also perhaps look into the representativeness and accuracy of the production data supplied by firms on a voluntary basis for computing the IIP, especially the data on the small-scale sector as the basis for collecting them by the concerned official agency appear suspect.[39]

As seen in Section II the concept of consumer durables appears to warrant a serious re-examination considering the pace of introduction of newer products in the recent years. Moreover, the method of capturing the growth of consumer goods, including durables, considering the rapid growth of the small-scale sector after the mid-sixties, also perhaps need to be thoroughly reassessed.

If our arguments on the improved performance of public sector in general and infrastructure in particular have any substance then they seem to raise a number of issues for further enquiry.[40] We would hypothesise that it is not merely the level and the rate of growth of public investment per se which seems to influence industrial growth, but also its composition and quality. In order to examine the issue what is perhaps required is not merely an analysis of the aggregated data on the growth of investment and its sectoral composition—as has been attempted, in a modest way, in this study using the *National Accounts Statistics*—but a more disaggregated examination of public investment projects to understand their efficacy from the stage of conception to the point when they begin to yield economic returns on a sustainable basis. Though no analytical framework may be readily available to address such a problem, attempts in that direction could probably be of considerable value especially for the practical problem of policy. Such exercises could also possibly shed some light on what constitutes structural- and policy-induced constraints on the efficient execution and functioning of public sector projects.

The proposition that there appears to have been a greater selectivity in public investment projects and possibly some improvement in decision-making resulting in relatively quicker yield in the eighties needs to be systematically assessed against data.

Though the desirability of reduction in direct (physical) controls and their replacement by fiscal and financial[41] ones has been widely debated, very few attempts appear to have been made to analyse the possible effects of the process of the policy reform on specific industries regions. The limited aggregated evidence adduced in this study suggests that at the sectoral level, while the output has displayed a faster growth rate, the rate of capital formation has not indicated that the causal links between policy and performance do not appear to be as simplistic as they are widely believed.[42] Closely conducted enquiries are also perhaps warranted to understand the response of various specific policy measures of the change over from physical to financial controls—like delicensing, broad banding and so forth—on the structure and behaviour of specific industries.

A thorough examination of the capital goods industry warrants a special mention since, as noted in the previous section, the increase in the rate of gross fixed capital formation in the economy appears to be getting neutralised by the relatively faster rise in the prices of output of this sector. In such enquiries the role of demand, domestic supply constraints and external factors of trade and technology, (preferably in a comparative perspective) perhaps need to be carefully articulated.

VI

CONCLUSION

The growth rate of manufacturing output in the eighties and its pattern has been a widely debated issue. Providing some further evidence to support our earlier findings we have shown that the growth rate of the manufacturing output, as recorded by the revised index of industrial production is lower than that according to *Annual Survey of Industries* for factory sector for the period 1980-81 to 1985-86. A disaggregated analysis of the ASI does suggest that the higher growth rate has been shared by a majority of industry groups.

As the relatively rapid growth of consumer durable goods in the eighties has attracted widespread adverse attention, we considered it appropriate to make a preliminary examination of empirical and analytical bases of the various arguments.

Locating the problem of industrial growth of the eighties in the context of the stagnation debate, we have attempted to systematically examine some of the prominent hypotheses on industrial growth in India. It was found that there appears to have been (i) some significant improvement in the rate and the pattern of gross domestic capital formation in general and public investment in particular, (ii) better performance of infrastructure industries as a consequence, and (iii) a decline in the unfavourable trends in intersectoral terms of trends in favour of non-agriculture. Though neither the growth of agricultural output nor its value added displays any statistically significant change over the 39-year period under consideration a perceptible increase in the use of manufactured inputs in crop production could have contributed to an additional demand for a certain range of manufacturing industries. These real factors, together with the changes in the trade and industrial policies could have accounted for to the observed improvement in the performance of the manufacturing sector.

Without attempting to speculate on the sustainability of the higher growth rate, we have, on the basis of an examination of the available evidence, attempted to highlight a few areas of concern which could possibly become binding constraints on maintaining the improved industrial growth. An important infrastructure industry which has witnessed a total stagnation in the six years of the eighties for which firm data is available is iron and steel industry, resulting in a sharp increase in its imports.

Though the crop output in the eighties has maintained the long-term trend growth rate, non-food crops and coarse cereals have witnessed a trend deceleration and oilseeds have recorded a lower trend growth rate since the mid-sixties. No statistically significant trend is discernible in the output of pulses since 1949-50. Moreover, gross fixed capital formation in agriculture has recorded a negative growth rate since the late seventies which could erode the very basis of a self-reliant growth process.

Despite considerable reduction of physical controls, a relatively liberal import of capital and technology and favourable climate for industrial investment, rate of growth of capital formation, especially in the registered manufacturing, appears to have remained relatively low in the eighties thus questioning some of the implicit assumptions underlying the arguments for liberalisation.

We conclude the study by raising a few issues for further enquiry, among others, on public investment behaviour and the effects of policy reform initiated in the eighties on the growth of the manufacturing sector.

Appendix

A-5.1

Constituents of Consumer Durables according to Various Use-Based Classifications

	IIP with 1960 as Base Year			*IIP with 1970-71 as Base Year*			*ISIC Use-Based Classification*			*NIC Use-Based Classification*			*Ahluwalia's Classification*	
	Industry	*Weight*		*Industry*	*Weight*		*Industry*	*ISIC Code*		*Industry*	*NIC Code*		*Industry*	*NIC Code*
1	Mfg. of metal products nec*	1.30	1	Commercial, office household equipment excluding air conditioner and refrigerators	0.22	1	Coir	239.4	1	Water proof textile such as oil cloth, tarpaulin, etc.	267	1	Mfg. of furniture and fixtures	26
2	Commercial, office, and household machines	0.53	2	Electrical fans	0.24	2	Artificial leather and oil cloth	239.5	2	Coir and coir products	268	2	Hurricane lanterns	350.9
3	Electrical appliances	0.56	3	Telecommunications	0.97	3	Linoleum and similar products	239.6	3	Textiles, nec	269	3	Mfg. of commercial, office and household equipment excluding refrigerators and air conditioners	360.11.3
4	Communication equipment	0.61	4	Motor cycles and bicycles	0.75	4	Gas mantels	239.7	4	Wooden furniture and fixture	276	4	Electrical fans	370.1.3
5	Motor cycles and bicycles	0.62	5	Professional and scientific instruments	0.37	5	Tarpaulins, tents, sails and other made-up canvas goods	239.8	5	Bamboo and cane furniture and fixtures	277	5	Tele-communications	370.2
6	Mfg. of textiles nec	1.28	6	Watches and clocks	0.13	6	Textiles nec	239.9	6	Furniture and fixtures primarily of metal	342	6	Motor cars	383.1
7	Mfg. of professional, scientific measuring and controlling instruments	0.20			**2.92**	7	Furniture and fixtures	260	7	Metal utensils, etc.	345	7	Motor cycles and bicycles	385
8	Mfg. of watches and clocks	0.02				8	Cutlery, locks, etc.	350.2	8	Refrigerators, air-conditioners and fire fighting equipment	355	8	Professional, and scientific measuring and controlling instruments	391
9	Mfg. of jewellery and related articles	0.17				9	Hurricane lanterns	350.9	9	Office, computing				
						10	Commercial, office and household equipment	360.11						
						11	Electrical fans	370.13						
						12	Electrical lamps	370.14						

Contd ...

... Contd ...

Constituents of Consumer Durables according to Various Use-Based Classifications

IIP with 1960 as Base Year		IIP with 1970-71 as Base Year		ISIC Use-Based Classification		NIC Use-Based Classification		Ahluwalia's Classification	
Industry	Weight	Industry	Weight	Industry	ISIC Code	Industry	NIC Code	Industry	NIC Code
10 Mfg. of furniture and fixtures	0.39			13 Household appliances, such as electric iron, heaters, etc.	370.19	and accounting machinery	358	9 Watches and clocks	393
	5.68			14 Telecommunications	370.2	10 Non-electrical a/c nec	359	10 Jewellery and related articles	394
				15 Phonographs	370.3	11 Electrical apparatus	363	11 Other repair services	39.8
				16 Motor cycles and bicycle	385	12 Radio and television	364		
				17 Professional, and scientific and controlling instruments	391	13 Motor cycles, scooters	375		
				18 Watches and clocks	393	14 Bicycles, cycle rickshaws	376		
				19 Jewellery and related articles	394	15 Medical, surgical and scientific equipment	380		
				20 Musical instruments	395	16 Watches and clocks	382		
						17 Jewellery and related articles	383		
						18 Minting of coins	384		
						19 Musical instruments	386		

Note: * nec refers to not elsewhere classified.

Sources: 1 *Reserve Bank of India Bulletin*, June 1970 and February 1977.
2 Chaudhuri (1989).
3 Ahluwalia (1985).

Notes

1. In economic terms liberalisation is largely once over change in supply, consequent upon a reduction in regulation, leading to a downward shift in supply curve and hence a greater equilibrium output at the same price level.
2. The procedure for arriving at gross value added figures from IIP is not clear from the explanatory notes provided in the NAS. Even the recently published *National Accounts Statistics: Sources and Methods* [CSO, 1989c] does not throw any further light on it.
3. Though the official source has given details about the items from the small-scale sector that are included in the revised IIP and their weight, it is silent on the method of collection of data from small firms (more about it later).
4. This is particularly puzzling as the former are said to be based on the estimates provided by the latter. We are not in a position to comment on the reason for the observed divergence as the *National Accounts Statistics: Source and Methods* [CSO, 1989c] also does not provide any explanation for the same.
5. Apparently wholesale price indices for manufactured products are increasingly getting unrepresentative of the true price movements in the economy. As this view has been expressed by officials in the development banks financing industrial projects, it perhaps needs to be systematically examined. We are grateful to S.L Shetty for pointing this to us.
6. It is interesting to discover from the official note on the revised IIP [*Reserve Bank of India Bulletin*, October 1988] that the weight of items deleted from the earlier index for lack of inadequate data at 6.9324 is higher than that of 53 items dropped on account of their slower growth at 4.8605.
7. Kelkar and Kumar [1990] have described some dimensions of industrial growth using IIP even at 4-digit level without really subjecting the data to any serious scrutiny. Their empirical evidence seems to contain some obvious, though perhaps not grave, computational errors. For instance, while the average of annual growth rate for 'chemical and chemical products' for 1980-81 to 1988-89 in Table 3 [Sl No. 12, last column, p 212] is only 6.26, it is 11.19 in Table 4 [Sl no. 3, last column; p 213]. Thanks to Sunil Mani for pointing this to me.
8. This argument does not appear to be a particularly new one. Documenting various dimensions of 'structural retrogression' that is said to have been set in after the mid-sixties, Shetty (1978) argued that "... many industries which directly or indirectly cater to the requirements of the rich and upper middle class sections of the community have registered phenomenal growth rates. For want of sufficiently disaggregated data in respect of individual industrial items, it is difficult to make a more systematic analysis of the phenomenon. However, disproportionately large increases in the output of man-made fibres, beverages, perfumes and cosmetics, commercial office and household equipment, watches and clocks, finer varieties of cloth—all signify the emergence of an output structure that was increasingly getting elite oriented" (p 198).
9. In their attempt to characterise the industrial growth in the eighties as 'consumption-led', as against 'investment-led' growth during the 'Mahalanobis period' of 1955-65, Kelkar and Kumar (1990) have seriously overstated the weight of consumer goods (35.97) and consumer durables (5.623) in their Table 4. Weighting diagrams for successive indices of industrial production with 1960-61, 1970-71 and 1980-81 as base years are shown in Table A. It is evident that the weight of CDs used by Kelkar and Kumar corresponds to the 1960-61 series and not to the latest index. Moreover, the weight for consumer goods used by the authors does not correspond to any of the three series.

Table A

Changing Composition of Use-Based Classification of Indices of Industrial Production

Use-Based Classification	*1956=100*	*1960=100*	*1970=100*	*1980=100*
1 Basic goods	22.33	25.11	32.28	39.42
2 Capital goods	4.71	11.76	15.74	16.43
3 Intermediate goods	24.59	25.88	20.95	20.51
4 Consumer goods	48.37	37.25	31.03	23.65
a) Consumer durables	2.21	5.68	2.92	2.55
b) Consumer non-durables		31.57	28.11	21.10
Total manufacturing	**100.00**	**100.00**	**100.00**	**100.00**

Source: RBI Bulletin, Feb 1977, June 1990; *Economic Survey,* 1989-90.

10. A detailed statistical examination [Nagaraj, 1990] of the alternative hypotheses on the long-term growth rate of GDP and its main sectors clearly suggests a statistically significant break in the series at 1979-80 and a higher trend growth rate thereafter. This result remains valid even when the observation for 1979-80, a statistical outlier, is dropped.

11. Despite a higher trend growth rate of CDs in the seventies and the number of items included remaining constant (though with some reclassification at 270,11, the weight of CDs has come down from 2.92 in the older series with 1970-71 as the base year to 2.55 in the revised series. This seems to indicate a possible underestimation of the weight of CDs.

12. For a clear exposition of various linkages between agricultural and non-agricultural sectors in India see, Vaidyanathan (1977). As Raj (1984) has shown there is a close relationship with one year lag, between the movements of agricultural and manufacturing value added. However, as the following estimated linear regression equation suggests only about 18 per cent of the yearly variation in real manufacturing gross value added (Y_t) can be 'explained' by the early variation [with one year lag] in real gross value added in agriculture (X_{t-1}).

$$Y_t = 4.252 + \underset{(2.467)}{0.394} X^{*}_{t-1} \quad R^2 = 0.179 \quad N = 30$$

Figure in the bracket refers to estimate 't' value which is statically significant at 95 per cent level. This convention is followed consistently in this paper, unless otherwise stated.

13. We have fitted the following widely used trend equations to arrive at the underlying constant growth rate, to test for acceleration/deceleration in the trend growth rate and to test for possible statistically significant 'breaks' in the series with changes in the trend growth rate in different sub-periods.

(i) $\text{Log } y = a + bt$

(ii) $\text{Log } y = a + bt + ct^2$

(iii) $\text{Log } Y = a + a_1 (D) + bt + B_1 (Dt)$

Where Y is the economic time series whose trend growth rate we want to find out, 't' is time and 'D' is dummy variable which takes values '0' or '1' for different sub-periods.

14. There is a sharp increase in foodgrain output of about 13 per cent, in 1988-89 over the previous year. Since such an observation in the terminal year of a time series could induce undue upward bias in the trend growth rate we did not include the observation.

15. Some recent studies have hypothesised a higher trend growth rate of agricultural output since the mid-seventies. Montek Ahluwalia (1988) has said: "By the early eighties, however, it became generally accepted that Indian agriculture had indeed entered a new phase with a discernible acceleration in agricultural growth. The compound growth rate of production for all crops has increased from about 2.5 per cent in the period 1950-51 to 1967-68, to about 3 per cent after the mid-seventies. The compound annual growth rate of the index of agricultural production in the more recent period from 1980-81 to 1985-86 is about 3.2 per cent" (p 348). The evidence adduced in Table 4 seems to reject such a proposition.

16. Dividing the period 1961-62 to 1987-88 into two, 1961-62 to 1974-75 and 1975-76 to 1987-88, Thamarajakshi (1990) has shown the growth rate in the latter sub-period to be higher than that in the former. However, as can be seen below, a rigorous testing of the proposition using the dummy variable test, seems to reject the hypothesis.

    $$\text{Log } Y = 4.374 + \underset{(4.489)}{0.024t^{*}} + 0.067\,D - 0.002\,Dt$$

    $R^2 = 0.073 \quad N = 27$

    Where Y is index numbers for foodgrains.

17. The relevance of the movements in intersectoral terms of trade has been of significance not merely for analysing industrial growth, but for a substantial theorising on India's overall economic development. More important, questioning Thamarajakshi's estimates Kahlon and Tyagi (1983) and their alternative estimates displaying a considerably different pattern of the movement of terms of trade has given rise to a major debate on the political and economic aspects of the development process. Considering the limited purpose of our study, and Thamarajakshi (1990) recent rebuttal of the arguments of Kahlon and Tyagi, we have restricted our discussion only to the relevant aspects of the contributions of Chakravarty and Mitra.

18. The following regression between the annual percentage change in output of all agricultural commodities (X) and annual percentage change in the terms of trade (Y) shows a statistically significant (at 90 per cent level of significance) negative relationship.

    $$Y = 0.970 - \underset{(1.991)}{0.191X} \qquad R^2 = 0.104 \quad N = 36$$

19. The small share of the corporate saving has to, however, be recognised in interpreting these results.

20. A greater willingness in the eighties to use imports, especially of essential items like vegetable oil, even at the risk of adverse external balance, seems to have checked rise in prices of agricultural commodities. This perhaps could have played a role in dampening the adverse movement of terms of trade for industry.

21. We have not addressed the question of decline of consumption demand, which was hypothesised to have been a reason for the relative stagnation after the mid-sixties [Nayyar, 1978]. Ahluwalia (1985) has conclusively shown that the consumer goods industries did not witness slower growth after the mid-sixties and that the deceleration was in 'investment goods' industries only. Moreover, Raj has found, as noted in the previous section, the growth of consumer goods industries to be consistent with the implicit income elasticity of demand.

22. As the domestic saving rate has lagged behind the rate of capital formation, the share of external finance has gone up significantly in the eighties. The ratio of external finance of GDP reached a high figure of 4.6 per cent in 1981-82. However, the average of this rate for 1980-81 to 1986-87 at 3.3 per cent is lower than the figure at 3.6 per cent for 1960-61 to 1964-65 [Sundrum, 1987].

23. Decline in the share of 'construction' in gross fixed capital formation need not necessarily be perceived as a favourbale trend in the long-term development of the economy if it has adversely affected public works [roads, docks, transport, water, electricity, schools, hospitals and government buildings]. As Arthur Lewis (1955) had

cautioned: "The great importance of construction is not generally realised, many people think of capital formation mainly in terms of installing machinery, while in truth it consists to a greater extent of building structures of one sort or another; civil engineering is the key industry in capital formation, with mechanical engineering following some distance behind" [p 213].

24. Chart 1, showing indices of cement production and real gross fixed capital formation in 'construction', for the period 1950-51 to 1987-88 appears revealing. While a sharp increase in the former since 1981-82 is clearly evident there is no corresponding increase in the latter suggesting an underestimation of GFCF contributed by construction. This could possibly have two kinds of implications for our argument. While it may vitiate our finding of a sharp fall in the share of construction in GFCF, it could also imply a much higher rate of GFCF than indicated by the NAS data.

Chart 1

Cement Output and Real GFCF in Construction, 1951-52 to 1987-88

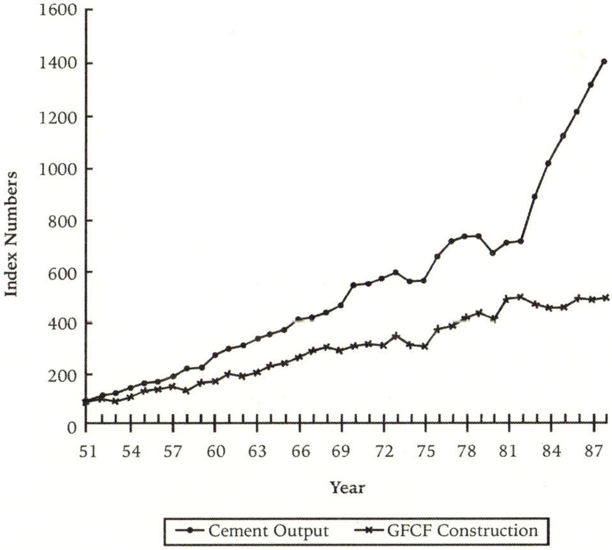

Source: CSO (1989b) and CSO (1990).
Economic Survey, various issues.

25. As can be seen from the following regression equation public investment has a statistically significant relationship not only with private corporate investment (equation 1), but also with total private investment (equation 2).

$$Y_1 = -19.246 + 2.310X \quad R^2 = 0.373 \quad (1)$$
$$(4.366)^* \quad N = 34$$

$$Y_2 = 5.448 + 0.439X \quad R^2 = 0.138 \quad (2)$$
$$(2.265)^* \quad N = 34$$

where X is annual percentage increase in public sector investment at current prices and Y_1 and Y_2 are annual percentage increases in private corporate and total private sector investment at current prices, respectively. While the above specification of the relationship between the investment in the public and private sectors could possibly be incomplete, our findings could perhaps be taken as a 'first a approximation' to investigate the relationship in a more precise manner. Though preliminary, our findings seem to be consistent with the critique of the widely accepted 'crowding out' hypothesis. Lance Taylor (1988), on the basis of some 18 country case studies, arrived at the following inference: 'There appear to be strong complementarities between public and private capital formation in the mixed economies that most developing countries have evolved, so that government project [ideally of good quality] stimulate entrepreneurs' (p 36).

26. A preliminary analysis of the data of the ministry of programme implementation shows, as can be seen from Tables B and C, a decline in the time and cost overruns of central government projects. Though these figures cannot perhaps be taken as firm evidence, they do nevertheless provide a basis for a more detailed examination of the official information.

Table B

Analysis of Major Projects

(Projects costing more than Rs. 100 crore)

Project Sanctioned	*Per cent Cost Overrun*	*Per cent Time Overrun*
Before 1975	184.8	158.3
Between 1975 and 1980	179.9	71.0
After 1980	34.1	16.7

Table C

Analysis of Medium-Sized Projects

(Projects costing between Rs. 20 crore and Rs. 100 crore)

Project Sanctioned	*Per cent Cost Overrun Index*	*Per cent Time Overrun Index*
Before 1975	257.4	82.0
Between 1975 and 1980	186.6	60.3
After 1980	25.1	26.5

Source: Neeraj Kaushal: 'Overruns Overcome', *Financial Express,* October 1984.

27. Chart 2 shows, quite similar to the observation made in endnote 23, that while cement production displays a sharp upturn since 1982 real GDP originating in construction does not show any increase in its growth indicating a possible underestimation of value added in this sector.

Chart 2

Cement Output and Real GDP in Construction, 1950-51 to 1987-88

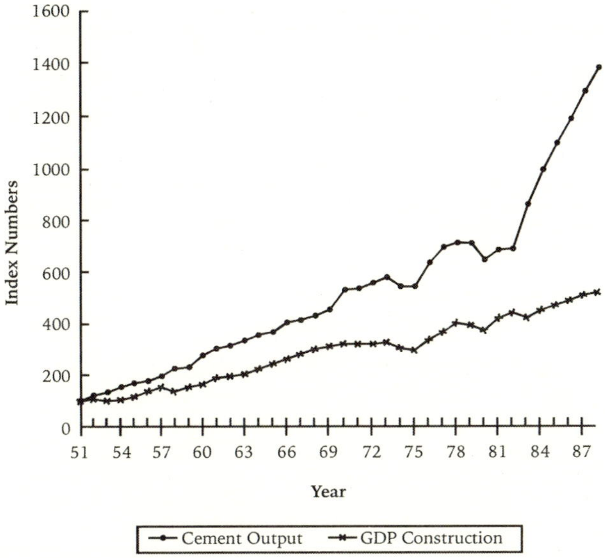

Source: CSO (1989b) and CSO (1990).
Economic Survey, various issues.

28. In fact, this is the only industry group at 3-digit NIC which has displayed zero growth rate. Therefore, we have clubbed it with other industries recording a positive growth rate of up to 5 per cent per annum.

29. This significant weakness of domestic manufacturing of steel appears to have been overlooked by scholars who have attributed the higher rate of growth of manufacturing sector to the improved performance of infrastructure [Rangarajan, 1990].

30. While a number of scholars [Bagchi, 1990, for instance] have criticised rapid growth of consumer durables (with alleged high import intensity) very few, not even the Economic Advisory Council (1989), have pointed to this serious shortcoming in the domestic production of basic metal industries (NIC 33) in general, and steel (NIC 330) in particular, resulting the steep rise in imports of basic metals. As reported earlier, [Nagaraj, 1989, Table 3], trend growth rate of basic metal industries during 1980-81 and 1986-87 at 3.9 per cent per annum is lower than that of total manufacturing sector at 8.3 per cent per annum during the same period.

31. There appears to have been some instances where domestic capital goods industries faced negative rate of protection mainly due to non-alignment of tariff and tax policies. How serious this problem has been for the manufacturing as a whole, we are not in a position to assess. The much publicised case of BHEL facing undue external competition could perhaps be perceived more as a reflection of domestic resource constraint since the government has apparently not been in a position to make available rupee resources due to fiscal stringency. Instead foreign supplier of power equipment seems to have been encouraged as they are packaged with (mostly bilateral) aid.

32. The shortcomings of the highly discretionary physical control in stifling domestic competition is by now widely acknowledged. While generally cautioning against uncritical acceptance of the (mainly external) liberalisation process, Raj (1985) was equally strong in his disapproval of the prevailing system of (domestic) controls on investment and output: 'For the industrial licensing system, as it grew over a period of nearly three decades, had accumulated much fat and filth. It had ceased to perform effectively most of the functions it was designed for earlier; had become a major source of political and bureaucratic corruption; and was being used by powerful vested interests (well placed in New Delhi in thinly-disguised embassies of their own) to throttle competition from potential rivals (less influential) within the country, and increase their monopolistic (or oligopolistic) power even in industries where no economies of scale to justify the growth of such enterprises ... Given the balance of political and economic forces in the country very little could be done to bring about radical improvements, in these forms of direct administrative controls and, in my view, it was wiser therefore to rather abandon the dishonesty and hypocrisy of it all than maintain a process (which deceived no one except perhaps some arm chair radicals) and create needless delays and inefficiencies all around.

33. Given its small share, rapid increase in exports since 1986-87 is unlikely to have influenced the overall industrial growth. Exports form merely 5.5 per cent of registered manufactured output in 1986-87. The share is likely to be even lower if adjusted for import content in exported goods and unregistered manufacturing is included in the denominator.

34. Rate of inflation, as measured by trend growth rate using the wholesale price index during 1980-81 and 1988-89 at 6.7 per cent per annum is lower than that in the seventies at 8.8 per cent per annum. This perhaps has some relation to the trade balance. As can be seen from the following estimated regression equation for the period 1950-51 to 1986-87 there appears to be a statistically significant inverse relationship between the rate of inflation and the trade balance.

$$Y = 2.109 - 1.662X \qquad R^{22} = 0.154$$
$$(2.492)^{*} \qquad N = 36$$

where Y is annual percentage change in implicit GDP deflator and X is trade balance as percentage of GDP.

35. These seem to be (a) low level external debt and debt service rates in the seventies compared to most other developing economies, (b) fairly high domestic savings and investment and (c) fairly comfortable food stock. It may not be inappropriate to suggest as hypothesis for further investigation, that the genesis of the policies reform introduced in the eighties can perhaps be traced to [ignoring the political changes] the short but significant years of of the mid-seventies when the economy found itself with surplus foodgrains and foreign exchange on the one hand the inadequate investment demand and little increase in the GDP growth rate on the other.

36. A similar comparison in Chart 3, for unregistered manufacturing appears to be even more interesting. The gap between the growth of output and investment in this sector has steadily widened since the early fifties indicating very poor (or negative) productivity growth. *Prima facie* the chart provides evidence in support of the argument of growing capital intensity (and hence of growing inefficiency) in the unregistered manufacturing which, constitutes the small manufacturing enterprise sector in India. However, one has to be extremely cautious in drawing such an inference on account of many empirical problems. First, capital formation in this sector could possibly include investment on construction which are also widely used as dwelling units [Nagaraj, 1985]. Moreover, considering the weakness in gathering data a substantial proportion of the output originating in the unregistered manufacturing may no get recorded [For more details on the problem of obtaining accurate output data from small firms see, Nagaraj, 1989].

Chart 3

GDP and GCF in Unregistered Manufacturing at 1980-81 Prices, 1951-52 to 1987-88

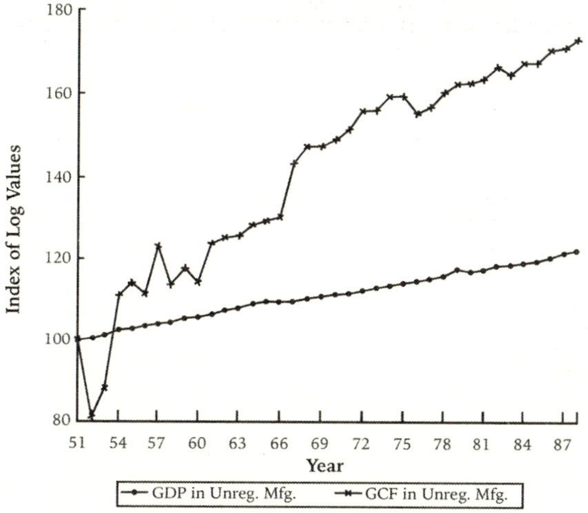

Source: CSO (1989b) and CSO (1990).
Economic Survey, various issues.

37. Though the import of cereals have come down after the mid-seventies with the rapid increase in the production of mainly wheat, import of oilseeds, whose income elasticity of demand is said to be greater than one, has gone up quite considerably.

38. This argument has been substantiated in greater detail by Shetty (1990).

39. The data on the small-scale sector published by the Development Commissioner, Small Scale Industries (DCSSI) has serious limitations. Though output of this sector is said to be estimated based on 1 per cent sample survey, the official source has nowhere provided any details on the methodology for collecting the data [for a detailed account of the limitation of the DCSSI data see, Nagaraj, 1984]. Since the official data base appears so weak, one suspects the quality of estimates supplied for the preparation of the IIP.

40. Currently, fashionable discussion on privatisation appears to be of marginal relevance in the Indian context, as has been pointed out by Montek Ahluwalia (1988), since such a change in ownership of industrial assets 'is not on the agenda' (p 354). Moreover, the use of the term privatisation in a loose manner meant to indicate any change in the demarcation between the 'public' and 'private' sectors in favour of the latter seems to be of little descriptive value, let alone for any serious analysis or policy reform.

41. Much of the recent literature on liberalisation in the developing economies appears to be of marginal value for analysing the recent policy reform in India since, as has been rightly pointed out by Montek Ahluwalia (1988), it is mostly domestic oriented intended to improve capabilities of domestic firms.

42. As the available evidence of the effects of policy changes on performance is not unambiguous there appears to be a case for examining the recommendation of the official committee [Report of the Committee to Examine Principles of Possible Shift from Physical to Financial Controls. Chairman: M. Narasimham] to systematically document the intentions and achievements of the policy changes and to analyse their major shortcomings. Such an attempt could, in our view, contribute towards initiating the necessary corrective measures. However, before making any such move, the Committee's full report needs to be made public to generate a meaningful debate.

References

Ahluwalia, Isher Judge (1985). *Industrial Growth in India: Stagnation since the Mid-Sixties*, Oxford University Press, Delhi.

Ahluwalia, Montek S. (1988). "India's Economic Performance: Policies and Prospects" in Robert E.B. Lucas and Gustav F. Papanek (eds.) *The Indian Economy: Recent Developments and Future Prospects*, Oxford University Press, Delhi.

Alagh, Y.K. (1985). "Some Aspects of Planning Policies in India," *Govind Vallabh Pant Memorial Lecture*, Allahabad.

Bagchi, Amiya Kumar (1990). "An Economic Policy for the New Government," *Economic and Political Weekly*, February 10.

Central Statistical Organisation (1989a). *National Accounts Statistics, 1980-81 to 1986-87*, Government of India, New Delhi.

————. (1989b). *National Accounts Statistics (New Series), 1950-51 to 1979-80*, Government of India, New Delhi.

————. (1989c). *National Accounts Statistics: Sources and Methods*, Government of India, New Delhi.

————. (1990). *National Accounts Statistics, 1990*, Government of India, New Delhi.

Chakravarty, Sukhamoy (1974). *Reflections on the Growth Process in the Indian Economy*, Administrative Staff College of India, Hyderabad.

————. (1987). *Development Planning: The Indian Experience*, Clarendon Press, Oxford.

Chandrasekhar, C.P. (1988). "Aspects of Growth and Structural Change in Indian Industry," *Economic and Political Weekly*, Special Number, November.

Chaudhuri, Sudip (1989). *Structural Changes and Fluctuation in Manufacturing Factory Sector: A Disaggregated Analysis, 1989 to 1984-85*, Indian Institute of Management Calcutta, mimeo.

Economic Advisory Council (1989). "Current Economic Situation and Priority Areas of Action," reproduced in the *Mainstream*, January 6, 1990.

Kahlon, A.S. and D.S. Tyagi (1983). *Agricultural Price Policy in India*, Allied Publishers, Delhi.

Kelkar, Vijay L. and Rajiv Kumar (1990). "Industrial Growth in the Eighties: Emerging Policy Issues," *Economic and Political Weekly*, January 27.

Kurien, C.T. (1989). "Indian Economy in the 1980s and on to the 1990s," *Economic and Political Weekly*, April 15.

Lewis, W. Arthur (1955). *The Theory of Economic Growth*, George Allen and Unwin, London.

Mitra, Ashok (1977). *Terms of Trade and Class Relations*, Frank Cass, London.

Nagaraj, R. (1984). "Sub-contracting in Indian Manufacturing Industries: Analysis, Evidence and Issues," *Economic and Political Weekly*, Annual Number, August.

————. (1985). "Trends in Factory Size in Indian Industry, 1950 to 1980," *Economic and Political Weekly*, Review of Management, February.

————. (1989). "Growth in Manufacturing Output since 1980: Some Preliminary Findings," *Economic and Political Weekly*, July 1.

————. (1990). "Growth Rate of India's Gross Domestic Product, 1950-51 to 1987-88: An Examination of Alternative Hypothesis," *Economic and Political Weekly*, June 30.

Nagaraj, Rayaprolu (1989). *Sub-Contracting in Indian Manufacturing Industries: The Bangalore Experience*, PhD thesis submitted to the Jawaharlal Nehru University, New Delhi.

Nayyar, Deepak (1978). "Industrial Development in India: Some Reflections on Growth and Stagnation," *Economic and Political Weekly*, Special Number, August.

————. (1988). "India's Export Performance, 1970-85: Underlying Factors and Constraints," in Robert E B Lucas and Gustav F Papanek (eds.) *The Indian Economy: Recent Trends and Future Prospects*, Oxford University Press, Delhi.

Patnaik, P. and S.K. Rao (1977). "Explanation of Crisis in a Mixed Underdeveloped Economy," *Economic and Political Weekly*, Annual Number, February.

Planning Commission (1988). *Seventh Five-Year Plan, 1985-90: Mid-Term Appraisal*, Government of India, New Delhi.

Raj, K.N. (1981). "Problem of Plan Implementation: Resource Mobilisation" paper presented at the conference on *Review of the Indian Planning Process*, Indian Statistical Institute, Calcutta, December 1981.

————. (1984). "Some Observations on Economic Growth in India over the Period 1952-53 to 1982-83," *Economic and Political Weekly*, October, 13.

————. (1985). "New Economic Policy," *V.T. Krishnamachari Memorial Lecture*, Institute of Economic Growth, Delhi.

Rangarajan, C. (1990). "Industrial Growth in the 80s: Facts and Some Issues," *Financial Express*, April 24.

Reserve Bank of India (1982). *Capital Formation and Savings in India, 1950-51 to 1979-80: Report of the Working Group on Savings* (Chairman: K.N. Raj), Bombay, Reserve Bank of India.

Shetty, S.L. (1978). "Structural Retrogression in the Indian Economy since the Mid-Sixties," *Economic and Political Weekly*, Special Number, August.

————. (1990). "Investment in Agriculture: Brief Review of Recent Trends," *Economic and Political Weekly*, February 17-24.

Srinivasan, T.N. and N.S.S. Narayanan (1977). "Economic Performance since the Third Plan and its Implications for Policy," *Economic and Political Weekly*, Annual Number, February.

Sundrum, R.M. (1987). *Growth and Income Distribution in India: Policy and Performance since Independence*, Sage Publications, New Delhi.

Taylor, Lance (1988). *Varieties of Stabilisation Experience: Towards Sensible Macroeconomics in the Third World*, Clarendon Press, Oxford.

Thamarajakshi, R. (1969). "Inter-Sectoral Terms of Trade and Marketed Surplus of Agriculture Product, 1951-52 to 1965-66," *Economic and Political Weekly*, June 28, Review of Agriculture.

————. (1977). "Role of Price Incentives in Stimulating Agricultural Production in a Developing Economy" in Douglas Ensmingar (ed.) *Food Enough or Starvation for Millions*, FAO.

————. (1990). "Inter-Sectoral Terms of Trade Revisited," *Economic and Political Weekly*, March 31, Review of Agriculture.

Vaidyanathan, A. (1977). "Constraints on Growth and Policy Options," *Economic and Political Weekly*, Vol. 12, No. 32, September 17.

Economic and Political Weekly, Vol. 25, No. 41, October 13, 1990.

6

Performance of India's Manufacturing Sector in the 1990s

Some Tentative Findings

INTRODUCTION

India's manufacturing sector accounts for about 16 per cent of measured GDP, 10 per cent of total workforce, and a slightly less than 80 per cent of merchandise exports. The registered manufacturing sector constitutes about 2/3rd of value added, and 1/5th of employment. It also represents import competing sector and it is a net importer. The unregistered manufacturing sector contributing 1/3rd of value added and 4/5th of employment, accounts for the bulk of manufactured exports.[1]

The manufacturing sector, though small relative to the economy, even in a comparative perspective, has received an overwhelming attention in India's development effort. In the Mahalanobis strategy—initiated in the mid-1950s that formed the basis for India's planning—development of 'heavy industry' (capital and intermediate goods industries) was vital for maximising long-term economic growth, and for pursuing economically self-reliant, politically autonomous path of development.

Such a structuralist development perspective has been widely criticised in the mainstream economic writings, especially in the face of the exceptional performance of the small, socially homogeneous, export-oriented economies of the East and South-East Asia. In the context of the 1991 external payment crisis, the protagonists of the orthodox reforms laid the blame for the crisis to the four decades of import substituting, public sector dominated, industrialisation strategy. According to Vijay Joshi and Ian Little, Indian economic strategy, as reflected in various controls was "not only microeconomically inefficient, but also macroeconomically perverse" [Joshi and Little, 1994: 3]. Therefore, the economic reforms initiated in 1991-92 sought to consciously move away from the earlier development path towards a market-oriented, export-led growth that was implemented as a package of stabilisation and structural adjustment programme.

The orthodox reforms initiated since 1991, probably based on the favourable experience with deregulation in the 1980s, dismantled most of the remaining (domestic) industrial output and investment controls, sharply reduced tariffs and removed restrictions on inward foreign direct investment (FDI). In principle, the reforms are expected to accelerate growth in output, investment and manufactured exports, after a brief dip—popularly called the 'J' curve. Further, these policy initiatives, in principle, are expected to improve allocative and productive efficiency.

This paper reports tentative findings on the trends in output and its composition, investment and employment after the reforms, by comparing them with the record of the 1980s. The study uses data from the *National Accounts Statistics* (NAS), *Annual Survey of Industries* (ASI) and the *Net State Domestic Product* (SDP) compiled by the Central Statistical Organisation. Empirical results reported are mainly based on the semi-log trend analysis, and graphical description of the time series. The study will conclude by making a brief and tentative assessment of the performance.

Output Performance

Variation in Yearly Growth Rates

Figure 6.1 shows the annual growth rate of manufacturing sector in the 1990s in terms of two indicators, namely, the Index of Industrial Production (IIP) for manufacturing and GDP in total manufacturing.[2] Both the series broadly show the same trend: the growth rate dipped sharply in 1991-92 (turning negative in the NAS series), and a sharp upturn in the next four years (1992-93 to 1995-96). In fact, the growth rate of 14 per cent in 1995-96 is perhaps the highest that has ever been recorded in the manufacturing sector in India. Such a sharp recovery after the initiation of a programme of

Figure 6.1

Manufacturing Growth in the 1990s

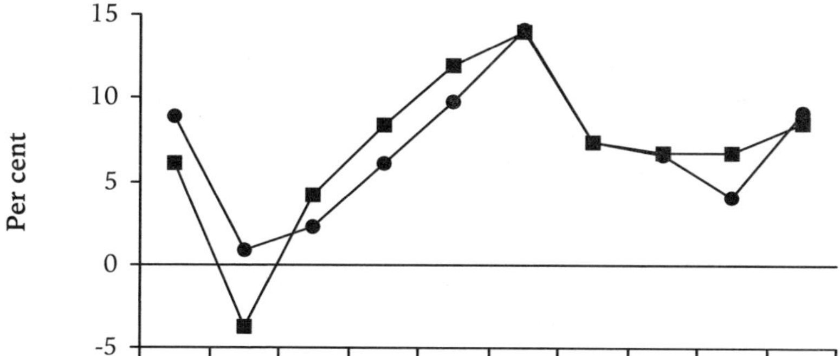

	1991	1992	1993	1994	1995	1996	1997	1998	1999	2000
—●— IIP	8.9	0.8	2.2	6.1	9.8	14.1	7.3	6.6	4.1	9.2
—■— NAS	6.1	-3.7	4.2	8.4	11.9	14	7.4	6.7	6.7	8.5

Year ending

stabilisation and structural reforms is consistent with the 'J' curve hypothesis.

But, quite contrary to the theoretical prediction, the growth rate fell sharply in the subsequent three years (1996-97 and 1998-99)—which is popularly termed as recession.[3] However, the growth rate recovered somewhat in 1999-2000 to about 9 per cent, though its sustainability appears suspect.

Trend Growth Rates

How does the manufacturing sector performance in the 1990s compare with that of the pre-reform period? To answer this question, we estimated the trend growth rates for the period, 1980-81 to 1998-99. A dummy variable test is conducted to find out if there was a statistically significant break in the trend growth rate in 1991-92. This analysis was also carried out for GDP in total manufacturing, as well for GDP in registered manufacturing, using the NAS data, for 2-digit industry groups (Tables 6.1 and 6.2).[4]

Annual growth rates of the total, as well as registered manufacturing GDP during the two decades since 1980-81 are 6.9 and

8.4, respectively. The growth rates for the period before the reforms (1980-81 and 1990-91) are 7.4 per cent and 7.6 per cent per year, respectively. The dummy variable test shows there is a statistically significant slowdown in the total manufacturing 'GDP growth rate after 1991-92. However, there are no statistically significant change in the trend growth rate of the registered manufacturing GDP after the reforms. Therefore, the slowdown in the total manufacturing growth rate has occurred entirely in the unregistered sector.

Table 6.1

Growth Rate of GDP in the Total Manufacturing Sector, 1980-81 to 1998-99, in 2-Digit Industrial Groups

(Per cent per year)

Code	*Industry Name*	*1981-99*	*1981-91*	*1992-99*	*Dummy Variable*	
					Sign	*Significance*
20-1	Food	7.3	9.0	8.4	–	Significant
22	Beverages	6.0	4.8	8.7	+	Not significant
23-6	Textiles	2.5	4.1	(-)1.1	–	Do
27	Wood	(-)0.9	(-)2.1	3.7	–	Do
28	Paper	7.1	8.6	6.6	–	Do
29	Leather	6.5	4.7	6.3	+	Significant
30	Chemicals	10.2	9.6	10.8	+	Not significant
31	Rubber	11.6	15.6	8.5	–	Significant
32	N.M. minerals	7.9	9.7	8.0	–	Not significant
33	Metals	7.6	5.2	11.6	+	Do
34	M. products	4.3	6.2	6.9	–	Significant
35	N.E. M/c	5.9	6.2	7.4	–	Not significant
36	Elec. M/c	9.0	12.7	7.4	–	Significant
37	Transport equip	7.2	6.2	12.2	–	Not significant
38	Others	7.3	11.4	8.7	–	Significant
39	Repairs	5.6	6.8	8.4	–	Do
	Total	6.9	7.4	8.5	–	Do

Source: NAS, various issues.

In the total manufacturing sector, in terms of 2-digit industry groups, leather industry (NIC 29) witnessed an improvement in its growth rate after the reforms. However, the growth rates of other industry groups, *viz.*, food (20-1), rubber (31), metal products (34), electrical machinery (35) and repair services (39), slowed down after 1991-92.

Table 6.2

Growth Rate of GDP in the Registered Manufacturing Sector, 1980-81 to 1998-99, in 2-Digit Industrial Groups

(Per cent per year)

Code	*Industry Name*	*1981-99*	*1981-91*	*1992-99*	*Dummy Variable*	
					Sign	*Significance*
20-1	Food	8.0	10.1	9.3	–	Significant
22	Beverages	8.2	8.6	7.6	–	Not significant
23	Cotton	2.5	3.6	2.8	–	Do
24	Wool, silk	7.6	6.2	9.9	+	Do
25	Jute	0.6	(-)1.8	4.1	+	Do
26	Textile products	15.3	12.0	8.6	+	Significant
23-6	Textiles	5.4	4.4	6.0	+	Not significant
27	Wood	1.3	4.9	(-)0.2	–	Do
28	Paper	6.7	6.6	7.3	–	Do
29	Leather	11.7	10.0	7.2	+	Do
30	Chemicals	10.4	8.9	11.7	+	Do
31	Rubber	11.8	16.6	6.8	–	Do
32	N.M. minerals	8.3	10.6	4.2	–	Do
33	Metals	7.0	4.2	15.9	+	Do
34	M. products	5.9	4.3	12.2	–	Do
35-6	N.E. M/c	7.2	7.2	8.7	+	Do
37	Transport equip.	7.5	4.9	16.9	+	Do
38	Others	12.7	9.3	15.9	+	Do
39+97	Repairs	12.5	13.9	12.2	+	Do
	Total	8.4	7.6	11.0	+	Do

Source: NAS, various issues.

In the registered manufacturing sector, the growth rate of textile products (26) improved after the reforms, while all other industry groups did not experience any change in their growth performance.

Thus, on a trend basis, there is a clear evidence of a modest slowdown in the total manufacturing sector growth rate after the reforms. This is entirely in the unregistered sector, as there are no statistically valid changes in the growth rates of the registered sector after the reforms.

Regional Distribution of Growth

How is the manufacturing sector growth distributed across the regions? This question is of considerable significance for policy, as it is popularly believed that after the reforms, states that have initiated the market-oriented policies have improved their growth performance. To answer this question, a similar exercise was carried out for the registered manufacturing sector for 17 major states, using the official estimates of net SDP at 1980-81 prices, for the period, 1980-81 to 1997-98, the latest year for which these estimates were available.[5]

The trend analysis shows that there is no statistically significant improvement in the growth rates of these states after 1991-92 (Table 6.3). But, four states, namely, Bihar, Haryana, Punjab and Uttar Pradesh, experienced statistically significant slowdown in their growth rates after the reforms.

Table 6.3

Growth Rates of NSDP in the Registered Manufacturing Sector in 17 Major States, 1980-81 to 1998

(Per cent per year)

	States	*1981-98*	*1981-91*	*Dummy Variable*	
				Sign	*Significance*
1	Andhra Pradesh	10.1	11.3	–	Not significant
2	Assam	1.8	0.7	–	Do
3	Bihar	3.7	11.7	–	Significant
4	Gujarat	9.7	9.0	–	Not significant
5	Haryana	6.9	8.6	–	Significant
6	Himachal Pradesh	15.8	19.8	–	Not significant
7	Jammu and Kashmir	7.7	7.3	–	Do
8	Karnataka	8.9	10.3	–	Do
9	Kerala	4.8	4.8	–	Do
10	Maharashtra	7.4	7.6	–	Do
11	Madhya Pradesh	8.3	8.1	–	Do
12	Orissa	7.2	12.9	–	Do
13	Punjab	8.7	9.7	–	Significant
14	Rajasthan	9.1	9.7	–	Not significant
15	Tamil Nadu	6.2	6.4	–	Do
16	Uttar Pradesh	8.5	14.2	–	Significant
17	West Bengal	3.2	2.4	–	Not Significant
	All-India	**7.7**	**8.3**	–	**Significant**

Source: Estimates of Net SDP, various issues.

An examination of the coefficient of variation (CV) of net SDP in the registered manufacturing sector strengthens this inference (Figure 6.2). The CV that was generally declining in the 1980s got reversed in the next decade. In fact, the inequality in 1997-98 is higher than what it was in 1980-81. These trends suggest that although there is no indication of an improvement in the growth rates of any of the major states after the reforms, industrial growth seems to be adversely affected in the backward states like Bihar and UP, as well as in the agriculturally advanced states of Punjab and Haryana. Though no evidence is available, one could argue that the observed growing inequality in the manufacturing sector might imply a greater efficiency, as the production decisions are increasingly driven by private profitability considerations.

Investment Performance

While the growth rate in value added shows no improvement after the reforms—if anything a slow down in the unregistered manufacturing—there has been a boom in gross fixed capital formation (GFCF) or fixed investment, in the registered manufacturing (Figure 6.3).[6] The average of the annual growth rate of GFCF went up from about 10 per cent per year in the 1980s to over 15 per cent per year, between 1991-92 and 1996-97. A similar analysis at a disaggregated level suggests that the increase in the rate of fixed investment has occurred across a wide range of industry groups (Table 6.4). These are textile products (26), wood (27), paper (28),

Figure 6.2

Regional Disparity in Industrial Development

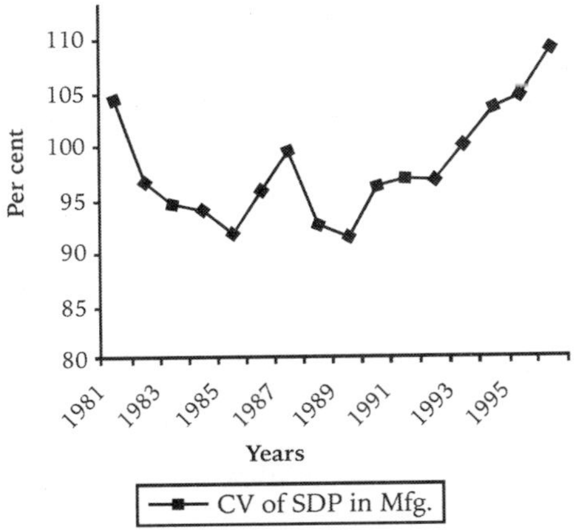

rubber (31), non-metallic minerals (32) metal products (34), transport equipment (37) and repair services (39).

Figure 6.3

Fixed Investment Growth in Registered Manufacturing

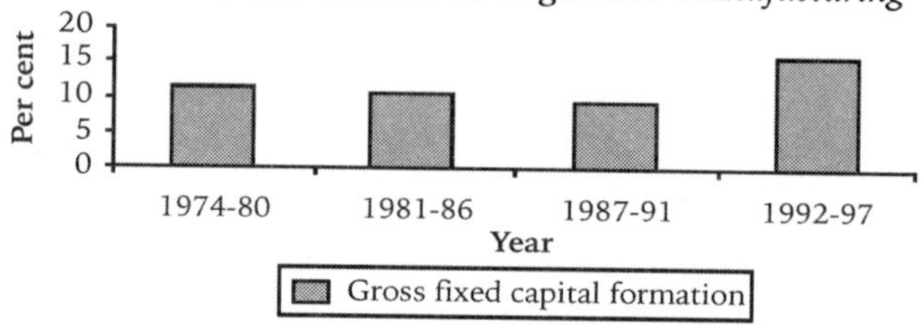

Table 6.4

Growth in Fixed Investment (GFCF) in the Registered Manufacturing Sector in 2-Digit Industrial Groups, 1981-98

(Per cent per year)

Code	*Industry group*	*Average of Annual Growth Rates*		
		1982-91	*1982-98*	*1992-98*
20-1	Food	13.2	10.5	6.6
22	Beverages	21.9	16.7	9.4
23	Cotton textiles	4.7	8.7	14.3
24	Wool, silk textiles	15.2	14.8	14.3
25	Jute textiles	n.a.	n.a.	9.0
26	Textile products	17.3	21.2	26.7
23-6	Textiles	6.5	9.6	14.0
27	Wood	35.7	28.5	18.2
28	Paper	10.0	22.1	39.3
29	Leather	18.6	12.6	3.9
30	Chemicals	10.4	14.9	21.3
31	Rubber	19.5	21.2	23.6
32	N.M. minerals	11.0	13.1	16.1
33	Metals	11.8	10.0	7.4
34	Metal products	8.7	12.6	18.3
35-6	N.E. M/c	10.7	8.7	5.9
37	Transport equipment	7.6	13.8	22.6
38	Others	18.0	21.2	25.7
39+97	Repair services	13.9	35.2	22.7
	Total	**17.3**	**12.3**	**15.3**

Source: ASI, various issues.

As there has been no perceptible improvement in the economy's aggregate investment rate, the observed change suggests that the composition of fixed investment has shifted in favour of the registered manufacturing sector and away from the rest of the economy—perhaps mainly from infrastructure. Moreover, within the manufacturing sector, GFCF in the unregistered sector has been adversely affected in the 1990s (Figure 6.4). In terms of growth rate, it fell from about 7 per cent per year in the 1980s to 5.6 per cent between 1991-92 and 1996-97.

Figure 6.4

Unregistered Manufacturing's Share in Total GFCF

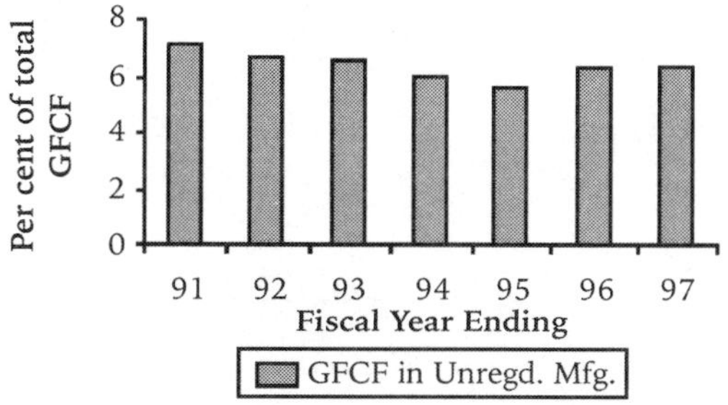

What explains the investment boom when the output growth has not improved? We would hypothesise, the deregulation and the rising business expectations generated by the reform euphoria drove the boom. Perhaps the stock market boom up to the mid-1990s also contributed to it, as it reduced costs of long-term capital.[7]

On the face of it, the decline in fixed investment rate in the unregistered manufacturing sector is puzzling, as the reforms were expected to strengthen the labour-intensive, export-oriented manufacturing, consistent with India's comparative advantage. The reasons for the decline in the fixed investment rate can perhaps be related to the decline in the credit availability and its high cost in response to the financial sector reforms that was carried out simultaneously. As Figure 6.5 shows, the share of the small-scale sector in gross bank credit declined from about 13 per cent in 1989-90, to less than 10 per cent in 1996-97.[8]

Employment Performance

While there was much to commend about the improved industrial growth in the 1980s—after nearly one and half decade of slow growth from the mid-1960 to the end of the 1970s—lack of a corresponding employment growth was a major cause for concern. In fact, the registered manufacturing witnessed a decade of 'jobless growth' that attracted considerable analyses, as it was perceived to be central to our understanding of the labour market performance in the organised sector.

Figure 6.5

SSI's Share in Gross Bank Credit

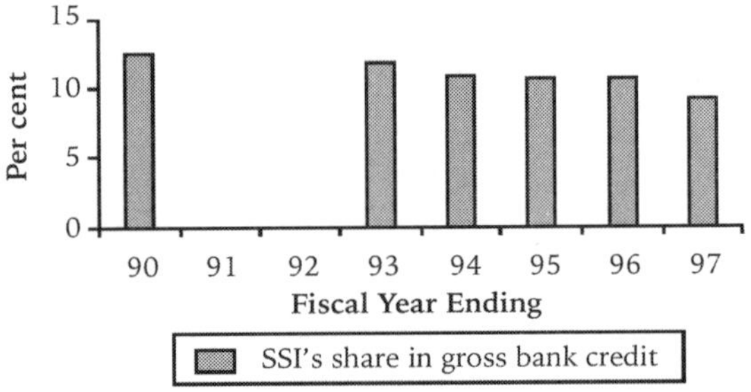

The mainstream economic writings suggested that the jobless growth in the 1980s reflected the growing rigidity in the industrial labour market, as employers substituted capital for labour since wages went up sharply [Ahluwalia, 1992; Fallon and Lucas, 1993]. However, their views have been widely contested [for instance, Nagaraj, 1994; Bhalotra, 1998]. Nagaraj (1994) showed, the rapid rise in workers' earnings in the 1980s represented growth in the mandays worked, while wage rate per manday—for the standard working day—grew at less than one-half the growth in per capita income in this period.

It is in this context that we examine the trends in the registered manufacturing employment in the 1990s. Many serious apprehensions were raised about the potential adverse effects of the reforms on employment. As shown in Figure 6.6, quite contrary to the trend in the previous decade, there is a steady growth in employment in the 1990s. The reforms in 1991-92 do not seem to have had any influence on this trend. A closer look at the data for the period since 1980-81 suggests, for four years during the mid-1980s (during 1982-83 and 1986-87) employment growth rate was actually negative. Thereafter, there has been a steady growth – at 3.2 per cent per year.

Figure 6.6

Employment in Registered Manufacturing

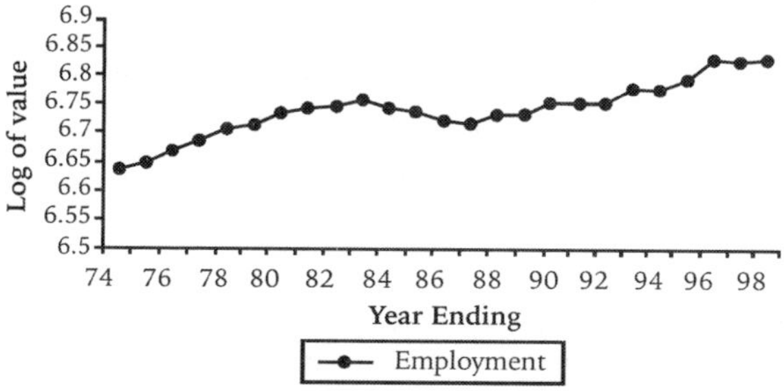

Continuing the earlier debate, Goldar (2000) argued that moderation in the wage growth accounts for the turnaround in employment in the 1990s. Nagaraj (2000) contested his view, by drawing attention to the analytical and empirical limitations of Goldar's proposition.

While employment trends in the registered sector attracted so much attention, perhaps more significant changes were taking place in the unregistered manufacturing that went unnoticed. An analysis of economic census data for the period 1978-79 to 1994-95 suggests a negative growth rate in employment as well as in the number of establishments between 1984-85 and 1994-95 (Table 6.5).* This observation seems broadly consistent with the slowdown in growth in output and fixed investment in unregistered manufacturing that was earlier discussed.

There is probably more to the fall in the employment growth rate in the unregistered manufacturing sector than the slowdown in the output and investment growth. Perhaps, the fall in employment growth was also because of the real incidence of adjustment problems to reforms faced in the organised sector, being passed on to workers and enterprises in the unorganised sector as the subcontracting relationship between the two sectors had grown during the last two decades.[9]

In sum, the manufacturing employment scenario after the reforms is perhaps not bright, although the registered manufacturing

* Admittedly this finding of a fall in employment is at variance with the NSS employment-unemployment survey data. Therefore, the data may be suspect. But the economic census data on establishment where quality is not in question, also shows a corresponding fall. For a careful analysis of the trends in the 1990s, it is necessary to contend with these divergent trends.

Table 6.5

Growth in Number of Establishments and Employment in Unregistered Manufacturing, 1985 to 1994-95 for all over India

(Percentage change over the previous period)

Year	*Establishments*	*Employment*
1978-79		
1984-85	15.1	12.8
1989-90	3.9	-0.8
1994-95	-9.5	-1.3

Source: Lalitha (1999).

employment turned around. There are competing explanations for the turnaround, requiring further research. Perhaps, the real brunt of the adjustment is borne by the workers in the unregistered sector which witnessed negative growth in employment and in the number of enterprises between the mid-1980s and the mid-1990s.

Summary and Conclusion

This preliminary study on India's manufacturing sector since the reforms of 1991-92 examined three aspects of performance, namely, output (value added), fixed investment and employment growth. This assessment is broadly based on comparing the performance after the reforms with that of the 1980s. The analysis is mainly based on NAS, ASI, and the SDP data, disaggregated by two-digit industry groups, as well as, by the registered and unregistered manufacturing.

In the literature on the economic reforms, it is widely believed that the industrial growth follows a 'J' curve—that is, output growth contracts immediately after initiating the stabilisation and structural adjustment programme. However, as the structural reforms take root, output growth rebound rapidly as supply responds to market signals in the deregulated environment. We examine if such a process of adjustment was evident in India in the 1990s.

As predicted, output growth dipped immediately after the reforms, but it turned around quickly to follow a 'J' curve during the four years since 1992-93. The growth rate in 1995-96, at 14 per cent, was the highest that was ever recorded. However, such a growth was not sustained, as there was a set-back in the second half of the 1990s.

On a trend basis, therefore, the total manufacturing sector growth rate during 1992-99 is slightly lower but statistically significant, compared to that during 1981-91. The slowdown after the reforms is entirely in the unregistered manufacturing, as the growth rate of the registered sector has remained the same.

The only industrial groups that experienced an improvement in the growth rate after the reforms are leather (NIC 29) in the total manufacturing sector, and textile products (26) in the registered manufacturing sector. However, a much wider range of industry groups, both in the total and the registered manufacturing sectors, witnessed a slowdown in their growth rates after the reforms.

How did the reforms affect industrial growth across the states? This is an important question for policy, as it is widely believed that the states that have initiated the reforms improved their performance. Our analysis suggests that there is no evidence of a statistically significant improvement in the registered manufacturing growth rates in any of the seventeen major states of India after the reforms. But the growth rates in four industrially backward and agriculturally advanced states of Bihar, UP, Punjab and Haryana actually witnessed a slowdown after the reforms. Therefore, inequality in industrial output across the states widened in the 1990s, reversing the declining trend of the previous decade.

Thus, on output performance, it seems reasonable to infer that the manufacturing growth rate evidenced a slowdown after the reforms. This slowdown affected the unregistered sector, a sizeable cross section of the industrial groups, and four states in north India. Inter-regional inequality in industrial growth turned adverse in the 1990s, after a decade of equalising growth. Whether the pattern of growth has improved efficiency is a moot point.

There has been a boom in fixed investment in the 1990s. But it is entirely in the registered sector, though widely distributed across the industry groups. However, the growth of investment in labour-intensive, export-oriented, unregistered manufacturing sector came down after the reforms. Abolition of various output and investment controls, and rising business expectations generated by the reforms seem to be responsible for the growth in investment. This was perhaps facilitated by the stock market boom in the first half of the 1990s that reduced the cost of long-term capital.

By most popular indicators, the reforms increased domestic and import competition with a favourable impact on relative prices. This was perhaps best illustrated by relative decline in capital goods prices for the first time in the 1990s [Nagaraj, 1997].

Investment boom in the registered manufacturing turned around employment growth, after a decade of stagnation. But, the growth in employment and in number of enterprises suffered in the unregistered sector, perhaps bearing the real brunt of adjustment in the organised sector—considering the close inter-firm linkages between the organised and the unorganised sectors in the product and labour markets. Perhaps, this also reflects the decline in credit availability and increase in its cost for small enterprises in response to the financial sector reforms that were simultaneously initiated in the 1990s.

Have the reforms enabled the manufacturing sector to overcome the microeconomic inefficiency and the macroeconomic perversity that Vijay Joshi and Ian Little talked about? Probably not, for the following reasons:

- The flip side of the investment boom without a corresponding increase in output growth was the increase in the levels of excess capacities and increase in incremental capital-output ratio.
- As there was no improvement in machanise export growth on a trend basis in the 1990s, macroeconomic vulnerability persisted.
- Much of the fixed investment growth accrued to the import competing sector, rather than for building export capability. Therefore, the economy's vulnerability to external shocks was not reduced.

In sum, the reforms surely brought in some notable improvements in the functioning of industrial markets due to greater competition and quality improvements. But, the reforms neither improved the output nor the employment growth rates, in the total manufacturing sector. The distribution of the growth across regions and between the organised and the unorganised sectors turned adverse. And above all, it seems hard to believe that the reforms enabled India to overcome the 'macroeconomic perversity', as India's exports or export capability have not improved on a sustained basis at least not as yet.

Notes

1. Registered manufacturing mostly consists of all factories employing 10 or more workers (20 or more workers without using power) using power. Unregistered manufacturing refers to those manufacturing activities that are outside the registered sector.
2. There has been a change in the base year of IIP and of NAS, to 1993-94, replacing the earlier series with 1980-81 as the base year. We have merged the two series to create consistent time series for the 1990s. NAS estimates for 1999-2000 are quick estimates, and may undergo revision. IIP has serious limitations as its quality has deteriorated over the decades [Nagaraj, 1999]. Yet, the data has some value at 1-digit level, as they are available with least time lag.
3. Strictly speaking, recession is defined as two consecutive quarters of negative growth rate. India did not witness negative growth rate in any quarter.
4. Unless otherwise stated, all variables in this study are at constant prices.
5. We did not use figures for the total manufacturing, as the state level unregistered manufacturing value added estimates reportedly have many problem of quality.
6. Shuji Uchikawa's paper in this project provides detailed quantitative picture of this boom.
7. Although there is no statistically valid association between GFCF and stock market mobilisation in the long run [Nagaraj, 1996], in the short to medium term, the relationship could be different.
8. It is widely known that small entrepreneurs are severely credit constrained; fixed investment in small enterprises in developing economies is largely a function of timely availability of credit.
9. This is perhaps similar to what was observed in the Japanese economy, in the 1970s, where the real brunt of adjustment to market fluctuation were borne by workers in the small firms [Dore, 1986].

References

Ahluwalia, Isher Judge (1992). *Productivity and Growth in Indian Manufacturing*, Oxford University Press, New Delhi.

Bhalotra, Sonia R. (1998). "Puzzle of Jobless Growth in Indian Manufacturing," *Oxford Bulletin of Economics and Statistics*, Vol. 60, No. 1, January.

Dore, Ronald (1986). *Flexible Rigidities: Industrial Policies and Structural Adjustment in the Japanese Economy, 1970-80*, Althone Press, London.

Fallon, Peter and Robert E.B. Lucas (1993). "Job Security Regulation and the Dynamic Demand for Industrial Labour in India and Zimbabwe," *Journal of Development Economics*, Vol. 40, No. 2, April-June.

Goldar, Bishwanath (2000). "Employment Growth in Organised Manufacturing in India," *Economic and Political Weekly*, Vol. 35, No. 14, 1-7 April.

Joshi, Vijay and Ian Little (1994). *India: Macroeconomics and Political Economy, 1961-1991*, Oxford University Press, New Delhi.

Lalitha, N. (1999). *Unorganised Manufacturing Sector in the National Employment and Gujarat State*, report submitted to NCAER, New Delhi.

Nagaraj, R. (2000). "Organised Manufacturing Employment," *Economic and Political Weekly*, Vol. 35, No. 38, 16 September.

————. (1999). "How Good are India's Industrial Statistics? An Exploratory Note," *Economic and Political Weekly*, Vol. 34, No. 6, 6-12 February.

———. (1997). "What has Happened since 1991? Assessment of India's Economic Reforms," *Economic and Political Weekly*, Vol. 32, Nos. 44-5, 8-14 November.

———. (1996). "India's Capital Market Growth: Trends, Explanations, and Evidence," *Economic and Political Weekly*, Vol. 31, Nos. 35-7, September.

———. (1994). "Employment and Wages in Manufacturing Industries: Trends, Hypotheses and Evidence," *Economic and Political Weekly*, Vol. 29, No. 4, 22 January.

Shuji Uchikawa (ed.): *Economic Reforms and Industrial Structure*. Manohar, Delhi, 2002.

7

Industrial Policy and Performance since 1980

Which Way Now?

INTRODUCTION

India's manufacturing sector currently accounts for about 17 per cent of real (measured) GDP, 12 per cent of total workforce, and close to 80 per cent of merchandise exports. Over the last half a century, this sector has grown at nearly 6 per cent per year; at over one-and-half times the growth rate of domestic output—representing a major break from the colonial past.[1]

The annual trend growth rate of total manufacturing gross value added (output, for short, hereafter) during the last two decades (1980-2000) is close to 7 per cent. While this represents a turnaround compared to the preceding period of 'relative stagnation' (1965-1980), the record is modest in contrast to China's (official) double-digit growth during this period, as also most other industrialising Asian economies (Table 7.1).

Table 7.1

Industrial Growth in Asian Perspective, 1980-2000

(Per cent per year)

Country	*Growth Rate*
India	**6.8**
China	12.8
Indonesia	10.2
Korea	9.4
Malaysia	11.2
Singapore	7.7
Thailand	9.8

Note: Data are in constant (1996) dollar terms.

Source: *World Development Indicators*, 2002.

I

EVOLUTION OF THE POLICY SINCE 1980

Industrial Upturn in the 1980s

Around 1980, the initial year of our study period, there was considerable gloom about the immediate prospects for industrial growth, despite having, a surplus of food and foreign exchange stocks for a few years in the late 1970s—widely regarded long-term constraints on India's economic growth. For a variety of reasons, lack of industrial demand, especially for investment goods, was widely accepted to be the principal reason for the relative stagnation since the mid-1960s. However, there was also an argument that the controls on output, investment and trade—popularly called the 'permit licence raj'—were stifling private initiative and wasting meagre public resources. Reportedly, the controls led to widespread inefficiency in resource use, as reflected, in poor total factor productivity growth, or in the economywide rise in incremental capital-output ratios in the 1970s [Ahluwalia, 1985; Rangarajan, 1982]. The gloom was perhaps accentuated by the oil price and agricultural supply shocks in the late 1970s, together with political uncertainty as the Indian democracy entered the coalition era at the national level for the first time in 1977.

However, from 1980 onwards, after the domestic political certainty had ended, the industrial policy witnessed greater pragmatism with a gradual loosening of the controls, and a greater willingness to import technology and foreign private capital to modernise the manufacturing sector. Greater realism in policy-making also included stepping up of public investment in infrastructure and energy production (to insulate the economy from external shocks), rural development for diffusion of the Green Revolution technology, and for a 'direct' attack on poverty. As the second oil shock was successfully met by increasing domestic oil production and by import substitution in fertilisers in a short time, the second half of the 1980s witnessed considerable de-licensing and relaxation of import controls to upgrade the industrial technology—as reflected in Rajiv Gandhi's political slogan of taking the country to the 21st century! To achieve these, there was a greater reliance on the private corporate sector with fiscal incentives provided for stock market based financing of industrial investment, as government faced a growing resource constraint to meet the ambitious planned investment target.

In the 1980s, many branches of manufacturing like automotive industry, cement, cotton spinning, food-processing, polyester filament yarn and so on, witnessed modernisation and expansion of scales of production. Industrial export growth also improved in the second half of the 1980s as import restrictions moved from quotas to tariffs (as a first phase of trade reforms) albeit set at very high levels, and a steady depreciation of the currency in nominal terms. The turnaround in industrial output growth in this decade has been variedly attributed to the liberalisation, improvement in public investment and public sector performance [Ahluwalia, 1992; Nagaraj, 1990].

Speeding up of Reforms in the 1990s

As part of the orthodox initiatives since 1991, industry and trade policy reforms got accelerated, while public investment contracted sharply to reign in the fiscal imbalance. Financing of industrial development changed considerably as part of the financial sector reform that cut directed lending, and abolished subsidised credit for the identified sectors since development banks' access to long-term credit from the Reserve Bank and SLR funds were terminated. Although, formal changes in the industrial labour laws were avoided due to lack of political consensus, there were adequate signals to employers that the government would not come in the way of restructuring industrial relations, layoffs and retrenchments of organised workers—giving up the implicit *compact* that had bound capital and labour together in the previous four decades. While the reforms appeared like a 'big bang' by Indian standards, the pace was gradual compared to, say, China, let alone Russia and the East European economies.

Proponents expected the reforms to accelerate domestic output and industrial growth, taking it close to those achieved by the successful Asian economies. "Uncaging the tiger", the metaphor that *The Economist's* Clive Crook coined caught the imagination of the policy-makers and public alike—just as the new government was about to be formed in 1991 amidst an external payment crisis.[2] Expectedly, the policy initiatives drew considerable criticism, apprehending deep retrenchment of output and employment as had happened in Latin America and towards 'dependent development.'

How did the industrial sector really perform in the 1990s? How does it compare it with the previous decade?

II

INDUSTRIAL PERFORMANCE, 1980-81 to 2001-02

Worst Fears were Unfounded

Quite unlike in Latin America where manufacturing sector's share in GDP declined sharply over the last two decades, in India in the 1990s the share has remained broadly the same with a marginal rise (Table 7.2). As Figure 7.1 shows, manufacturing sector's share in workforce has remained roughly constant at around 12 per cent. Registered manufacturing employment—in factories regularly employing 10 or more workers constituting about one-fifth of total manufacturing employment – has steadily risen from around the mid-1980s for over a decade, without a trace of the effect of the 1991 reforms in the trend (Figure 7.2). Thus, in the aggregate, the worst fears did not come true (more about this later).[3]

Table 7.2

Share of Manufacturing in GDP in Selected Latin American Economies, 1980 to 2000

Country	*1980*	*1990*	*2000*
Argentina	29.5	26.8	17.6
Brazil	33.5		24.0
Chile	21.5	19.6	15.9
Mexico	22.3	20.8	20.7
India	**13.8**	**16.6**	**17.2**

Source: World Development Indicators, 2002; NAS, various issues.

Trend Analysis

Table 7.3 provides the trend growth rates of output for the total and registered manufacturing for varying time periods between 1980-81 and 2001-02. Evidently, the growth rates are, in general, lower in the 1990s compared to those in the previous decade. However, a dummy variable to test for a break in the series in 1991-92 does not

Figure 7.1

Share of Employment, Output and Investment in Total Manufacturing

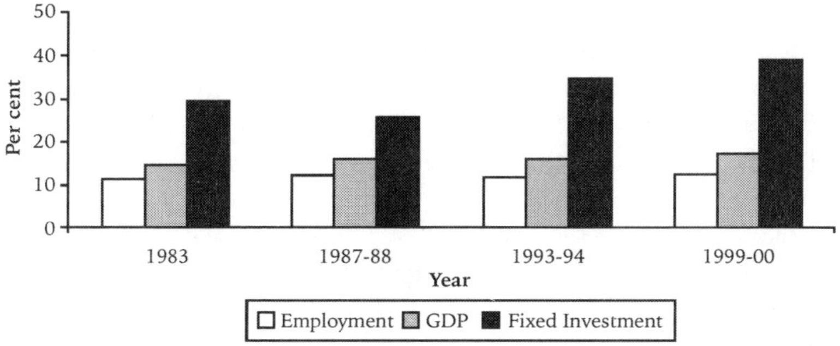

Figure 7.2

Employment in Registered Manufacturing

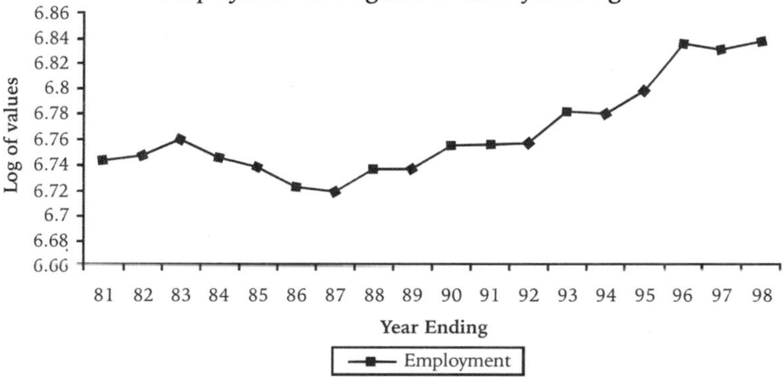

Table 7.3

Manufacturing Sector Growth, 1980-81 to 2001-02

(Per cent per year)

Period (year ending)	*Total Manufacturing*	*Registered Manufacturing*	*Dummy Variable Test*	
			Sign	*Statistical Significance*
1981-02	6.7		+	Not significant
1981-91	7.4	8.2		
1992-02	6.3			
1981-01		7.4	+	Not significant
1993-01		6.6		
1981-00	6.9			

Source: NAS, various issues.

show any statistically significant change in the growth rates. Thus, industrial growth during the last two decades have remained roughly the same, both for the total and registered manufacturing.

Results of a similar exercise for disaggregated (2-digit) industry groups are reported in Table 7.4. During the two-decade periods, in total manufacturing, chemicals (NIC 30), rubber and petroleum (NIC 31), and electrical machinery (NIC 36) have grown at above average growth rates by a reasonable margin. The same is true separately for each of the two decades. Similarly, textile products (NIC 26), leather, chemicals, rubber and petroleum (NIC 29-31), and repair services (NIC 39+97) grew faster than the average in registered manufacturing.

Table 7.4

Growth by 2-Digit Industry Groups, 1980-81 to 1999-2000

Industry	*Total Manufacturing*			*Registered Manufacturing*		
Group (NIC)	*1981-91*	*1992-00*	*1981-2000*	*1981-91*	*1992-00*	*1981-2000*
20-21	7.0	4.9	6.1	9.5	5.2	7.3
22	2.9	10.8	5.2	8.5	8.4	7.8
23-26	5.5	3.7	4.9			
23				5.6	6.3	3.2
24				5.8	13.8	7.6
25				1.9	4.4	0.9
26				12.8	1.6	14.8
27	(-)2.7	2.0	(-)0.8	7.3	4.7	0.9
28	9.1	4.3	6.2	9.2	0.6	5.3
29	3.8	5.1	6.0	9.7	3.7	10.4
30	9.3	10.4	10.0	9.4	10.6	10.3
31	14.7	5.5	9.9	17.6	5.5	11.4
32	9	9.9	7.4	11.8	7.7	7.9
33	5.7	8.1	7.4	5.4	8.4	7.2
34	6.0	6.9	4.3	6.5	7.9	6.2
35	6.0	8.7	6.1	6.0	8.5	6.0
36	12.5	12.3	10.0	10.7	13.0	9.6
37	5.5	6.3	5.3	5.4	5.5	6.5
38	11.1	7.6	7.1	7.7	7.0	7.3
39+97	7.1	8.3	5.4	15.3	6.8	13.2
Total	7.7	7.5	7.2	8.5	7.4	8.0

Source: NAS, various issues.

Growth by Use-based Industrial Groups

Many believe, the sharp reduction in tariffs for capital goods in the 1990s have severely affected their domestic output—"massacre of machine building," to use Ashok Desai's (2001) graphic description. Initial assessments, based on the index of industrial production (IIP) with different base years gave conflicting evidence in this regard. We now have a better basis to assess this proposition using the ASI data for the period 1980-81 to 1997-98 (Table 7.5).[4] The capital goods sector has grown at 6.7 per cent per year during 1981-98, and at 5.7 per cent per year during 1992-98; but there is no statistically significant break in the trend growth rate in 1991-92. The same is true for all the use-based industrial groups. Thus, the trend in output growth in the decades of 1980s and the 1990s are broadly similarly—in the aggregate, by 2-digit industry groups are well as by use-based classification of output.

Table 7.5

Growth in Registered Manufacturing according to Use-based Classification of Output, 1980-81 to 1997-98

(Per cent per year)

	Use-based Group	*1980-81/ 1997-98*	*1980-81/ 1990-91*	*Dummy Variable Test*
1.	Basic goods	8.3	8.0	(-) Not Sig.
2.	Intermediate goods	10.7	11.2	(-) Not Sig.
3.	Capital goods	6.7	5.3	(+) Not Sig.
4.	Consumer goods	9.1	8.9	(-) Not Sig.
	4.1 Consumer durable goods	12.5	12.0	(+) Not Sig.
	4.2 Consumer non-durable goods	8.5	8.3	(-) Not Sig.

Source: *EPW* Research Foundation (2002).

However, these trends seem to hide significant variations across specific products and industries. Within capital goods, passenger car—a widely accepted indicator of conspicuous consumption in a poor country—production (in numbers) went up from about 31 thousand in 1980-81 to about 5.8 lakh in 2000, representing an annual growth rate of 15 per cent during the two decades.

Its contrast with machine tool industry—the heart of domestic machine building capability—is telling. Gross value added in this industry grew at a mere 1.7 per cent per year during 1981-97, witnessing a negative growth thereafter. Indian Machine Tool Manufactures' Association says, "Output by domestic metalworking machine tool manufacturers in 2001 calendar year declined by 14 per cent to Rs. 5,137 million marking the fourth year of decline, since 1997, for the Indian machine tool industry" (*http://imtma.org/aimti.htm*). Domestic machine tool production stagnated at a time when the industrial investment really boomed (discussed later). Evidently, much of the incremental demand was met by imports, as the import-to-consumption ratio nearly doubled from 29 in 1990s, to 56 per cent in 1995.[5]

Due to the differing growth rates over nearly two decades, the relative weights of the use-based industrial groups have changed considerably. To discern their long-term changes in registered manufacturing, we have looked at their shares in every decade since 1960-61 (Table 7.6). During nearly three decades since 1970-71, the shares of consumer goods have gone up by 7 percentage points from 35 per cent to 42 per cent – mainly on account of consumer durable goods. Shares of basic and intermediate goods have gone down, while that of capital goods increased marginally by about 1 percentage point.

Table 7.6

Changes in the Use-based Classification of Registered Manufacturing Output, 1960-61 to 1997-98

Use-based groups	*1960-61*	*1970-71*	*1980-81*	*1990-91*	*1997-98*
1. Basic goods	27.5	30.7	21.3	23.7	23.0
2. Intermediate goods	21.0	19.0	16.3	16.8	17.0
3. Capital goods	10.7	15.2	21.2	17.5	16.3
4. Consumer goods	40.8	35.1	41.1	42.0	43.6
4.1 Consumer durable goods	2.5	2.8	4.8	6.8	8.8
4.2 Consumer non-durable goods	38.3	32.6	36.4	35.2	34.8

Note: Data for the years 1960-61 and 1970-71 are from Ahluwalia (1985: 9).

Though informative, the above findings are incomplete, as it excludes unregistered sector that constitutes one-third of total manufacturing value added. Moreover, with the diffusion of technology and skills, spread of electricity, and in response to a variety of policies to encourage small enterprises, many industries have got diffused in the unorganised sector in this period. While such a process is more likely in consumer goods industries, it is probably true to a lesser extent in machinery manufacturing also, since technology in these industries is amenable to division of labour and specialisation. But we cannot satisfactorily capture these changes, as use-based classification of the unorganised sector output is not available.

However, as a proxy for capital goods, we take the share of NIC 35 to NIC 37 in total manufacturing output (Figure 7.3). Expectedly, the capital goods share in total manufacturing is smaller than that in registered manufacturing. The two shares move in parallel, though there seems to be some narrowing of the gap between the two, suggesting a notable diffusion of capital goods production in the unorganised sector.

Figure 7.3

Machinery Sector's Share in Manufacturing Output

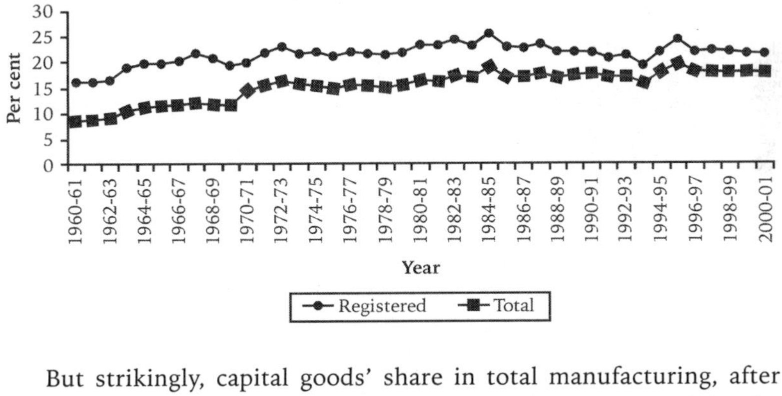

But strikingly, capital goods' share in total manufacturing, after peaking at about 18 per cent in 1984-85 has stagnated in the following one and half decade. Thus, the reforms have severely affected the sector—at least in the aggregate. Arguably, the steep rise in imports reflects poor capability of the domestic industry and its high prices. While there may be some merit in such argument, it is hard to believe that such an outcome was inevitable with policy reforms.

Capital Goods Prices

But the flip side of the above is, the real price of capital goods—the ratio of prices of capital goods to the GDP deflator—has steadily come down during the last two decades with the decline in tariffs, especially since 1993-94 (Figure 7.4). The same holds true for real price of construction – a positive effect of gradual decontrol of cement industry since 1982 leading to substantial capacity creation, entry of new firms and technological upgradation (moving from wet to dry process, thus lowering of the energy intensity of output). As the real price of fixed investment has gone down, and the share of machinery in GFCF has risen steadily, the additions to the capital stock is much more productive. This, in principle, would have economywide effects on potential output and productivity growth.

Figure 7.4

Real Price of GFCF by Type of Assets

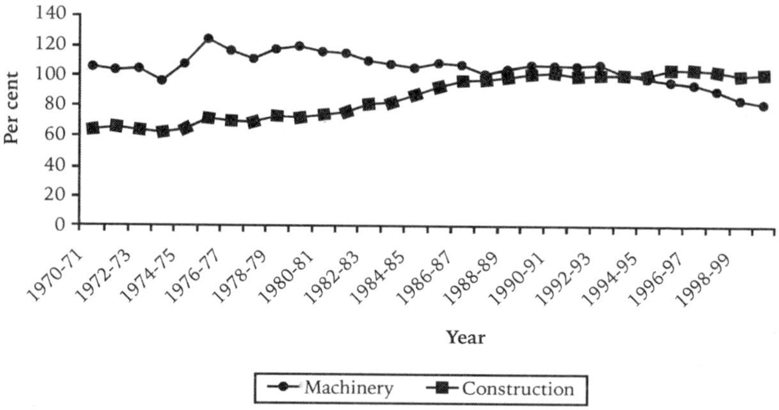

Growth of Construction Sector

With relaxation of supply constraints on cement and steel, and a fall in their real prices, there seems to have been a steady growth in construction sector. Though not evident from the domestic output estimates, employment figures seem to show a clearer picture.[6] The employment (usual status) share in construction for all India has nearly doubled from 2.3 per cent of total workforce in 1983, to 4.4 per cent in 1999-2000 [Chadda and Sahu, 2002]. Therefore, quite contrary to the popularly held view, the employment share of the industrial sector (mining, manufacturing, construction and utilities) shows a moderate increase in the last two decades, despite stagnation in manufacturing's share (Figure 7.5).

Figure 7.5

Workforce Distribution, 1983-2000

Better Functioning of Industrial Market

Undoubtedly, the economic reforms have increased domestic and external competition, providing greater consumer choice. A relative cheapening of capital goods under pressure from import competition has made fixed investment more productive, the gains of which are increasingly passed on to consumers by price reduction, or quality improvement. Firms can no longer implicitly operate on a 'cost plus' pricing principle. The shift in the market conditions is perhaps best reflected in manufacturers' growing use of consumer credit to induce sales of durable goods.

Moreover, the widely commented corruption in the industrial licensing system at the level of the central government has got largely eliminated, as entrepreneurs now have to merely register their proposed project with the concerned ministry, while state governments compete with each other for private investment with incentives. These are certainly significant gains of the gradual reforms over the last two decades.

On a closer look, however, there are many causes for concern.

III

A CLOSER LOOK AT THE 1990s

While the trend growth rate in the 1990s is the same as in the previous decade, the yearly growth rates show an interesting pattern (Figure 7.6). After an expected contraction in response to the external payment crisis in 1991-92, industrial output rebound rapidly in the following four years, peaking in 1995-96. In fact, the annual growth rate of output of over 14 per cent in that year is perhaps the highest ever recorded in India. The sharp upturn is widely credited to the policy reforms—with the expectation of further acceleration with more reforms.

Figure 7.6

Manufacturing Output Growth, 1991-2002

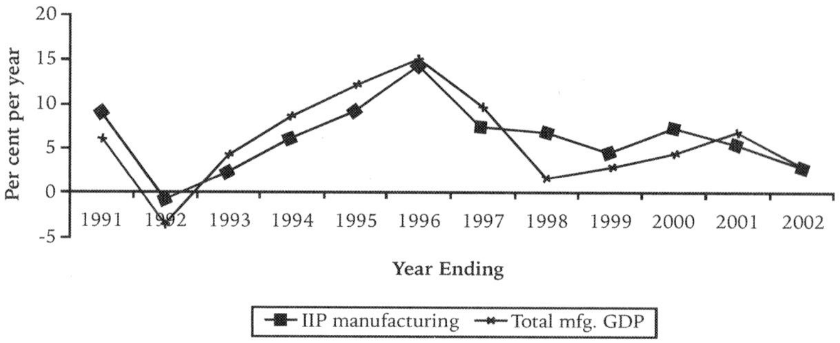

But the growth rate steadily decelerated in the following seven years now, except for a minor improvement in 1999-2000. Though it is not yet evident as a statistically significant break in the trend growth rate, the perceptible slowdown for so many years is surely a matter of concern. The deceleration is even sharper in fixed investment that has turned negative in the last few years (Figure 7.7). As there was an investment boom in manufacturing without a corresponding rise in the output growth, there is now a huge excess capacity, especially in consumer durable goods, automotive industry—and more generally in capital goods.

Figure 7.7

Fixed Investment Growth in Total Manufacturing

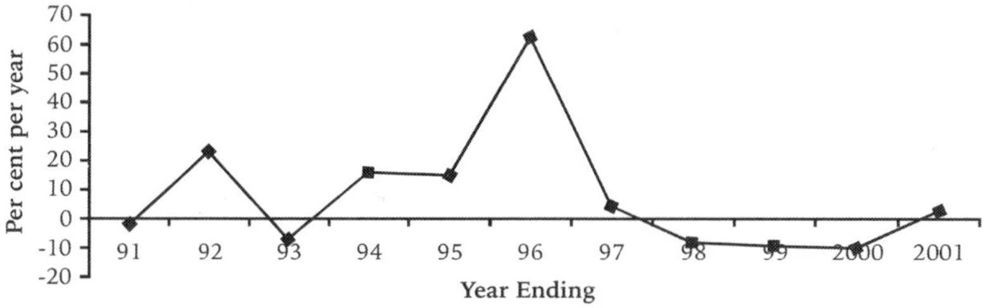

Divergence in Performance

By doing away with the reported import substitution bias in the industrial policy, the reforms were expected to boost output and exports of labour-intensive manufactures. If we accept the distinction of registered and unregistered sectors as proxies for import competing and export-oriented manufacturing respectively (as is widely done in the literature), then the experience of the 1990s seems to be at variance with *a priori* expectation.

While there was an investment boom in the registered sector, the unregistered sector has suffered. The unregistered sector's share in total manufacturing GFCF has nearly halved from around 45 per cent in the mid-1980s to less than 20 per cent by the end of the 1990s (Figure 7.8). What explains this? The investments seem to have been driven by the potential size of the domestic market, and the expectation of its growth in the liberalised regime.[7] This is particularly true of the consumer durable goods and automotive industry, largely driven by a surge in foreign direct investment [Nagaraj, 2003]. Many incumbent, domestic, firms responded to the threat of new entry by modernisation, expansion and strengthening distribution network, thus contributing to the investment boom. However, this did not translate into output growth as the size of the market was found to be much smaller than projected.

Investment in unregistered manufacturing was probably hurt by high interest rates in the initial years of the reforms.[8] While the interest rates came down in the second half of the 1990s, commercial banks have resisted lending for productive sector as they found it profitable to invest in risk-free government securities. As a proxy for access to fund investment, bank credit to small-scale sector in unregistered manufacturing—as proportions of (i) total non-food credit, and (ii) net bank credit—has declined from over 16 per cent in the late 1980s to less than 12 per cent a decade later (Figure 7.9). In other words, in the liberalised regime and without a change in the legal environment, commercial banks had little incentive to lend to small enterprises.

Figure 7.8

Unregistered Sector's Share in Manufacturing Fixed Investment

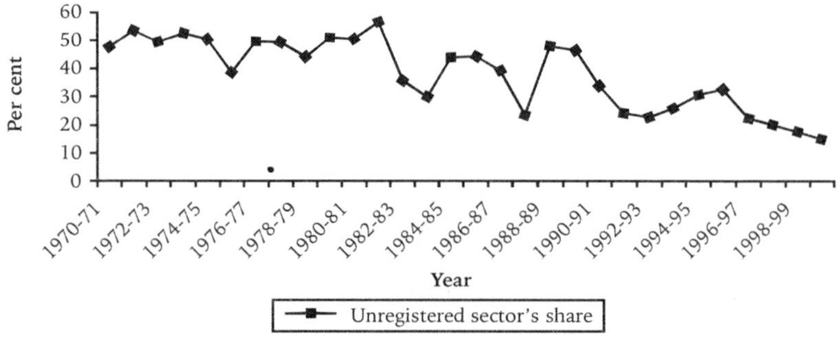

Figure 7.9

Bank Credit to SSI, 1980-81 to 2000-01

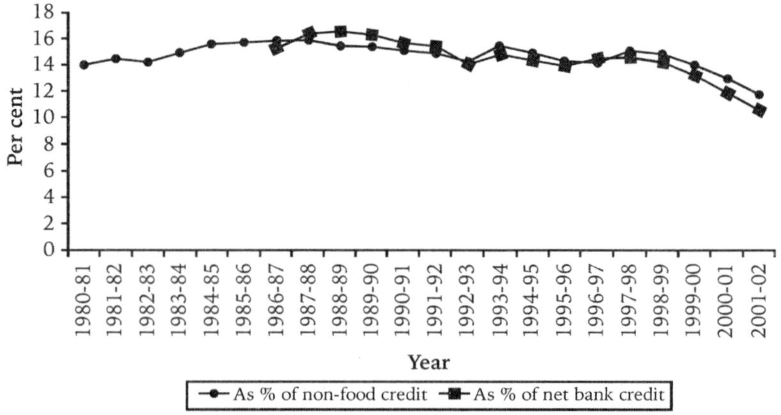

Thus, after over two decades of "creeping liberalisation"—to borrow Pranab Bardhan's (1998) phrase—there is now a widespread gloom with decelerating growth for nearly seven years since the mid-1990s with a huge excess capacity in many industries. This is in sharp contrast to the euphoria that marked the initiation of the orthodox economic reforms little over a decade ago.

Evidently, there is an uncanny resemblance of the current industrial outlook with what it was around 1980 that we described at the beginning. Why did the reforms not lead to an acceleration of output growth with a greater share of labour-intensive manufactures and exports? More pertinently perhaps, why has the growth tapered off after the mid-1990s although there were no significant policy reversals? If anything, regardless of the political dispensation in power, successive governments have sought to iron out the wrinkles in the reform process. Is it a question of the reforms being too little and too late? Or is it a mere failure of implementation of a sound design (political and bureaucratic inertia)?

These are serious questions that have a bearing not just on industrial performance, but also perhaps on the validity of the analytical model that underpins much of the current policy discourse.

IV

TOWARDS AN EXPLANATION

The policy initiatives in the 1990s were based on considerable support from the mainstream economics. They were, in principle, expected to set right what was widely believed to have been wrong with India's industrialisation effort. As T.N. Srinivasan argued, "They [the reforms] were solidly based on an understanding of what went wrong with Indian development strategy since 1950 that delivered neither rapid growth nor appreciably greater equity." [Srinivasan, 1993: 258]. In Jagdish Bhagwati's view, the three main elements of India's policy framework that stifled growth and efficiency were: "extensive bureaucratic controls over production, investment and trade; inward looking trade and foreign investment policies, and a substantial public sector, going well beyond the conventional confines of public utilities and infrastructure" [Bhagwati, 1993: 48]. Joshi and Little (1994) contended, "India's control system was not only microeconomically inefficient but macroeconomically perverse" [Joshi and Little, 1994: 3] —implying that the industrial policy was responsible for persistent fiscal deficits and periodic balance of payment crises.

Broadly, none of these features of the policy framework remain any more after 1991. Why, then, has the manufacturing sector growth slowed down so precipitously after the mid-1990s? Why haven't the budgetary imbalances disappeared with doing away of the allegedly worst features of the policy framework?

Ashok Desai (2001), among others, has argued that credit squeeze in 1996 and rise in interest rates throttled the boom of 1993-96. While it might have been true in the short run, why has industry not revived despite the steady loosening of the credit constraint and the fall in interest rates over the last seven years?

Many attribute the slowdown (lack of sustained improvement in the 1990s) to the stalled reforms. They believe a quick and sharp reduction in tariffs to the average levels of many Asian economies, pulling down the remaining restrictions on foreign direct investment, and removal of the policy-induced rigidities in the industrial labour market would deliver the desired fruits of reforms. These arguments merit closer examination.

If such an argument is valid, then the hastening of the reforms in the 1990s, compared to the previous decade ought to have improved the industrial growth rate, which evidently has not happened. Moreover, in comparative experience, there is little evidence to suggest an unambiguous positive association between the scope (and speed) of reforms and economic outcomes. If one can cite cases from Asian economies, as successful examples of following the orthodoxy, there are equally compelling cases from Latin America with adverse outcomes.

Thus, there are no clear signals as to how to reverse the trend of decelerating industrial growth, except for the fond hope that further relaxation of the rules governing the use of capital (domestic and foreign) and labour would somehow do the trick.[9] Moreover, the view that the "reforms have not gone far enough," resembles the arguments in the earlier times when repeated failure of the Five-Year Plans to meet the targets was attributed to "not enough planning," or "lack of political will," despite the growing evidence of the economy's structural weaknesses, or the heavy hand of bureaucracy. Therefore, such arguments in favour of more reforms do not seem to be based on an application of economic reasoning and examination of the evidence. Thus, there is a reason for us to look for an alternative explanation.

It is perhaps useful to start with the classical economic view. As Arthur Lewis once asked, "What limits the size of the manufacturing sector?" His preliminary answer was, "productivity of farmers whose marketable surplus will exchange for manufactures" [Lewis, 1984: 121]. As India is still a large and poor agrarian economy with 3/5th of workforce still dependent on agriculture (in Bihar it is close to 3/4th), with land productivity being one-third of China's, per capita value added in manufacturing is the lowest among the newly industrialising economies; and one-fourth of China's (Table 7.7).

Table 7.7

Manufacturing Value Added Per Capita in Selected Industrialising Economies

Countries	*Value Added Per Capita in Manufacturing In US$ in 1998*
Argentina	1253
Brazil	1078
Mexico	821
Hong Kong	1738
Korea	2142
Singapore	6064
India	**70**
China	286
Malaysia	946
Indonesia	115
Thailand	582
Turkey	501
Memo: High Income Economies	5344

Source: Weiss (2001): 15.

If we accept, following Chenery's stylised fact, that large countries, in general, have low trade ratios, and that India does not have abundant natural resources for exports, then industrial growth largely boils down to the size (and growth) of the domestic market. This, in turn, yet largely depends on how the agriculture performs. The rich discourse on India's industrialisation experience has shown that in a poor agrarian economy lack of demand could be a binding constraint on industrial growth. To quote, K.N. Raj:

> Private consumer demand in a country such as India depends to a large extent, ... on how things go in the agricultural sector. If output and income in this sector are rising rapidly, consumer demand for both agricultural and non-agricultural products can also be expected to increase rapidly, the latter being even more than the former since higher proportions are generally spent on non-agricultural products as levels of income rise. Output and incomes in the agricultural sector need not, of course, always rise together since the effect of sharp increases in output could well be to lower the prices of agricultural products more than proportionately; this is in fact an important factor governing agricultural income in some regions of the country characterised by serious year-to-year variation in climatic conditions and water supply [Raj, 1986: 225i].

Without denying that long-term constraint in a developing economy is one of supply of savings and investment, Sukhamoy Chakravarty, argued that under specific circumstances that India faced, lack of aggregate demand could become a binding constraint [Chakravarty, 1979 and 1984].

From a variety of analytical perspectives, it is widely accepted that autonomous public investment in a developing economy helps create large demand for industrial goods as well as relieve infrastructure supply constraint [Narayana and Srinivasan, 1977; Patnaik and Rao, 1977]. Pandit's (1995) survey of macroeconometric evidence seems to unambiguously support the view that public investment 'crowds-in' private investment. International evidence also suggests that public investment in infrastructure does not displace private investment, but crowds it in [Serven, 1996].

Combining the above arguments, one can perhaps contend that industrial growth in India is largely run on the twin engines of agriculture productivity and public investment. Apparently, neither of these was functioning well in the 1990s.

Agricultural Performance

In the aggregate, there are no signs of a statistically significant slowdown in the growth of GDP in agriculture in the 1990s [Nagaraj, 2001]. However, there are other pieces of evidence, mainly based on physical output growth, at the disaggregated level, that seems to suggest a different tendency.

A comparison of land productivity of all major crops (and crop groups) between the 1980s and the 1990s shows a distinctly lower trend growth rate in the 1990s compared to the previous decade, except for wheat (Figure 7.10).[10] If the above evidence has any merit, then poorer agricultural performance could have adversely affected the demand for industrial goods.

Figure 7.10

Trends in Agricultural Production, 1980-81 to 1999-2000

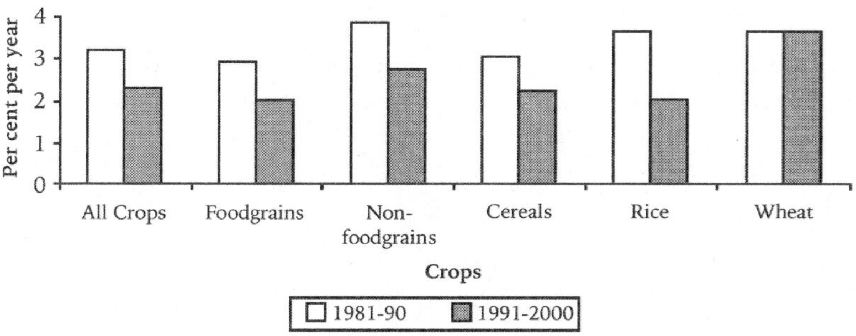

The indifferent agriculture performance in the 1990s is perhaps associated with much commented slowdown in public investment in this sector. Although an improvement in private investment seems to have partially compensated for the decline in public investment, there is an undeniable decline in total agricultural investment growth [Roy and Pal, 2002; Gulati and Bathla, 2001].

Poor agricultural performance seems to be also evident in lower labour demand in rural areas. Chadda and Sahu (2002) show that between 1993 and 2000, unemployment rates have gone up, while it had come down in the previous decade. This is found to be true by all measures of unemployment.

Thus, piecing together the above evidence seems to suggest a deterioration of agricultural performance in the 1990s that could perhaps have adversely affected industrial output growth.

Public Investment

It is widely accepted that as part of the economic reforms, public investment—over one-half of which is in infrastructure—was deliberately reduced.[11] Figure 7.11 shows the share of infrastructure (mining, utilities and transport) and manufacturing in total gross fixed capital formation (GFCF) for the period since 1970-71. Evidently, the decline in infrastructure's share started in the second half of the 1980s that became sharp in the mid-1990s. Interestingly, its mirror image can be found in the manufacturing sector's increasing share in GFCF. If we take a longer time-period (not shown here), we discover that the share of public investment in the late 1990s at about 30 per cent of total GFCF has fallen close to the level it was in the early 1950s when India initiated planned economic development. In physical terms the decline in public investment is perhaps best captured in the precipitous fall in the growth of electricity generation capacity from 8 to 10 per cent per year in the 1980s to 4 to 6 per cent in the 1990s (Figure 7.12). The fall in public investment has been so drastic that it is now—to rephrase Bhagwati's earlier quote—well *behind* the conventional confines of public utilities and infrastructure.

Figure 7.11

Share of Manufacturing and Infrastructure in GFCF

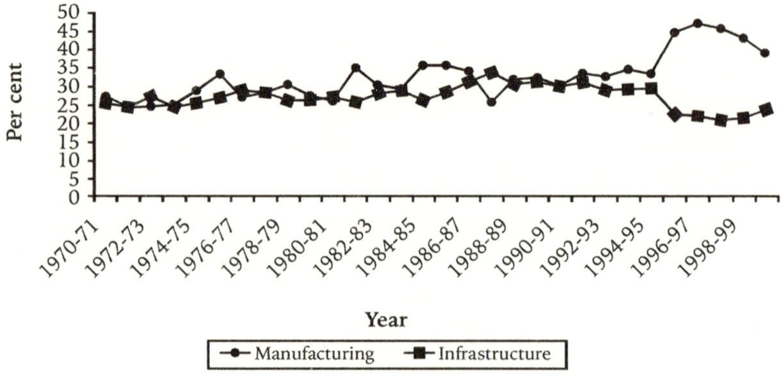

Figure 7.12

Annual Growth in Electricity Generating Capacity, 1981-2001

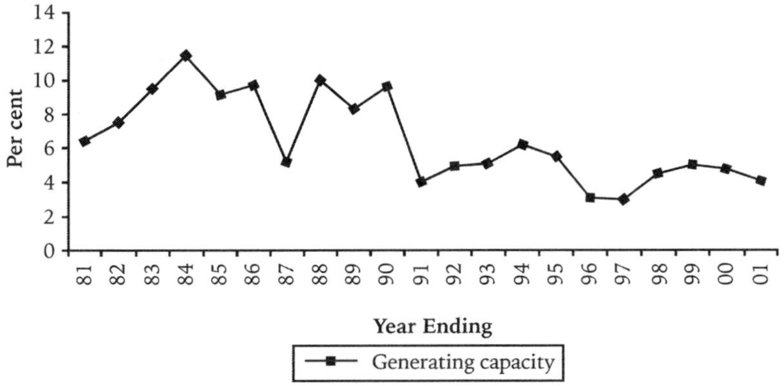

While some may applaud this 'achievement' at dismantling the public sector's role in the provision of social overhead capital, this has not led to a surge in investment and employment in labour-intensive manufactures. But the fall in infrastructure investment seems to have constrained industrial output and export growth, and also perhaps the inflow of foreign direct investment.

Economic theory seems fairly clear that when markets fail, as often happens in the industrial sector which has considerable externalities, economies of scale, scope and network, state intervention, in principle, improves social welfare. Such a view is increasingly countered by arguing that in developing economies, the costs of 'state failures' due to inefficiency, waste and corruption could outweigh the costs of market failure.

As such disputes cannot be resolved analytically, we have to look at evidence on market failure versus state failure in the course of industrialisation. The experience of successful industrialisation in the 20th century does not seem to support the state failure hypothesis in the aggregate: if anything, the sustained ability at acquisition of technical capability in late industrialising economies has gone hand in hand with substantial, yet responsive, state action [Amsden, 2001]. On the other hand, leaving more and more economic decisions to markets uncritically during the last two decades seem to have led to de-industrialisation, as measured by workforce distribution [Weiss, 2002].

Chile is probably the prime example of Latin America's most industrialised nation getting transformed to a primary producer of exotic (counter seasonal) agricultural produce.

V

POLICY OPTIONS AND CONSTRAINTS

If the foregoing discussion has any merit, then what should be done for industrial revival? There is widespread support from diverse analytical perspectives for stepping up public infrastructure investment, but the endorsement wares thin as to how to finance it. Financing by increasing user charges and cutting down delays and waste in public sector (reducing X-inefficiency) are obviously the first-best solution, but it is a gradual and politically difficult—but perhaps not an insurmountable—in a democratic set-up. Probably the best practical option in the medium-term is to use the available food and foreign exchange reserves for stepping public infrastructure investment—perhaps on the lines that Shetty (2001) suggested. Given the overflowing food stocks and considerable excess capacity in industry, the inflationary potential of such a stance is likely to be modest. But, what if such a policy accentuates the existing fiscal imbalance? But it need not necessarily happen, as is often believed. As Mihir Rakshit argued:

> Even in mainstream economics it is recognised that the fiscal deficit cannot be a primary policy parameter, but is the outcome of the working of the entire system. ...[in] India almost all industrial units producing heavy machinery, equipment and basic metals belong to the public sector; and the wage bill in the large majority of these enterprises constitutes a fixed rather than a variable cost in the short- and medium-run. This implies that (i) an increase in the demand for fixed capital goods met from domestic sources raises public sector savings by an almost identical amount; and (ii) the value of the investment multiplier is close to unity. Thus, even the short-run effects of public consumption and investment on aggregate demand are quite different [Rakshit, 1994: 269-70].[12]

Within the mainstream economics there are many who argue that after the economic reforms the markets may be less imperfect, but may not 'naturally' lead to improved growth performance.

Dornbusch famously argued, "Stabilisation may be inevitable, but it is not a ticket for prosperity. ... One should not presume that the market automatically solves the coordination problems..." [Dornsbusch, 1990: 42-43]. A large and credible public investment programme—besides creating the well known economywide supply and demand linkages—could go a long way in stabilising private sector's business expectations, and provide powerful signals as to the broad direction of the economic policy, and the commitment of the policy-makers to it. Further, it would perhaps not be incorrect to argue that in a poor and inequitous, agrarian economy like ours public infrastructure investment contributes towards efficiency as well equity.[13]

Agriculture has received less policy attention in the recent years as food stocks have risen well beyond the needs of safe levels for food security. But such a policy overlooks the fact that what is procured and distributed by public distribution system forms a small part of total food production and consumption; and, a sizable (though declining) share of food output is not marketed at all. Therefore, what share of rural income is left for non-food consumption depends on food production (and its prices), as poor and marginal farmers are net buyers of food.

VI

SUMMARY AND CONCLUSIONS

To sum up, industrial output growth during the last two decades has improved compared to the previous period of 'relative stagnation.' But contrary to both the euphoria and apprehension, with the acceleration of the reforms there has been little change in the trend growth rate of output in the 1990s, compared to the previous decade. Moreover, since the mid-1990s, there are distinct signs of a slowdown in growth for seven years now.

Gradualism in industry and trade policy reform during the last two decades has some notable achievements to its credit. Industrial markets have become more competitive, and product quality and variety have improved substantially. A relative cheapening of machinery and construction have made fixed investment more productive. An improved supply of cement and steel, and a fall in their real prices has spurred the construction sector whose share in total workforce has nearly doubled—increasing industrial sector's share in the total workforce.

Quite contrary to many apprehensions, the trend growth rate of capital goods sector in registered manufacturing has not declined during 1992-98 compared to the period 1981-91. While the capital goods sector's share in registered manufacturing has increased by about 1 percentage point in the 1990s, the share in total manufacturing has virtually stagnated since the mid-1980s, clearly suggesting the negative effect of the reforms on this sector. Moreover, the aggregate performance seems to hide more than it reveals. To illustrate, the number of passenger car produced increased at 15 per cent per year for two decades now. But machine tool industry—making the mother machines—has barely grown as imports to consumption ratio nearly doubling in the 1990s.

The much expected restructuring of production away from domestic market orientation, and towards labour-intensive manufactures and their exports has not happened—at least not as yet. If anything, import competing organised manufacturing has been strengthened by the investment boom, while unregistered manufacturing suffered in the 1990s. Much of the boom went into production for the home market. Quite contrary to Joshi and Little's (1994) contention, elimination of the import substitution bias and the decline in public sector's role in manufacturing have not resulted in decline in macroeconomic perversity, as evident from persistent fiscal imbalances even after a decade of economic reforms.

Why did industrial and export growth not accelerate in the 1990s with the speeding up of the orthodox reforms? More precisely, why did the growth momentum of the 1980s taper off so sharply after a mere four-year boom in the early 1990s? The experience seems to suggest that the much argued positive association between the reforms and growth seems suspect, or over done. What, then, should we do to revive industry?

'Stalled,' reforms since around the mid-1990s are widely believed to be responsible for the industrial deceleration. Such a view presumes a positive association between speed (and depth) of reforms and output growth—a view sustainable neither in principle nor in comparative experience. Successive governments in the 1990s have, by and large, sought to operationalise the reforms and remove various bottlenecks rather than go back on them—but with little effect.

Therefore, it needs to be recognised that the industrial sector currently suffers from a lack of demand especially of investment, and not of supply—constrained by policy. In a poor, agrarian economy there are many structural features that can constrain industrial demand, although low capital stock per head continues to be the long-term constraint. Lack of demand seems to be on account of poor to indifferent agricultural performance in the 1990s and a deep cut in public infrastructure investment since the late 1980s.

Following the classical economic percepts, there is an urgent need to refocus policy on stimulating agricultural productivity that creates rural demand. With growing capital intensity of crop production, such a move will not only augment demand for consumer goods, but also for capital and basic goods. Stepping up public infrastructure investment would not only generate investment demand, but also ease the constraints on infrastructure supply that could bring in domestic investment, and probably the much sought after foreign investment as well. Given the structural features of the Indian economy, a carefully crafted strategy of financing such investment may not worsen the budgetary imbalance as widely apprehended—on the contrary it may improve it, if the utilisation of excess capacity stimulates internal savings of enterprises.

Notes

1. Unless mentioned otherwise, the growth rates in this paper refer to log-linear trend growth rates, and all economic aggregates are measured at constant prices.
2. Clive Crook wrote, "India is a caged tiger. The tiger, set free, can be as healthy and vigorous as any in Asia. ... What needs to be done is clear. ... The government must dismantle an unbelievably complicated system of restraints and rewards that, over the past four decades, has securely enclosed every aspect of Indian life. The first and necessary step is to see these restraints and rewards as the cage that they are" (*The Economist: India Survey*, May 4, 1991: 5).
3. Reportedly, there have been large-scale retrenchments in older industries and locations like Mumbai though the official estimates do not seem to reflect the reality, as the system of reporting of labour statistics has deteriorated. Howell and Kambhampati (1999) gives a grim picture of textile workers in Ahmedabad.
4. The latest ASI data are available up to 1999-2000. We are unable to use the information for the last two years of the 1990s, as there is, once again, a change in

the industrial classification and the census and sample sectors within factory sector have also been redefined. We believe the broad trends reported in this study are unlikely to change by adding the data for the latest two years. In this study we have used the consistent time series compiled by *EPW* Research Foundation (2002).

5. High level of import-to-consumption ratio in machine tools would not have mattered, if their exports were also growing rapidly. Machine tools are a highly traded good, even among countries like the US, Germany and Japan and considerable economies in specialisation.

6. While output has boomed since the cement decontrol in 1982, neither fixed capital formation in construction nor domestic output in construction shows a corresponding increase, suggesting a growing underestimation of value addition in this sector [Nagaraj, 2001].

7. Much of this investment was predicated on the estimated size of the domestic market for consumer durable goods to be around 200 million—based on private market research and consumption surveys.

8. Many believe, the reservation policy for the small-scale industries (SSIs) is responsible for lack of investment in unregistered sector. While de-reservation surely merits attention, the policy cannot perhaps explain the fall in investment, as the reservation is restricted to a small number of industries, with a modest share in SSIs' output.

9. This view is well reflected in the official *Economic Survey* since the early the 1990s.

10. I owe an earlier version of this graph to G.S. Bhalla.

11. Usually infrastructure includes mining, utilities, transport and communications. However, if investment in major irrigation and flood control were also included, keeping in view the agrarian nature of the economy, its share would be even higher.

12. Economic Advisory Committee's report (1987) under the chairmanship of Sukhamoy Chakravarty had worked out numerical exercises to examine the effects of stepping up investment in infrastructure on domestic output and public saving.

13. Bardhan said, "... there are many projects which by relieving the severe constraints faced by poor and improving their conditions can help economic growth in the process. This runs somewhat contrary to the preoccupation of mainstream economies with equity-efficiency trade-offs, with its emphasis on the various costs of redistribution in terms of reduced economic incentives and performance ... ."

    Then there are important dynamic externalities which can arise from community or neighbourhood—specific characteristics. These may refer to physical infrastructure (like roads, communications, irrigation and power systems) improving the productivity of private investment ... ." [Bardhan, 1996: 1346-7].

References

Ahluwalia, Isher (1992). *Productivity and Growth in Indian Manufacturing*, Oxford University Press, Delhi.

————. (1985). *Industrial Growth in India: Stagnation since the Mid-Sixties*, Oxford University Press, Delhi.

Amsden, Alice H. (2001). *The Rise of "The Rest": Challenges to the West from Late-Industrialising Economies*. Oxford University Press, New York.

Bardhan, Pranab (1998). *The Political Economy of Development in India*, Expanded Edition with an Epilogue on the Political Economy of Reform in India, Oxford University Press, Delhi.

————. (1996). "Efficiency, Equity and Poverty Alleviation: Policy Issues in Less Developed Countries," *Economic Journal*, Vol. 106, September.

Bhagwati, Jagdish (1993). *India's Economy: The Shackled Giant*. Clarendon Press Oxford.

Chadda, G.K. and Sahu, P.P. (2002). "Post-Reform Setbacks in Rural Employment," *Economic and Political Weekly*, Vol. 37, No. 22, May 25.

Chakravarty, Sukhamoy (1984). "Aspects of India's Development Strategy for the 1980s," reprinted in Chakravarty's *Selected Economic Writings*, Oxford University Press, Delhi, 1993.

————. (1979). "On the Question of Home Market and Prospects for Indian Growth," *Economic and Political Weekly*, Vol. 14, Nos. 30-32, August, Annual Number.

Desai, Ashok (2001). "A Decade of Reforms," *Economic and Political Weekly*, Vol. 36, No. 50, December 15.

Dornsbusch, Rudiger (1990). "Policies to Move from Stabilisation to Growth," *Proceedings of the World Bank Annual Conference on Development Economics*. World Bank, Washington DC.

Economic Advisory Council (1987). *Public Enterprises in India: Some Current Issues*, Economic Advisory Council, New Delhi.

EPW Research Foundation (2002). *Annual Survey of Industries, 1973-74 to 1997-98: A Data Base on the Industrial Sector in India*, Mumbai.

Gulati, Ashok and Seema Bathla (2001). "Capital Formation in Indian Agriculture Re-visiting the Debate," *Economic and Political Weekly*, Vol. 36, No. 20, May 19.

Howell, Jude and Uma Kambhampati (1999). "Liberalisation and Labour: The Fate of Retrenched Workers in the Cotton Textile Industry in India," *Oxford Development Studies*, Vol. 27, No. 1, February.

Joshi, Vijay and IMD Little (1994). *India: Macroeconomics and Political Economy, 1961-1991*, Oxford University Press, Delhi.

Lewis, W. Arthur (1984). "Development Economics in the 1950s," Gerald Meier and Dudley Seers edited, *Pioneers in Development*, Oxford University Press, New York.

Nagaraj, R. (2003). "Foreign Direct Investment in India in the 1990s: Trends and Issues," *Economic and Political Weekly*, Vol. 38, No. 17, April 26.

————. (2001). "National Income and Balance of Payments Statistics: A Review," in C P Chandrasekhar and Jandhayala BG Tilak edited, *India's Socio-Economic Database: Surveys of Selected Areas*, Tulika, New Delhi.

————. (1990) "Industrial Growth: Further Evidence and Towards an Explanation and Issues," *Economic and Political Weekly*, Vol. 15, No. 41, October 13.

Narayana, N.S.S. and T.N. Srinivasan (1977). "Economic Performance since the Third Plan and its Implications for Policy," *Economic and Political Weekly*, Vol. 12, Nos. 6-8, February, Annual Number.

Pandit, V. (1995). "Macroeconomic Character of the Indian Economy: Theories, Facts and Fancies," in Prabhat Patnaik edited, *Macroeconomics*, Oxford University Press, Delhi.

Patnaik, Prabhat and S.K. Rao (1977). "Towards an Explanation of a Crisis in a Mixed Underdeveloped Economy," *Economic and Political Weekly*, Vol. 12, Nos. 6-8, February, Annual Number.

Raj, K.N. (1986). "Growth and Stagnation in Indian Industrial Development," *Economic and Political Weekly*, Vol. 11, Nos. 5-7, February, Annual Number.

Rakshit, Mihir (1994). "Issues in Structural Adjustment of Indian Economy," in Edmar L Bacha (edited) *Economics in a Changing World: Development, Trade and Environment*, Vol. 4, St. Martin Press, London.

Rangarajan, C. (1982). "Industrial Growth: Another Look," *Economic and Political Weekly*, Vol. 17, Nos. 14-16, April, Annual Number.

Roy, B.C. and Suresh Pal (2002). "Investment, Agricultural Productivity and Rural Poverty in India: A State-Level Analysis," *Indian Journal of Agricultural Economics*, Vol. 57, No. 4, Oct-Dec.

Serven, Luis (1996). "Does Public Capital Crowds Out Private Capital? Evidence from India," *Policy Research Working Paper* No. 1613, World Bank, Washington D.C.

Shetty, S.L. (2001). "Reviving the Economy: Some Explorations," *Economic and Political Weekly*, Vol. 36, No. 30, July 28.

Srinivasan, T.N. (1993). "Demand Deficiency and Indian Industrial Development," in Pranab Bardhan *et al.*, edited, *Development and Change: Essays in Honour of K N Raj*, Oxford University Press, Delhi.

Weiss, John (2002). *Industrialisation and Globalisation: Theory and Evidence from Developing Countries*, Routledge, London.

Economic and Political Weekly, Vol.38, No. 35, August 30-September 5, 2003.

Part III

Some Aspects of Economic Policy

8

Public Sector Performance in the Eighties

Some Tentative Findings

The role of the public sector in India's macroeconomic performance in general and in that of industrial sector in particular is widely acknowledged. In the first 15-year period of planned economic development since 1950, the public sector is credited to have been instrumental in securing rapid import substituting industrialisation and providing the much needed economic infrastructure for initiating a self-reliant growth process, though perhaps not in the desirably cost-effect manner. The period of 'relative stagnation' of industrial sector in the subsequent decade and a half or so has been attributed, among other factors, to a perceptible slowing down of the growth of public investment [for instance, Srinivasan and Narayana, 1977; Patnaik and Rao, 1977].

Somewhat in parallel, the unsatisfactory performance of public sector in generating adequate surplus for sustaining a non-inflationary growth process in India has been subjected to considerable analyses in the tradition of political economy [Raj, 1973; Bardhan, 1984]. Documenting the changing mode of financing of the decelerating public investment in India, Rubin (1986), following Bardhan, anticipated little possibility of stepping it up[1] to secure a higher desired growth rate of domestic output. More recently, in the context of the policy changes initiated in the 1980s, Raj (1985) reiterated his earlier position as to the reasons for the continued unsatisfactory performance of public sector.[2]

In the present context, inability of public sector enterprises to generate a reasonable rate of return on capital invested is widely perceived as an important cause for the serious and growing fiscal imbalance in the 1980s. Commenting on the poor financial performance of public sector enterprises, Jalan (1991) said: "... As far as public enterprises are concerned, the after-tax profit of central government commercial enterprises as a ratio of capital employed was 4.5 per cent in 1989-90. The performance of state level PSEs has been even worse. These enterprises had net losses of Rs. 1928 crore in 1990-91" (p 177). Vaidyanathan (1991) identifies their unsatisfactory resource generation record as an important failure of planning in India: "Subsidies, both implicit and explicit, are also part of the reason for low return to investment in public enterprises. The inability of public enterprises to generate surpluses for reinvestment and to become a progressively more important source of both aggregate savings and finances for public investment has been a major failure of our planning" (p 6).

While there could be considerable merit in these arguments, it is perhaps important to assess empirically (i) whether the financial performance of public sector enterprises has, in fact, deteriorated over a period of time, and (ii) if so, whether such a trend can be considered an important, if not the principle, cause for the growing fiscal imbalance in the 1980s. This exploratory exercise attempts to document the long-term trends in some aspects of public sector performance for the period since 1960-61. More specifically, it seeks to examine the validity of the foregoing propositions on the resource mobilisation effort of public sector enterprises. We rely mainly on *National Accounts Statistics* as this is the most comprehensive, long-term and internationally comparable data source using a consistent set of economic categories.

I

GROWTH IN PUBLIC SECTOR OUTPUT

India's economic performance in terms of real (measured) GDP has shown a distinctly higher trend growth rate[3] since 1980-81 [Nagaraj, 1990a] and the decade ended with a growth rate of 5.3 per cent per annum [Nagaraj, 1991b]. There is little evidence to suggest a decline in the trend growth rate of GDP originating in public sector since 1980-81; nor of a statistically unambiguous increase in that of private sector [Nagaraj, 1991a]. However, while the growth rate of total manufacturing in private sector increased from 4.4 per cent per annum during 1960-61 and 1979-80 to 6.5 per cent per annum thereafter, manufacturing in public sector continued to grow at an unchanging rate of 6.6 per cent per annum during the entire period since 1960-61 [Nagaraj, 1991a].

We have earlier argued [Nagaraj, 1990b] that an improvement in some aspects of public sector performance in the 1980s could be, among other factors, an important explanation for the higher tend growth rate of manufacturing industries. Gross fixed capital formation (GFCF) in public sector has grown at 6.2 per cent per annum during 1980-81 and 1988-89 compared to, 4.2 per cent per annum during 1965-66 and 1979-80.[4] Moreover, there is little evidence of a perceptible increase in the rate of inflation in the 1980s compared to the preceding period – inflation measured by implicit GDP deflator was 7.2 per cent per annum during 1965-66 and 1979-80 and 7.8 per cent during 1980-81 and 1988-89.

Share of public sector in total gross domestic capital formation (GDCF) has gone up from about 40 per cent during 1970-75 to about 52 per cent during 1986-88. A distinct shift in the composition of GFCF is discernible in favour of 'machinery and equipment'[5] and a corresponding decline in the share of construction. Moreover, the sectoral composition of public investment has shifted in favour of 'industry' (mining and quarrying, manufacturing and electricity, gas and water) and 'infrastructure' (mining and quarrying, electricity, gas and water and transport). As a result, perhaps, infrastructure industries have shown a distinct improvement in their output growth in the 1980s. We further hypothesised [Nagaraj, 1990b] that, in the 1980s, there appears to have been a relatively greater selectivity in public sector projects and concentration of the available resources in completing the ongoing ones which could have not only favourably influenced output growth but, as a corollary, brought down the incremental capital-output ratios (ICORs) in the relevant sectors.

II

PUBLIC SECTOR PERFORMANCE: A DISAGGREGATED VIEW

Continuing our empirical investigation, we now report some further results on the trends in public sector performance disaggregated by type of institution. *National Accounts Statistics* provides a break-up of public sector into (a) administrative departments[6] (ADs), (b) departmental enterprises[7] (DEs) and (c) non-departmental enterprises[8] (NDEs). As is widely known, NDEs have accounted for an increasing share of public sector investment and output over the last four decades. During 1980-81 and 1988-89, GDP (or simply output for convenience) originating in the three constituents of public sector recorded growth rates of 7.6 per cent, 5.6 per cent and 9.4 per cent per annum, respectively. However, there appears to have been a deceleration in the growth rate of NDEs as the relative shares of the three components in the total public sector output (at current prices) have remained roughly constant in the 1980s[9] (Figure 8.1). In other words, this decade witnessed a relative decline in the growth rate of NDEs and an increase in that of ADs compared to the preceding two decades. As DEs form a relatively small part of public sector GDP (around 15 per cent in the 1980s) and since our focus is on the relative performance of ADs and NDEs, DEs are ignored in the rest of this exercise.

Figure 8.1

Public Sector GDP–Relative Shares by Type of Institution at Current Prices, 1960-61 to 1988-89

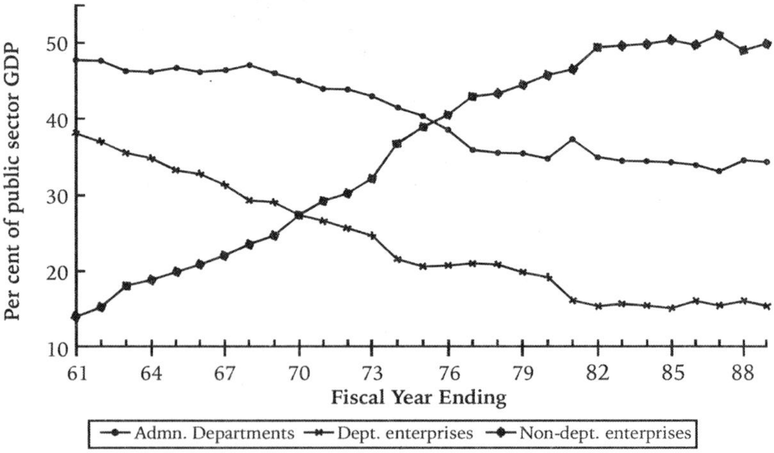

Soruce: CSO (1983), (1991).

Public Expenditure and Investment

Over the entire period since 1960-61, government final consumption expenditure[10] (GFCE) has grown at a faster rate than gross domestic capital formation (GDCF) in public sector as well as private final consumption expenditure (PFCE) (Figure 8.2). Moreover, a distinctly higher and uninterrupted growth rate in GFCE is discernible since 1974-75[11] (at 6 per cent per annum) which is faster than, though marginally, that of public sector GDCF (at 5.6 per cent per annum) as well as PFCE (4.6 per cent per annum). However, as a percentage of real GDP at market prices (GDPmp) (Figure 8.3) GFCE and GDCF in public sector show considerable yearly fluctuation, though increasing their share over time. While GFCE displays a steady and steep increase from around 10 per cent GDP in 1987-88, public sector GDCF has not registered any increase after reaching about 11 per cent of GDP in 1986-87.[12] Moreover, as can be seen in the figure, such a sharp increase in GFCE over a short period of four years did not occur during any period since 1960-61. More important, the rate of public sector GDCF after reaching its peak in 1982-83, declined in the rest of the 1980s, though with considerable yearly fluctuation.

Figure 8.2

Public Expenditure and Investment, 1960-61 to 1988-89

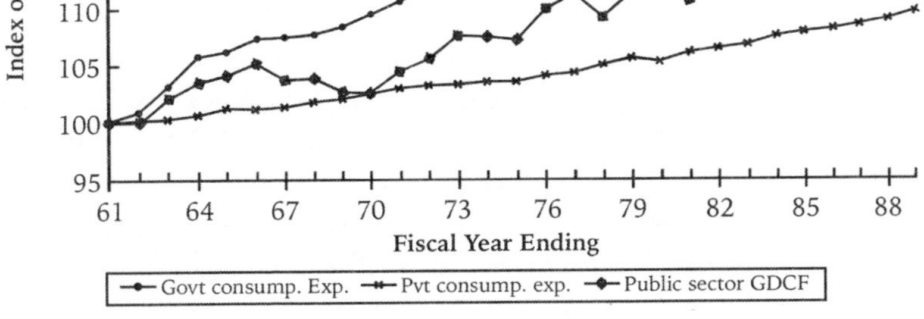

Soruce: CSO (1983), (1991).

Figure 8.3

Public Expenditure and Investment as per cent of GDPmp, 1960-61 to 1988-89

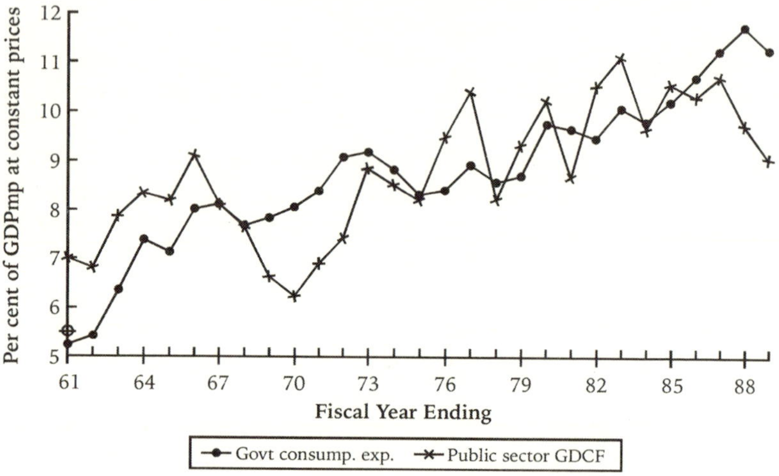

Soruce: CSO (1983), (1991).

Financing of Public Expenditure and Investment

How have the increasing public expenditure and investment been financed? Total taxes (direct plus indirect taxes minus subsidies) as a proportion of the sum of GFCE and public sector GDCF at current prices have increased since 1984-85, after remaining fairly constant in the preceding eight years. Contribution of gross saving[13] of public sector declined steadily since 1976-77 (Figure 8.4). Therefore, an increasingly large share of public sector expenditure and investment is being financed by borrowing.

However, it is interesting to discover from the same figure that while the share of public sector *as a whole* in financing of public expenditure and investment has declined, the contribution of NDEs has, in fact, steadily increased and especially so since 1980-81—although from an extremely low base. Correspondingly, the share of saving of ADs declined sharply since 1981-82, turning negative since 1984-85.

The perceptibly sharp increase in the gross saving of NDEs prompted us to look closely into the data base. An enquiry with the concerned official source revealed that, in fact there has been a minor change in the revised series of *National Accounts Statistics,* which apparently has not found a mention in the official *Sources and Methods* [CSO, 1989b]. Port trusts which were earlier included under DEs have been brought under NDEs in the revised series. However, a careful perusal of the unpublished data on gross saving of NDEs excluding the port trusts shows marginal, if any, difference to the foregoing trend. Therefore, one can infer with a reasonable degree of confidence that the observed improvements in the saving performance of NDEs is not on account of statistical discrepancy or changes in concepts and definitions.

Figure 8.4

Financing of Public Sector Expenditure and Investment, at Current Prices, 1960-61 to 1988-89

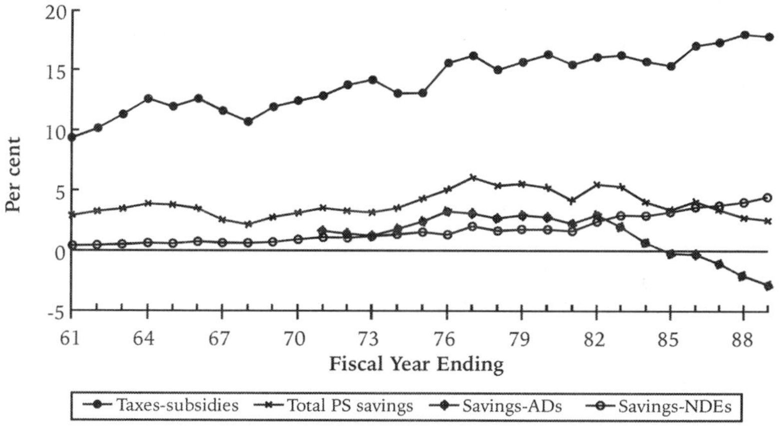

Soruce: CSO (1983), (1991).

Increase in the gross saving is also reflected (Figure 8.5) in the share of operating surplus[14]—defined as gross value added minus compensation to employees—as a proportion of gross value added of NDEs (at current prices). After steadily declining during the period of 1964-65 and 1973-74, the ratio begins to move up thereafter. Ignoring the observation for 1976-77—which could have been influenced by political emergency in the country—the rate of operating surplus has improved since the late 1970s, although with considerable yearly fluctuation. A perceptible decline in the ratio of compensation to employee as a proportion of gross value added of NDEs—a mirror image of the rate of operating surplus—is also discernible from the same figure; thus questioning the widely held perception that workers and employees in public sector enterprises have been appropriating an ever increasing share of their output.

Figure 8.5

Share of Wages and Surplus in Non-Departmental Enterprises at Current Prices, 1960-61 to 1988-89

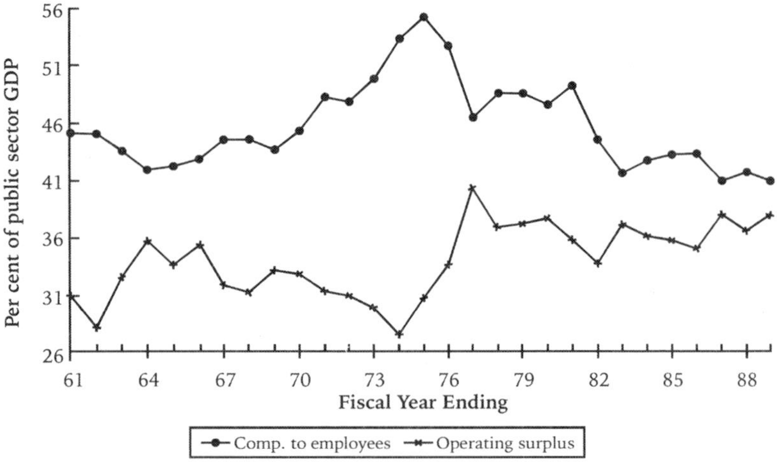

Soruce: CSO (1983), (1991).

Admittedly, a substantial proportion of the gross saving of the NDEs is constituted by non-departmental financial (NDF) enterprises[15] which merely reflects the returns to the public sector from its near monopoly over the financial resources in the organised sector of the economy. Figure 8.6 suggests that while the gross saving of NDF enterprises has steadily increased from around 1 per cent in 1966-67 to over 5 per cent of gross domestic saving in 1986-87, the relatively sharper increase, since 1980-81, in the rate of saving is unambiguously more pronounced with respect to non-departmental non-financial (NDNF) enterprises. Saving of NDNF enterprises increased not only as a proportion of gross domestic saving, but also

Figure 8.6

Saving of NDNF Enterprises Disaggregated into Financial and Non-Financial Enterprises, 1960-61 to 1988-89

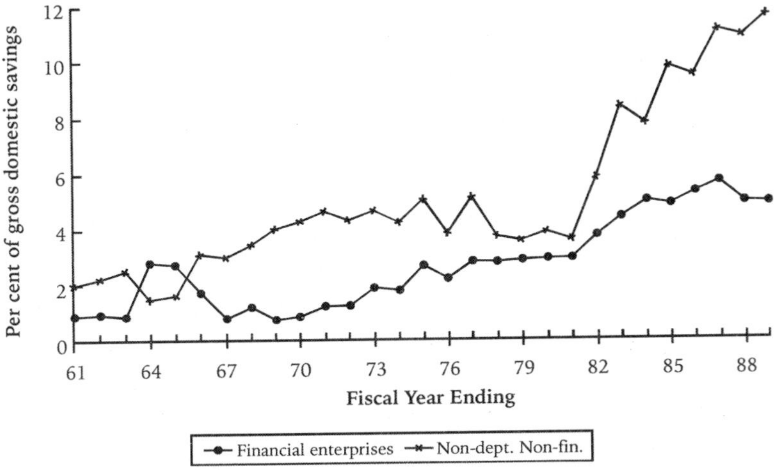

Soruce: CSO (1983), (1991).

Figure 8.7

Share of Internal Resources in Financing GDCF of NDNF Enterprises, 1960-61 to 1988-89

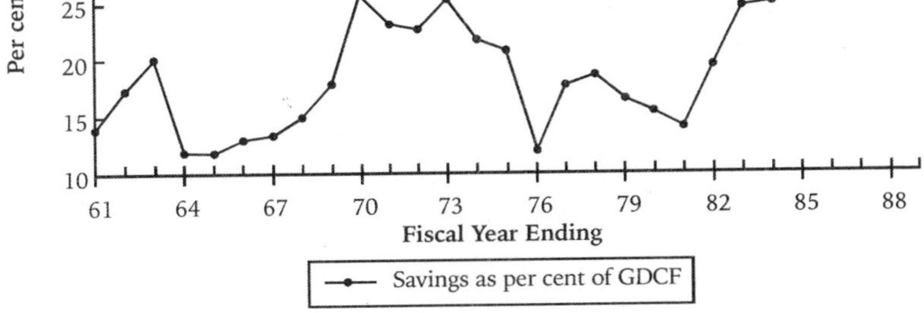

Soruce: CSO (1983), (1991).

as a proportion of gross domestic capital formation in that sector (Figure 8.7), thus suggesting that an increasing share of internal resources in financing public investment and a corresponding decline in the share of borrowed funds. The share, which declined during the period 1969-70 and 1980-81 from around 25 per cent of gross domestic capital formation to about 15 per cent, shows an unambiguous increase thereafter attaining a level of 43 per cent in 1988-89.

Quite conceivably, a major part of the saving in NDNF enterprises could be surplus from petroleum industry which is a result of a macroeconomic policy and may not reflect efficiency use of the industry. Since *National Accounts Statistics* does not provide further disaggregation of NDNF enterprises into specific industrial sectors, we use *Bureau of Public Enterprises'* annual surveys[16] to discern the performance of central government's PSEs, excluding the contribution of petroleum industry.

Figure 8.8 shows that profitability[17] of PSEs—defined as gross profit as a proportion of total capital employed—for the period 1973-74 to 1989-90. For PSEs as a whole, the ratio increased sharply from around 8 per cent in 1980-81 to about 13 per cent in the

Figure 8.8

Profitability of PSEs, 1973-74 to 1989-90

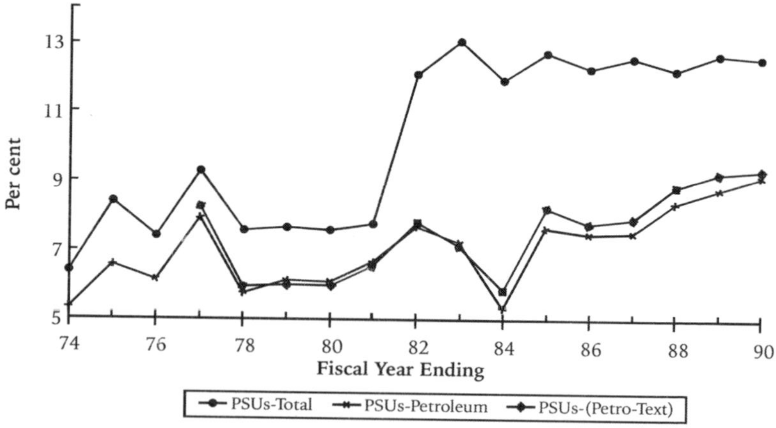

Soruce: Public Enterprise Surveys.

Profitability is defined as gross profits as per cent of total capital employed.

following year and remained roughly at that level, with perhaps a marginal decline towards the end of the decade. But the profitability of PSEs excluding petroleum industry—ignoring the sharp dip in 1983-84 for which we have no explanation—shows a steady increase since 1977-78, reaching a figure of about 9 per cent in 1989-90.[18] Moreover, the profitability rates achieved since 1984-85 are higher than any earlier year since 1973-74. If textile industry is also excluded—as a proxy for 'sick' private corporate firms which became a part of public sector consequent upon nationalisation—the profitability of PSEs increases marginally, though displaying an identical movement over time.

The foregoing evidence seems to suggest that the problem of declining saving rate of public sector as a whole is on account of the growing expenditure and subsidies of ADs relative to their revenue receipts and is not on account of a deteriorating performance of NDEs as is widely believed. In fact, the latter displayed a distinct improvement in surplus generation in the 1980s, albeit from a very low level. The finding seems to be valid even after adjusting for changes in the definition of NDEs, and netting out the contributions of NDF enterprises and petroleum industry.[19]

The observed improvement in surplus generation in NDNF enterprises could be on account of an improvement in efficiency and/or an increase in administered prices. Since implicit price deflator of public sector GDF in the 1980s has increased at a faster rate (9.4 per cent per annum) than that of implicit GDP deflator (7.9 per cent per annum) (Figure 8.9), at least a part of the favourable trend is, admittedly, due to price changes.[20] However, it needs to be appreciated that one of the widely accepted reasons for the poor performance of public sector enterprises has been their inability (or government's unwillingness to allow them to do so, for non-economic considerations) to adjust their prices adequately to compensate for increases in their costs of production. The above evidence suggests that in this respect the experience of the 1980s seems to be some what different from that of the preceding two decades.

No firm evidence is available on the productivity trends in public sector enterprises to assess if the improvement in surplus generation is, at least partly, attributable to an increase in efficiency.[21] However, limited evidence is available on the improvement in capacity utilisation and production in specific sectors such as electricity and coal [Nagaraj, 1990b].

Figure 8.9

Implicit Price Deflators—GDP and Public Sector GDP, 1960-61 to 1988-89

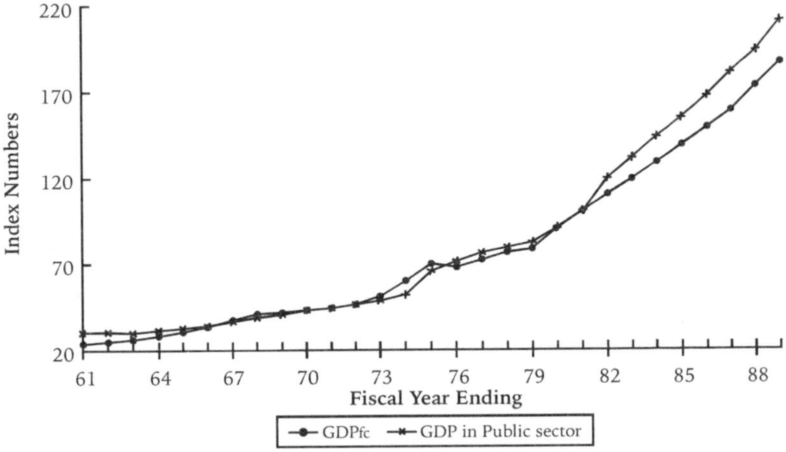

Soruce: CSO (1983), (1991).

Implications of Observed Trends

If the foregoing trends in gross saving of NDNF enterprises have any validity, then they seem to have a significant implication for further analysis and policy. The evidence begs the question as to the reasons for the observed improvement. In other words, what changes, in the 1980s, in the policies at the macroeconomic and sectoral levels on the one hand and management practices at the firm level on the other, could have brought about the favourable trend?[22] Notwithstanding the persistence of the widely documented microeconomic inefficiencies and the *need for substantial reform* to secure a better resource use, the observed improvement in gross saving in the 1980s—admittedly from a very low base—seems to suggest the possibility of securing a better financial return from public sector enterprises within the framework of public ownership and control. This empirical result could be of considerable value in the present context of policy reform with an overwhelming emphasis on change in ownership as a—predominant, if not the sole—means of improving the public sector performance. Moreover, since there is no theoretically valid relationship between ownership and performance[23] [Yarrow, 1986], a close examination of the reasons for the observed improvement in gross saving in the eighties—reversing the deteriorating performance of over a decade—could possibly provide a more meaningful basis for public sector policy reform.

CONCLUSION

Objective of this exploratory exercise is to document the long-term trends in some aspects of public sector performance and in particular, to discern plausible changes in them in the 1980s using *National Accounts Statistics* and disaggregated by type of institution. More specifically, the note attempts to examine in some detail the resource mobilisation effort of public sector enterprises—a widely accepted shortcoming.

While there is little evidence of a deceleration in the growth rate of public sector output in the 1980s, growth rate of ADs appears to have increased (relative to the previous two decades) and that of NDEs has declined. During the entire period since 1960-61, in absolute terms, public consumption (PFCE) has grown at a faster rate than public investment (public sector GDCF), especially since 1974-75. The 1980s witnessed a favourable turn not only in the rate and pattern of public sector capital formation, but more significantly, in gross saving by NDEs as well, admittedly from a very low base. This improvement has come about after a period of a deteriorating record since around the late 1960s to the mid-to-the-late 1970s. The declining contribution of public sector as a whole in gross domestic saving is found to be on account of the deteriorating saving record of ADs (ignoring the relatively small share of DEs) and is *not* on account of NDEs. Moreover, saving of NDEs has improved even after adjusting for change in definition of NDEs and excluding the contribution of the financial sector and the petroleum industry. Although a part of the improvement is evidently on account of relatively faster rise in prices of public sector output, we do not have adequate information to assess the contribution, if any, of productivity increase in securing the same.

A careful examination of the recent experience could be of considerable value for designing a package of reform measures to reinforce the favourable trend of the 1980s. Such an attempt appears to be all the more urgent and significant in the present context of policy reform with an overwhelming emphasis on change in ownership, since neither in theory nor in practice (as evident from the developing countries) is the change in ownership and control correlated with performance.

Notes

1. Based on his empirical analysis, Rubin (1986) arrived at the following conclusion: "The ultimate political fall out, of failing to mobilise the resources, means, if not stagnation, at least a continuation of a slow growth path that gives little hope of satisfying the aspirations of either the consumption-oriented middle classes or subsistence-oriented masses" (p 1950).
2. To quote Raj (1985): "...while there has been much verbal support for public enterprises on conventional as well on radical grounds, perhaps the most important reason why they have not been able to grow, in the manner once hoped and expected, was simply that there has not emerged any political force in the country generally interested in making such enterprises yield adequate profits and savings on their own."
3. Growth rates reported in this paper are all based on log-linear trend analysis and are at constant (1980-81) prices, unless otherwise stated.
4. As GFCF in public sector for the period prior to 1980-81 are not available at constant prices, we have estimated them by deflating the current price series by implicit price deflator for total GFCF series at 1980-81 prices.
5. This is true not only for the total GFCF, but also for GFCF in public sector.
6. Administrative departments "...comprise government departments, offices and other bodies of the central, state/union territories and local authorities, whose function is to organise for the community, but not normally sell those services which cannot be otherwise conveniently and economically provided" [CSO, 1989b, p 291].
7. "Departmental enterprises ... are unincorporated enterprises owned, controlled and run directly by public authorities. These enterprises normally do not hold or manage financial assets and liabilities apart from their working balances and business accounts payable and receivables. ... The criteria followed to distinguish enterprise activity from administrative activity are: (i) use of commercial accounting methods to determine profit and loss and (ii) control of productive capital in the form of equipment such as machines, plant and stocks" [CSO, 1989b, p 292].
8. "Non-departmental enterprises comprise of (i) government companies (in which not less than 51 per cent of the PUC is held by the central government or state government or partly by central government and partly by one or more state governments) and subsidiaries of government companies; and (ii) statutory corporations set up under special parliament or state legislatures" [CSO, 1989b: p 292].
9. As the public sector GDP series by type of institution for 1960-61 to 1979-80 are not available at constant prices, we could only present the trends in terms of their relative shares.
10. It is comprised "... the consumption expenditure of the government and it consists of purchase of non-durable goods and services by the government. By convention, expenditure on durable goods which are used for defence are also treated as part of consumption expenditure of the government" [CSO, 1989b: p27].

11. It is widely believed that public administration and defence (PAD) accounts for an increasing share of public final consumption expenditure. However, Chart A shows that PAD as a proposition of GFCE, after reaching a peak (about 46 per cent in 1974-75), has come down sharply during the eighties.

Chart A

Public Expenditure as Per Cent of Public Final Consumption Expenditure, 1960-61 to 1988-89

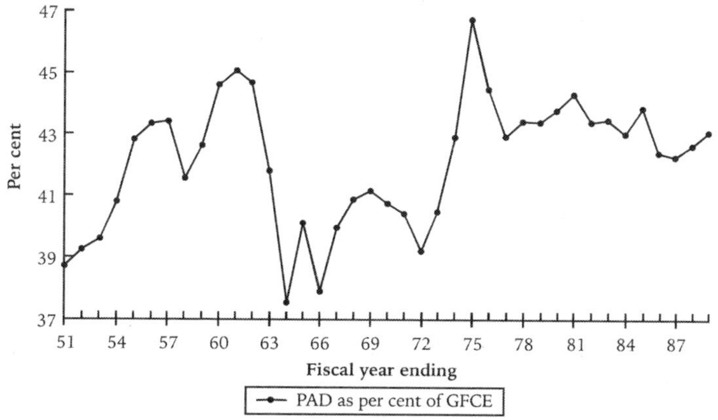

Soruce: CSO (1989a), (1991).

12. This is not inconsistent with our earlier finding [Nagaraj, 1990b] of an increasing share of public sector in total GDCF.

13. Ideally, one should have presented trends in gross as well as net saving in public sector. However, due to major changes in the methodology of computing consumption of fixed capital in the revised series, one does not have a comparable estimates of the latter since 1960-61.

14. An important shortcoming of the data on NDEs needs to be stated at the outset. As mentioned in *National Accounts Statistics: Sources and Methods* [CSO, 1989b], due to delay in obtaining annual accounts of all the enterprises, estimates are prepared by 'blowing up' the data obtained from the responding enterprises. We are not in position to ascertain the quality of the estimates since the size and the representativeness of the sample used are not known.

15. Non-departmental financial enterprises comprise of: "... (i) nationalised banks and the banking department of RBI, (ii) financial corporations, and (iii) LIC, GIC and its subsidiaries and Employees State Insurance Corporation (ESIC)" [CSO, 1989b: p 293].

16. Bureau of Public Enterprises (BPE), Government of India, presents to the parliament every year a detailed report of the functioning of all central government's enterprises, excluding the departmentally-run enterprises and banking institutions. Enterprises included in the BPE surveys would form a significant subset of NDNF enterprises, notable exceptions being the statutory corporations like the electricity boards and road transport corporations, and the large number of enterprises owned and operated by state governments/union territories.

17. One is conscious that profitability is strictly not comparable to the various measures used to describe the foregoing trends. However, it would be analytically correct to argue that an increase in profitability rate is consistent with an increase in the rate of surplus generation.

18. Ideally, one should be able to compare the profitability of public and private corporate sector to judge their relative financial performance. However, such an attempt has a number of limitations. For instance, it is not easy to arrive at strictly comparable sets of firms and industries. Second, public and private corporate sectors do not operate under similar conditions of market and protection from external trade. Thirdly, a sizeable proportion of capital employed at any time in public sector is 'work in progress,' which enhances its capital costs. Fourthly, there appears to be considerable variation in accounting practices not only between public and private corporate sectors, but within the public sector.

19. It is arguable that the improvement in the saving rate of NDNF enterprises could have been on account of a shift of implicit subsidies from the enterprises to ADs with a view to relieve the former of their 'social responsibility.' There is, however, no evidence of such a trend. Moreover, as Mundle and Rao (1991) have shown, NDEs received only about 16 per cent of government's estimated implicit subsidies in 1987-88.

20. The results do not change even if prices of petroleum products are excluded from both the implicit price deflators.

21. BPE annual surveys provide frequency distribution of number of enterprises according to their capacity utilisation (in per cent). Since public sector enterprises vary enormously in size, any trend based merely on number of firms, without any information on their weightage in value added or capital employed, could be misleading.

22. It may not be incorrect to argue that the previous decade witnessed a number of attempts to grapple with the problem of public sector reform. Several committees were instituted to suggest organisational changes, for instance, the Expert Committee on Public Sector Management and Performance (Chairman: Md. Fazal, 1982), Committee to Review Policy for Public Enterprises (Chairman: Arjun Sengupta, 1984) and Economic Administrative Reforms Committee on Government and Public Enterprise (Chairman: L.K Jha, 1985).

    We do not have any systematic documentation of various measures initiated to reform public sector management and their possible effects on the performance. For instance, some holding companies have been formed and more recently, the Memorandum of Understanding (MoU) has been introduced to bring about a greater clarity of roles and responsibilities between government and the enterprises. It is quite conceivable that some of these measures could have yielded positive results, though it remains a matter for closer examination.

23. The growing evidence from developing countries seems to increasingly question the empirical validity of the impact of privatisation on enhancing efficiency. For instance, Yotopoulos (1989) for Chile, and Naqvi and Kemal (1991) for Pakistan. We quote from the latter study's emphatic conclusion to highlight their empirical findings: "The basic message that comes out clearly from the preceding analysis is that changing the locus of ownership of industries is by itself neither necessary nor sufficient condition for an efficient operation of specific industrial enterprises" [Naqvi and Kemal, 1991: p 131].

References

Bardhan, Pranab (1984). *Political Economy of Development in India,* Oxford University Press, Delhi.

Central Statistical Organisation (1983). *Transactions of Public Sector, 1960-61 to 1979-80,* Government of India, New Delhi.

————. (1989a). *National Accounts Statistics,* New Series, 1950-51 to 1979-80, Government of India, New Delhi.

————. (1989b). *National Accounts Statistics: Sources and Methods,* Government of India, New Delhi.

————. (1991). *National Accounts Statistics,* 1991, Government of India, New Delhi.

Jalan, Bimal (1991). *India's Economic Crisis: A Way Out,* Oxford University Press, Delhi.

Mundle, Sudipto and Govind Rao G. (1991). "Volume and Composition of Government Subsidies in India, 1987-88," *Economic and Political Weekly,* May 4.

Nagaraj, R. (1990a). "Growth Rate of India's Gross Domestic Product, 1950-51 to 1987-88: An Examination of Alternative Hypotheses," *Economic and Political Weekly,* June 30.

————. (1990b). "Industrial Growth; Further Evidence and Towards an Exploration and Issues," *Economic and Political Weekly,* October.

————. (1991a). "Increase in India's Growth Rate," *Economic and Political Weekly,* April 13.

————. (1991b). "Excess Growth of Tertiary Sector? A Reply," *Economic and Political Weekly,* September 14.

Naqvi, Syed Nawab Haider and A.R. Kemal (1991). "The Privatisation of Public Industrial Enterprises in Pakistan," *Pakistan Development Review,* Vol. 30, No. 2.

Patnaik, P. and S.K. Rao (1977). " Towards a Explanation of Crisis in a Mixed Underdeveloped Economy," *Economic and Political Weekly* Vol. 12, Nos. 6-8, February, Annual Number.

Raj, K.N. (1973). "The Politics and Economics of 'Intermediate Regimes'," *Economic and Political Weekly,* July 7.

————. (1985). "New Economic Policy," *V.T. Krishnamachari Memorial Lecture,* Institute of Economic Growth, Delhi.

Rubin, Barnett R. (1986). "Financing Gross Capital Formation in Indian Public Sector: A Quantitative Model," *Economic and Political Weekly,* November 18.

Srinivasan, T.N. and N.S.S. Narayana (1977). "Economic Performance since the Third Plan and its Implications for Policy," *Economic and Political Weekly,* February, Annual Number.

Vaidyanathan, A. (1991). "Emerging Issues in Policy Planning," *The Economic Times,* March 11, 1991.

Yarrow, George (1986). "Privatisation in Theory and Practice," *Economic Policy,* Vol. 1, No. 2

Yotopoulos, Pan A. (1989). "The (Rip) Tide of Privatisation: Lessons from Chile," *World Development,* Vol. 17, No. 5.

Economic and Political Weekly, Vol. 26, No. 50, December 14, 1991.

9

Macroeconomic Impact of Public Sector Enterprises

Some Further Evidence

Public sector enterprises (PSEs) have been getting a bad press these days. They are widely perceived as an important reason for the increasing fiscal imbalance in recent years and for the widespread, and allegedly growing, inefficiencies in the non-farm sectors of the economy. A gradual reduction in the role of the public sector, especially in the sphere of production, is, therefore, widely perceived to be an integral element in the policy reform to restore sustainable—if lower, but consistent with the economy's real resources—economic growth.

In the context of the recent stabilisation efforts and structural adjustment in India, the Statement of Industrial Policy (July 24, 1991) stated: "Public enterprises have shown a very low rate of return on capital invested. This has inhibited their ability to regenerate themselves in terms of new investment as well as in technology. The result is that *many of the public enterprises have become a burden rather than being an asset to the Government*" (emphasis added).

The 'Programme for Structural Reform' submitted to the International Monetary Fund (IMF) on November 11, 1991 to secure its financial assistance for the ongoing reform process stated:

> India's severely constrained budgetary circumstances create both the need and opportunity for rationalising the scope of public sector activity, and *for placing greater reliance on the private sector for resource mobilisation and investment*. Public enterprises have absorbed large amounts of budgetary support for their expansion or operations, but in many cases they have failed to generate adequate returns on the investment of public money and *contributed significantly to the public sector saving gap and fiscal*

deficit (Reproduced in *Reserve Bank of India Bulletin*, April 1992, p 789, emphasis added).

Such views seem to be shared by many policy advisors as well. In his introduction to a recently published set of essays on the Indian economy, Bimal Jalan (1992) opined that "the public sector has *become a big drain on the exchequer*" (emphasis added).

Considering the significance of these pronouncements for the policy reforms in India, the underlying premises of the aforementioned views warrant a close empirical scrutiny. A preliminary attempt has been made in Nagaraj (1991) at discerning the long-term trends in the performance of PSEs in general and in their resource mobilisation in the 1980s in particular, mainly using *National Accounts Statistics* and *Transactions of Public Sector* [CSO, 1983] as together they provide a comprehensive and consistent time series since 1960-61, disaggregated by type of institution. The institutional categories used are: administrative departments (ADs), departmental enterprises (DEs) and non-departmental enterprises (NDEs); NDEs are further subdivided into non-departmental financial enterprises (NDFEs) and non-departmental non-financial enterprises (NDNFEs).[1] Our study concerned itself with NDNFEs, as they include all the non-financial PSEs in the economy. Although DEs should be strictly included to fully capture the production activities of the government, we have ignored them as they form a relatively small and declining proportion of the total public sector. Moreover, aggregating them with NDNFEs posed some operational difficulties. NDNFEs, nevertheless, form a substantially comprehensive category as they include not only the PSEs owned and managed by the central government, but also those of other (administrative) levels of the Indian union which are quantitatively significant, such as the state electricity boards and road transport corporations. Our study showed, among other things that:

(1) While the share of the public sector in financing the sector's expenditure and investment declined since the mid-1970s (and there was hence an increasingly greater recourse to debt), the contribution of NDEs to public saving has steadily increased. The problem of growing fiscal imbalance, therefore, appears to be on account of the growing expenditure and subsidies of the ADs and not on account of the publicly owned enterprises, ignoring the DEs.

(2) Reversing the trend of about a decade ending in the late 1970s, operating surplus as a proportion of value added in NDEs and the share of NDNFEs in gross domestic saving and their internal resource as a proportion of their gross domestic capital formation have increased steadily in the 1980s, although from a very low level.

(3) The observed improvements in resource generation and profitability appear to hold even after excluding the contributions of NDFEs and the petroleum sector.

Admittedly, our earlier exercise has some limitations. It could not reject the hypothesis that the growing fiscal imbalance could be due to the increasing deficit of the public enterprise sector,[2] or trace its financial burden on the budget. Moreover, the study did not isolate the contributions of (i) increases in administered prices, and (ii) improvements, if any, in resource utilisation to the observed upturn in NDNFEs' resource mobilisation in the 1980s.

Continuing our enquiry, this note attepts to address the following questions, using more or less the same data sources:

(1) Has the deficit of the public enterprise sector increased over the years? If yes, does it account solely or predominantly for the growing gross fiscal deficit?

(2) Has the financial burden of the NDNFEs on the budget increased over the years?

(3) Is the internal resource generation of NDNFEs lower than that of the private corporate sector in recent years? Has the trend for the former declined while that of the latter increased?

(4) Is the observed improvement in resource generation in the 1980s entirely on account of increases in administered prices?

I

Although concern over the PSEs' alleged poor financial performance has been growing, not many serious efforts seem to have been made to quantify and assess the PSEs' contribution to the deteriorating macroeconomic and fiscal imbalances. The International Monetary Fund's attempt [Short, 1984] to grapple with the problem is, to our knowledge, a major effort to fill the analytical and empirical gap. In this study, Short estimated the broad dimensions of the size, role and impact of PSEs for selected years to arrive at a significant conclusion that their growing deficit forms an important reason for the stabilisation problems of a large number of countries.[3] While the generalisation, based on estimates for selected years could be questioned for lack of required empirical rigour, Short's methodology appears useful for a more careful enquiry. Therefore, using some of his measures, this study traces the macroeconomic impact of PSEs in India. Besides providing evidence on the Indian experience, this attempt could also enable assessment of the validity of Short's generalisation with time-series data, albeit limited to one country.

Overall Deficits of PSEs: These are defined as "the difference between (1) current plus capital expenditure; and (2) revenue plus receipts of current transfers and of non-governmental capital transfers. Government capital transfers are also conventionally included in receipts in defining the overall deficit" [Short, 1984; 144].[4] Figure 9.1 shows the trends in (i) the combined gross fiscal deficit of central and state governments in India, and (ii) the overall deficit of the public enterprise sector as a proportion of the gross domestic product at current market prices for the period 1960-61 to 1989-90.[5] The figure suggests, ignoring the observation for 1973-74, a secular deterioration in the fiscal deficit, with some fluctuation from (-)4.3 per cent in 1969-70 to over (-)10 per cent in the latter half of the 1980s. Although the overall deficit of PSEs has also deteriorated from (-)1.4 per cent in 1972-73 to (-)3.7 per cent in 1986-87, the trend in it is significantly less sharp than that of the fiscal deficit, as reflected in the sharply widening gap between the two curves. Moreover, a distinct reduction in the PSEs' overall deficit is discernible since 1987-88, taking its level back to that during the early 1970s. The visibly divergent trends in the two series would seem to indicate that the growing fiscal deficit is perhaps not attributable to the overall deficit of the public enterprise sector.[6]

Admittedly, the foregoing finding does not take into account revenue from the oil account. To the extent, it represents a macroeconomic measure of taxation, PSEs' deficits are understated. However, as shown in our earlier exercise [Nagaraj, 1991], profitability of PSEs, even excluding the oil sector, showed a distinct improvement in the 1980s. Hence, there is a reasonable basis to argue that the overall deficit of the public enterprise sector is not a reason for the observed deterioration of the fiscal deficit of the economy. This seems to be consistent with our earlier finding [Nagaraj, 1991] that the deteriorating fiscal deficit is mainly on account of ADs' declining saving which has turned negative since the mid-1980s, rather than on account of the alleged decline in surplus generation of the enterprise sector.

Figure 9.1

Public Enterprise Sector Deficit and Fiscal Deficit as per cent of GDPmp

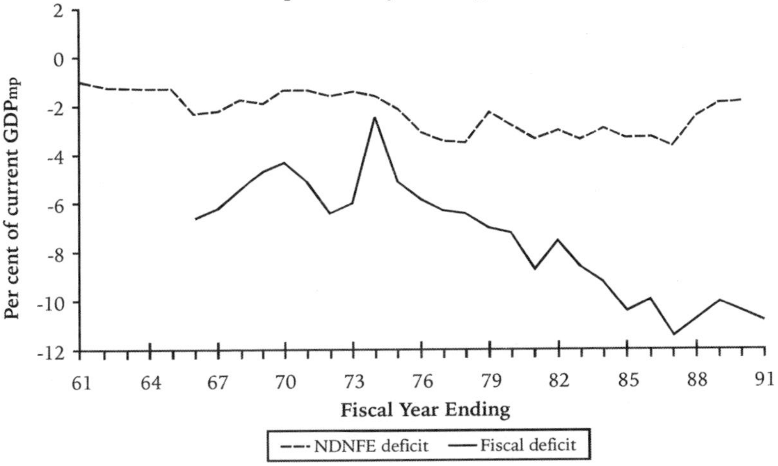

Sources: CSO (1983), NAS (various issues), Public Finance (various issues).

'Budgetary Burden' of PSEs: Another indicator to assess PSEs' macroeconomic impact is their 'budgetary burden', as defined by Short to be the government's contribution of equity capital and loans, net of dividend and interest payment.[7] As it is not possible to net out PSEs' dividend payment and repayment of loans due to inadequate disaggregation, our estimates overstate their 'burden' on the budget to that extent. However, the tax-free bonds floated by some PSEs since 1986-87 have increased the burden to the extent of the tax revenue foregone. But, since the tax revenue foregone cannot be estimated, we have provided a variant of the budgetary burden in

which the tax-free bonds are equated with government loans, although, such an adjustment further overstates the budgetary burden.

Figure 9.2 [(i) and (ii)] traces PSEs' budgetary burden measured as equity capital, loans and net capital transfers to NDNFEs as a proportion of (i) GDP at current market prices, and (ii) gross expenditure[8] of NDNFEs, for the period 1960-61 to 1989-90. Budgetary burden as a proportion of GDP increased from 1.4 per cent in 1972-73 to 3.5 per cent in 1977-78 and fluctuated around that level for about a decade. However, a sharp fall in it is discernible since 1986-87 after reaching 3.7 per cent, bringing it back to the level attained in the early 1970s. The budgetary burden as a proportion of the gross expenditure of NDNFEs has steadily declined from about 34 per cent in 1961-62 to less than 7 per cent in 1989-90. The inclusion of tax-free bonds as loans from the government in both the measures of budgetary burden, although it exaggerates the PSEs' budgetary dependence, does not affect the above trend materially. The estimates would have been further lower if PSEs' dividend payments and repayments of loans were taken into account. The evidence suggests,

Figure 9.2 (i)

Budgetary Burden of PSEs as per cent of GDPmp

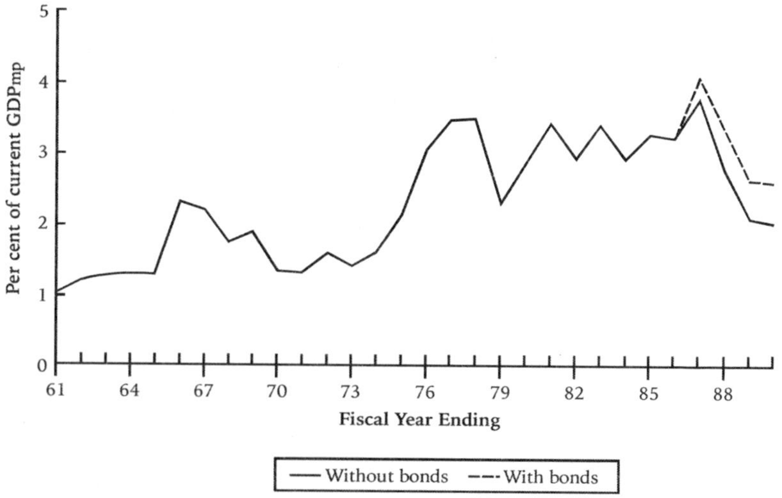

Sources: CSO (1983), NAS (various issues).

contrary to the widely held opinion, a sharp decline in budgetary support for the PSEs' expenditure and hence, their burden on the government. Even as a proportion of GDP, a sharp fall in the burden in the latter half of the 1980s is undeniable.

Figure 9.2(ii)

Budgetary Burden on PSEs as per cent of PSEs Gross Expenditure

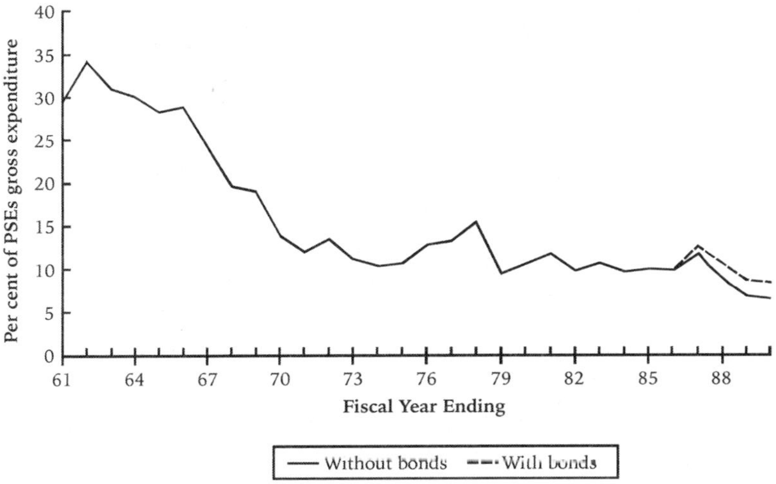

Sources: CSO (1983), NAS (various issues).

Self-Financing Ratio: We have shown earlier [Nagaraj, 1991] that this ratio—defined as gross saving of NDNFEs as a proportion of their gross capital formation at current prices—has improved distinctly in the 1980s, thus reducing NDNFEs' dependence on the government for financing their growth. Figure 9.3 compares self-financing ratios for NDNFEs and private corporate sector[9] for the period 1960-61 to 1988-89. While the ratio for the public enterprise sector shows generally an upward trend, especially in the 1980s, almost the obverse seems discernible for the private corporate sector, with the two ratios converging to more or less similar levels of around 40 per cent towards the end of the decade.[10] This finding seems to question the basis for the commitment given to the IMF for placing greater reliance on the private corporate sector for mobilising resources for industrial growth, as evident from the official memorandum quoted earlier.[11]

Figure 9.3

Share of Internal Resources in Public and Private Corporate Sectors

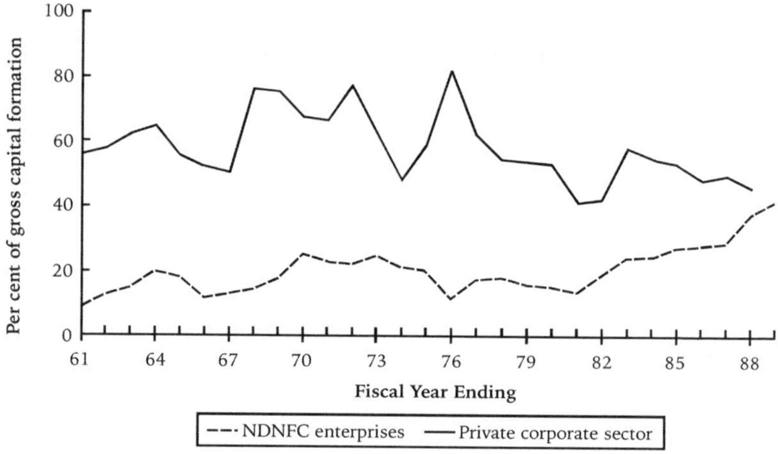

Sources: CSO (1983), NAS (various issues), RBI Bulletin (various issues).

Trends in Capacity Utilisation in PSEs: Highlighting the significant improvement in surplus generation in the 1980s, our earlier study [Nagaraj, 1991] admitted its inability, due to the limitations of the data, to ascertain if any part of it was attributable to improvement in resource use. As is widely known, capital or total factor productivity measurements have numerous conceptual, methodological and empirical problems [Griliches, 1987]. As a measure of operational performance, we have computed a weighted average index of capacity utilisation of 14 central public sector enterprises, accounting for about 55 per cent of this subset of PSEs' capital employed and value added in 1990-91. Two variants of the index are computed by taking as weights their shares in (i) capital employed, and (ii) in value added. The results suggest a statistically significant trend growth rate of over 1 per cent per annum in capacity utilisation over the period 1979-80 and 1990-91 (Figures 9.4 and 9.5).[12] Hence, the hypothesis that the observed improvement in resource generation in the 1980s is entirely

Figure 9.4

Index of Capacity Utilisation
(Weighted by Capital Employed)

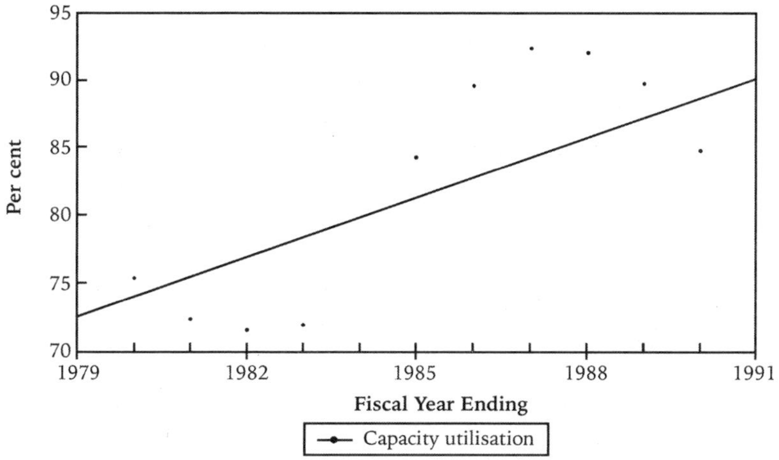

Source: Public Enterprise Surveys.

Figure 9.5

Index of Capacity Utilisation
(Weighted by Value Added)

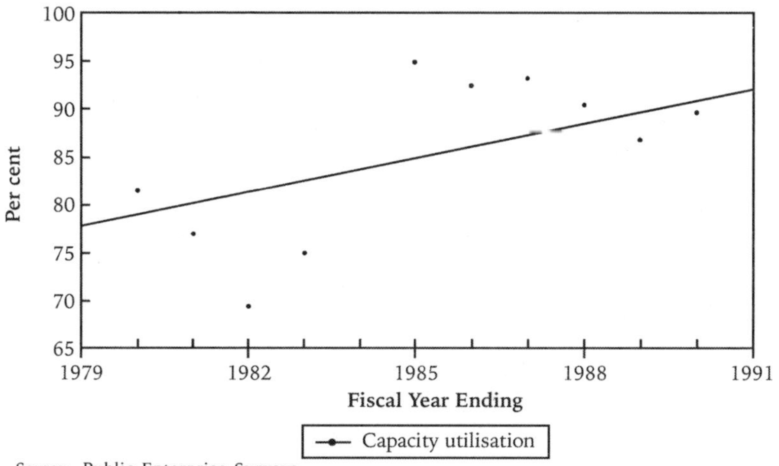

Source: Public Enterprise Surveys.

on account of increases in administered prices can be rejected. Better operational performance has also contributed to the increase in resource generation.

II

The foregoing evidence seem to be significant in many respects. Highlighting the merits of Time Series analysis, our findings question Short's generalisation, based on a cross-country comparison for selected years, of deteriorating PSEs' deficits as a principal cause of the stabilisation problems in a number of developing countries.

The main findings of this study, in terms of the questions posed at the begining, can be summarised as follows: Although the overall deficit of PSEs has increased marginally over two decades, the increase seems insignificant compared to the sharp deterioration in the gross fiscal deficit. The widening gap between the two suggests that the deterioration in gross fiscal deficit is not on account for the overall deficit of the enterprise sector. The budgetary burden of the PSEs measured as a proportion of (a) GDP at current market prices shows a definite decline since the mid-1980s, and (b) PSEs' current and capital expenditure shows a secular decline from about 34 per cent in 1961-62 to 7 per cent in 1989-90. While the share of internal resource generation in financing investment in PSEs has increased in the 1980s, the same for the private corporate sector has declined, both converging to around 40 per cent by the end of the 1980s. A statistically significant improvement in capacity utilisation, during 1978-79 and 1990-91, is discernible which would partly account for the observed improvement in resource mobilisation of PSEs, besides the increases in administered prices.

These results seem seriously to question the underlying premises of the current policy reforms with their overwhelming emphasis on diluting public ownership. Moreover, such a stance cannot be justified on analytical considerations either, since *a priori* economic theory does not postulate a positive association between nature of ownership and performance.[13]

Notes

1. For the definitions of these categories see CSO (1989) and Nagaraj (1990).
2. In this study terms PSEs, NDNFEs, public enterprise sector and publicly-owned enterprises are used synonymously.
3. To quote Short (1984: 180-81): "It is clear that the overall deficits of public enterprises are extremely large in many countries. As a result, public enterprises make sizeable demands on governments, bank credit and foreign borrowing. The precise effects of these demands will vary from country to country depending on economic circumstances. However, their large size strongly suggests that, in many developing countries, public enterprises have been a major cause of stabilisation problems and, as a result, have contributed significantly to inflation and balance of payments difficulties... . As a consequence, measures to reduce the overall deficits of public enterprises may often be particularly appropriate for countries facing stabilisation problems."
4. This measure is arrived at, using the NAS, in the following manner: Overall deficit = (total revenue – total expenditure)/GDPmp at current prices. Total revenue is gross output – (net current transfers + net property income + all loans excluding those from government + net capital transfer); and total expenditure is intermediate consumption + compensation to employees + (indirect taxes – subsidies) + direct taxes + gross investment + net acquisition of financial assets.
5. Gross fiscal deficit is defined as excess of total government expenditure over revenue receipts and grants as a proportion of GDP at current market prices. As a relatively comprehensive measure we have used consolidated accounts of the centre and the states and union territories rather than that of merely the central government, as is widely done. For justification, see Blejeer and Cheasty (1991).
6. The documentation of the overall deficit of PSEs should not be construed as its justification, even if it has not increased significantly over the long period. Such a justification, if any, should be based on the impact of the deficit on the economy's efficiency of resource use and social well-being.
7. However, as Short admits, this is incomplete since it ignores the tax revenue collected from PSEs on the one hand and subsidised credit provided by government financial institutions and purchase preference given to PSEs. As these are difficult to quantify, Short restricts his estimate to the measurable aspects of the budgetary burden.
8. Gross expenditure is defined as sum of intermediate consumption, compensation to employees and gross investments of NDNFEs.
9. The internal resources of private corporate sector are defined as retained earning plus depreciation.
10. This result, based on a long time series analysis, questions the World Bank's (1988) findings of a higher internal resource generation by the private corporate sector based on the average for the first five-year period of the 1980s. To quote the report: "The saving performance of CPEs, which financed only 26 per cent of their investments from internal resources during 1980-85, has been substantially lower than that of the private corporate sector, where internal resources financed 55 per cent of investments on the average during the same period" [World Bank, 1988: 2].
11. Perhaps the declining self-financing ratio in the private corporate sector is related to the increasing share of dividends as a proportion of profit before tax, which has gone up from 19.4 per cent in 1980-81 to 27.5 per cent in 1987-88 [RBI, 1990]. This observation is tentative, subject to closer scrutiny.
12. The estimated trend equations are as follows:

$$\text{Log } Y_1 = 1.89 + 0.007t \quad R^2 = 0.41,\ N = 13$$
$$(0.0025) \quad t = 2.77$$

$$\text{Log } Y_2 = 1.88 + 0.006t \quad R^2 = 0.34,\ N = 13$$
$$(0.0026) \quad t = 2.38.$$

where Y_1 is the weighted average capacity utilisation of 14 central government PSEs accounting for 55 per cent of capital employed; and Y_2 is the same with weights being value added. The estimated coefficients of 't' in both the equations are statistically significant at 95 per cent confidence level.

13. A growing analytical literature questions the widely posited positive relationship between ownership and performance. See Vickers and Yarrow (1991) and Estrin and Perotin (1991). Arguing against premature obituaries of market socialism, Bardhan and Roemer (1992: 101-2) say: "Our claim is that competitive markets are necessary to achieve an efficient and vigorous economy, but that full-scale private ownership is not necessary for the successful operation of competition and markets. Contrary to popular impression, this claim has not yet been disproved by either history or economic theory." Even in management literature one does not find any analytical support for the alleged superior efficiency of private ownership. Reviewing 11 studies on privatisation, Goodman and Loveman (1991: 38) conclude: "Ownership of a good or service is far less important than the dynamics of the market or institutions that produce it... . Accountability and consonance with the public's interest should be the guiding lights. They will be found where competition and organisational mechanism ensure that managers do what, we, the owners, want them to do."

References

Bardhan, Pranab and John E. Roemer (1992). "Market Socialism: A Case for Rejuvenation," *Journal of Economic Perspectives,* Vol. 6, No. 3, Summer.

Blejer, Mario I. and Adrienne Cheasty (1991). "The Measurement of Fiscal Deficits: Analytical and Methodological Issues," *Journal of Economic Literature,* Vol. 29, December.

Central Statistical Organisation (1983). *Transactions of Public Sector, 1960-61 – 1979-80,* Government of India.

————. (1989). *National Accounts Statistics: Sources and Methods,* Government of India.

Estrin, Saul and Virginie Perotin (1991). "Does Ownership Always Matter?," *International Journal of Industrial Organisation,* Vol. 9.

Goodman, John and Gary W. Love (1991). "Does Privatisation Serve the Public Interest," *Harvard Business Review,* November-December.

Griliches, Zvi (1987). "Productivity: Measurement Problems" in *The New Palgrave: A Dictionary of Economics,* Vol. 3, Macmillan.

Jalan, Bimal (1992). *The Indian Economy: Problems and Prospects,* Viking, Delhi.

Nagaraj, R. (1991). "Public Sector Performance in the Eighties," *Economic and Political Weekly,* December 14.

Reserve Bank of India (1990). *Selected Financial and Other Ratios in Public Limited Companies, 1980-81 to 1987-88: All-India,* Vol. 1.

Short, R.P. (1984). "The Role of Public Enterprises: An International Comparisons" in Robert H. Floyd, Clive S. Gray and R.P. Short (eds): *Public Enterprise in Mixed Economies: Some Macroeconomic Aspects,* International Monetary Fund, Washington DC.

Vickers, John and George Yarrow (1991). "Economic Perspectives on Privatisation," *Journal of Economic Perspectives,* Vol. 5, No. 2, Spring.

World Bank (1988). *India: Review of Public Enterprises – Propositions for Greater Efficiency in the Central Government Public Enterprises,* Volume II – Main Text, Report No. 7294-IN, October 12.

Economic and Political Weekly, Vol. 28, No. 3-4, January 16-23, 1993.

10

Employment and Wages in Manufacturing Industries

Trends, Hypothesis and Evidence

The decline in the growth of employment in the manufacturing sector in the 1980s and in particular the fall in the number of workers in registered manufacturing are by now accepted facts. While the growth rates in real net value added and real earnings per worker (earnings, hereafter) in registered manufacturing improved, the absolute number of workers employed declined (Figure 10.1). These tendencies are discernible in a number of major industry groups (Table 10.1).[1] Perceiving them to be part of an economywide phenomenon, the Planning Commission (1990) favoured serious changes in the development strategy.[2]

Isher Ahluwalia, however, identified policy-induced rigidities in the labour market as the principal reason for the decline in employment, though she mentions other possible reasons like the growth of contract labour and spillover of employment into the unregistered sector. Identifying consumer non-durable goods industries in registered manufacturing as accounting for the bulk of the decline, she argued: "The sharp increase in the capital-labour ratio in the first half of the 1980s was associated with a sharp increase in the real wage rate during this period... . While the cause and effect can be debated at length, the data seem to suggest that the consumer non-durable goods sector experienced the maximum increase in capital intensity as well as the maximum increase in the real wage rate during this period" [Ahluwalia, 1992: 82-84]. Associating the increase in the real wage rate with the reportedly growing labour market rigidities—citing evidence on the increase in disciplinary action against workers between 1960 and 1975 and the Indian worker's preference for job security than for higher earnings—she further said: "This makes for inflexibility in hiring and firing possibilities and rigidities in the labour market" [Ahluwalia, 1992:84].

Table 10.1

Trends in Employment and Earnings in Registered Manufacturing, 1973-74 to 1988-89

Industry Group	*Employment Growth in*		*Earnings Per Worker*		*Share of Employment*
	1973-74 to 1979-80	*1980-81 to 1988-89*	*1973-74 to 1979-80*	*1980-81 to 1988-89*	
20-21	0.3	(-)3.8	5.7	8.9	13.2
22	4.5	(-)0.3	3.1	5.1	4.6
23	(-)1.6	(-)3.6	2.1	2.0	20.0
24	4.4	2.9	3.0	1.2	3.2
25	(-)1.6	(-)3.4	3.0	2.9	5.7
26	3.8	3.7	1.8	1.2	1.3
27	(-)0.2	(-)1.5	3.1	3.7	1.4
28	1.0	(-)0.8	3.1	2.7	4.5
29	5.2	5.1	1.7	(-)0.3	0.9
30	4.2	2.6	2.8	3.9	2.0
31	3.5	2.0	3.5	3.2	5.4
32	3.5	1.9	2.4	2.2	5.5
33	2.8	1.1	2.5	2.2	8.1
34	0.9	0.4	3.7	3.3	3.2
35	1.6	(-)0.1	3.5	3.2	5.5
36	2.4	1.6	3.5	3.1	4.2
37	2.4	(-)1.6	3.7	3.4	7.1
38	1.3	2.4	3.4	3.7	1.2
97	—	1.1	3.3	4.3	2.8
Total	1.4	(-)0.6	3.2	3.6	100.0

Source: ASI Summary Results for the Factory Sector, various issues.

The World Bank also offers a similar explanation. Claiming that the real wage rate increased at 7.2 per cent per annum in the first half of the 1980s, the Bank argued: "... employers responded [to the increase in wage rate] by virtually stopping new hiring and retrenching existing workers to the extent possible." The study added: "The estimates ... point to a significant trade off between the higher real cost of labour and employment. This suggests that the faster growth of real wages in 1980s indeed did play an important role in slowing employment creation" [The World Bank, 1989: 109-10].

Figure 10.1

Trends in Employment, Earnings and Value Added in Registered Manufacturing, 1973-74 to 1988-89

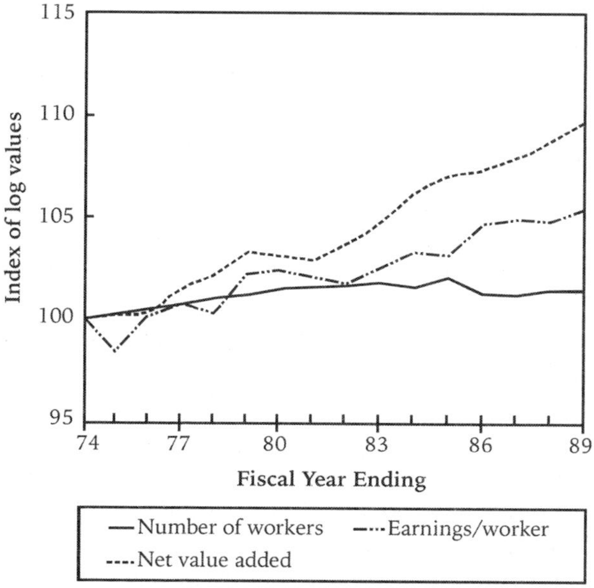

Source: ASI Summary Results.

These views are consistent with the trade theoretic perspective on the principal problem with India's industrial policy. Analysing Indian experience between 1960 and 1980, Robert E.B. Lucas attributes low employment growth to import substituting industrialisation in general and the policy-induced rigidities in non-agricultural labour markets in particular: "...[a] rising industrial wage has been a significant factor in the observed move toward more capital intensive techniques... . Since the scope and coverage of these job security laws has increased through time, it again seems likely that they have contributed to the trend towards reliance on more capital-intensive techniques within many manufacturing industries" [Lucas, 1988: 189-90].

These propositions—based on (simplistically) neoclassical percepts—form a serious viewpoint, especially in the present context of policy reforms.[3] Their analytical and empirical validity can, however, be contested on a number of substantive issues. Firstly, these studies seem to have ignored the possible role of human capital variables—namely, skill, education and experience—in increasing the wages as these could be considerable in a period of structural changes in the composition of industrial sector.[4] Second, the orthodox view seems to ignore the effect of a reduction of wages, mediated by aggregate demand, on output growth [Taylor, 1988]. Third, evidence on the relationship between the labour market institutions and economic performance is ambiguous, as discernible from the recent European experience in general and the Scandinavian experience in particular, where corporatism seems to have positively influenced industrial relations and hence macroeconomic performance [Freeman, 1988].

Given such ambiguity, both in theory as well in experience, a close look at the orthodox view could, therefore, be of value in understanding the relationship between labour market behaviour and output performance in India's manufacturing sector. In doing so, we propose to examine (a) the concept of wage rate/wages as used in the studies mentioned above (Section I), (b) evidence on the reportedly growing rigidities in the non-agricultural labour market (Section II), and (c) the validity of the postulated relationship between wages, capital-labour ratio and employment at a disaggregated level (Section III). Before concluding, a provisional alternative explanation for the observed decline in registered manufacturing employment in the 1980s is suggested (Section IV).

I

DISTINCTION BETWEEN WAGE RATE AND EARNINGS

Ahluwalia and the World Bank use *Annual Survey of Industries* (ASI) data on 'wages to workers' to compute the wage rate (or wages).[5] As the ASI definition includes all payments made to workers—excepting lay off payments not made by the employer and the imputed value of benefits in kind—it evidently refers to workers' *total earnings,* which covers not only the wage rate—that is, the basic wage plus dearness allowance, wherever applicable—but also all *additional* remuneration for workers' *additional* effort.[6] Conceptually, earnings per worker is a function of the wage rate for the standard working day, remuneration for additional hours of work (and more shifts) and incentive income for more intensive work that is linked to output. In the decade beginning 1979-80, while the employment growth turned negative, total person days (or mandays) worked in registered manufacturing—and hence mandays per worker—recorded a positive trend growth rate; suggesting that the observed increase in earnings per worker could, at least partly, represent his (or her) compensation for greater effort and may not *necessarily* imply an increase in the wage rate, as has been argued (Figure 10.2).[7]

Figure 10.2

Number of Workers Employed and Mandays Worked in Registered Manufacturing, 1979-80 to 1988-89

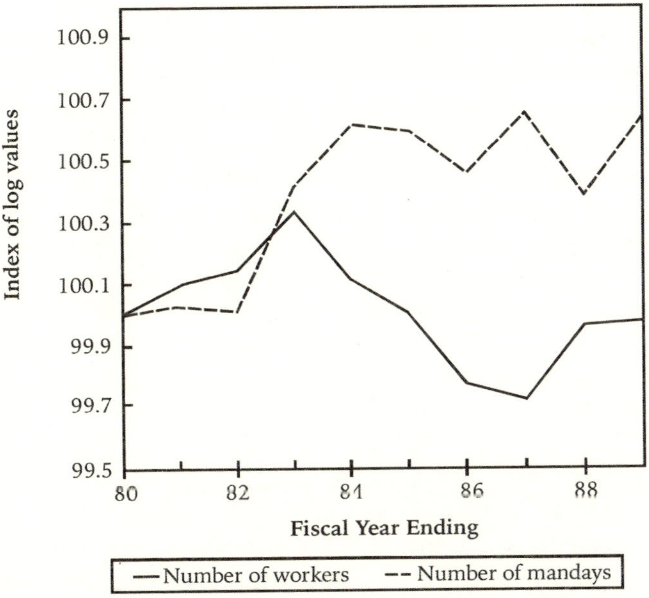

Source: ASI Summary Results.

Admittedly, since the definition of workers in ASI includes contract (or casual) workers, it is arguable that all or most of the additional mandays worked may well have been done by contract workers at the market clearing wage rate, with little additional effort by the supposedly unionised permanent workers. This proposition is examined using the labour statistics data for the census sector of ASI.[8] The share of casual workers in the total employment more than doubled from 4.6 per cent in 1980-81 to 10 per cent in 1986-87. However, as their proportion in the total mandays worked in 1986-87 is only 8.9 per cent, contract workers' contribution to mandays worked does not seem to be disproportionate to their share in employment. An estimate—assuming that the proportion of contract workers in total employment in the census sector is the same for ASI as a whole and that the share of mandays worked by casual workers in 1980-81 is same as in 1986-87—suggests that between 1980-81 and 1986-87 while the mandays per worker for *all* workers increased by 16 per cent, the same for casual and permanent workers increased by 15.8 per cent and 16.7 per cent, respectively. There is, thus, little basis to argue that casual workers account for all (or most) of the observed increase in mandays worked in the 1980s, though their share in total employment has gone up.

We examine the trends in earnings per worker and earnings per manday, although the latter as a proxy for the wage rate ignores additional remuneration due to plausible intensification of the working day. While earnings per worker in registered manufacturing increased at 3.2 per cent in the decade beginning 1979-80, earnings per manday increased at only 1.6 per cent per annum, which is less than the corresponding real per capita GDP (hereafter per capita income) growth rate during the same period (2.7 per cent) (Table 10.2). At a disaggregated level, growth in earnings per manday ranges from (-)1.3 per cent in leather (NIC 29) to 3.7 per cent per annum in repair services (NIC 97), with no statistically valid trend for (i) beverages, (ii) cotton textiles, and (iii) wool and synthetic fibre textiles (NIC 22, 23 and 24).

A comparison of the trends by use-based industrial classification for the same period suggests that in consumer non-durable goods industries, accounting for nearly half the registered manufacturing employment, while earnings per worker increased at 3 per cent, earnings per manday rose by a mere 0.5 per cent per annum, which is less than one-third the average for registered manufacturing (1.6 per cent). The observed divergence between the two measures of wages in these industries seems to be consistent with the decline in employment at the rate of 1.6 per cent and the growth in mandays per worker 2.3 per cent per annum; corresponding figures for registered manufacturing are (-)0.5 per cent and 1.5 per cent per annum, respectively.

Table 10.2

Growth Rates in Registered Manufacturing, 1979-80 to 1988-89

	Employment of Workers	*Mandays per Worker*	*Earnings per Worker*	*Earnings per Manday*
Intermediate goods	0.5*	1.0*	2.6*	1.6*
	(0.336)	(0.870)	(0.843)	(0.751)
Capital goods	(-)0.02	0.3	3.0*	2.7*
	(0.0)	(0.134)	(0.900)	(0.965)
Consumer durable goods	1.6*	0.7	2.7*	2.0*
	(0.791)	(0.181)	(0.776)	(0.588)
Consumer non-durable goods	(-)1.6*	2.3*	3.0*	0.5*
	(0.706)	(0.750)	(0.829)	(0.653)
Registered manufacturing	(-)0.5*	1.5*	3.2*	1.6*
	(0.301)	(0.663)	(0.579)	(0.800)

Notes: (1) * Indicates statistical significance of the estimated coefficient at 90 per cent confidence level and above.

(2) Employment growth rate for registered manufacturing is for the nine-year period since 1980-88 as the same for the period since 1979-80 is statistically significant at 80 per cent confidence level.

Source: ASI Summary Results of Factory Sector, various issues.

Ahluwalia, as noted earlier, observed that inverse movement between employment and wage rate in these industries was associated with an above average increase in capital-labour ratio. The foregoing evidence, however, suggests that while earnings per worker undoubtedly went up in the 1980s, it was mainly on account of an above average increase in the number of days worked per worker. The rise in earnings per manday in consumer non-durable goods industries, as shown above, is considerably lower (0.5 per cent per annum) than the average for registered manufacturing (1.6 per cent per annum). If these findings are valid, then they not only question Ahluwalia's evidence of increase in the wage rate, but also perhaps the postulated associations between the wage rate, capital-labour ratio and the decline in employment.

Though these findings seem interesting, they remain partial since earnings per manday is not the same as wage rate due to a possible intensification of the working day. We examine *Occupational Wage-Surveys*[9] (OWS) which take into account the distinction between the wage rate per worker per day (hereafter wage rate)[10] and earnings per worker per day (hereafter earnings).[11] As these surveys have been conducted four times since 1958-59, using consistent definitions and methodology covering almost the entire registered manufacturing sector, they could be useful to discern the long-term movements in wages, disaggregated by industries. Our preliminary attempt, however, ignores the variation in wage rate and earnings on account of education, skill and experience, though considerable scope seems to exist to do a more detailed exercise. Moreover, the figures reported here are simple averages of the minimum and maximum wage rate/ earnings reported in OWS.

Fourteen industries for which data are available for all the rounds since 1958-59 account for about 40 per cent of registered manufacturing employment. In seven industries—accounting for about a quarter of registered manufacturing employment in 1980-81—the compound growth of wage rate between 1958-59 and 1986-87 is lower than the corresponding per capita income growth of 1.3 per cent per annum (Table 10.3).[12] In one industry, namely, bicycle manufacturing, the wage rate has, in fact, declined by 7 per cent in 1986-87 compared to 1958-59. In the remaining industries, wage rates have grown in the range of 1.3 per cent (ship building) to 2.9 per cent per annum (electrical machinery). The *tentative* inference from these long-term trends is that while the wage rates across industries under consideration have not remained constant, increases in them do not appear to be disproportionately large compared to per capita income growth in the same period. This result, consistent with the foregoing evidence on the trends in earnings per manday in the 1980s for registered manufacturing based on ASI data, seems to provide a basis to question Ahluwalia's and the World Bank's finding of a disproportionate increase in the wage rate.

It is, however, interesting to discover from the same table that between the Third and the Fourth Round of the OWS (between 1975-76 and 1986-87) in almost all the 17 industries for which data are available, earnings increased much faster than the wage rate.[13] While the increase in the wage rate is in the range of (-)0.1 per cent (iron and steel) to 5 per cent (prime movers) per annum, earnings have went up between 1.3 per cent (garments) and nearly 7.9 per cent (electrical machinery) per annum.[14] If it is conceded that the definitions of the wage rate (by Ahluwalia) and wages (by the World Bank) represent earnings per worker, then these diverging trends seem to suggest that much of the reported increase in the wage rate or wages noted by them represents additional remuneration for workers' extra effort—which is likely to get reflected in higher labour productivity (Figure 10.10)—and perhaps not a substantial increase in the wage rate for the standard working day.

Table 10.3

Trends in Wage Rate and Earnings in Selected Manufacturing Industries

Industry	*Compound Growth Rate*		
	Wage Rate between I and IV Round OWS	*Between III and IV OWS*	
		Wage Rate	*Earnings*
Cotton textiles	1.0	0.5	4.2
Jute textiles	1.8	2.0	2.4
Woolen textiles	0.7	1.6	4.3
Silk textiles	0.2	1.1	2.8
Garments	0.4	1.3	1.3
Ship building	1.5	1.5	7.4
Locomotive	2.0	3.4	3.8
Motor vehicle	0.7	2.6	6.4
Bicycle	-0.3	0.2	2.3
Aircraft	1.8	0.3	5.0
Iron and steel		0.3	2.7
Casting and forging		2.7	5.9
Agricultural machinery	0.9	1.6	4.0
Electrical machinery	2.9	4.5	7.9
Machine tools	1.9	2.0	6.7
Prime movers		5.0	7.6
Textile machinery	0.2	0.9	6.7

Notes: (i) I Round: 1958-59, II Round: 1963-66, III Round: 1974-75, IV Round: 1986-88.

(ii) Consumer price indices for industrial workers for all India are used. In order to reduce yearly fluctuations, we have used three-year averages around the year of survey to deflate the money wage rate and earnings.

Source: Occupational Wage Survey, various reports.

To recapitulate: wage rate according to the OWS and earnings per manday as per ASI data have not gone up disproportionately as has been suggested by the studies quoted earlier. The wage rate over a long period in half the number of industries for which data are available (OWS) and earnings per manday for registered manufacturing in general and consumer non-durable goods industries in particular in the 1980s (ASI) has not kept pace with growth of per capita income. However, earnings per worker increased faster than per capita income in registered manufacturing as well as in consumer non-durable goods industries since workers have evidently worked a larger number of days. Although, analytically, more intensive work could also account for a part of the discernible growth in earnings per worker, we have no basis to test the proposition.[15]

II

STRENGTH OF ORGANISED WORKING CLASS

The increase in the wage rate that is presumed to have taken place is seen as an evidence of the growing rigidities in the labour market—namely, minimum wage legislation (growing) strength of trade unions and increasingly stringent job security laws—as reflected in the power of organised labour to appropriate a share of output disproportionate to their contribution, at the expense of additional employment generation and with a socially undesirable rise in capital intensity. Robert E.B. Lucas, for instance, showing an increase in the *absolute* number of mandays lost in industrial disputes in the *organised sector as a whole,* argued: "... it is clear that the comparative power of unions in pressing for wage settlements has grown substantially and the incidence of strikes has consequently risen as reflected in the number of mandays lost in strikes and lockouts ..." [Lucas, 1988: 189]; he reiterates this view in a more recent study as well [Fallon and Lucas, 1993].

Lucas' measure seems incorrect for three reasons. One, the *absolute* number of mandays *lost* in industrial disputes has little meaning when the number of mandays *worked* has also grown. Two, as industrial disputes could be due to either strikes or lockouts—which he evidently recognises—an increase in the total number of mandays lost does not necessarily imply an increase in the proportion of strikes.

Three, his data refer to the organised sector of the economy and not to the registered manufacturing industries which he has examined; the latter is a subset of the former.

Following Lucas in examining the trends in union power as a proxy for the alleged rigidities, our evidence questions his contention.[16] In his measure of mandays lost in disputes in registered manufacturing, when normalised for mandays worked, no statistically valid trend is discernible during the two decades beginning 1970-71. There are only fluctuations in the range of 0.7 per cent to about 2.3 per cent of the number of mandays worked (Figure 10.3). Union density – the proportion of workers unionised in registered manufacturing – fell from around 45 per cent in the late 1970s to around 30 per cent towards the end of the 1980s, (Figure 10.4).[17] The proportion of strikes in the total number of mandays lost in the disputes, ignoring the sharp dip during the 'emergency,' has also steadily declined to less than half in the latter half of the 1980s. This implies that in the recent years a greater share of industrial disputes has been on account of lockouts by employers and not because of strikes (Figure 10.5).[18] Finally, declining share of mandays lost due to strikes in the total is discernible in a period when the total number of workers involved in industrial disputes has dropped from 38 per cent in 1973-74 to less than 10 per cent in 1988-89 (Figure 10.6).[19]

The decline in the strength of unionised labour is accompanied by changes in the structure of employment as well.[20] The share of registered sector in total manufacturing employment fell from around 30 per cent in 1977-78 to about 23 per cent a decade later (Figure 10.7). Moreover, within the factory sector, employment growth is positive in factories employing less than 1,000 workers; and a statistically significant negative correlation exists—with R^2 of 0.66—between the size class of factories and employment growth between 1979-80 and 1988-89 (Figure 10.8).[21] Since the average wage rate is lower in smaller-sized factories and the likelihood of power of unions is also lower, *a priori* one could argue that these structural changes would have further contributed towards reducing policy-induced rigidities in the labour markets and exerting downward pressure on wage rate and earnings within the registered manufacturing sector.

Figure 10.3

Number of Mandays Lost in Industry Disputes as per cent of Number of Mandays Worked, 1973-74 to 1988-89

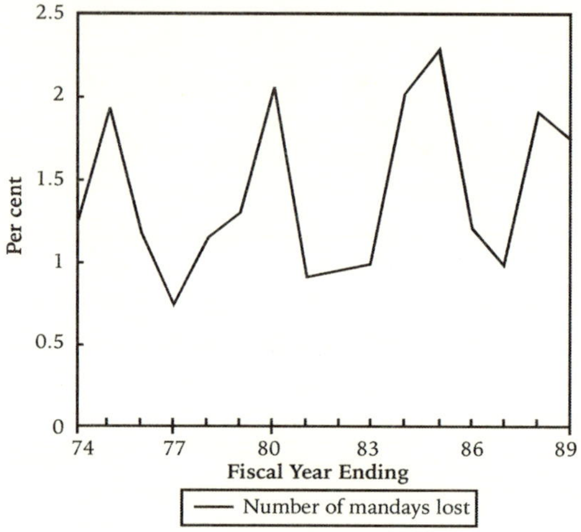

Source: Indian Labour Yearbook, various issues.

Figure 10.4

Union Density: Percentage of Workers Unionised in Registered Manufacturing, 1973-74 to 1987-88

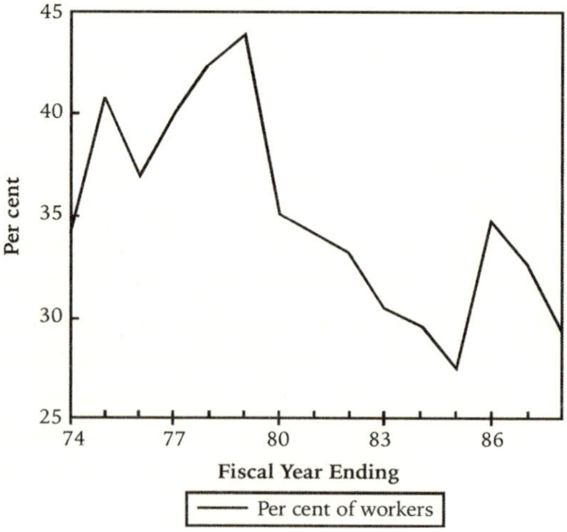

Source: Indian Labour Yearbook, various issues.

Figure 10.5

Share of Strikes in Total Number of Mandays Lost in Industries Disputes, 1970-71 to 1988-89

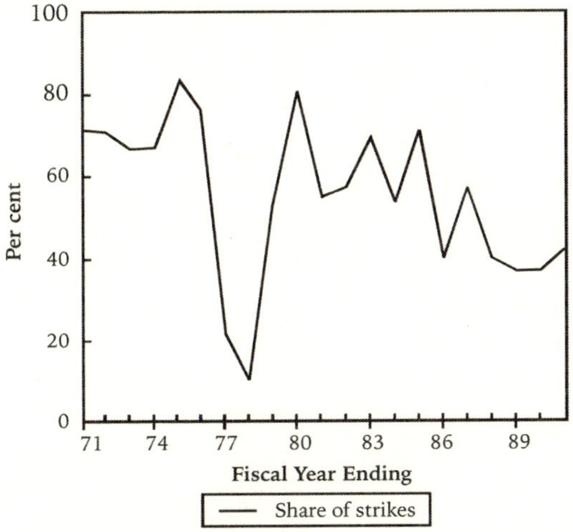

Source: *Indian Labour Yearbook*, various issues.

Figure 10.6

Percentage of Workers Involved in Industries Disputes, 1973-74 to 1988-89

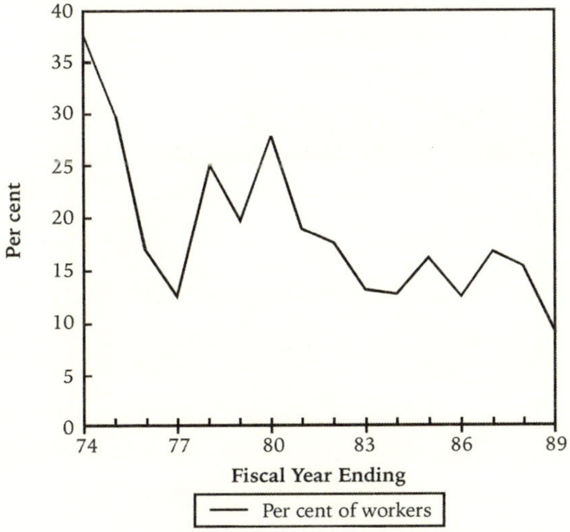

Source: *Indian Labour Yearbook*, ASI Summary Results, various issues.

Figure 10.7

Share of Registered Manufacturing in Total Manufacturing Employment, 1977-78 to 1987-88

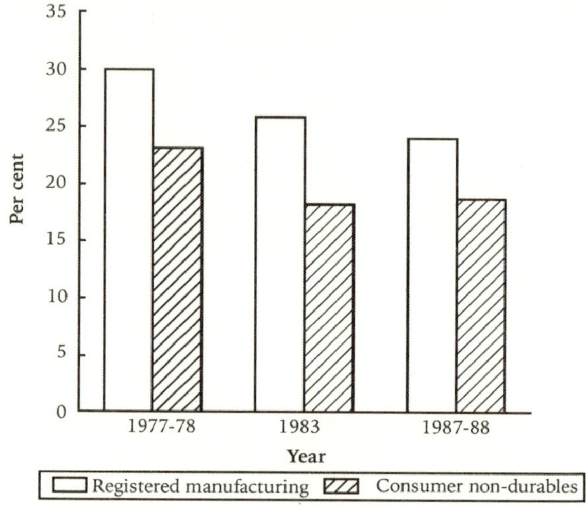

Sources: NSS, ASI various issues.

Figure 10.8

Employment Growth in Registered Manufacturing by Employment Size Class, 1979-80 to 1988-89

Note: Employment size-class by number of workers, 1: 0-49; 2: 50-99; 3: 100-199; 4: 200-499; 5: 500-999; 6: 1000-1999; 7: 2000-4999; 8: 5000+.

Arguably, these changes reflect the response of firms to the labour market rigidities. While there could be some validity in such a view, it would perhaps be incorrect to attribute the structural changes mainly or entirely to the behaviour of the labour market, as there could be a number of other reasons. These changes seem to form part of the long-term tendencies in the size structure of manufacturing to correct for the historical bias in favour of large-sized plants in India [Nagaraj, 1985]. This could also reflect the outcome of various policies to promote small-scale manufacturing and institutional changes in financing industrial development. Moreover, diffusion of skills, entrepreneurship and technologies could also have favoured modern small- and medium-scale firms.

The foregoing evidence unambiguously shows a decline in the strength of the organised labour. Hence, it seems reasonable to suggest that, in a period of declining bargaining power of organised workers and structural changes in employment within registered sector towards smaller-sized establishments, unionised labour is unlikely to have secured a disproportionate increase in the wage rate, especially at a time when the share of registered manufacturing employment in the total is itself declining.

While registered manufacturing accounted for about 30 per cent of total manufacturing employment in 1977-78, for consumer non-durable goods industries it was only about 24 per cent (Figure 10.7). Moreover, the average size of a factory in these industries declined from around 70 workers in 1973-74 to less than 55 workers per factory in 1988-89, as in registered manufacturing (Figure 10.9). Since employment in consumer non-durable goods industries is predominantly in the unregistered sector and since within the registered sector their average factory size has declined considerably, it is quite unlikely, contrary to what Ahluwalia has suggested, that organised workers in these industries could have succeeded in securing notable increases in the wage rate.

This is not to deny that organised workers command any bargaining power in the labour market. They perhaps do in large firms, in the public sector and in some locations. But at an aggregated level, the foregoing evidence seems to question the proposition of growing rigidities in non-agricultural labour markets.

Figure 10.9

Factory Size in Registered Manufacturing Industries, 1973-74 to 1988-89

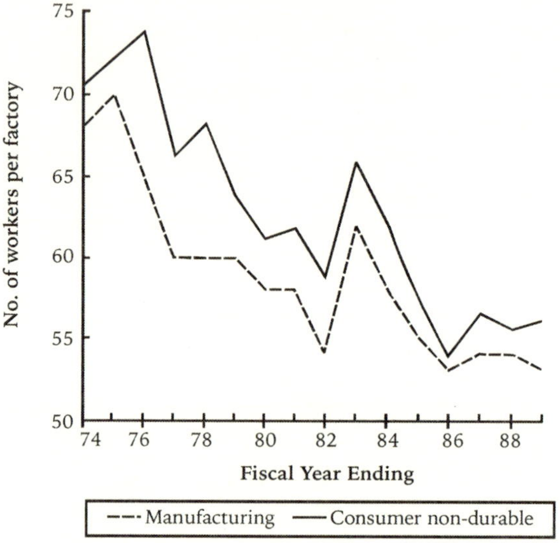

Source: ASI, Summary Results of Factory Sector, various issues.

III

TESTING THE HYPOTHESIS

The evidence adduced by Ahluwalia, the World Bank and Lucas on the postulated relationship between the wage rate, capital-labour ratio and employment seems to have an analytical shortcoming. They have shown trends in the wages/wage rate and the rigidities in the labour market without considering the changes in the cost of capital. Analytically, what matters in the choice of technique is not the wage rate per se, but the wage-rental ratio. Perhaps, these studies implicitly assume the cost of capital to have remained constant. Admittedly, its measurement is fraught with numerous conceptual and empirical problems. The simple and widely used measure is real interest rates, which increased steeply in the 1980s, even ignoring the spikes in the series (Figure 10.11).[22] Therefore, there is a need to qualify the findings of Ahluwalia and others in this respect.

This section re-examines the postulated associations between increase in earnings per worker, increase in capital intensity (capital-labour ratio), and a decline in employment growth in registered manufacturing. The cost of capital is not included to minimise computational difficulties. Simple correlations across 42 three-digit industries for the period 1973-74 and 1986-87 are calculated between the growth rates of: (i) earnings per worker and capital intensity; and (ii) capital intensity and employment.[23] Three variants of associations are explored: (i) growth over the entire period of 14 years; (ii) increase in sub-period I (1973-74 and 1979-80) and in sub-period II (1980-81 and 1986-87); and (iii) average of the annual growth rates in sub-period I and average of annual growth rates in sub-period II, thus obtaining five sets of correlations.[24]

Evidence suggests that although the results are partially consistent with the hypothesis, in none of the variants does one find consistent and statistically significant results with the expected sign for the coefficients (Table 10.4). For instance, in variant I—that is over the entire period—while the correlation between the growth rates of capital-labour ratio and employment is statistically significant with the expected negative sign, the correlation between the growth rates of earnings per worker and the capital-labour ratio is not statistically different from zero. Similarly, in variant III—that is, average of annual growth rates in sub-period II—while the correlation coefficient between the growth rates of earnings per worker and the capital-labour ratio is statistically significant with the expected positive sign, the correlation between the growth rates of capital-labour ratio and employment is positive and statistically significant, which is inconsistent with the hypothesis.

We have also computed the above-mentioned correlations separately for the time series data of 42 industries. To minimise autocorrelation problems the first differences in each series are correlated. The findings shows that in only nine out of 42 industries the postulated relationship is statistically valid with the expected sign for the estimated coefficients. These results, therefore, seem to suggest that the relationship between earnings per worker, capital intensity and employment is more complex than postulated by the hypothesis. Moreover, if we accept that real interest rate has gone up during the period it would further dilute the strength of the observed associations between the three variables.

Table 10.4

Correlation Coefficients between Growth Rates of Employment, Earnings Per Worker and Capital-Labour Ratio

	Simple Correlation Coefficient between Growth Rates of	
	Earnings/ Worker and Capital-Labour Ratio	Capital-Labour Ratio and Employment
1 Trend growth rate during 1973-74 and 1986-87	0.142	(-)0.362*
2 (i) Percentage change in sub-period I	0.479*	(-)0.215
(ii) Percentage change in sub-period II	0.014	0.001
3 (i) Average of annual growth rates in sub-period I	0.193	(-)0.108
(ii) Average of annual growth rates in sub-period II	0.436*	0.348*

Notes: (i) Sub-period I: 1973-74 and 1979-80; and sub-period II: 1980-81 and 1986-87.
(ii) Correlation coefficients are computed for growth rates across 42 three-digit industry groups.
(iii) * Refers to statistically significant at 90 per cent level and above.

Source: *ASI Summary Results of Factory Sector,* various issues.

IV

TOWARDS AN ALTERNATIVE EXPLANATION

The causal connection between the wage rate, capital intensity and employment is, admittedly, an equilibrium condition. In a labour surplus dual economy, evolved under certain institutional conditions and witnessing an upturn in growth after a prolonged period of 'relative stagnation,' the observed decline in employment could have multiple causes, not necessarily originating in the reported increase in wage rate.[25] In an attempt at exploring an alternative explanation, without offering an analytical model, we propose to identify a set of factors which could have influenced employment.

Changing Composition of Output: Part of the explanation for the decline in the 1980s seems to lie in the changing composition of output in favour of less labour-intensive industries. For instance, industry groups food products (20-21), rubber, plastic, petroleum and coal products (30), chemical and chemical products (31), non-metallic mineral products (32), and electrical machinery (36) witnessed above average growth in value added, but have a below average share of wages in value added. The correlation between (i) growth rate in real gross value added and share of wages in gross value added across 19 two-digit industry groups, for the period 1980-81 to 1988-89, is (-)0.51 and statistically significant. The relatively faster growth rate of these industries, especially chemical- and petroleum-based industries perhaps reflects conscious efforts to import substitute these products in response to the oil price hikes in the 1970s and the exploitation of newly discovered mineral oil deposits to reduce adverse effects of external economic shocks; and perhaps less driven by the evolution of relative prices.

Overhang of Employment: The upturn in output growth (and the corresponding negative growth rate in employment) in manufacturing in the 1980s, as is well known, was witnessed after a prolonged period of relative stagnation since the mid-1960s when employment growth was sustained at over 3 per cent per annum despite a deceleration in output growth, resulting in a narrowing of the gap between the growth of earnings per worker and labour productivity. More specifically, during the seven-year period since 1968-69 while net value added grew at 2.6 per cent per annum, employment kept growing at 3.9 per cent per annum; hence, labour productivity was increasing at a lower rate than earnings per worker, resulting in an unsustainable situation in the long run (Figure 10.10).

Intuitively, one could argue that when demand picked up in the 1980s firms would have first used their existing stock of labour (as well as capital) intensively before deciding to employ additional workers. This could perhaps partly account for the lack of employment growth in registered manufacturing, despite an upturn in output growth.

Changing Market Conditions: Analytically, changes in the product and financial markets are likely to affect the demand for labour. Studying the interdependence between market structure and technology, Desai

Figure 10.10

Earnings and Labour Productivity in Registered Manufacturing, 1960-61 to 1988-89

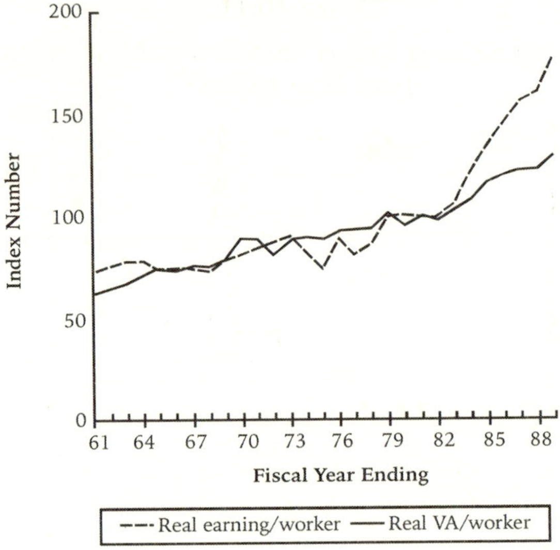

Source: ASI Summary Results.

(1985) suggested an increase in competition during the period 1963-64 to 1978-79.[26] Considering that liberalisation was initiated in the 1980s one could hypothesise that industrial markets have become more competitive exerting firms to reduce costs. We, however, do not have any evidence to support the proposition.

In response to the public sector's growing borrowing requirement on the one hand and the policy directive of priority sector lending on the other, the cost of credit for the private (non-agricultural) sector seems to have increased significantly in the 1980s. Figure 10.11 shows a steady increase in interest cost as a proportion of total income in medium and large public limited companies and the trend seems to be positively associated with an increase in the real interest rate in the 1980s.[27]

A priori, one would expect an increase in the cost of capital in a period of increasing competition to result in substitution of labour for capital and hence an increase in employment. However, given the differential wage-rental ratios in the registered and unregistered sectors, firms would perhaps have found it profitable to shift the production to unregistered sector adversely affecting employment in the former.

Figure 10.11

Share of Interest Cost in Cost of Production and Real Interest Rate, 1960-61 to 1988-89

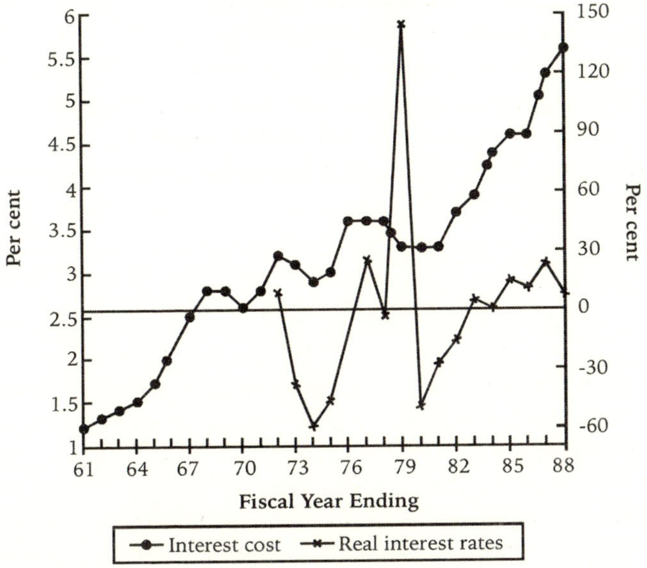

Source: *RBI Bulletin*, *National Accounts Statistics*, various issues.

Modalities of Adjustment: Based on field experience [Nagaraj, 1989], we would hypothesise the following plausible adjustment process. As demand picked up for manufacturing output, firms (i) used their workforce intensively by increasing incentives for workers at the shop floor level, linking wage agreements to productivity norms, (ii) reorganised shop floor and workers' job-content, (iii) farmed out manufacturing of relatively simpler components and products to secure economies of specialisation and used contract labour for labour-intensive services, and (iv) increasingly employed part-time workers especially small firms. While capital investment and automation form elements of restructuring, these are more likely only after the other options are fully explored, unless dictated by technological consideration. However, the adjustment behaviour of public sector firms is likely to be more constrained by policy. These modalities of rationalisation of labour use in registered manufacturing were feasible in the 1980s as a result of diffusion of skills, spread of infrastructure and various policies to promote small firms.

The foregoing explanation, however, would imply an increase in the growth rate of employment in the unregistered sector. Since employment growth in unregistered manufacturing has also declined [Planning Commission, 1990], one is inclined to further hypothesise that in the non-factory sector there is a much more intensive use of labour for longer hours and in a flexible manner. Moreover, there appears to be an increasing trend of workers taking up more than one job, especially among skilled workers, which could further restrict employment generation.

V

CONCLUSION

A reportedly sharp rise in the wage rate in the 1980s in registered manufacturing—due to increasing policy-induced distortions in the labour market—is widely hypothesised to have led firms to substitute capital for labour, resulting in the observed decline in employment. Consciously avoiding getting into the theoretical debate on the causal relationship between the labour market and economic growth, this study provided evidence to suggest that the wage rate (using OWS) and earnings per manday (using ASI) did not increase disproportionately as has been argued. However, earnings per worker increased at a faster rate than per capita income growth mainly due to an increase in the number of mandays per worker. Our findings also suggest a distinct decline in the power of organised labour, used as a proxy for the reported rigidities in the labour market. Moreover, structural changes are discernible in employment in manufacturing industries in favour of the unregistered sector and within registered manufacturing towards smaller sized factories. These long-term tendencies would have further undermined the power of the organised working class to induce flexible use of labour. Finally, not much of a systematic relationship could be discerned in the postulated relationship between earnings per worker, the capital-labour ratio and employment at a disaggregated level.

Exploring an alternative explanation, it was argued that (i) mainly in response to the macroeconomic compulsions of the 1970s and the discovery of appropriate natural resources, the composition of output changed in favour of less labour-intensive industries, (ii) there was a overhang of employment that had built up during the prolonged period of relative stagnation in the 1970s, and (iii) increasing competition in the product market due to domestic liberalisation and increase in the cost of borrowed funds could account for the decline in employment in registered manufacturing in the 1980s. It was further hypothesised that there was (a) a restriction on fresh employment in large factories so as to use the existing workforce more intensively, (b) shop-floor reorganisation and changes in workers' job-content, (c) contracting out of (mostly unskilled) labour-intensive services and farming out of production, and (iv) an increasing use of part-time workers in small firms permitting flexible use of labour.

Finally, if evidence and arguments outlined above have any validity, they seem to suggest the limitation of the orthodox view in explaining the labour market behaviour and hence question the policy implications that follow from such a view.[28]

Notes

1. Unless otherwise stated, growth rates reported in this study are computed using log-linear trend equation.
2. Visaria and Minhas (1991) question the Planning Commission's findings since in three out of the four years in which the NSS data were collected happen to be 'bad' rainfall years and hence the employment in these years could have been affected adversely. However, such a problem is likely to be unimportant for the manufacturing sector since: (i) output witnessed a sustained growth with very little yearly fluctuation, and (ii) bad agricultural harvest is found to affect manufacturing output with one year lag.
3. Recently published official 'Discussion Papers' on economic reforms echoes the foregoing views: "... we must review and reform the current legislations for employment and industrial disputes to ensure that excessive rigidities are removed and long-term growth facilitated. The operation of the current Industrial Disputes Act (in particular, the requirement for prior approval by government for closure of sick units and retrenchment of labour) needs to be reviewed as it affects incentive for investment and as well as increased employment... . Rigid rules limiting the flexibility with which labour can be hired and retrenched have the effect of pushing entrepreneurs into more capital-intensive technology and reduce the number of workers they have to deal with" [Government of India, 1993:34].
4. It is perhaps pertinent to cite South Korean example in this context. Despite strict laws prohibiting trade union activity, real wage rate in that country increased at a trend growth rate of 5 per cent per annum over a long period. Amsden (1990) attributes it to intensive learning, education and skill of the Korean workers.
5. "Wages are defined to include all remuneration capable of being expressed in monetary terms and also payable more or less regularly in each pay period to workers as compensation for work done during the accounting year. It includes (a) direct wages

and salary (i.e, basic wages, salaries, payment of overtime, dearness compensatory, house rent and other allowances), (b) remuneration for period not worked, (c) bonus and ex-gratia payment paid both at regular and less frequent intervals..." (ASI, 1988-89: Summary Results of Factory Sector, p 78).

6. For conceptual clarity, Maurice Dobb's distinction seems instructive in this context: "When we speak of a wage rate, we usually refer to the amount paid to the worker per hour per normal working day or for performing a certain job. In other words, we are speaking about what the worker receives in return for a given output of work on his part... . When we talk about the standard of life of the worker and his family, we are concerned with the total *earnings* of the family-unit... . *We cannot judge what is happening to the former wage rate solely from the figures about the latter earnings* and for a number of reasons these two quantities may change quite differently" [Dobb, 1959: 27; emphasis added].

7. Due to possible changes in the definition and methodology, data on mandays prior to 1979-80 are not comparable with the subsequent years.

8. Census sector of ASI includes all factories employing 50 or more workers with power and 100 or more workers without power.

9. The Labour Bureau, Government of India in order to obtain "accurate and up-to-date wage statistics" [*Indian Labour Year Book* 1992: 45] has periodically conducted *Occupational Wage Surveys*. The four rounds have been conducted so far in 1958-59, 1963-65, 1974-79 and 1985-88. The coverage has steadily increased over the successive rounds; from 44 plantation, mining and manufacturing industries in the first round to 53 in the fourth. These surveys include firms in the *organised* sector of these industries covered under the relevant acts. Complete results of the fourth round are awaited.

10. To quote OWS: "Wage rate should include basic wage rate, cost of living allowance and other guaranteed and regularly paid allowances, but exclusive of overtime payment, bonuses, gratuities, family allowance and other social security payments made by employers."

    "For the purpose of this survey, wage rate has been defined as the sum of basic wage and dearness allowance in respect of workers who receive both these components while for other workers the actual consolidated amount earnings represent their wage rate" [*Occupational Wage Survey* (Fourth Round), Report on Textile Industries (1986-87), Labour Bureau, 1989: 46].

11. "For the purpose of this survey, pay roll earnings have been defined as all those components of remuneration received by workers more or less on regular basis. Thus basic wage, DA, production and incentive bonus, attendance bonus, overtime allowance, shift allowance, cycle/transport allowance, washing allowance, etc., are included in the data on pay roll earnings. They also include money value of benefits/concessions accruing to workers on more or less regular basis." [*Occupational Wage Survey* (Fourth Round), Report on Textile Industries (1986-87), Labour Bureau, 1989: 106].

12. These are cotton textiles, woolen textiles, silk textiles, garments, bicycle, agricultural machinery and textile machinery.

13. As the coverage has expanded in successive rounds of OWS, a comparison of more recent rounds enables one to include greater number of industries.

14. The observed increases in wage rate and earnings perhaps get overstated due to a conceivable reduction in them during the emergency. A close perusal of the data confirms the suspicion.

15. Robin Marris observed a similar variation between wage rate and earnings for the UK manufacturing industries in the 1980s, by comparing the official earnings enquiry with employers' associations' statistical series on 'settlements' which relates to "agreed increases in basic rates for standard work under standard conditions" [Marris, 1987: 48].

16. Though these are official figures and are the only source to discern the long-term trends, their quality, according to some union analysts, leaves much to be desired. It

is believed that trade unions often do not file returns on time, especially the smaller ones and firm-based independent unions.

17. However, at a disaggregated level, trend decline in union density is statistically significant in only eight out of 18 major industry groups and in only one industry, namely, cotton textiles (NIC 23) the trend is positive and statistically significant. In the remaining cases, due to considerable yearly fluctuation in union membership, the trends are not statistically significant, though have the expected negative sign.

18. Although this is a widely used, and is a valid simplification at an aggregate level, we are conscious that, at a microeconomic level lockout by management may well represent a pre-emptive measure to prevent a strike by workers or vice versa.

19. Even this figure is perhaps an overestimate since it is not uncommon for workers to be members of more than one union.

20. That registered manufacturing constitutes a small and declining proportion of the total manufacturing employment is not adequately appreciated by many. For instance, the World Bank (1989), unable to reconcile the employment figures from the ASI and the population census seems to infer that the latter are an overestimate.

21. Information on employment by size class of factories is available only for factory sector. Since manufacturing accounts for over four-fifths of the factory employment, our finding is unlikely to be incorrect.

22. Though widely used, real interest rate as a measure of the cost of capital has many limitations, since it ignores tax rate and depreciation rules. We estimated trends in the cost of capital for the RBI's medium and large non-financial public limited companies using the equation: (D/D + E) (1-t) r + (d/d + E) (return on equity), where D is debt, E equity capital, t tax rate and r interest rate. A few variants were tried using different measures of return on equity. In all the cases the cost of capital is found to have increased on a trend basis since 1970-71. I am grateful to Subir Gokam for enlightening me a great deal on the analytical and empirical issues in computing cost of capital.

23. In this exercise, the critical data are estimates of capital stock series, which we have taken from Aggarwal (1991). Since the 42 three-digit industries account for 72 to 75 per cent of net value added at current prices in the entire period, our exercise can be considered reasonably comprehensive.

24. We computed averages for the years 1973-74/1974-75, 1978-79/1979-80 and 1985-86/1986-87 and the increments for each industry. These series were used for computing correlations, as mentioned in the text.

25. Mazumdar (1989), for instance, is conscious of the complexity of the labour market behaviour in developing economies and seems to argue for a closer study of individual economies before arriving at simplistic generalisations.

26. To quote Desai: "Many industrial markets in India are competitive and accommodate a large number of firms.... Rather than a tendency for monopoly, the market structures display a tendency towards intense competition..." [Desai, 1985: 168].

27. Real interest rate is equal to [(1+interest rate)/(1+inflation rate)]. We have used scheduled commercial banks' deposit rate for one year and above maturity and inflation rate is derived from implicit GDP deflator.

28. Freeman's (1993a and 1993b) assessment of the evidence on the validity of the 'distortionists' and 'interventionists' views on the labour market, against the background of structural adjustment in a large number of developing countries, seems instructive:

    In the 1980s many economists came to view institutional interventions in the labour market as major impediments to growth and employment... . Concerns were expressed that these and related interventions would prevent labour market adjustments necessary for stabilisation and structural adjustment.

    For the subset of countries that have been studied intensely, the evidence dispels fears that government or union interventions invariably impede labour-market adjustments... .

> In short when you arrive in developia and find the economy a mess, don't look to government or union labour-market intervention as the prime cause of the trouble [Freeman, 1993b: 404-05].

References

Aggarwal, Ashok K. (1991). *Estimates of Fixed Capital Stock in Registered Manufacturing Sector in India,* W P No 937, Indian Institute of Management, Ahmedabad.

Ahluwalia, Isher Judge (1992). *Productivity and Growth in Indian Manufacturing,* Oxford University Press, Delhi.

Amsden, Alice (1990). "South Korea's Record Wage Rates: Labour in Late Industrialisation," *Industrial Relations,* Vol. 29, No. 1, Winter.

Desai, Ashok (1985). "Market Structure and Technology: Their Interdependence in Indian Industry," *Research Policy,* Vol. 14.

Dobb, Maurice (1959). *Wages,* Cambridge Economic Handbooks, Cambridge University Press.

Fallon, Peter R. and Robert E.B. Lucas (1993). "Job Security Regulations and the Dynamic Demand for Industrial Labour in India and Zimbabwe," *Journal of Development Economics,* Vol. 40.

Freeman, Richard B. (1988). "Labour Market Institutions and Economic Performance," *Economic Policy,* Vol. 3, No. 1, April.

————. (1993a). "Labour Market Institutions and Policies: Help or Hindrance to Economic Development?," Annual Conference on Development Economics, 1992, Supplement to the *World Bank Research Observer,* March.

————. (1993b). "Labour Markets and Institutions in Economic Development," *American Economic Review,* Vol. 83 No. 2, May.

Government of India (1993). *Economic Reforms: Two Years After and the Task Ahead,* Department of Economic Affairs, Ministry of Finance.

Lucas, Robert E.B. (1988). "India's Industrial Policy" in Robert E.B. Lucas and Gustav F. Papanek (eds.), *The Indian Economy: Recent Development and Future Prospects,* Oxford University Press, Delhi.

Marris, Robin (1987). "Does Britain Really Have a Wage Problem?," *Llyods Bank Review,* April.

Mazumdar, Dipak (1989). "Microeconomic Issues of Labour Markets in Developing Countries: Analysis and Policy Implications," *EDI Seminar Paper* No. 40, World Bank, Washington DC.

Nagaraj, R. (1985). "Trends in Factory Size in Indian Industry, 1950 to 1980," *Economic and Political Weekly,* Review of Management, February.

————. (1989). *Sub-Contracting in Indian Manufacturing Industries: The Bangalore Experience,* PhD Thesis (Centre for Development Studies, Trivandrum), Jawaharlal Nehru University, New Delhi.

Planning Commission (1990). "Employment; Past Trends and Prospects for 1990s," *Working Paper,* New Delhi.

Taylor, Lance (1988). *Varieties of Stabilisation Experience: Towards Sensible Macroeconomics in the Third World,* Clarendon Press, Oxford.

Visaria, Pravin and B.S. Minhas (1991). "Evolving an Employment Policy for the 1990s: What Do the Data Tell Us?," *Economic and Political Weekly,* April 13.

World Bank (1989). *India: Poverty, Employment and Social Services,* Washington DC.

Economic and Political Weekly, Vol. 29, No. 4, January 22, 1994.

11

India's Capital Market Growth: Trends, Explanations and Evidence

For some time now, the capital market in India is much in news.[1] There is a widespread appreciation of the private corporate sector's (corporate sector, hereafter) ability to issue a growing volume and variety of marketable securities, as this suggests an increasing role for markets in the economy's resource allocation. It also raises many questions. What does the trend imply for the economy's aggregate saving rate and its composition, and for corporate performance. Is it necessary and desirable for the economy's long-term development prospects? This study seeks to explore these and related questions.

Section I describes long-term trends in India's capital market growth. To understand them, Section II briefly reviews the recent literature. On this basis, Section III examines the implications of the observed trends for the economy and the corporate sector. Summarising the main findings, the concluding section raises some questions that seem to follow from the capital market development.

I

TRENDS

After remaining dormant for nearly two decades since around 1960, resource mobilisation in the primary capital market showed an upturn from the late 1970s (Figure 11.1). The growth accelerated towards the end of 1980s. The market capitalisation ratio went up from about 5 per cent of GDP in 1980-81 to 63 per cent in 1992-93.[2] In eight years after 1986, the average daily turnover in the secondary market grew at about 35 per cent per year.[3] Between 1980-81 and 1992-93, the RBI index of securities prices increased almost thrice (20.7 per cent per year) as fast as the wholesale price index (7.6 per cent per year). This, in principle, reduces cost of equity capital and increases prospects for capital gains.

Figure 11.1

Capital Raised in India's Primary Capital Market in Nominal Terms, 1960-61 to 1992-93

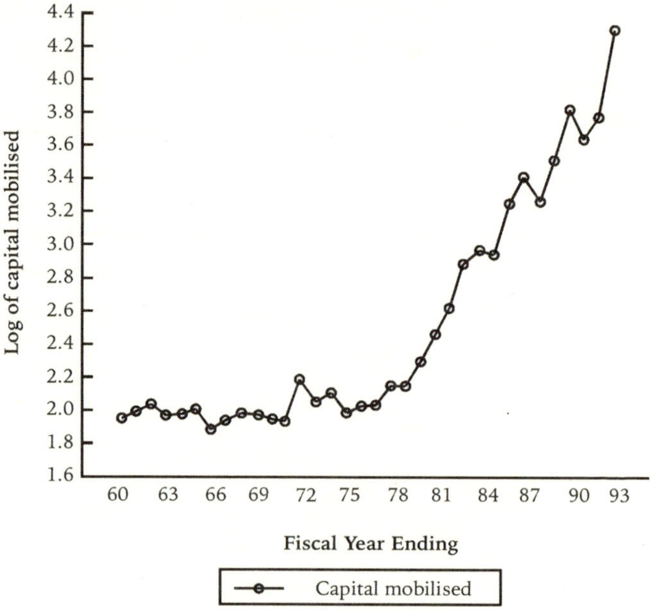

Source: RBI Report of Currency and Finance, various issues.

However, much of the growth is for debt securities. About a third is for convertible debentures.[4] Proportion of equity (or risk) capital in market mobilisation came down from about 90 per cent in the early 1970s to about 30 per cent two decades later (Figure 11.2). However, in absolute terms, nominal value of fresh equity capital raised grew at 18 per cent per year. Promoters' contribution in this more than doubled, from 21 per cent in 1970-71 to 45 per cent in 1990-91. This, in principle, is a favourable change as they now have a greater stake in the companies' financial success (Table 11.1).[5] Proportion of equity underwritten also rose steadily, reflecting the stock market's growing maturity [Samuel, 1996a]. Moreover, the market witnessed growth of new financial institutions offering a variety of services and tradable instruments with varying components of debt, equity, maturities and risk.[6]

Table 11.1

*Proportion of Promoters' Subscription to Equity Capital Raised, 1970-71 to 1990-91**

Year	*Per cent*
1970-71	20.7
1975-76	9.0
1980-81	22.5
1986-87	24.0
1987-88	38.3
1988-89	28.5
1989-90	56.9
1990-91	45.0

* 'Promoters' include collaborators and employees.

Source: *RBI Report on Currency and Finance*, 1991-92.

Figure 11.2

Share of Equity in Total Capital Mobilised, 1960 to 1992

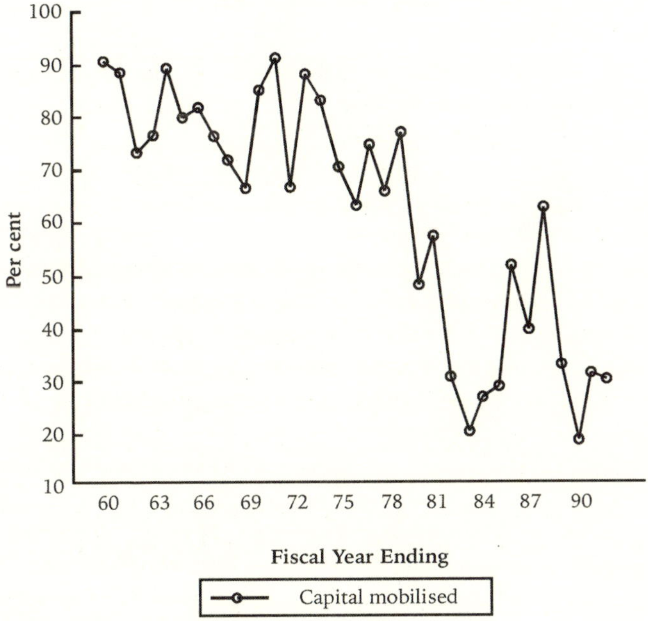

Source: *RBI Report of Currency and Finance*, various issues.

How does India compare with other 'emerging market economies' (EME)? Reportedly, India is the biggest among them with about 8,000 quoted companies in 1995, an increase of over 70 per cent over the last decade (*The Economist*, July 6, 1996).[7] In market capitalisation, India ranked seventh in 1995 (*The Economist*, July 15, 1995).[8] However, as Indian firms are small (measured by market capitalisation), they do not figure in the list of top 30 firms in EMEs (*The Economist*, August 12, 1995).

What explains the capital market growth? Proximate causes are a series of policy initiatives since around the late 1970s when, as mentioned, the stock market had a marginal role in financing industry.[9] Initially, dilution of equity holding in foreign-controlled rupee companies—popularly called the 'FERA companies,' as they attracted this 1973 Act—was perhaps a conscious effort to stimulate the primary capital market [Morris, 1985].[10] FERA companies' success was probably significant for further development of the market.

This broadly coincided with the rise in nominal interest rates and the financial sector's growing resource constraint.[11] With increasing reserve requirement and 'priority sector' lending targets at concessional interest rates, commercial banks reportedly could not meet the industrial sector's credit needs. In these circumstances, development finance institutions (DFI) persuaded firms to raise part of the required funds from the capital market.[12] Anticipating corporate sector's resource constraint in the Sixth Plan (1981-85), government initiated many steps to encourage flow of household saving into capital market [Planning Commission, 1982].[13] These included hike in interest rates on debt instruments, their convertibility into equity, raising of tax exemption limits on dividend income and easing its (and interest) deduction at source. Similarly, corporate tax rates were reduced.[14] Thus capital market reforms since 1991 perhaps reflect a continuation of a trend initiated over a decade ago.[15]

What do these trends (and policies that seem to underpin them) imply for long-term development? Do they represent a 'natural' evolution of a 'repressed' financial system towards a more 'market-oriented' system with a greater need for regulation, as the Narasimham Committee noted [Government of India, 1991]. Does it necessarily mean a greater allocative efficiency as resource use is increasingly market determined? Are there alternative 'models' or 'systems' of financial development to choose as our trajectory. To explore these questions, the recent analytical literature and comparative experience is briefly reviewed below.

II

AN ANALYTICAL SKETCH

For much of the recent literature on financial markets, Mckinnon (1973) and Shaw (1973) form the points of departure. These studies argue that state intervention in setting interest rates and quantitative measures of resources allocation—defined as financial repression—adversely affect not only allocative efficiency, but also depress the aggregate saving rate (hence investment) in less developed countries (LDCs). Therefore, they advocate liberalisation of financial markets. However, their arguments are mostly related to interventions in banking, like interest rates ceiling, statutory reserve requirements and directed lending programmes at concessional interest rates. Extending their thesis, Cho (1986) argued that financial market liberalisation may remain incomplete without an efficient market for equity capital as a means of spreading risk (and reward).[16]

In principle, stock market, as a part of a well organised financial system, has many advantages. It allows efficient risk sharing. Stock market induces gathering of information which gets reflected in stock prices. These prices are then signals for resource allocation. In the secondary market, stock prices are powerful signals for managerial incentives and corporate governance.

Attributing part of the debt crisis of the 1980s in LDCs to inadequate development of their financial markets, the *World Development Report* (WDR), 1989 [World Bank, 1989] broadly reflects the preceding analytical position. However, recognising information failure that can be acute in financial markets, the report argues for a sound supervisory mechanism and institutions to ensure their efficient functioning. On these considerations, the World Bank (and its affiliate, International Finance Corporation) makes policy-based lending and offers technical assistance for capital market development. Stock market growth in many LDCs in recent years perhaps reflects these policies and financial incentives. In India too, of late, much of the policy discussion seems to follow this dominant thought.

Till some time ago, shortage of long-term capital was believed to be a major constraint on industrialisation, since banks supply only short-term loans. As capital markets were practically non-existent (or reportedly inefficient) in most LDCs, state promoted DFIs (often supported by World Bank's advice and lines of credit) were expected to make up for the absence of an efficient capital market. Keynes' precepts about inefficiency (and fickleness) of the stock market and banks' limitation in meeting long-term financial needs of industrialisation perhaps underpinned much of the earlier policy.[17] Gerschenkron's (1962) historical account offered an empirical support for it.[18]

Many believe one of the reasons for the post-war success of Japanese and German growth and productivity is the difference in their institutional set-up for financing industry [Zysman, 1983; Dore, 1985; Dimsdale and Prevezer, 1994]. In these economies, large firms and banks have close financial (and managerial) links, while stock markets are relatively small and illiquid. Hence, firms reportedly take a long-term view of corporate success. In contrast, firms in the US and UK have arms length relations with banks. Firms are apparently more concerned about short-term prospects as their market valuation depends on quarterly/half-yearly financial performance.[19] A growing opinion seems to find the US system of stock market—though efficient and liquid—unsatisfactory for corporate governance. [Bhide, 1994].

Another reason for questioning capital markets' role in financing development is the recent empirical research that revived the 'financing hierarchy' hypothesis in corporate finance literature [Koch, 1943; Donaldson, 1961]. Contrary to the widely held belief, Mayer found, using company balance sheet data, that internal resources finance bulk of corporate (physical) investment in major OECD countries and stock market's role (net of redemption) is very limited. To quote him:

> The first is that retentions are the dominant source of finance in all countries ... where external finance is raised, it generally comes from banks rather than from securities market ... stock markets contribute very little to new sources of finance for companies: new equity issues account for well under 10 per cent of the total sources of finance raised by companies in all major OECD countries ... bond markets are a relatively minor source of finance for industry in aggregate in all countries other than the US and Canada. [Mayer, 1992: 465].[20]

Reiterating the same stylised fact, Stiglitz, highlights problems of information failure that are severe in financial markets and notes the need for state intervention [Stiglitz, 1991 and 1993]. He says, "... we must bear in mind the quite limited role that they [market for equity] play in raising capital in developed countries. Hopes of raising substantial amounts of capital in this form within LDCs appear to me to be unreasonable." In a footnote, he further adds, "Today, investors in LDCs bring to bear the full experience of how equities have been abused, even in societies with fairly well functioning legal systems. This should make them wary about what would happen in LDCs" [Stiglitz, 1991: 11].

Thus, we seem to have two broadly competing perspectives. One, the financial liberalisation thesis that emphasises centrality of stock market in resource allocation and the secondary market's disciplining role (with independent supervision) on managerial behaviour. Two, information economics theorists who, on theory and history, argue for its limited role.

In development economics, stock market did not receive adequate attention as it is a recent phenomenon in LDCs. To our knowledge, Singh and Hamid (1992) and Singh (1995), analysing corporate financing pattern of top 50 (100) private corporate firms in nine (ten) EMEs in 1980s, are significant efforts.[21] Contrary to the OECD experience they find, on average, equity capital finances about 40 per cent of corporate investment growth in these economies.[22] However, noting the limitations of sample size and methodology, Cobham and Subramaniam (1995) seriously qualify Singh's finding. Following Mayer's methodology, they show a much limited role for equity in financing corporate growth in India. To quote them:

> ... India is broadly comparable to ... . France and Italy which have relatively small stock market (with no market for corporate control), large sectors of medium and small-sized companies and a banking system which lends substantial amounts to companies but does not have very close ties with firms and cannot exert the same influence and control over them typical of Japanese banks [Cobham and Subramaniam, 1995: 31].

Mindful of the OECD experience and analytical limitations of the financial liberalisation thesis, Singh (1992) suggested that the real test for capital market in developing economies is its effect on saving, investment and growth. To quote him:

> ... the important question is whether the development of the stock markets in these economies has led to an increase in *aggregate* savings or whether it simply represents the substitution of one form of saving (say bank savings or government bonds) for another (purchase of corporate shares in stock market)... it could be argued that the stock market is still useful insofar as it leads to a more efficient allocation of these savings or to better corporate performance as a result of stock market exposure (p 38-39, emphasis as in the original).

The preceding brief review helps us ask relevant questions about the recent Indian experience. What does capital market growth mean for domestic saving rate, corporate investment rate and output growth? What proportion of physical investment is financed by internal resources? Has it changed since the capital market boom? Does capital market mobilisation represent additional resources for investment or a substitution of external finance for internal resources? Has the composition of external finance changed in recent years? Is capital market boom associated with improved corporated performance? The following section examines these questions empirically.

III

EVIDENCE

India's Corporate Sector: A Brief Account

In this study, the corporate sector is defined as non-financial, non-government joint stock companies. As this sector accessed bulk of the capital market resources, it will be useful to begin by describing the broad dimensions of this sector. In 1994, it consisted of about 3.4 lakh registered companies [Department of Company Affairs, 1995]. Slightly less than half of them are engaged in manufacturing and about a quarter in 'finance, insurance, real estate and business services'. However, bulk of corporate value added originates in registered manufacturing. Only about 12 per cent of the corporate sector are public limited companies, yet they account for about 80 per cent of the total paid up capital. Among public limited companies, the top 670 companies accounted for 43 per cent of net value added in the corporate sector in 1986-87.[23] Only about 2 per cent of public limited companies accessed capital market in 1993-94.

Corporate sector constituted 11 per cent of current GDPfc in 1986-87 (about 9 per cent in 1960-61), and about 27 per cent of non-agriculture, private sector GDPfc.[24] Within the corporate sector, public limited companies' share in value added declined by 10 per cent (from 80 per cent), over two and a half decades from 1960-61. This seems to broadly correspond to faster growth in the number of private limited companies. In other words, private limited companies, representing mostly small and closely held firms, increased their share in corporate sector value added.[25] These statistics show the relative size of India's corporate sector and the (skewed) distribution of firms in it.

Trends in Aggregate Saving and its Composition

As is widely known, India's gross domestic saving rate (GDS) after peaking at 23 per cent of GDP at market prices (GDPmp) in 1978-79, fluctuated around 21 per cent for about a decade, till it regained the earlier level in 1990-91. Figure 11.3 shows five-yearly average in GDS since 1950-51.[26] The share of financial saving in GDS rose steadily from 20 per cent in 1970-71 to about 55 per cent in 1984-85.

Figure 11.3

Gross Domestic Saving as per cent of GDPmp, 1950-51 to 1993-94

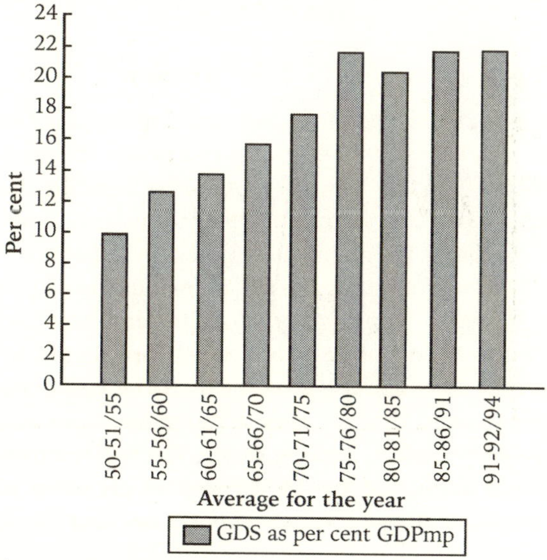

Source: National Accounts Statistics, various issues.

However, it declined to about 40 per cent in the second half of 1980s, though it has improved somewhat subsequently (Figure 11.4). Therefore, no association exists between capital market growth and aggregate saving rate (or its share in financial assets).[27]

However, in the 1980s financial saving's composition shifted away from bank deposits to 'shares and debentures,' with little change in the share of resources accruing to government through contractual saving schemes, like provident fund (Table 11.2). Between 1980-81 and 1992-93, the proportion of 'shares and debentures' in financial saving increased four times, from 5 per cent to 21 per cent. Therefore, the growth of (primary) capital market mobilisation represents a substitution of tradeable securities for (fixed interest rate) bank deposits. Higher than bank interest rate on debentures, with opportunities for capital gains (in case of convertible debentures) and tax saving (in case of tax-free public sector bonds) are perhaps responsible for the shift in the portfolio.[28]

Figure 11.4

Share of Financial Saving in Gross Domestic Saving, 1960-61 to 1991-92

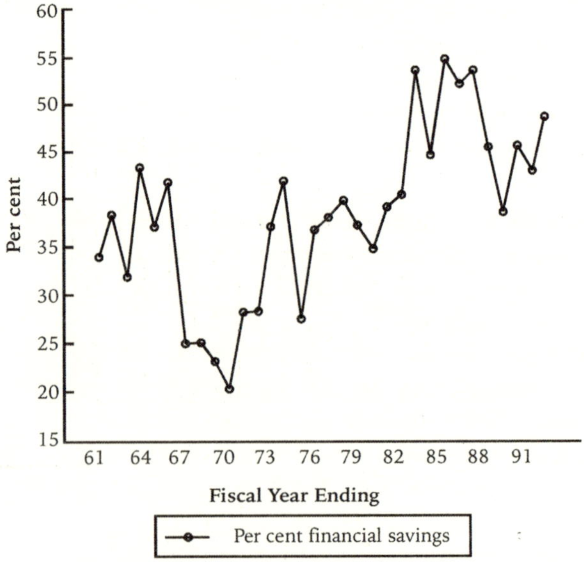

Source: National Accounts Statistics, various issues.

Table 11.2

Changing Composition of Net Financial Saving, 1960-61 to 1993-94

Year	*Bank Deposits*	*Shares and Debentures*	*Government*
1960-61/64-65	23.4	14.3	57.1
1965-66/69-70	29.9	11.2	55.0
1970-71/74-75	42.8	3.8	52.5
1975-76/79-80	44.9	3.3	51.2
1980-81/84-85	38.8	6.0	54.1
1985-86/90-91	26.9	11.8	59.1
1991-92/93-94	29.6	22.6	44.3

Notes: Government includes net claims on government life insurance fund and provident and pension funds

Source: National Accounts Statistics, various issues.

Changing Pattern of Corporate Finance

This subsection uses three sets of time series data: (i) Dutta Roy Choudhury (1992) for 1955-56 to 1986-87, (ii) RBI finances of medium and large non-financial public limited companies, 1960-61 to 1991-92, and (iii) flow of funds (FoF) of private corporate business sector, for 1951-52 to 1991-92.[29] We use balance sheet data as well as FoF table covering overlapping time periods to ensure robustness of our findings. Our effort seems an improvement over Singh (1995) as well as Cobham and Subramaniam (1995) since we use data for the entire private corporate sector, and for three to four decades.

A significant long term trend is a decline in share of internal finance in corporate physical investment. According to the Dutta Roy Choudhury series, gross internal finance as a proportion of (nominal) gross fixed capital formation at (GFCF) declined from a high of 126.5 per cent to 39 per cent between 1966-70 and 1985-87 (Table 11.3, column 1). In the RBI series (column 3), ratio of gross internal finance and (nominal) gross capital formation (GCF) also show a similar trend, though the extent of decline is less. The trend is broadly similar on a 'net' basis as well.[30] In the Dutta Roy Choudhury series, ratio of net retention (retained earning) and (nominal) net fixed capital formation peaked during 1971-75 and reached a low of 5 per cent during 1986-87 (column 2). Using *National Accounts Statistics* (NAS) also, the ratio shows a similar trend, though it improved by early 1990s (column 4). The FoF data for four decades since 1951-52 confirms these changes.[31] This seems significant, as it is at variance with the trends in the developed economies. As mentioned earlier, Mayer showed that in all major OECD countries internal finance forms a high and stable proportion of capital formation.

Table 11.3

Share of Retention in Financing Corporate Physical Investment, 1956-57 to 1991-92

Year	Dutta Roy Choudhury Series		RBI	NAS
	Gross Retention[1]	Net Retention[2]	Series[3]	Series[4]
	(1)	(2)	(3)	(4)
1956-57/59-60	64.4	34.2		34.5
1960-61/64-65	67.1	54.3	60.1	50.5
1965-66/69-70	126.5	55.6	61.9	94.8
1970-71/74-75	95.2	92.5	64.3	119.0
1975-76/79-80	86.7	75.0	62.4	89.7
1980-81/84-85	58.5	37.9	49.6	16.3
1985-86/86-87	39.4	5.0		30.1
1985-86/89-90			49.5	42.3
1990-91/91-92			50.1	

Notes: 1. Gross saving (retained earnings plus depreciation) as per cent of gross fixed capital formation at current prices.
2. Net saving (retained earnings) as per cent of net fixed capital formation at current prices.
3. Gross saving as per cent of gross capital formation for medium- and large- non-financial public limited companies.
4. This includes financial companies and cooperative banks and societies. But since non-financial companies form over 90 per cent of the total, these figures are broadly comparable with the rest of the table.

Source: Dutta Roy Choudhury (1992); *RBI Bulletin*, various issues.

In India, the share of internal finance fell, despite a secular decline in corporate tax provision as a proportion of gross profit, from about 40 per cent in mid-1970s to about 15 per cent by the end of 1980s (Figure 11.5). This perhaps questions the widely held view that tax reduction increases corporate sector's internal resource generation.

Figure 11.5

Tax Provision as percentage of Corporate Sector's Gross Profit, 1960-61 to 1990-91

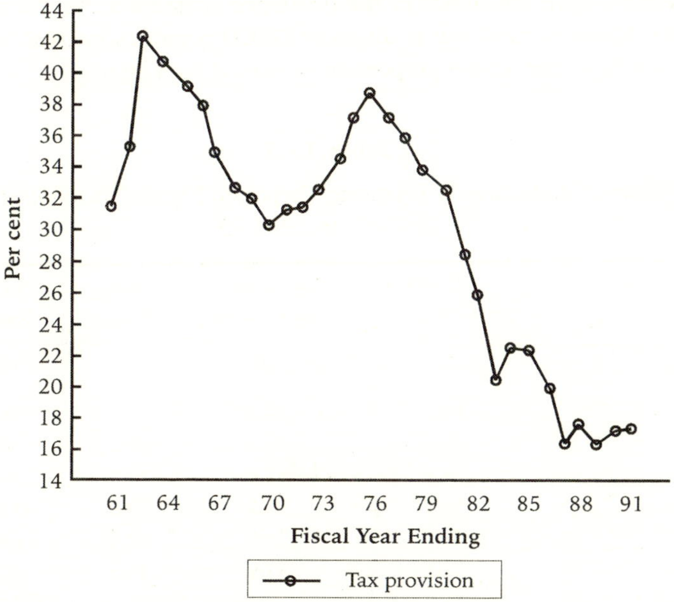

Source: National Accounts Statistics, various issues.

What happened to the composition of external finance with capital market growth? The RBI series show that the share of fresh paid-up capital (including premiums) in total external finance increased from 4.4 per cent during the second half of 1970s to 11.3 per cent a decade later (Table 11.4). This level of equity financing is comparable to that during 1960s.[32] A similar change in external finance's composition is evident as a proportion of corporate gross capital formation also.

However, the share of borrowing has remained stable at over one-half of external finance in 1980s. Therefore, an increase in equity finance has compensated for the decline in the share of trade credit. However, composition of 'borrowing' has changed: shares of banks and fixed deposits have come down significantly, with a corresponding increase in the proportion of debentures (Table 11.5).

Table 11.4

Changing Composition of Corporate Sector's External Finance, 1961-62 to 1990-91

Years	As per cent of Total External Finance			As per cent of Gross Capital Formation		
	Paid-up Capital	Borrowing	Trade Credit	Paid-up Capital	Borrowing	Trade Credit
1961-62/64-65	17.3	52.6	30.0	10.6	33.2	18.9
1965-66/69-70	10.9	56.4	32.5	7.5	38.7	22.1
1970-71/74-75	5.7	40.9	54.5	2.7	23.6	31.9
1975-76/79-80	4.4	46.6	48.7	4.2	45.0	46.4
1980-81/84-85	4.0	55.2	40.2	3.6	50.2	36.3
1985-86/89-90	11.3	55.7	33.5	10.4	57.8	39.3
1990-91/91-92	11.8	54.5	33.6	11.5	55.1	34.0

Note: Paid-up capital includes share premium.
Source: *RBI Bulletin*. various issues.

Table 11.5

Changing Profile of Corporate Borrowing, 1961-62 to 1990-91

Year	Share in Total Borrowing			
	Banks	Debentures	Fixed Deposits	Others
1961-62/64-65	63.3			36.7
1965-66/69-70	62.0			38.0
1970-71/74-75	72.9			27.1
1975-76/79-80	55.6			44.4
1980-81/84-85	30.0	22.0	13.3	34.7
1985-86/89-90	38.3	28.0	6.8	26.9
1990-91/91-92	26.6	23.7	2.7	47.0

Source: *RBI Bulletin*, various issues.

The FoF data since 1951-52 are also consistent with these observations, suggesting that much of the growth of capital market represents substitution of securitised debt for bank credit, trade credit and fixed deposits (with a limited increase in equity financing) (Table 11.6).

In principle, greater reliance on external finance subjects firms to the constant scrutiny of capital market. If an increase in share of

Table 11.6

Financing of Corporate Business Sector, 1951-52 to 1991-92

Year	Deficit Financed by Sectors						Deficit Financed by Instruments				
	Banking	Other Fin. Institution	Government	HH Sector	Rest of the World	Others	Currency	Securities	Loans	Trade Credit	Others
51-52/55-56	15.1	9.6	7.0	66.1	1.9	-	-11.5	47.8	57.5	5.8	-
56-57/60-61	38.6	8.7	10.1	29.9	6.5	6.2	-3.4	31.2	81.6	-7.5	-1.8
61-62/65-66	50.9	22.2	7.2	15.8	3.9	-	-3.8	28.6	80.8	-5.6	-
66-67/70-71	54.9	19.7	6.9	15.3	2.7	0.5	-5.1	19.7	85.6	-2.3	2.4
71-72/75-76	35.5	14.4	6.8	35.2	3.0	5.1	10.7	9.7	45.4	16.6	17.6
76-77/80-81	20.6	18.9	5.7	35.5	0.6	18.6	4.7	14.1	43.6	10.6	26.9
81-82/85-86	29.6	24.1	0.8	24.6	0.7	20.2	-2.8	18.6	47.5	4.0	32.7
86-87/89-90	37.4	48.7	-0.2	8.7	1.1	4.3	-1.4	30.7	43.5	1.0	26.2
90-91/91-92	10.7	77.9	-0.7	8.6	7.4	-3.8	-17.4	29.8	54.4	5.2	38.0

Source: RBI Bulletin, various issues.

external finance boosts corporate investment rate, it may be desirable since, as Singh and Hamid noted, many rapidly industrialising economies like South Korea display such a pattern. As Table 11.7 shows, in India corporate GFCF as a proportions of (i) GDPmp, and (ii) aggregate GFCF increased in the second half of 1980s.

Table 11.7

Gross Fixed Capital Formation, 1955-56 to 1993-94

Year	*Corporate GFCF as per cent of*	
	GDPmp	*Total GFCF*
1955-56/59-60	1.6	12.3
1960-61/64-65	2.5	17.6
1965-66/69-70	1.4	9.5
1970-71/74-75	1.6	10.6
1975-76/79-80	1.6	8.8
1980-81/84-85	3.4	17.5
1985-86/89-90	3.5	16.3
1990-91/93-94	5.7	26.0

Note: All values at current prices.
Source: *National Accounts Statistics*, various issues.

However, is this association statistically significant? Over three decades since 1961-62, (nominal) annual growth rates of capital raised and corporate GFCF have a statistically significant positive correlation (Table 11.8). However, the correlation turns statistically insignificant for the period since 1980-81, when the capital market boomed. The same finding holds with one year lag also. Therefore, on the face of it, the hypothesis that capital market resource mobilisation could have favourably influenced corporate physical investment growth does not seem valid.

Arguably, capital market boom may have contributed to output growth by encouraging better use of existing capital stock. This does not seem to be true either. Growth rate of real net value added in corporate manufacturing is lower than that of registered manufacturing as a whole (Table 11.9).[33] This holds for 1973-74 to 1990-91 as well as for its sub period, 1980-81 to 1990-91, when manufacturing output growth witnessed an upturn. This means (as noted earlier), small sized, non-corporate firms have contributed more to the improvement in manufacturing growth rate in 1980s than the corporate sector.

Table 11.8

Simple Correlation Coefficients between Nominal Annual Growth Rates of Capital Raised and Gross Fixed Capital Formation in Corporate Sector

Year	*No. of Observations*	*Correlation Coefficient*	*No. of Observations*	*Correlation Coefficient*
(1)	*(2)*	*(3)*	*(4)*	*(5)*
1961-62/91-92	31	0.361*	30	0.0
1961-62/79-80	19	0.446*	18	(-)0.424*
1980-81/91-92	12	0.246	11	0.0

Notes: 1. Columns 4 and 5 refer to a lagged relationship between capital raised in year 't' with nominal GFCF in year (t+1).

2. * Statistically significant at 90 per cent confidence level.

Source: National Accounts Statistics, various issues.

Table 11.9

Growth Rates of Real Net Value Added in Registered Manufacturing and Corporate Manufacturing Sectors

(Per cent per year)

Years	*Registered*	*Corporate*
1973-74 to 1990-91	5.7	4.4
1980-81 to 1990-91	7.1	6.3

Note: Implicit registered manufacturing GDP deflators are used to compute real values.

Source: Annual Survey of Industries: Summary Results of Factory Sector, various issues.

Is the capital market boom then associated with improved corporate profitability? Dutta Roy Choudhury data suggest that profitability (gross profit as percentage of capital employed) fell sharply by 7 per cent, from around 19 per cent during 1981-87 (Figure 11.6). This is consistent with Singh and Hamid's estimates for top 50 companies for 1980-88. During the three decades since 1960-61, corporate sector's profit margin (profit before tax as percentage of total income) has come down by more than half (Table 11.10). Profit before tax as percentage of net assets and profit after tax as percentage of net worth (representing return to investor) show a gradual decline since the mid-1970s. However, these trends may have changed somewhat in the 1990s, though the evidence is limited for two years.

One could argue that real efficiency gain in securities market is likely to come from contestability of managements through threat of takeover. This question is as yet largely hypothetical, since this route to possible efficiency gains is legally restricted in India.

To answer the questions that we posed (quoting Singh) in the last section; there is little association between capital market resource mobilisation and aggregate saving rate, and corporate physical investment and output growth rates. As Singh speculated, primary stock market growth seems to represent households sector's substitution of 'shares and debentures' for bank deposits. Firms

Figure 11.6

Corporate Profitability: Gross Profit as percentage of Capital Employed, 1955-56 to 1986-87

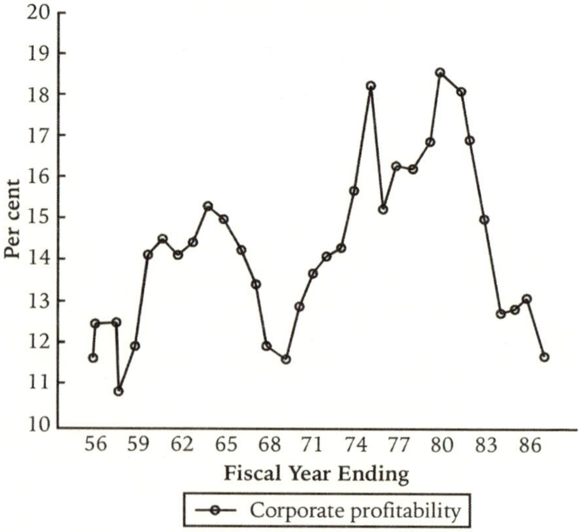

Source: Dutta Roy Choudhury (1992).

Table 11.10

Corporate Profitability, 1960-61 to 1991-92

Years	*PBT as per cent of Total Income*	*PBT as per cent of Net Assets*	*PAT as per cent of Net Worth*
1960-61/64-65	9.0	14.0	9.7
1965-66/69-70	6.9	11.5	8.3
1970-71/74-75	7.3	15.5	11.5
1975-76/79-80	5.9	15.0	10.2
1980-81/84-85	4.7	11.2	11.1
1985-86/89-90	3.7	6.8	7.7
1990-91/91-92	5.9	10.0	12.8

Note: PBT – Profit before tax; PAT – Profit after tax.

Source: RBI Bulletin, various issues.

securitised their debt, instead of getting it from banks, or as trade credit and fixed deposits. These developments represent financial disintermediation that many OECD countries witnessed about a decade ago.[34] No statistically valid relationship exists between growth rates of capital market mobilisation and corporate physical investment (and output) in manufacturing. Significantly, corporate profitability declined in 1980s when capital market boomed.[35] In other words, with capital market growth, an increasing share of loanable funds have accrued to a sector that contributed relatively less to output growth and that did not improve its investment rate either.

IV

CONCLUSIONS

In sum, India's capital market witnessed a rapid growth since around 1980. It accelerated by the end of the decade. This is also significant in comparison with other emerging market economies. Increases in nominal interest rates since early last decade, incentives offered on traded securities, and changes in related policies (and procedures) seem responsible for this development.

The financial liberalisation thesis posits its likely positive effect on the economy's saving, investment and efficiency. A well functioning stock market also has a screening and monitoring role. However, recent advances in analytical literature highlights the possible inefficiencies in financial markets due to imperfect information that could be acute in LDCs, and underscores the need for state intervention. Further, reviving the financing hierarchy hypothesis, the new evidence on corporate financial structure in major OECD countries shows that the stock markets contributed very little to fixed investment. Secondary market's role in improving corporate governance is also open to a serious debate both on theoretical and empirical grounds. In the light of these competing perspectives, this study examined the implications of the India's capital market boom for the economy and the corporate sector.

Capital market growth has changed domestic financial saving's composition from bank deposits to 'shares and debentures', without favourably influencing domestic saving rate, or its share in financial assets. Equity capital's share in the total capital market mobilisation declined, as bulk of such mobilisation is in the form of debt securities. However, growth rate of fresh equity capital raised is substantial. Promoters' contribution to it has more than doubled. This could possibly improve financial performance as promoters have a greater stake in their firms.

Over the last two decades, the corporate sector that secured most of these resources witnessed a long-term decline in the share of internal finance in corporate physical investment. In mid-1980s, retained earning accounted for less than 10 per cent of gross internal resources. This happened, despite a steady fall in tax burden (tax provision as proportion of gross profits). These changes are quite at variance with the developed countries' experience, where internal finance forms the largest and stable source of finance for corporate capital formation.

In 1980s, composition of external finance shifted away from trade credit to equity capital (including share premium), while the proportion of borrowing remained high and increased somewhat. However, within borrowing, debentures replaced bank credit and fixed deposits.

There is no statistically valid association between capital market resource mobilisation and growth in corporate fixed investment or growth in this sector's real value added. Thus, we have witnessed, mainly, financial disintermediation, with little effect on aggregate saving rate and corporate investment and output growth rates. This seems similar to what happened in many developed economies with financial deregulation about a decade ago. All indicators of corporate profitability show a decline in 1980s.

If our findings are valid, they appear significant. The widely held view of positive effects of stock market growth on the economy's real sector, perhaps, needs to be taken with caution. Moreover, the findings seem to raise many questions. How could corporate sector access such large resources when its profitability was steadily declining? Why did the share of retained earning decline when the corporate tax burden fell? Is the fall in profitability related to decline in share of internal finance? Finally, and perhaps more fundamentally, if capital market has little relation to corporate investment rate and output growth rate, what does capital market growth mean for the economy? Is it, then, merely a side show?[36]

Capital market is not just an institution for resource mobilisation, but equally important, a market for corporate control that necessarily follows. Assume that, over time, widely perceived capital market imperfections are overcome with better regulation and technology. Are we, then, prepared for contestability of corporate management through mergers and takeovers in the secondary market? Assuming such a market is organised efficiently, does it necessarily improve corporate performance? These widely debated issues in developed economies seem to have an increasing relevance for India.

The Anglo-Saxon 'model' of corporate governance reportedly leads to 'shortism' as investors have arms length relation with managers. Threat of takeover apparently leads managers to resort to short-sighted policies, at the expense of long-term goal of growth and technical progress. In contrast, German and Japanese firms, that have close links with their banks, are said to be free from such pressures to show immediate results, and hence are able to take a long-term view of the firm's prospects.

In other words, the critical question is, what sort of a market economy we intend to move towards: is it the Anglo-Saxon 'model' with the primacy of capital market emphasising 'efficiency' and liquidity with the attendant shortism of corporate managements, or the German and Japanese styles of bank centric corporate governance with limited role for stock market but primacy to long-term growth and technical progress.[37]

These issues perhaps cannot be ignored any longer.

Notes

1. In this paper 'capital market' is used narrowly to refer to India's stock markets. Strictly, stock market refers to issuing and trading of equities. Since the bulk of resources mobilised in Indian stock markets are debt securities, we prefer, for convenience, using the term capital market.
2. Market capitalisation ratio, is the market value of all traded shares, as a proportion of current gross domestic product at factor cost (GDPfc). This is a widely used measure of stock market size.
3. Though the secondary stock market has grown substantially both in absolute and comparative terms, one has to recognise its narrow base. In 1992-93, top 50 firms account for over two-thirds of trading volume in Bombay Stock Exchange that does over 70 per cent of trading in all stock exchanges in India [CMIE, 1994; Machiraju, 1995].
4. A convertible debenture is a debt instrument, which is (or can be) partially or fully converted into equity share(s) at predetermined time and ratio, as specified in the initial public offer.
5. Increased promoters' contribution could partly be an illusion, as those eligible for contributing to promoters' share may have been enlarged. One suspects that in a regime of licensing and capital controls with booming securities prices, promoters' quota could have been used to dispense favours, similar to Japan's 'Recruit scandal' some years ago.
6. In 1980s a number of financial services firms like merchant bankers, underwriters, mutual funds, custodial services, etc., came into existence, mostly by existing public sector banks and financial institutions. Some of them were discredited in the 1992 stock market scam. However, since 1991 private sector firms including many with foreign origin also entered these newer industries. Instruments are convertible debentures, variety of mutual funds, etc. See Machiraju (1995) for descriptive details.
7. This is an overestimate due to double counting. We know, a significant proportion of firms is listed in more than one stock exchange in India. Bombay Stock Exchange, oldest and busiest of all, listed 2,601 companies in 1992 [CMIE, 1994]. This figure, we guess, is more accurate.
8. Demirguc-Kunt and Levine's (1995) stylised facts seem to underestimate size of India's stock market. In their set of 41 countries. India ranks 31st in market capitalisation, with 16 per cent of GDP, during 1986-93.
9. Documenting India's financial development up to 1977, Goldsmith (1983) said: "The open capital market has been only a secondary source of funds for corporate business... Thus, the market for corporate issues seems not to have developed since independence, and, in addition, to have lost considerably in importance" (pp 204-06).

   In describing India's financial system and structure, Raj (1992) perhaps did not find capital market significant enough to mention it.
10. Foreign Exchange Regulation Act (FERA). 1973, required all foreign-controlled rupee companies to dilute foreign equity hold to 40 per cent, though the law's implementation depended on the firms' relative bargaining power *vis-à-vis* the government. However, in most cases, these firms did not disinvest their holding. Instead, they issued fresh equities to Indian public, thus reducing their share in the paid-up capital, without losing their controlling interest in most cases.
11. Rao's (1980) conclusion aptly reflects the dominant opinion before the capital market boom, "... industrial units have relied heavily for finance on the public financial institutions and banks, and have raised relatively little capital from the market... with reordering of priorities over the last decade, an increasing proportion of resources of the commercial banks are channelled to other uses such as meeting increased reserve requirements and credit to priority sectors... . Industrial expansion, therefore, must rely on raising more capital from the market ... industrial units can be.... . encouraged to meet their financing requirement from a wide range of investors through marketable securities that can assist in the development of capital market" (p 153-54).

12. Observing that firms depend on banks and DFIs for finance, and households invest in bank deposits. Patil (1979) argued for greater participation of household sector in financing firms' equity capital. This led to an interesting debate, mostly by practitioners of finance, on the need to develop capital market as a source of risk capital. See also, Chitale (1980).
13. Lall (1983) offers a critical comment on the assumptions underlying the Committee's recommendation that seem relevant even now.
14. CMIE (1986) documents these changes in policies and procedures.
15. *World Development Report, 1989* highlighted success of India's capital market reforms [World Bank, 1989: 108].
16. To quote Cho, "In a credit market with imperfect information, liberalisation of the banking system... would not, by itself, be sufficient to achieve full efficiency... This is due to the adverse selection effect (and also the moral hazard effect) that occurs when debt contracts are used in the presence of asymmetric information... Equity contracts, however, are free from adverse selection effects and could thus overcome inefficient allocation of capital when the same degree of imperfect information on borrowers exists as in the case of debt contracts" [Cho, 1986:198].
17. To quote Keynes' well known remark on Wall Street, "... In one of the greatest investment market in the world, namely, New York, the influence of speculation ... is enormous ... . Speculators may do no harm as bubbles on a steady stream of enterprise. But the position is serious when enterprise becomes the bubble on a whirlpool of speculation. When the capital development of a country becomes a by-product of the activities of a casino, the job is likely to be ill done. The measures of success attained by Wall Street, regarded as an institution of which the proper purpose is to direct new investment into most profitable channels in terms of future yields, cannot be claimed as one of the outstanding triumphs of *laissez-faire* capitalism..." [Keynes, 1936].
18. To quote Gerschenkron, "Depending on a given country's degree of economic backwardness on the eve of industrialisation, the course and character of the latter tended to vary in a number of important respects. Those variations can be readily compressed into the short hand of six propositions... . The more backward a country's economy, the greater was the part played by institutional factors designed to increased supply of capital to the nascent industries..." [Gerschenkron, 1962].
19. Dore (1985) says, "The senior British manager, it is said, is bothered about the bottom line in his next half-yearly results: the Japanese manager about his market share in five years time. The Japanese manager is more concerned with long-range planning, more assiduous in gathering information about the probable state of markets and the directions to be taken by technological development over the long-term" (p 10).
20. Quite at variance with the WDR view, Mayer's background study for the report cautions against a benign view of stock market development. Tilting it provocatively, *Myths of the West* Mayer (1989) makes following 10 observations, based on his studies using corporate balance sheet data:

    Retentions are the dominant source of finance in all countries (p 9).

    There are some marked variations in self-financing ratios across countries. In UK and US more than three quarters of investment is funded from retentions. In France, Japan and Italy, appreciably more is raised externally. Canada and Germany lie somewhere between the two groups (p 9-10).

    In no country do companies raise substantial amount of finance from securities market (p 10).

    Banks are the dominant source of external finance in all countries.

    Bank finance is particularly pronounced in France, Italy and Japan. It represents a surprisingly small proportion of German corporate financing.

    UK investment has been consistently financed from retentions (91 per cent on average). Bank finance has contributed close to zero (3 per cent on average) on a net basis.

There is a strong inverse relation between the proportion of expenditure financed from retentions and bank credit.

Securities markets have declined in significance as source of finance for British industry. Trade credit increased in importance at the end of 1960s and early 1970s.

Small- and medium-sized firms are considerably more reliant on external finance than large firms. A smaller proportion of small than large company finance comes from securities market.

Bank (and short-term) finance account for approximately two-thirds of UK companies total debt but more than five-sixth of small companies debt.

21. Demirguc-Kunt and Levine (1995) is the other significant study that collects and compares stock market development indicators in a cross-country perspective, from 1986 to 1993. This study's focus is on the characteristics of secondary market and relates them to financial development.

22. Singh is very circumspect on the implications of this findings. However, on their basis IFC seems to justify its efforts in promoting stock markets in these economies.

23. This is estimated using CMIE (1994) and Dutta Roy Choudhury (1992).

24. These estimates are based on Dutta Roy Choudhury (1992) and *National Accounts Statistics.*

25. These numbers should be interpreted cautiously. Private limited companies should not be simplistically viewed as 'independent' and/or 'small' firms doing better than large ones. As Hazari had revealed long ago, a sizeable proportion of private limited companies are closely related to large firms, in terms of ownership and management — often called 'satellite' companies in popular parlance. Moreover, many holding companies that control India's large business houses are private limited companies. Very often, newer entrepreneurial groups that emerge in capital market usually do so after their success with a number of private limited companies and family-owned business.

26. The average for the second half of 1980s is extended by a year to include 1990-91 as this marks an end of a certain policy regime. In this and subsequent graph, we avoid interpreting the trends since 1990-91, as the saving estimate is disputed.

27. Interestingly, the period of rapid rise in the share of financial saving ratio is associated with rapid geographical expansion of banking services though offered negative real interest rates.

28. During 1989-90 and 1991-92, public sector tax-free bonds formed 40 per cent of capital market mobilisation.

29. RBI's surveys of medium- and large- non-financial public limited companies, using uniform definitions and concepts since 1949, accounting for over four-fifths of private corporate sector's paid-up capital and sales forms the basis of this study.

    Using RBI company finance data, Dutta Roy Choudhury (1992), has arrived at 'population' estimates for the non-financial private corporate sector and relate them to national income aggregates. Thus we have consistent time series for about three decades since the mid-1950s.

    We also use RBI's flow of funds table for 'private corporate business'. This includes non-financial private corporate sector plus non-financial cooperative sector. Since the latter is very small, private corporate business can be proxied for the corporate sector.

30. These, we guess, are strictly comparable to Mayer's estimates as we use company balance sheet data, and on a 'net' basis.

31. Gross saving financed two-thirds of gross capital formation in private corporate business during the First Plan (1951-52 to 1955-56). The ratio came down to a little over one-third in the Seventh Plan (1986-87) to 1987-88) [Ramachandra Rao, 1989].

32. But, unlike then, when DFIs used to subscribe much of it as underwrites (as Goldsmith suggested), in 1980s public seems to hold bulk of the fresh equity.

33. Following Shanta's (1992) method, using *Annual Survey of Industries,* we estimate private corporate manufacturing value added by subtracting proprietary and partnership firms' share from that of 'wholly privately owned' firms.

34. According to Goodhart (1992), "disintermediation is ... said to occur when some intervention, usually by government agencies for purpose of controlling, or regulating, the growth of financial intermediaries, lessens their advantages in the provision of financial services and drives financial transfers and business into other channels. In some cases the transfer of funds that otherwise would have gone through the books of financial intermediaries now pass directly from saver to borrower" (p 683).
35. We are very circumspect in interpreting this trend, since 1980s also witnessed an increase in competition in industrial goods markets in response to gradual loosening of investment licensing and import restrictions.
36. This is a widely debated issue in recent literature developed country context. For a brief review of the literature and fresh evidence for the US, see Samuel (1996b).
37. *The Economist,* (May 5, 1990) in a perceptively titled survey, "Capitalism: In Triumph, In Flux," raised some of these issues, for a wider audience.

References

Bhide, Amar (1994). "Efficient Government and Deficient Governance," *Harvard Business Review,* Vol. 27, No 6, November-December.

Centre for Monitoring Indian Economy (1986). *The Liberalisation Process,* Bombay.

————. (1992). *Key Financial Data on Larger Business Units,* Bombay.

————. (1994). *Basic Statistics: India,* Volume 1, Mumbai.

Chitale, R.P. (1980). "Finance for Industry," *Economic and Political Weekly,* April 26.

Cho, Y.J. (1986). "Inefficiencies from Financial Liberalisation in the Absence of Well-functioning Equity Markets," *Journal of Money, Credit and Banking,* Vol. 18.

Cobham, David and Subramaniam (1995). "Corporate Finance in Developing Countries: New Evidence from India," *Discussion Paper* No. 9512, Centre for Research into Industry, Enterprise, Finance and the Firm, University of St. Andrews, Scotland.

Demirguc-Kunt, Asli and Levine, Ross (1995). "Stock-market Development and Financial Intermediaries: Stylised Facts," *Policy Research Working Paper* 1462, the World Bank, Washington, DC.

Department of Company Affairs (1995). *Annual Report, 1994-95,* Ministry of Law, Justice and Company Affairs, Government of India, New Delhi.

Dimsdale, Nicholas and Martha Prevezer (eds.) (1994). *Capital Market and Corporate Governance,* Clarendon Press, Oxford.

Donaldson, Gorden (1961). *Corporate Debt Strategy: A Study of Corporate Debt Policy Determinants of Corporate Capacity,* Harvard University Press, Boston.

Dore R.P. (1985). "Financial Structures and the Long Term View," *Policy Studies,* No. 6, July.

Dutta Roy Choudhury, Uma (1992). "Finances of the Private Corporate Sector: 1955-56 to 1986-87," *Journal of Indian School of Political Economy,* Volume 4, No. 4.

Gerschenkron, Alexender (1962). *Economic Backwardness in Historical Perspective,* Harvard University Press, Cambridge, Massachusetts.

Goldsmith, Raynold W. (1983). *The Financial Development of India, 1960-1977,* Yale University Press, New Haven.

Goodhart, Charles (1992). "Disintermediation," *The New Palgrave Dictionary of Money and Finance,* Volume 2, Macmilan, London.

Government of India (1991). *Report of the Committee on the Financial System* (Chairman: M Narasimham), New Delhi.

Keynes, J.M. (1986). *General Theory of Employment, Interest and Money,* Harcourt Brace and Co. New York.

Koch, Alfred R. (1943). *The Financing of Large Corporations. 1920-39,* NBER, New York.

Lall, Vinay D. (1983). "Financing of Private Corporate Sector," *Economic and Political Weekly,* August 6.

Machiraju, H.R. (1995). *The Working of Stock-Exchanges in India,* New Age International Publishers, New Delhi.

Mayer, Colin (1989). "Myths of the West: Lessons from Developed Countries for Development Finance," *WPS* 301. The World Bank, Washington, DC.

———. (1992). "Corporate Finance," *The New Palgrave Dictionary of Money and Finance,* Volume 2, Macmillan, London.

McKinnon, R.I. (1973). *Money and Capital in Economic Development,* Brooking Institution, Washington, DC.

Morris, Felipe (1985). "India's Financial System: An Overview of its Principle Structural Features," *World Bank Staff Working Paper* No. 739, The World Bank, Washington. DC.

Patil, R.H. (1979). "Tax Treatment of Interest Cost in the Context of Increasing Reliance on Debt Financing," *Economic and Political Weekly,* September 22.

Planning Commission (1982). *Report of the Study Group on Financing of the Private Corporate Sector in the Sixth Five-Year Plan* (Chairman: C Rangarajan), Government of India, New Delhi.

Raj, K.N. (1992). "India: Monetary and Financial System," *The New Palgrave Dictionary of Money and Finance,* Volume 2, Macmilan, London.

Rao, D.C. (1980). "The Structure of Corporate Finance and Some Related Policy issues," *Reserve Bank of India, Occasional Papers,* Vol. 1 No. 2.

Rao, K.S. Ramachandra (1989). "Financing of Sectoral Investment During Plan Period," *Reserve Bank of India, Occasional Papers,* Vol. 10, No. 4, December.

Samuel, Cherian (1996a). "The Stock Market as a Source of Finance: A Comparison of U S and Indian Firms," *Policy Research Working Paper* 1592. The World Bank, Washington, DC.

———. (1996b). "Stock Market and Investment: The signaling Role of the Market," *Policy Research Working Paper* No 1612, The World Bank, Washington, DC.

Shanta, N. (1992). "Trends in Private Corporate Savings," Centre for Development Studies, *Occasional Paper Series,* Trivandrum.

Shaw, Edward (1973). *Financial Deepening in Economic Development,* Oxford University Press, New York.

Singh, Ajit (1992). "The Stock Market and Economic Development: Should Developing Countries Encourage Stock Markets?," *UNCTAD/OSG/DP/49.*

———. (1995). "Corporate Financial Patterns in Industrialising Economies: A Comparative International Study," *Technical Paper* 2, International Finance Corporation, The World Bank, Washington, DC.

Singh, Ajit and Javed Hamid (1992). "Corporate Financial Structures in Developing Countries." *Technical Paper 1,* International Finance Corporation, The World Bank, Washington, DC.

Stiglitz, Joseph E. (1991). "Government, Financial Markets and Economic Development," *NBER Working Paper* No. 3669.

———. (1993). "The Role of State in Financial Markets," *World Bank Research Observer,* Proceedings of the Bank Annual Conference on Development Economics, 1993.

World Bank (1989). *World Development Report, 1989,* Washington, DC.

Zysman, John (1983). *Governments, Markets and Growth: Financial Systems and Politics of Industrial Change.* Cornell University Press, Ithaca.

Economic and Political Weekly, Vol. 31, Nos. 35-37 (Special Number), September 1996.

12

Foreign Direct Investment in India

Trends and Issues

Introduction

Compared to most industrialising economies, India followed a fairly restrictive foreign private investment policy until 1991—relying more on bilateral and multilateral loans with long maturities. Inward foreign direct investment (FDI, or foreign investment, or foreign capital hereafter) was perceived essentially as a means of acquiring industrial technology that was unavailable through licensing agreements and capital goods import. Technology imports were preferred to financial and technical collaborations. Even for technology licensing agreements, there were restrictions on the rates of royalty payment and technical fees. Development banks largely met the external financial needs for importing capital equipment. However, foreign investment was permitted in designated industries, subject to varying conditions on setting up joint ventures with domestic partners, local content clauses, export obligations, promotion of local R&D and so on—broadly similar to those followed in many rapidly industrialising Asian economies.

Foreign Exchange and Regulation Act (FERA), 1974 stipulated foreign firms to have equity holding only up to 40 per cent, exemptions were at the government's discretion. Setting up of branch plants was usually disallowed; foreign subsidiaries were induced to gradually dilute their equity holding to less than 40 per cent in the domestic capital market. The law also prohibited the use of foreign brands, but promoted hybrid domestic brands (Hero-Honda, for instance). However, pragmatism prevailed to ensure stable domestic supply at reasonable prices.

Such a restrictive policy is believed to have retarded domestic technical capability (as reflected in the poor quality of Indian goods);

it also meant a loss of export opportunity of labour-intensive manufactures—in contrast to many successful East Asian economies. Moreover, such a policy is said to have encouraged 'rent seeking' by domestic partners on imported technology—with little efforts to improve product quality, undertake innovation, and seek export markets [Ahluwalia, 1985]. This popular perception was perhaps best illustrated by the passenger car industry that produced obsolete (and fuel-inefficient) models of the 1950s at very high costs in small numbers.

Without denying some of these arguments and evidence, others have shown that the regulation reduced costs of technology imports [Subramaniam, 1991], and promoted export of goods with relatively stable technologies where domestic firms had the opportunity of 'learning by doing' by catering to the large domestic market—as illustrated by successful firms like TELCO (commercial vehicles) and BHEL (heavy electrical equipment) [Lall, 1982]. The recent international achievements of some Indian pharmaceutical firms (Cipla, Ranbaxy, Dr. Reddy's Laboratories, for instance) are also attributed to the regulatory and promotional policies, and the patent laws [Chaudhuri, 1999] that sought to encourage domestic production to reduce drug prices.

However, the 1980s witnessed a gradual relaxation of the foreign investment rules—perhaps best symbolised by the setting up of Maruti, a central government joint venture small car project with Japan's Suzuki Motors in 1982. It was followed by Pepsi's entry in the second half of the decade, to primarily export processed-food products from Punjab, and also to bottle its well known beverages for the domestic market.

Reforms in the 1990s

All this changed since 1991. Foreign investment is now seen as a source of scarce capital, technology and managerial skills that were considered necessary in an open, competitive, world economy. India sought to consciously 'benchmark' its policies against those of the rapidly growing south-east Asian economies to attract a greater share of the world FDI inflows. Over the decade, India not only permitted foreign investment in almost all sectors of the economy (barring agriculture, and, until recently, real estate), but also allowed foreign portfolio investment—thus, practically divorcing foreign investment from the erstwhile technology acquisition effort. Further, laws were changed to provide foreign firms the same standing as the domestic ones.[1]

What are the trends in the quantum and composition of the FDI inflow; and what are their benefits and costs to the economy? This paper seeks to provide a preliminary answer for these questions. To do so, we first discuss, very briefly, the recent literature on foreign investment and economic development (Section I). The limitations of the available data to test the propositions following from the analytical literature are discussed in Section II. As a first step in our assessment, Section III describes the trends in FDI in the 1990s. Section IV contains a brief comparison of foreign investment in India and China—an issue that has a bearing on the current policy discussion. Based on the available, limited and preliminary, information, Section V makes an initial assessment of foreign investment by raising some issues for further work, Section VI suggests a more realistic policy on the basis of the analytical discussion and comparative experience. Section VII concludes by summarising the study's main findings.

I

A BRIEF ANALYTICAL REVIEW

Much of the currently held perceptions of foreign investment's role essentially take a macroeconomic view: it is a source of additional external finance (and of risk capital), augmenting fixed investment, potential output and employment.[2] Such a positive view gained currency mainly after the crises in Latin America in the early 1980s, more recently in east Asia, when other forms of capital inflows quickly dried up (or reversed), accentuating the macroeconomic vulnerability of these economies. As against portfolio investment, FDI is also seen as a source of technology and managerial skills, creating tangible (and intangible) assets in the host economy. Foreign firms seek not only the domestic market, but also provide access to external markets by sourcing manufactured products (and services) from domestic firms.

The crux of the policy, therefore, is how the benefits of such investments are distributed between the foreign firms and the host country, as also between the various factors of production within the host country. In other words, the real question is the cost of foreign capital to the host economy: is it too high, compared to the alternative sources of external finance and technology, in the short and the long run?

However, in a microeconomic perspective, a different set of questions is usually asked: What does FDI do to the working of the domestic markets, and their effect on output and productivity growth [Caves, 1996]. If, as is often the case, the entry of a foreign firm results in the creation of a domestic monopoly, then the benefits of such investment may be limited, unless accompanied by a sound anti-trust law (or competition policy). Similarly, if FDI inflow results in the displacement of domestic monopolies with the foreign ones, then again, social benefits of such investments may be marginal (if any), as any monopolist, regardless of its origin, would maximise profits either by varying price or output (or both). Moreover, the host government may have considerable difficulty in enforcing domestic laws adequately, as foreign firms often seek protection under complicated legal structures.[3]

In industrial organisation literature, from a variety of analytical perspectives, foreign firms are seen as having firm-specific advantages —including significant market power that they seek to exploit in many countries.[4] Availability and costs of these resources for the host economy depend on the relative bargaining strength of the foreign firms *vis-a-vis* the domestic firms (and the host government). While the foreign firms' advantages lie in their size, control over technology and marketing strength worldwide, the host country can use its domestic market, access to cheap labour, location and quality of infrastructure (all of which go to reduce the cost of production to service the international market) to bargain with the foreign firms.

Thus, a social cost benefit approach is perhaps a meaningful method to assess the potential effects of FDI. If such a view is valid, then what countries should do is perhaps not to maximise foreign investment inflow per se, but to channel it in the desired directions to maximise long-term returns to the economy. From the development economics perspective, the questions one asks could get even deeper.

In a world with unequal resources and technological capabilities (including brand names), how does FDI affect the ownership and control of industrial firms? In the market for industrial technologies that is invariably oligopolistic, does foreign capital inflow augment or reduce access to technology and domestic R&D efforts? Does foreign capital improve exports (and export capability) from the host country? What is the cost of FDI over a long period; is it necessarily lower than that of external debt [Helleiner, 1989]?[5]

It is perhaps worth reiterating that markets for industrial technologies continue to be imperfect and probably have got accentuated with the recent international agreements like the TRIPS. Moreover, the experience of the last half a century clearly suggests that countries with liberal FDI and technology import policy are not necessarily the examples of successful industrialisation [Bruton 1989]. They may have become either outposts of foreign firms servicing regional markets (like Singapore), or partners in the international division of labour with limited mastery over production technology and generation of domestic brand names (Brazilian automobile industry, for example).

In the development literature, well reflected in the Indian discourse, there is a wide consensus that regulation reduces costs of imported technology [Lall, 1989]. One of the ways to acquire the disembodied technology is to 'unbundle' the package that foreign firms offer, and to buy the technology outright, while providing for capital investment by the domestic financial system. This has been the time-tested method of all the successful late industrialising economies [Amsden, 2001].[6]

II

DATA ON FDI AND THEIR LIMITATIONS

To understand how the recent changes in foreign investment policy have influenced the economy, quantitative information is needed on broad dimensions of the investment (and its distribution) across industries, regions and by size of projects; firm and industry level production accounts, and audited financial statements. However, such information is scarce. The most easily available (and widely used) data in India are on FDI approvals (contracted), by broad industry group

(1-digit ISIC), by country of origin, and by states (regions) of destination. This represents mere intentions of investment. The actual (or realised) foreign investment is not available by the same classification, but according to the administrative and institutional channels of the inflow. Therefore, it is not possible to compare the realised with the intentions, in any meaningful manner. Apparently, even the concerned official agency does not seem to know—let alone monitor—how the actual inflows are translated into capital formation, transfer of assets or change in managerial control.

The actual FDI inflow is recorded under five broad heads: (i) Reserve Bank of India's (RBI) automatic approval route for equity holding up to 51 per cent, (ii) Foreign Investment Board's discretionary approval route for larger projects with equity holding greater than 51 per cent, (iii) acquisition of shares route (since 1996), (iv) RBI's non-resident Indian (NRI) schemes, and (v) external commercial borrowings (ADR/GDR route). Reportedly, the Indian definition of FDI differs from that of the IMF, as well as of the UN's *World Investment Report*. IMF's definition includes external commercial borrowings, reinvested earnings and subordinated debt, while the *World Investment Report* excludes external commercial borrowings.[7]

Ideally, FDI inflow should get reflected in (i) capital formation, (ii) formation of new firms and factories, (iii) increase in foreign equity holding in the existing firms, and (iv) mergers and acquisitions of existing firms and factories (or parts of them). However, the availability of information on them depends on their legal status. We know very little about those registered outside the country, and in tax shelters, like Mauritius. For instance, Enron's Dabhol Power Company —the largest foreign investment project yet—is incorporated in India as an unlimited liability company. But it is a shell company that Enron controls through at least six holding companies registered in various offshore locations [Mehta, 1999].[8]

Similarly, fully owned private limited companies of foreign firms (or branch plants) reveal very little information about their investment and output. An increasingly large proportion of foreign firms have set up fully owned subsidiaries that have become manufacturers (and distributors) by acquiring domestic firms. They provide very little audited financial information to assess the impact of the firms on the industry, and the corporate sector.[9] Considering these legal problems, many of their operations do not seem to get recorded in the RBI's survey of financial performance of foreign controlled companies—a valuable data source in the earlier times.

Therefore, the assessment of foreign investment reported in this study remains preliminary. However, based on the preceding discussion, the issues raised below can perhaps be taken as working hypotheses for further research.

III

THE TRENDS

FDI Approvals and Its Composition

Approved FDI rose from about Rs. 500 crore in 1992 to about Rs. 55 thousand crore in 1997 [*Economic Survey,* 2001-02] (Figure 12.1). Cumulative approved foreign investment during 1991 and 2000, in dollar terms, is about $ 67bn—at an average exchange rate of Rs. 40 to a dollar. A fifth of it is from the US (Table 12.1). Mauritius is the second largest source; reportedly a conduit for many US-based firms, as India has a tax avoidance treaty with it since 1982. In Asia, South Korea has emerged as a new source of foreign investment.[10] A quarter of the approved FDI is for power generation (Table 12.2), followed by telecommunications (mobile phone firms) at 18.5 per cent, and electrical equipment (mainly software) at 10 per cent. While

Figure 12.1

FDI into India, 1992-2000

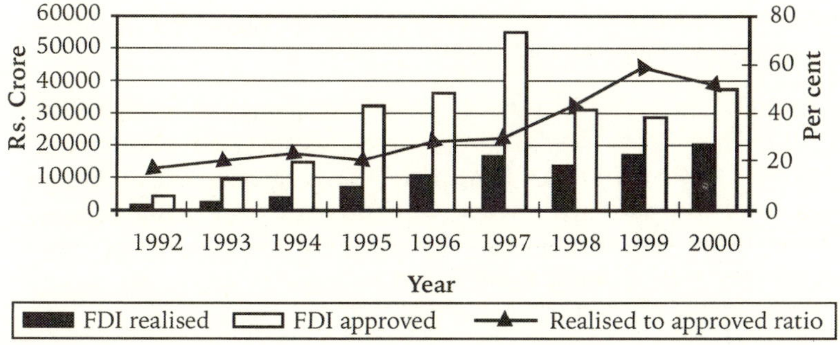

Table 12.1

Top 10 Investing Countries in India, 1991-2000

Country/Region	*Share (in Per Cent)*
US	20.4
Mauritius	11.9
UK	6.4
Japan	4.0
South Korea	3.9
Germany	3.4
Australia	2.7
Malaysia	2.3
France	2.1
Netherlands	1.9

Note: In addition to the countries, external commercial borrowings and non-resident Indians (NRIs) contributed 17.2 and 3.9 per cent of the FDI approvals.

Source: *Handbook of Industrial Policy and Statistics, 2001.*

Table 12.2

Sectoral Distribution of FDI Approvals, 1991-2000

Sector	*No. of Approvals*	*Approved Investment (Rs. Billion)*	*Share (in Per Cent)*
Power and fuel	541	634531.2	25.7
Telecommunications	579	458845.0	18.5
Services sector	790	152389.0	6.2
Chemicals (other than fertilisers)	809	123016.2	5.0
Food processing	648	87574.9	3.5
Transport sector	722	184467.6	7.5
Metallurgical industries	304	143796.8	5.8
Elec. equipment (incl. software)	2491	245791.5	10.0
Textiles	548	33617.8	1.4
Paper and paper products	111	31580.6	1.3
Industrial machinery	530	22438.5	0.9
Others	2404	348976.2	14.2
Total	11965	2467025.3	100.0

Note: Data is for the period, August 1991 to March 1998.

Source: *Handbook of Industrial Policy and Statistics, 2001.*

the proportion of projects with investment up to Rs. 5 crore is high, their share is less than 5 per cent in value. At the other end of the distribution, larger projects with Rs. 100 crore and above account for over two-thirds of the total value of approvals (Table 12.3). Evidently, very little of the FDI has gone to augment exports that are mostly from labour-intensive unregistered manufacturing. The economically advanced states of Maharashtra, Delhi, Karnataka, Tamil Nadu and Gujarat have attracted one-half of the approved foreign investment (Table 12.4).

Table 12.3

Distribution of FDI by Size of Investment, 1991-97

Investment	*No. of FDI Approvals*		*Quantum of FDI Approved*	
(Rs. Crore)	*Number*	*Share (in Per Cent)*	*Amount*	*Share (in Per Cent)*
0-1	3040	49.2	919.4	0.9
1-5	1686	27.3	3800.8	3.6
5-25	906	14.7	10046.0	9.5
25-50	212	3.4	7503.5	7.1
50-100	128	2.1	8828.4	8.4
100-500	173	2.8	38699.0	36.6
Over 500	38	0.6	35992.4	34.0

Note: This distribution is for the approvals during August 1991 and May 1997,
Source: Rao and Murthy (1999).

Table 12.4

Top Five Destinations of Approved FDI among the Indian States

State	*No. of Financial Collaborations Approved*	*Approved FDI ($ Million)*	*Share (in Per Cent)*
Maharashtra	2015	11135.9	16.9
Delhi	1226	9226.7	13.1
Karnataka	1078	5247.1	8.1
Tamil Nadu	1223	5073.8	7.7
Gujarat	458	3129.6	4.5
State not indicated	3119	19476.4	27.9

Source: Handbook of Industrial Policy and Statistics, 2001.

Table 12.5 provides the actual FDI inflow as estimated by four different agencies, for 1991 to 2000. IMF's and the *World Investment Report's* estimates of the cumulative inflow during the 1990s are roughly the same—at about $ 17bn. The *Economic Survey* estimate is about $ 22bn, while that by RBI is $ 17.3bn. The difference between the last two estimates is mainly on account of ADR/GDR inflows. While the *Economic Survey* classifies them as FDI, RBI records them under foreign portfolio investment.

Table 12.5

Alternative Estimates of the Actual FDI, 1991-2000

Year	*Economic Survey (Rs. Crore)*	*RBI (Rs. Crore)*	*International Financial Statistics (Million $)*	*World Investment Report (Million $)*
1991	351	316		155
1992	675	965	276.5	261
1993	1787	1836	550.1	586
1994	3289	4126	973.3	947
1995	6820	7172	2143.6	2144
1996	10389	10015	2426.1	2591
1997	16425	13220	3577.3	3613
1998	13340	10358	2634.7	2614
1999	16868	9338	2168.6	2154
2000	19342	10686	2315.1	2315
Total	89286	68034	17065.3	17080

Sources: *Economic Survey*, various issues; RBI's *Handbook of Statistics on Indian Economy, 2001;* IMF's *International Financial Statistics* CD-ROM; UN's *World Investment Report*, various issues.

As there has been a gradual improvement in the actual inflow from a low base, and a slowdown in the approvals after 1997, there is an increase in the ratio of the actual-to-approved FDI in the last few years. On average, it is a little over one-third in the 1990s (Figure 12.1). India's share in the world foreign investment increased from 0.5 per cent in 1992, to 2.2 per cent in 1997 (Figure 12.2).

Figure 12.3 describes the actual inflow by various routes discussed in the previous section. The FIPB route—representing larger projects requiring the government's discretionary approval—accounts for the bulk of the inflow, though its share is somewhat declining. Automatic approval route *via* RBI meant for smaller sized investments received modest inflow; and the NRI route's share has declined sharply. Proportion of the inflow to acquire shares in the domestic firms, and flotation of ADRs/GDRs have gained in prominence in the second half of the 1990s.

Figure 12.2

India's Share in World FDI

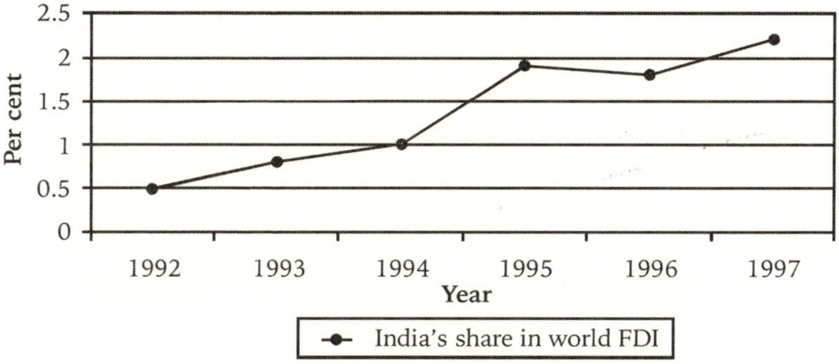

Figure 12.3

Actual FDI by Different Routes

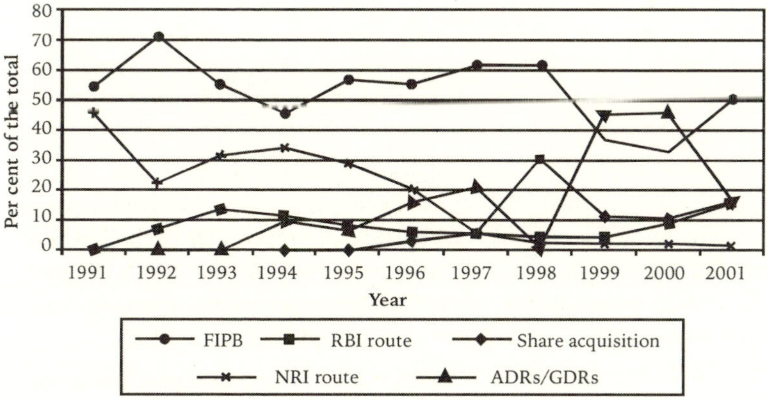

Interpreting the Trends

Though it is not possible to compare the actual with the approved FDI for the reasons discussed earlier, some broad generalisation can perhaps be made based on the available qualitative information. While the bulk of the approvals is for infrastructure, the actual inflow seems to be largely in registered manufacturing—more precisely, in consumer durable goods and automotive industries; very little of it has gone into capital goods industries. The inflow in telecommunication industry is probably to get licences for mobile phone operations, not for manufacturing equipment. The investments in electrical machinery industry are apparently to set up local offices to produce computer software.

Much of the realised FDI has also come in as fully owned subsidiaries (or branch plants) of their parents abroad. Table 12.6 provides an illustrative list of such foreign entities. Most of them have not issued IPOs in the domestic bourses, hence are not quoted companies. Quite contrary to the earlier period, the government has so far not insisted on enforcing its policy in this respect (more about this later).

Table 12.6

An Illustrative List of Foreign Firms Not Listed in the Domestic Stock Market

Product Group	*Foreign Firms*
Automobiles and allied products	GM, Ford, Mercedes Benz, Honda, Hyundai, Fiat, Toyota, Volvo, Yamaha, Cummins, Goodyear
Food and beverages	Coca-cola, Cadbury Schweppes, Kellogg, Heinz, Seagram, Hiram Waker, United Distillers, Perfitti, Wrigley, KFC, McDonalds
Consumer durable goods	Daewoo, Samsung, Sony, General Electric, LG Electronics, Black and Decker, Kimberley Clark
Personal care products	Revlon, L'Oreal, Cussons, Unilevers

Source: Rao, Murthy and Ranganathan (1999).

About 40 per cent of the inflow seems to have been used for acquiring existing industrial assets, and their managerial control (Table 12.7 (i)); and, there seems to be a gradual increase in such merger and acquisitions in the 1990s (Table 12.7 (ii)). Further, Table

12.8 provides an illustrative list of plants (and divisions) of Indian controlled firms acquired by foreign firms in the 1990s. This is also evident from the fact that foreign firms seem to use a larger proportion of their total funds for such acquisition than for capital formation, compared to Indian owned firms in the private corporate sector, the ratio of fixed capital formation to total uses of funds by foreign firms is lower than that by the domestic companies [Nagaraj, 1997].

Table 12.7 (i)

Share of M and A as in FDI Inflows in India

Year	*FDI Inflow ($ Million)*	*M and A Fund ($ Million)*	*Share of M and A Fund in FDI Inflow (Per cent)*
1997	3200	1300	40.6
1998	2900	1000	34.5
1999 (Jan-Mar)	1400	2800	39.4

Source: Kumar (2000: 2852).

Table 12.7 (ii)

Foreign Firms Related M and A in India

Year	*Mergers*	*Acquisitions*	*Total*
1993-94	4	9	13
1994-95	-	7	7
1995-96	-	12	12
1996-97	2	46	48
1997-98	4	61	65
1998-99	2	30	32
1999-00 (up to Jan 2000)	5	74	79
Total	17	239	256

Source: Kumar (2000: 2852).

Predominance of acquisitions in India as a route to FDI is similar to the trends in many developing economies. For instance, in Brazil, the ratio is as high as 70 per cent mainly fuelled by privatisation drive in the 1990s.[11] Foreign firms seem to find it a quick and cheaper route to enter a new market, and secure a sizeable market share.

Table 12.8

An Illustrative List of Units/Divisions Transferred to Foreign Firms

Units to be Transferred/Transferred	*Remark*
Apar Lighting Division	Transferred to the joint-venture (JV) GE-Apar Ltd.
Compressor unit of Kirloskar Brothers	Transferred to Kirloskar Copeland
Compressor unit of SIEL and Kelvinator	Taken over by Tecumseh Venture
Engine valve division of Kirloskar Oil Engines	Proposed to be transferred to a JV with MWP, subsidiary of Mahel Germany
Halol Plant of Hind Motors	Transferred to a JV with GM, of the US
Hinditron Computers	Acquired by Digital Equipment Corp.
India Linoleum	Transferred to a JV with DLW of Germany
Premier Auto	Taken over by Fiat
Luxar Pen	Transferred to a JV with Gillette
Electric meters of VXL Ltd.	Transferred to VXL Landys Gys. Ltd.
Motorcycle division of Escorts	Transferred to Escorts Yamaha Ltd.
Oral Care division of Parle	Acquired by Gillette
Refrigerator division of Godrej & Boyce	Transferred to Godrej-GE appliances
Specialty chemicals div. of Max India	Transferred to Max-Atotech
Stabiliser division of Jan Auto	Taken over by NHK Jai Suspensions Ltd.
Sugar machinery div. of KCP Ltd.	Transferred to FCB-KCP Ltd.
Ceat's two- and three-wheeler tyre plant	Transferred to South Asia Tyres Ltd. with Goodyear

Source: Rao, Murthy and Ranganathan (1999).

Table 12.9

An Illustrative List of Foreign Firms Moving to De-List from Domestic Bourses

Sl. No.	*Company*	*Acquirer's Current Holding (Per Cent)*	*Offer Price (Rs.)*	*Post-offer Holding (Per Cent)*
1	Cabot	60	100	92
2	Cadbury	51	500	90
3	Carrier Aircon	51	100	86
4	Centak Chemicals	75	200	93
5	Hoganas	51	100	85
6	Otis	69	280	79
7	Phillips	51	105	83
8	Reckitt & Colman	51	250	Yet to open
9	Sandvik	73	850	89

Source: Business India, April 1-14, 2002: 118.

Of late, taking advantage of the changes in the rules governing the stock market listing, in a situation of low share price level, many existing foreign firms are re-purchasing their equity to exit from the domestic bourses. Table 12.9 provides an illustrative list of such firms. This represents a reversal of the positive effect that the foreign firms' domestic listing has had on the development of the primary stock market since the late 1970s [Nagaraj, 1996].

IV

A COMPARISON OF FDI IN INDIA AND CHINA

Though the actual FDI inflow in India in the 1990s increased significantly over the past, it is modest compared to many Asian economies (Figure 12.4); and, it pales into insignificance in comparison to China (Figure 12.5).[12,13] UNCTAD's ranking of countries in terms of foreign investment (relative to the size of the economy) for the period 1998-2000 is 119 for India, and 47 for China. The ranking a decade ago was 121 and 61, respectively (*The New York Times,* August 28, 2002). It shows that even at the start of the reforms, China's ranking was way ahead of India's; China moved up in the ranking much faster than India did in the 1990s.

Figure 12.4

FDI in Selected Asian Economies, 1991-2000

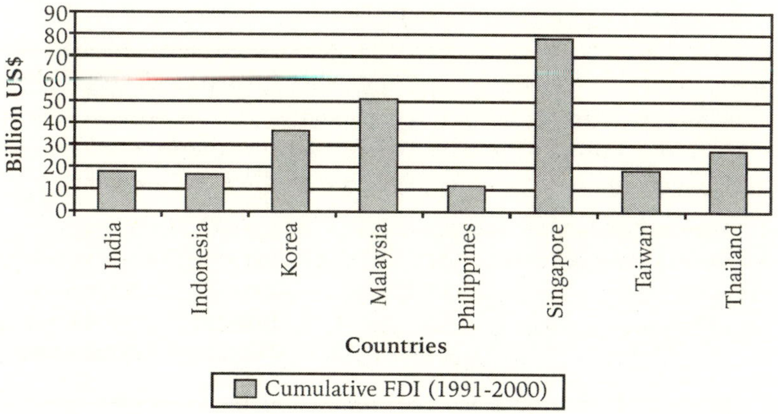

These statistics are widely seen as an evidence of the failure of India's reforms, since greater inflow of foreign capital in China is believed to be largely responsible for its exceptional growth and export performance. As this perception is much discussed in the current policy discourse, we examine the quality of the Indian and the Chinese estimates, and the evidence on the role of FDI on economic performance in the recent years.

Figure 12.5

FDI in India and China

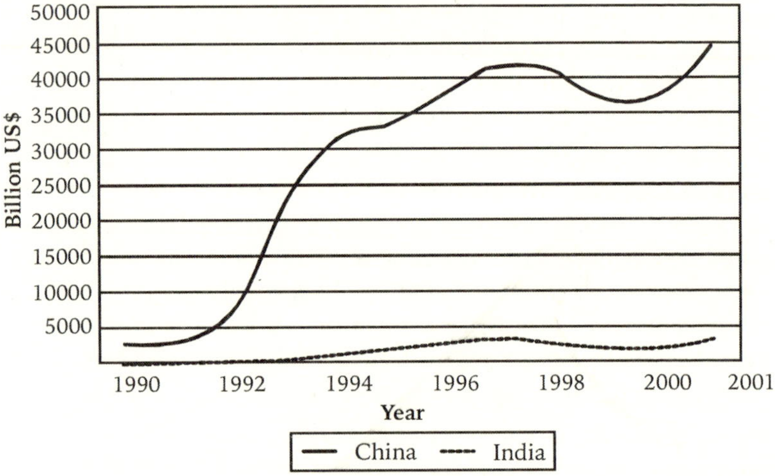

According to IFC (2002), India does not follow the standard IMF definition as it excludes (i) external commercial borrowings, that is ADRs/GDRs, (ii) reinvested profits, and (iii) subordinated debt.[14] IFC is probably right, but only partially. As noted earlier, the *Economic Survey* estimates include external commercial borrowings, but not the remaining two items. Thus, notwithstanding the underestimation of FDI in the Indian statistics, there is little doubt that foreign investment inflow in India is negligible as compared to China.

However, it is well recognised that a large share of the investment inflow in China represents 'round tripping'—recycling of the domestic saving via Hong Kong to take advantage of tax, tariffs and other benefits offered to non-resident Chinese. This is estimated to be in the range of 40-50 per cent of the total FDI (*Global Financial Report, 2002, IFC*).

Further, about a quarter of the inflow in China is invested in real estate [Tseng and Zebregs, 2002]. Some of the Chinese coastal cities have attracted considerable speculative capital in this sector in the 1990s after the collapse of the property prices in Hong Kong. It is widely accepted, especially after the east Asian financial crisis, that foreign investment in real estate is inherently problematic, as this sector can easily give rise to financial bubbles, with potentially adverse macroeconomic consequences.

Of the remaining, only a small fraction has gone into large-scale manufacturing that can potentially augment domestic capability and exports. In fact, FDI from the advanced economies that could bring in newer technology and managerial practices are limited, as the Chinese still seem to have a fairly strict regulation on such inflows. Reportedly, in 31 industries China does not allow wholly foreign owned enterprises; and in 32 others, Chinese partners must hold majority share holding.[15]

Based on the foregoing, the International Finance Corporation's study of business environment, in fact, places India marginally ahead of China – from the viewpoint of foreign investors [IFC, 2002]. The study also found that the quantum of FDI inflow in China and India, as proportions of their respective GDP, is roughly comparable. Thus, the widely held view of China's ability to attract enormous foreign capital needs to be taken with considerable circumspection.

Do countries that attract larger FDI inflow necessarily grow faster? In other words, is there a positive association between foreign investment inflow and GDP growth? Evidence is far from unambiguous. If China's exceptional performance is believed to be largely on account of the foreign capital inflow, then one also has to contend with the recent Brazilian experience that proves the contrary. It has probably attracted the largest FDI from the industrialised economies since 1994. As noted earlier, much of it has gone to acquire domestic assets that were privatised on a large scale. But neither Brazil's growth or its export performance improved in the recent years.

Firm level studies also do not show any evidence that foreign investments improve output and productivity growth [Caves, 1996]. There are, however, numerous cross-country studies that provide conflicting evidence on this issue. But, they often suffer from serious methodological problems. A recent study that seeks to address many of the concerns associated with such exercises, seems to find no evidence of a positive association between FDI inflow and output growth [Carkovic and Levine, 2002].[16]

Thus, the quantum of FDI inflow into China, and its positive effect on the economy are perhaps overstated. Without getting into simplistic comparisons, what we need to appreciate from the Chinese experience is perhaps how to take advantage of the openness to investment and trade, to expand domestic capability and get access to external markets for its labour-intensive manufactures.

V

A PRELIMINARY ASSESSMENT

Focus on Domestic Market

As noted earlier, India's seemingly large (and growing) domestic market is probably the main attraction for foreign firms. For instance, international soft drinks producers and fast food chains that were unknown a decade ago have acquired a visible presence in the metropolitan cities, though their quantitative significance may yet be marginal. These firms have brought with them the oligopolistic market structures and firm rivalries that are evident in the developed economies. While such market structures may have some desirable properties, if they lead to tacit collusion to bar new entry, then it may not be a positive development in the long run.

Similarly, almost all major international automobile companies have set up assembly and manufacturing facilities in varying extent. The same probably holds true for washing machines, refrigerators and entertainment electronics. Such large-scale entry of firms has resulted in increased price and non-price competition, leading to a greater choice and quality improvement—a desirable outcome for consumers.

Initially, there were considerable apprehensions that international firms with their superior technology, marketing skills and financial strength would wipe out domestic firms (and brand names) in many of these industries. To some extent this has indeed happened—in the aerated drink market, for instance. The same is partly true in the automotive industry as well: Fiat gradually acquired Premier Auto (its erstwhile licensee); Hindustan Motors (an erstwhile GM licensee) has largely become a sub-contractor for GM and Ford, producing engines and transmission equipment.

But many technologically strong and financially sound domestic firms seem to have withstood the growing competition—at least so far. In some cases, domestic firms have severed their ties with their foreign collaborators to assert their managerial independence after some years of association, though such cases are only a few.[17] Further, contrary to many early apprehensions, bulk of the domestic firms (and brand names) have not been displaced from the market. Dominant domestic firms have sough to protect their market shares by expanding capacity and distribution networks, contributing, among other factors, to the boom in fixed investment in registered manufacturing in the 1990s [Nagaraj, 2002].

Though foreign firms have acquired a visible presence in consumer durable goods industries, by and large, it has apparently not been an easy entry for them. While, again, no definitive estimates are available, popular reports suggest many of them overestimated the size (and the growth) of the domestic market, and the appeal of international brands, and thus now suffer from excess capacity and poor profits (*Financial Times*, April 25, 2002). Foreign firms seem to have realised the smallness of the domestic market, and price sensitivity of its consumers.[18] Reportedly, a few foreign firms have left India, while many others have staggered their investment and expansion plans.[19]

However, realising the narrowness of the domestic market, many foreign firms are discovering the way out is to indigenise production to reduce costs and secure economies of scale. Moreover, there seems to be a growing appreciation of the cost advantage of domestic manufacturing for exports. For instance, discovering that their car was too expensive for the domestic market, Ford has now found it profitable to use its Indian facilities for the external market. Reportedly, it has exported 30,000 CKD kits to China and South Africa last year [*Business World*, December 2, 2002]. Samsonite is apparently expanding its Indian operations for exports, while closing down its Europe plants. There are similar reports from ABB (electrical equipment manufacturer) and Cummnis (Diesel engine manufacturer) as well. If such a tendency gathers momentum, India could possibly emerge as a competitive manufacturing base in these firms' global production networks.

Problems with Infrastructure Investment

Foreign investment in power generation that attracted the largest approved FDI was predicated on securing a high and assured rate of return on invested capital—modelled after Enron's DPC. It was the first of its kind, offering exchange rate guaranteed 16 per cent rate of return on investment on power purchase by the Maharashtra State Electricity Board. The agreement was not based on competitive bidding, violating many established norms of investment planning for a project of that size and scope. This was apparently done in the early years of the reforms to signal India's eagerness to invite foreign investment.

Most of these power projects did not fructify, as they were based on unrealistic assumptions regarding the profitability and the market size. Moreover, as the Enron's Indian saga unravelled, most foreign firms discovered the state governments' inability to ensure the guaranteed return, hence cancelled their investment plans. The speed and secrecy, with which the Enron project was launched, ignoring the checks and balances in public decision-making, invoked considerable debate in the press, parliament and academia. In retrospect, many of the criticisms seem valid, denting foreign investment's popular image (and the credibility of its exponents).

However, there are probably other reasons as well. Much of the projected demand for power that formed the basis for inviting such a large FDI in this sector was apparently inflated.[20] After the industrial slowdown since the mid-1990s, the demand-supply gap was found to be relatively modest [Nagaraj, 2002]. Moreover, cost of production of the thermal power plants of many state electricity boards using domestic raw material and capital equipment were found to be lower than that of the proposed FDI (invariably using imported feedstock). With hindsight—consistent with much of what the critics maintained—the problem with the power sector was not so much the inefficiency of generation, but pricing and recovery of the user charges. Despite the much publicised reforms in the 1990s, the average revenue-to-cost ratio in the power sector has not improved.

Net Foreign Exchange Inflow

For long it has been held that foreign firms bring in limited net resources in the host economy, as they usually take a large surplus out of the country as dividends and royalties [Chandra, 1991]. This, to some extent, is probably true of what happened in India in the early 1990s, though it may be hard to substantiate. One of the earliest changes in the foreign investment rules after the reforms was to remove the restriction on the foreign equity holding in the existing foreign firms—reversing the policy initiatives of the earlier period. Foreign firms were quick to seize the opportunity to issue large equity to themselves at a fraction of the market prices (when the stock market was booming). This meant, in principle, a substantial FDI inflow in the book of accounts during 1991-94, but in reality it was simply a book transfer without any fresh capital inflow. With a larger proportion of equity held by the parent firms, it is now possible for them to take out an ever-larger share of surplus in perpetuity.[21] Table 12.10 provides an illustrative list of the foreign firms that followed such a practice, and their gains due to the discount on the issue price of the fresh equity.

Table 12.10

An Illustrative List of Foreign Companies that Issued to themselves Shares at a Concession

Sl. No.	*Company*	*No. of Shares Allotted (in million)*	*Preferential Issue Price (in rupees)*	*Market Price on Allotment Date (rupees)*	*Gain to the Company (in million rupees)*
1	Colgate	11.3	60	700	7227.5
2	Castrol	3.5	110	1050	3325.7
3	Sesa Goa	3.3	120	1025	2968.4
4	Asean Brown Boveri	4.8	60	325	1260.0
5	Bata	4.7	35	325	936.7
6	Coats Viyella	7.5	65	260	1444.7
7	Alfa Lavel	3.4	73	290	738.8
8	Nestle	4.8	70	285	1021.6
9	Glaxo	4.5	75	255	808.0
10	Hoechst	2.2	70	370	645.3
11	Lipton	3.5	105	380	972.4
12	Procter & Gamble	4.8	70	285	1021.6
13	Procter & Gamble	1.9	225	340	223.1
14	Phillips	7.7	40	205	340.0
15	Rickitt & Colman	3.0	100	380	848.4
	Total gain to the foreign firms				24737.0

Source: Jain (2001: 219).

It only goes to show how sensitive foreign firms are about the managerial control. In the absence of suitable regulations, they would like to retain an absolute control that may not be desirable for the host country. However, it is often argued that majority equity holding is necessary for international firms to be assured enough to bring in the latest technology that could potentially have positive spillover in the host economy. This view seems suspect. There is some evidence to show it is not the majority control, but the market structure that determines innovation and the introduction of new technology. Mani (1983), in a case study, showed that in the 1970s when the world's leading firms dominated the Indian automotive tyre industry, it was the new Indian entrants like Apollo and Vikrant Tyres that introduced innovations, and not the incumbent firms. Faced with such a threat, foreign firms quickly followed suit to protect their market shares.

Technology Spillovers

As noted earlier, one of the argument in favour of FDI is the potential positive externality of technology into the host economy. However, in reality, the process may not be that simple. We have seen, that foreign investment does not necessarily lead to fixed capital formation; moreover, technical spillovers depend on the extent of value addition that is carried out in the host economy. For instance, assembly operations or production of simple consumer products is likely to have marginal externality.

For instance, most automobile firms—barring Hyundai and to a less extent Ford—have essentially set up minimal facility to assemble and paint their imported CKD kits, leading to a proliferation of firms and models with modest rise in domestic production and technological capability.[22,23]

In other durable goods industries too, foreign firms have acquired dormant domestic firms and/or resorted to contract manufacturing with the existing firms rather than set up green field plants.[24] While these may be efficient strategies for the firms concerned, the social benefit of such arrangements may remain modest. Our contention is consistent with Richard Caves's observation:

> ... While productivity spillovers from foreign subsidiaries to local firms are apparently widespread, they are neither ubiquitous nor independent of firms' market ambient structure ... Spillovers may be a justification

> for LDC government policies to encourage flow of foreign direct investment ... . Justification is likely to be conditional on the country's state of development and the structure of particular industries in which foreign subsidiaries might alight [Caves, 1999: 17].

Decline in Competition

FDI, in principle, brings in greater market discipline on the incumbent firms by increasing competition. But, as we have seen, foreign firms often acquired dominant positions by taking over domestic firms (and brands). This, again, is best illustrated by Coca Cola's acquisition of the dominant domestic competitor, Thumps Up; and Hindustan Lever's—Indian subsidiary of Unilever—acquisition of its largest domestic rival, and the second largest firm in the industry, TOMCO, and the largest cosmetics firm, Lakme.

In principle, in a well-functioning market economy such acquisitions would have attracted the provisions of the competition law. But they went unchallenged in India as the MRTP Act—the anti-trust law—was practically abolished as part of the economic reforms. Further, the government ignored the public and academic criticisms of such acquisitions, as it was keen to signal a positive outlook towards FDI. Thus, our examples show, the widely held view of foreign investment *per se* leading to greater competition needs to be taken with caution.

Foreign Exchange Earnings

One of the common apprehensions against foreign investment is the net drain of foreign exchange in the host countries. Many countries seek to overcome this problem by imposing foreign exchange neutrality clauses. Reportedly even the UK applied such a clause while permitting Japanese automotive firms in the early years of conservative reforms in late 1970s and the early 1980s. Many states in the US apply conditions of job creation while offering incentives for Japanese automotive firms. Though, we do not have data to examine net foreign exchange outgo on account of foreign firms that came into India in the 1990s, the government, reportedly, has been lax in enforcing this clause or has diluted it.[25] This could be a serious matter, especially with many automotive firms that have set up are largely limited assembly plants.

Brand Names

In consumer goods industries intangible assets like brand names matter most; and, it takes a long time and effort to create them. A large home market is widely accepted to be advantageous in building such assets before 'exporting' them. India followed a prudent policy in this respect up to the 1980s. However, in the 1990s, as mentioned earlier, in soft drink industry, Coca Cola bought rival brand Thumps Up; Gold Spot and Limca; Pepsi purchased Mongola, Dukes and so on. The foreign firms destroyed many of the purchased brands that competed with their international ones. Coca Cola 'killed' all competing brands except Thumps Up, as it was too uneconomical to do so. Reportedly, even now, this Cola drink sells four times as much as the worldwide brand of Coke. It only seems to show how 'path dependent' brand loyalty can be in consumer goods. Therefore, there seems to be considerable merit in promoting indigenous brands that have the potential to compete in the world market. Such hasty policy changes could prove a costly mistake in the long run for India, as consumer goods are nothing, but their brand names.[26]

Loss of Bargaining Power in the Technology Market

It is well accepted that dominant international firms have substantial market power, and many developed countries widely intervene in the technology market to protect and promote interests of their firms.[27] Indian policy, after the reforms, practically ceased to intervene in the technology market, significantly weakening domestic firms' bargaining position.

With the increasing role of financial collaborations, foreign technical agreements as a source of technology have steadily dwindled in the 1990s—both in absolute and relative terms (Figure 12.6) [*Economic Survey, 2001-02*]. Evidently, foreign firms do not want to part with their technology, as they can now come into India without a domestic partner.

Considering their superior financial and technical strengths, many foreign firms in the capital goods industry seem to have wrested managerial control in the existing joint ventures in the 1990s. For example, Caterpillar bought out Birla's stake in their joint venture manufacturing earthmoving equipment although the firm was doing well in the market. Many automotive firms started as joint ventures,

Figure 12.6

Decline in Technical Collaborations Agreements

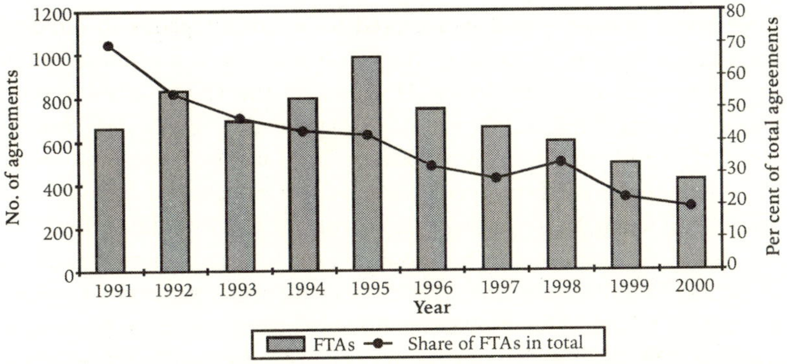

but gradually foreign partners increased their financial stake by buying out domestic partners, as Indian partners were unable to bring in the resources to make up for the losses in the early years of the firms' operations. This happened at a time when the domestic interest rates were higher than the international rates. Foreign partners found it an inexpensive way to acquire a greater managerial control, especially as the currency was steadily depreciating.

For instance, Honda bought out the Sriram group, and Ford acquired Mahindra's stake in their joint venture car projects. However, more recently, there are instances of the converse, where Indian firms have bought out their foreigner partners; for instance, TVS Motors and Suzuki, Kinetic motors and Honda, and LML and Piaggio. But such instances seem far fewer.

Arguably, the above examples illustrate the virtues of a market-driven process for corporate control that is best left to it. Such a benign view may not necessarily favour developing countries and their consumers in the long run. For instance, the demise of Spanish automotive firms with its integration in the European Union, and the lack of technological and market dynamism in the Brazilian auto industry—despite substantial investment and output growth—probably suggests that strategic intervention to support domestic firms and industry are not incompatible with securing dynamic comparative advantage and export competitiveness.

In sum, while the entry of foreign firms has increased competition and improved the variety and quality of consumer goods, there are some disturbing signals. Foreign investment in infrastructure is a failure. Gradual loss of managerial control in many industrial firms, decline in competition in some industries, extinction of some leading domestic brand names and limited improvement in domestic production capability seem to be signs of concern.

VI

TOWARDS A REALISTIC FDI POLICY

It is widely believed that India has not done enough of policy reforms to attract substantially more foreign investment. Moreover, it is not the financial incentives but the lack of adequate infrastructure, bureaucratic delays and above all, the rigid industrial labour laws that have come in the way of attracting more investments [Bajpai and Sachs, 2001]. This view seems to have many limitations. For instance, there is no evidence of a positive association between the extent of market-oriented reforms and FDI inflows across developing economies [Easterly, 2001]. Moreover, as discussed earlier, greater foreign investment inflow does not necessarily mean faster output and export growth. What, then, should guide India's foreign investment policy?

If history is any guide, foreign investment in infrastructure is potentially problematic. Latin America witnessed a wave of foreign infrastructure investment from the US in the 1930s, only to leave with the bitter experience of nationalisations in a couple of decades. It bears repetition that infrastructure is inherently capital-intensive with long gestation lags, and low (but stable) returns over a long period. Market failures are ubiquitous in these industries, with considerable network economies necessarily inviting wide and deep state intervention. In a world consisting of politically independent nations with a growing number of democracies, the pricing of infrastructure is bound to be a political decision. Foreign firms with short pay-back periods invariably find it hard to stay on, as it conflicts with the goals of developing economies caught in an increasingly uncertain world economy.[28]

There are also perhaps some India specific factors for the relatively small foreign capital inflow. It seems worth reiterating that India is still largely an agrarian economy, with land productivity being a third of China's, where the average disposable income after meeting food and clothing (wage goods) requirement is still relatively small. Price-income-ratio of most consumer goods that foreign firms usually sell is high by domestic standards, accentuated perhaps by cultural factors and regional heterogeneity of markets [*Financial Times,* April 25, 2002].

In infrastructure industries, the rupee cost of electricity supply by foreign firms seems high. Given India's fairly diversified industrial capability, and low labour costs, foreign firms may not have a cost advantage over the domestic producers—especially with the currency depreciating in nominal terms. This is perhaps best illustrated, again, by the Enron's DPC. With imported capital goods and fuel, and high operating cost due to international norms of costing, Enron's cost of production was found to be higher than the comparable new plants using domestic capital equipment [Morris, 1996].

At the same time, Hyundai's large investment with consciously built-in high domestic content secured through economies of scale has succeeded in producing a small car that seems competitive both in price and quality. Reportedly, Hyundai proposes to use its Indian plant as a global hub for its small car [*The Economic Times,* January 2, 2003]. Thus, the key to increasing FDI inflow seems to lie in industries (and products) with relatively high technology that have large economies of scale, with substantial domestic content.

However, the foregoing reasoning still does not explain why foreign investment does not come to use cheap labour and skills for export of labour-intensive manufactures—as it has happened in China. We are inclined to believe that the foreign investment policy lacks a clear focus. Unlike China, India has not invested in export infrastructure. In fact, as is widely accepted now, the share of infrastructure in fixed capital formation has declined sharply for nearly one and half decade now [Nagaraj, 1997]. Further, what is needed is perhaps not large investment but suitable inducement to international marketers—trading houses and retail chains—to set up purchase offices and testing facilities to tap the potential of the domestic manufacturers.[29] It is widely acknowledged that China's export success largely lies in marrying its low cost manufacturing capability in Town and Village Enterprises (TVEs) with Hong Kong's highly developed trading houses and other long-established commercial organisations catering to international trade. While it is out of question for India to replicate the locational and historical advantage of Hong Kong for China, investment in export infrastructure in strategic locations and carefully tailored incentives to international trading houses (and retailers) merit a serious consideration. Similarly, such investments are perhaps equally necessary to tap the growing potential for using India's labour cost advantage for doing back office jobs—business processes outsourcing—for international firms [*The Economist*, May 5, 2001].

Realistically, what is it that India expects from foreign investment, and how to secure it? In principle, openness to foreign investment should be strategic, not passive (or unilateral). History does not seem to support such an uncritical international integration as a proven route to growth and efficiency. If the recent experience is any guide, foreign capital is far from a major provider of external savings for rapid industrialisation of any large economy. It can only supplement the domestic resources, wherever they necessarily come bundled with technology, and access to international production and distribution networks. The terms of foreign investment will depend on the relative bargaining power of the foreign firm *vis-a-vis* domestic firms, backed by the state. Indian advantages are the availability of skilled workforce, cheap labour, and the size of the domestic market, which it should leverage as most successful countries have done. A telling instance of it is perhaps Korea's big leap in semi-conductor and telecom equipment manufacturing in the recent years, as it seems to have tied liberalisation of domestic market to sharing of production technology.

If this view has any value, then how should we go about inviting FDI that is consistent with the economy's long-term interests? Foreign investment should be allowed mainly in manufacturing to acquire technology, and to establish international trading channels for promoting labour-intensive exports.

VII

SUMMARY AND CONCLUSION

Ending its long held restrictive foreign investment policy in 1991, India sought to compete with the successful Asian economies to get a greater share of the world's FDI. Cumulative approved foreign investment since then is about $67bn, but the realised amount is about a third of it—the ratio roughly comparable to China's. While the foreign investment inflow represents a substantial jump over the 1980s, it is modest compared to many rapidly growing Asian economies, and minuscule compared to China. While the bulk of the approved FDI is for infrastructure, the realised investment is largely in manufacture of consumer durable goods and the automotive industry seeking India's seemingly large and growing domestic market. Foreign investment in telecom and software industries has also been significant. Approved FDI has largely gone to a few developed states—similar to its concentration in the southern coastal provinces in China. A sizable part of the foreign investment seems to represent a gradual increase in foreign firms' equity holding (hence managerial control) in the existing firms, and acquisition of industrial assets (and brand names).

China's ability to attract a phenomenal amount of foreign investment is a puzzle for many. About 40-50 per cent of China's FDI represents its domestic saving recycled as foreign investment via Hong Kong to take advantage of economic incentives—popularly called the 'round tripping.' Another 25 per cent or so, seems to represent investment in real estate by overseas Chinese that is potentially problematic, as such investments could easily give rise to property bubbles. Thus the quantum of foreign investment from the advanced economies that could improve domestic production capability is perhaps not very different from that in India, in relation to its domestic output. Contrary to the popular belief, China's foreign investment regime is said to be more restrictive than India's. Therefore, what India should be concerned about is not so much the absolute quantum of the inflow, but how effectively it uses its external openness to augment the domestic capability, and access foreign markets for its labour-intensive manufactures.

For a careful economic analysis of the effects of foreign investment, considerable detailed statistical information is required—both at the aggregate and at the firm or industry level. In their absence, much of our analysis is indicative in nature, raising questions for further enquiry.

As the 1990s experience shows, quite contrary to the popular perception, the size of India's domestic market is relatively small, given the low levels of per capita income. After meeting the needs of food and clothing (wage goods), income let for spending on products that most foreign firms offer seems small; their price-income ratio too high for Indian consumers. Therefore, many of them seem to be making efforts to indigenise production to reduce costs and secure economies of scale. In this process, many foreign firms are discovering the potential of low cost of manufacturing for exports.

Much of the approved FDI in infrastructure did not fructify, as the rupee cost of electricity supply by foreign firms is too much high for Indian consumers. This seems true for two reasons: one, prices of goods like electricity are widely subsidised, and cannot be increased without inviting public opposition; second, India produces much of these services at lower cost using domestic raw material and capital equipment.

Foreign investment in consumer goods industries has increased domestic competition, resulting in greater choice and quality improvement. While FDI inflow displaced some domestic firms (and brand names), the bulk of them have—at least yet—largely been able to withstand the competition by making large capital investment, and in expanding distribution networks.

However, in industrial goods there have probably been sizable acquisitions of domestic firms (and factories) whole details are not known. There are many instances of foreign firms gradually acquiring controlling interests, edging out domestic partners. Whether these firm-level changes get reflected in industrial efficiency in the aggregate—as many expected—is a moot point.

What should be done to increase foreign investment? It is popularly believed that a more liberal policy regime, industrial labour market reforms, and infrastructure investment are needed. While infrastructure improvement surely merits a close attention, one is not so sure if the extent of the reforms and the quantum of foreign investment inflow are positively related. Moreover, there is little evidence that greater FDI inflow ensures faster output and export growth. Such simplistic associations, usually based on cross-country analysis, seem to have support neither in principle nor in comparative experience.

What is needed is a strategic view of foreign investment as a means of enhancing domestic production and technological capability, and so also to access the external market for labour-intensive manufactures—as China has precisely done. It seems valuable to reiterate what K.N. Raj, a perceptive observer of comparative economic development, noted early on in China's liberalisation drive, "It is certainly not without good reason that China has chosen to be hospitable even to multinationals with worldwide ramifications like IBM, evidently in the expectation of securing the know-how for building up semi-conductor industry of its own. Those who do not realise the implications of all this for India are living in a dream world of their own... ." [Raj, 1986].

Such interventions need selectivity, and strategic intent. Comparative experience seems to clearly favour such a policy stance.

Notes

1. For a chronological account of the policy reforms, see appendix of Bajpai and Sachs (2001). For detailed official statements on the policy changes, refer to the Ministry of Industry's annual publication, *Handbook of Industrial Statistics*.
2. There is some evidence to support this view. For instance, using cross-section data for 58 developing countries during 1978-95, Bosworth and Collins (1999) show that a dollar of FDI translates into an equivalent domestic investment, while no such association was found with respect to foreign portfolio investment.
3. For a long time developing countries have complained about foreign firms, as they seemed to hide their true operations from the host country rules. But in the recent years under easier capital flow regime, the same legal maze seems to have begun to hurt tax compliance in the developed countries as well. Recently a report in the *New York Times* sought to unveil the legal maze of such operations [Johnston, 2002].
4. Though largely ignored in the mainstream economic writings, much of the literature on the behaviour of international firms builds on Stephen Hymer's (1976) original contribution that focused on firm-specific characteristic, including their market power.
5. It has long been held in the development literature that while short-run cost of foreign debt is high, the long-term costs of FDI could be even higher [Lewis, 1953]. In fact, it is such a view that prevailed in the successful industrialisation efforts of Japan, Korea and Taiwan that carefully regulated foreign investment inflow.
6. However, some recent literature in mainstream economics has argued that while the state may have succeeded in steering these economies in the past, there is little guarantee that in the developing countries today the state has similar capability to repeat the performance [World Bank, 1993].
7. "*Flow of FDI* comprises capital provided (either directly or through other enterprises) by a foreign direct investor to an FDI enterprise or, capital received from an FDI enterprise by a foreign direct investor. There are three components in FDI: equity capital, reinvested earnings, and intra-company loans." (*World Investment Report*, 2001: 275.)
8. Apparently, there is a discrepancy in Enron's declaration of its equity holding in the Indian entity. To the US bankruptcy court it has declared that it holds 50 per cent, but here it has declared that it owns 65 per cent equity.
9. The law requires all closely held (private limited) companies to submit their annual audited accounts to the department of company affairs that are, in principle, available to the public. But practice seems different as the law enforcement seems poor.

10. Korean firms have aggressively moved in to India, since they perceive it as their only chance to get into the last unexplored market, to beat their established corporate rival from Japan and the US.

11. Assessing the Brazilian reforms, Rocha (2002) said, "Mergers and acquisitions of private firms have been equally central to the restructuring of the Brazilian economy ... A recent study shows that between 1995 and 1999 there were 1,233 mergers and acquisitions in which multinational corporations acquired control or participation in Brazilian industries—the devaluation of the real since 1999 making such purchases cheaper. A KPMG survey reveals that 70 per cent of all acquisitions in Brazil during the same period were undertaken by multinationals, to the tune of some $50 billion of FDI inflows" [Rocha, 2002: 23].

12. Data for this graph is from the various issues of the UN's *World Investment Report.*

13. Figure 12.5 is from IFC (2002). In this graph, x-axis represents years, and y-axis measures FDI in million US dollar.

14. I am grateful to Cherian Samuel for providing this unpublished study.

15. Quoting an OECD study, *China in the World Economy*, Srinivasan (2002) reports that majority of Chinese equity holding is mandatory in coal mining, design and manufacture of aircraft, oil and gas, printing and publishing, agricultural production in grains, cotton and oil seeds, domestic commerce, foreign trade, medical instruments and repairs, design and manufacture of ships.

16. I am grateful to Edward Graham for this unpublished paper.

17. For instance, in the two-wheeler industry, TVS, Kinetic and LML have terminated their technical and/or financial collaboration with Suzuki, Honda and Piaggio, respectively, to introduce indigenously developed motorcycle/scooter models that have been well received in the market. Bajaj has stopped making motorcycles in joint brand name with Kawasaki for the domestic market, to introduce its own brand of motorcycles. In consumer products, Godrej, a leading domestic firm, terminated its comprehensive ties with Proctor and Gamble, and repromoted own brands to regain its lost market share. In wristwatch industry, Titan industries ceased its collaboration with Timex to expand internationally.

18. External liberalisation was predicated on the proposition that India has a core of about 200 million consumers with purchasing power close to that in the developed economies. After a decade's experience, many market research agencies have reportedly pruned the estimate to a quarter of the original.

19. For instance, BMW (motorcycles), Piaggio (scooters), Nine Gold (broadcasting), Kokna and Haier (Chinese electronics firms), Roche, Merck (pharmaceuticals), Blue Bunnies (ice cream) and so on have left India (*Business Standard*, October 28, 2002).

20. During the earlier policy regime, the Central Electricity Authority—an autonomous body—was responsible for looking into the techno-economic feasibility keeping in view the network externality of power generation and distribution system. Apparently after the deregulation, such official scrutiny was largely ignored in the belief that, 'markets know the best'. Hence, based on power demand projections drawn up by private consultants, large numbers of projects were approved.

21. Admittedly, the share of foreign controlled firms in the private corporate sector is, by most reckoning, small. However, they account for a substantial share of total profits and dividend in this sector.

22. In fact, considering the fragmented nature of the market, many automotive firms view their Indian operations as mainly distribution and 'brand building' exercises, rather than manufacturing ones. Therefore, it is hard to expect such operations to have significant positive spillovers.

23. According to knowledgeable sources, the Indian auto industry now is as fragmented as the Brazilian industry was when it liberalised its industry some 30 years ago. While Brazil failed to climb up the technology ladder, it was strategic technology importing countries like Japan and Korea that produced world-class automotive manufactures. If

the present trend persists it seems likely that India will follow the Brazilian path, rather than the Japanese and the Korean one.

24. To illustrate, Hyderabad Allwyn, acquired by Voltas, after privatisation, has been engaged in contract manufacturing for the Korean firm Samsung [*Business Standard*, November 11, 2002].
25. Reportedly, Coca Cola has repeatedly refused to comply with the law in diluting its equity in the domestic capital market for the past six years [Guha, 2002].
26. Apparently, the US tax laws provide tax credit for promotion of American brands abroad. We do not have evidence to substantiate this claim.
27. The US protection of the super computers manufacturer, Cray, despite competing products by Japan's Hitachi and Fijitsu being much cheaper is a well known case. Recently when, for the first time, the US department of agriculture bought a Fujitsu super computer, *The New York Times* considered the decision news worthy to report it (June 14, 2002).
28. Writing at the height of the foreign infrastructure investment boom in the 'emerging markets' in the mid-1990s, Wells and Gleason (1995) cautioned the American businessman against rushing into such investment precisely on the above arguments.
29. In fact, it was Mrinal Datta Chaudhuri (1981) who long ago emphasised the role of large domestic and international trading houses as market institutions in promoting manufactured exports from Korea and Taiwan.

References

Ahluwalia, Isher (1985). *Industrial Growth in India – Stagnation Since the Mid-Sixties*, Oxford University Press, Delhi.

Amsden, Alice (2001). *The Rise of 'The Rest': Challenges to the West From Late-Industrialising Economies*, Oxford University Press, New York.

Bajpai, Nirupam and Jeffery D. Sachs (2001). "Foreign Direct Investment in India: Issues and Problems," HIID, *Development Discussion Paper* No. 759, March.

Bosworth, Barry P. and Susan M. Collins (1999). "Capital Flows to Developing Countries: Implications for Savings and Investment," *Brooking Papers on Economic Activity*, No. 1.

Bruton, Henry (1989). "Import Substitution" in *Handbook of Development Economics*, Vol. 2, edited by Hollis Chenery and T.N. Srinivasan, North Holland, London.

Carkovic, Maria and Ross Levine (2002). *Does Foreign Investment Accelerate Economic Growth?* Finance Department, University of Minnesota, Mimeo.

Caves, Richard E. (1999). "Spillovers from Multinationals in Developing Countries: The Mechanisms at Work," *Working Paper* No. 247, Department of Economics, Harvard University.

———. (1996). *Multinational Enterprise and Economic Analysis*, 2nd Edition, Cambridge University Press, London.

Chandra, Nirmal (1991). "Growth of Foreign Capital and Importance in Indian Manufacturing," *Economic and Political Weekly*, Vol. 26, Nos. 11-12.

Chaudhuri, Sudip (1999). "Growth and Structural Change in the Pharmaceutical Industry in India," *WP No.* 356/99 Indian Institute of Management Calcutta.

Datta Chaudhuri, M.K. (1981). "Industrialisation and Foreign Trade: The Development Experiences of South Korea and Philippines" in E. Lee (ed.) *Export-led Industrialisation and Development*, ILO, Geneva.

Easterly, William (2001). "The Lost Decades: Developing Countries Stagnation in spite of Policy Reforms 1980-1998," *Journal of Economic Growth*, Vol. 6, June.

Guha Thakurta, Paranjoy (2002). "Coke: Arrogance of a Multinational," *www.rediff.com*, July 20.

Helleiner, G.K. (1989). "Transnational Corporations and Direct Foreign Investment" in *Handbook of Development Economics*, Vol. 2, H. Chenery and T.N. Srinivasan (eds.), Elsevier Science Publishers B.V.

Hymer, Stephen (1976). *The International Operations of National Firms: A Study of Foreign Direct Investment*, MIT Press, Massachusetts.

International Finance Corporation (2002). "Business Environment and Surveys," (mimeo), Washington DC.

Jain, Virendra (2001). *Investors Beware*, Macmillan India, Delhi.

Johnston, David Cay (2002). "Tax Treaties with Small Nations Turn into a New Shield for Profit," *The New York Times*, April 16.

Kumar, Nagesh (2000). "Mergers and Acquisitions by MNEs: Patterns and Implications," *Economic and Political Weekly*, August 5.

Lall, Sanjaya (1989). *Learning to Industrialise*, Macmillan, London.

————. (1982). *Developing Countries as Exporters of Technology*, Macmillan, London.

Lewis, W. Arthur (1953). *Aspects of Industrialisation*, Bank of Egypt, Cairo.

Mani, Sunil (1983). *Industrial Concentration and Economic Behaviour: Case Study of Indian Tyre Industry*, Centre for Development Studies, Trivandrum.

Mehta, Abhy (1999). *Power Play: A Study of the Enron Project*, Orient Longman, Hyderabad.

Morris, Sebastian (1996). "Political Economy of Electric Power in India," *Economic and Political Weekly*, Vol. 31, No. 21, May 25.

Nagaraj, R. (2002). "Performance of India's Manufacturing Sector in the 1990s: Some Tentative Findings" in Shuji Uchikawa (ed.) *Economic Reforms and Industrial Structure in India*, Manohar, Delhi.

————. (1997). "What has Happened Since 1991? Assessment of India's Econmic Reforms," *Economic and Political Weekly*, Vol. 32, No. 44-45.

————. (1996). "India's Capital Market Growth: Trends, Explanations and Evidence," *Economic and Political Weekly*, Vol. 31, Nos. 35-37 (Special Number), 1996.

Raj, K.N. (1986). *New Economic Policy*, Oxford University Press Delhi.

Rao, K.S. Chalapati, M.R. Murthy and K.V.K. Ranganathan (1999). "Foreign Direct Investment in the Post-Liberalisation Period: An Overview," *Journal of Indian School of Political Economy*, Vol. 11, No. 3, Jul-Sept.

Rao, Chalapati K.S. and M.R. Murthy (1999). "Foreign Direct Investment" in *Alternataive Economic Survey, 1991-98: Seven Years of Structural Adjustment*, Alternative Survey Group, New Delhi.

Reserve Bank of India (2001). *Handbook of Statistics on Indian Economy*, Mumbai

Rocha, Geisa Maria (2002). "Neo-Dependency in Brazil," *New Left Review*, No. 16, July-August.

Srinivasan, G. (2002). "Secret of China's FDI Riches," *Business Line*, December 6, 2002.

Subramaniam, K.K. (1991). "Technological Capability under Economic Liberalism: Experience of Indian Industry in the Eighties," *Economic and Political Weekly*, Vol. 26, No. 35, August 31.

Tseng, Wanda and Harm Zebregs (2002). "Foreign Direct Investment in China: Some Lessons for other Countries," *IMF Policy Discussion Paper* (PDP/02/03), Washington DC.

Wells, Louis, T. and Eric, S. Gleason (1995). "Is Foreign Infrastructure Investment Still too Risky?," *Harvard Business Review*, September-October.

World Bank (1993). *The East Asian Miracle: Economic Growth And Public Policy*, Oxford University Press, New York.

Economic and Political Weekly, Vol. 38, No. 17, April 26, 2003.

Index

C

D

G

M

T

U

V

W

Y

Z